Part 6: SPEAKING TO INFORM

Chapter 13
The Informative Speech
228

The process for informative speaking 230
What informative speaking is 232
Choose and research an informative topic 234
  Get to know the audience and situation 234
  Create an idea bank 235
  Select and narrow your topic 235
  Determine the type of speech 236
  Identify your specific purpose 236
  Identify your central idea 237
  Create a working outline 238
  Conduct your research 239

Recognize your organizational strategy 242
Commit to a strategy 242
Construct main points 244
Organize support materials 244
Compose your introduction, conclusion 245
Present or evaluate an informative speech 252
  Put your speech on its feet 252
  Evaluate the message and presentation 253

Part 7: SPEAKING TO PERSUADE

Chapter 14
Tools for Persuading
256

What a persuasive speech should do 258
  Narrow listeners' options 258
  Seek a response 258
  Support a proposition of fact, value, or policy 259
  Rely on varied, valid support materials 260
  Use highly structured organization 260
  Use different appeals 260
  Highlight emotive, stylistic language 261
  Emphasize powerful, direct delivery 261
  Acknowledge freedom to decide 261
Traditional appeals 262
  Pathos 262
  Mythos 263
  Ethos 264
  Logos 265

Modern appeals 266
  Need 266
  Harmony 268
  Gain 269
  Commitment 269
Parts of an argument 270
  Claim 270
  Evidence 270
  Warrants 271
Types of arguments 272
  Deduction 272
  Induction 274
  Analogy 275
  Cause 275
  Authority 275
Faulty arguments 276

Chapter 15
The Persuasive Speech
278

The process for persuasive speaking 280
Choose and research a persuasive topic 282
  Get to know the audience and situation 282
  Create an idea bank 283
  Select and narrow your topic 284
  Determine the type of speech 285
  Identify your specific purpose 286
  Identify your central idea 287
  Create a working outline 288
  Conduct your research 289

Construct a persuasive outline 290
Organize a persuasive speech 292
  Recognize your organizational strategy 292
  Commit to a strategy 293
  Construct main points 294
  Organize support materials into arguments 294
  Compose your introduction, conclusion 295
Present or evaluate a persuasive speech 304
  Put your speech on its feet 304
  Evaluate the message and presentation 305

Part 8: SPEAKING ON SPECIAL OCCASIONS

Chapter 16
Speeches for Special Events
308

The process for special occasion speaking 310
Special occasion speech purposes 312
  To celebrate 313
  To commemorate 313
  To inspire 313
  To entertain 313
Writing a special occasion speech 314
  Determine the purpose 314
  Clarify the type of speech 315
  Analyze the audience 315
  Focus on a central idea 316

Research your speech 316
Create your outline 317
Practice the speech 317
Evaluate the speech 317
Types of special occasion speeches 318
  Eulogy or tribute 318
  Speech of introduction 319
  Toast or roast 320
  Speech of award presentation 321
  Speech of award acceptance 321
  After-dinner speech 322
  Speech of inspiration 323

D0219625

DK Speaker

LISA A. FORD-BROWN

Columbia College

Pearson

Boston Columbus Indianapolis New York San Francisco
Upper Saddle River Amsterdam Cape Town Dubai
London Madrid Milan Munich Paris Montréal Toronto
Delhi Mexico City São Paulo Sydney Hong Kong Seoul
Singapore Taipei Tokyo

PEARSON

Text design, page layout,
and cover design:
Stuart Jackman

Editor-in-Chief, Communication: Karon Bowers
Director, Market Research and Development: Laura Coaty
Development Editor: Brenda Hadenfeldt
Editorial Associate: Megan Sweeney
Senior Digital Editor: Paul DeLuca
Digital Editor: Lisa Dotson
Senior Marketing Manager: Blair Zoe Tuckman
Managing Editor: Linda Mihatov Behrens
Production Manager: Raegan Keida Heerema
Project Coordination: Integra
Visual Research Manager: Annette Linder
Senior Manufacturing Buyer: Mary Ann Gloriande
Printer and Binder: RR Donnelley & Sons Company/Crawfordsville
Cover Printer: Lehigh-Phoenix

For permission to use copyrighted material, grateful acknowledgment is made to the copyright holders on pp. 351–352, which are hereby made part of this copyright page.

Microsoft and/or its respective suppliers make no representations about the suitability of the information contained in the documents and related graphics published as apart of the services for any purpose. All such documents and related graphics are provided "as is" without warranty of any kind. Microsoft and/or its respective suppliers hereby disclaim all warranties and conditions with regard to this information, including all warranties and conditions of merchantability, whether express, implied or statutory, fitness for a particular purpose, title and non-infringement. In no event shall microsoft and/or its respective suppliers be liable for any special, indirect or consequential damages or any damages whatsoever resulting from loss of use, data or profits, whether in an action of contract, negligence or other tortious action, arising out of or in connection with the use or performance of information available from the services. The documents and related graphics contained herein could include technical inaccuracies or typographical errors. Changes are periodically added to the information herein. Microsoft and/or its respective suppliers may make improvements and/or changes in the product(s) and/or the program(s) described herein at any time. Partial screen shots may be viewed in full within the software version specified.

Microsoft® windows®, and microsoft office® are registered trademarks of the microsoft corporation in the u.S.A. And other countries. This book is not sponsored or endorsed by or affiliated with the microsoft corporation.

Library of Congress Cataloging-in-Publication Data

Ford-Brown, Lisa A.
DK speaker/Lisa A. Ford-Brown.
    p. cm.
Includes bibliographical references.
 ISBN-13: 978-0-205-87012-7
 ISBN-10: 0-205-87012-0
1.   Public speaking—Handbooks, manuals, etc. I. Title.
PN4129.15.F673 2012
 808.5'1—dc23   2012012870

3 4 5 6 7 8 9 10—DOC—15

www.pearsonhighered.com

ISBN-13: 978-0-205-87012-7
ISBN-10:   0-205-87012-0

This book is dedicated to my past, present, and future students.

How to Use This Book

This book contains eight parts. **Parts 1–5** explain the creative process for public speaking, and **Parts 6–8** discuss the basic types of speaking. The **brief contents** shown in the charts to the right give a quick overview.

Detailed contents appear at the beginning of each chapter, as well as inside the front cover of the book. Chapter headings in the book are in question-and-answer format to ask common questions that beginning speakers have and to provide clear answers. Each chapter-opening contents section also serves as a list of **learning objectives** for that chapter.

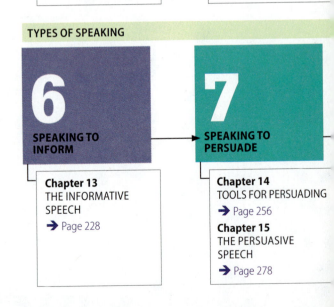

THE CREATIVE PROCESS FOR PUBLIC SPEAKING

1 STARTING

OVERVIEW OF PUBLIC SPEAKING
→ Page 2

Chapter 1
GETTING TO KNOW YOUR AUDIENCE AND SITUATION
→ Page 20

Chapter 2
SELECTING YOUR TOPIC AND PURPOSE
→ Page 34

2 RESEARCHING

Chapter 3
LOCATING SUPPORT MATERIALS
→ Page 52

Chapter 4
SELECTING AND TESTING SUPPORT MATERIALS
→ Page 74

TYPES OF SPEAKING

6 SPEAKING TO INFORM

Chapter 13
THE INFORMATIVE SPEECH
→ Page 228

7 SPEAKING TO PERSUADE

Chapter 14
TOOLS FOR PERSUADING
→ Page 256

Chapter 15
THE PERSUASIVE SPEECH
→ Page 278

3

CREATING

Chapter 5
OUTLINING YOUR SPEECH
➜ Page 96

Chapter 6
ORGANIZING THE SPEECH BODY
➜ Page 122

Chapter 7
INTRODUCING AND CONCLUDING YOUR SPEECH
➜ Page 136

4

PRESENTING

Chapter 8
USING LANGUAGE SUCCESSFULLY
➜ Page 152

Chapter 9
DELIVERING YOUR SPEECH
➜ Page 162

CHAPTER 10
USING PRESENTATION AIDS
➜ Page 178

5

LISTENING & EVALUATING

Chapter 11
LISTENING
➜ Page 204

Chapter 12
EVALUATING SPEECHES
➜ Page 216

8

SPEAKING ON SPECIAL OCCASIONS

Chapter 16
SPEECHES FOR SPECIAL EVENTS
➜ Page 308

NCA STUDENT OUTCOMES FOR SPEAKING AND LISTENING
➜ Page 325

GLOSSARY
➜ Page 340

BIBLIOGRAPHY
➜ Page 349

NOTES
➜ Page 350

CREDITS
➜ Page 351

INDEX
➜ Page 353

Preface

This book was inspired by a 2008 study by a leading research institution concluding that students use a textbook for less than 15 percent of their study time for their public speaking course. The picture that emerged from 25 hours of interviews and more than 300 diary entries was this: Although students found textbooks to be useful when studying for quizzes, they did not find them at all useful for guidance while developing their speeches. Responding to this need, *DK Speaker* gives students the practical information and examples they seek right up front, supported with the concepts and theories instructors know students need.

This guide pairs the benefits of a brief text—condensed explanations and examples, a "how to" focus, streamlined chapters—with an engaging design that presents concepts in full-color visuals, supported by text. It provides a lively, pedagogically effective option for covering the core skills and helping students meet their biggest challenges when creating a speech.

Combining its concise coverage with the powerfully visual DK design, *DK Speaker* offers an easy-to-navigate resource with dynamic visuals, current examples, and clear instruction that will equip students with the tools and confidence to be effective speakers.

FEATURES

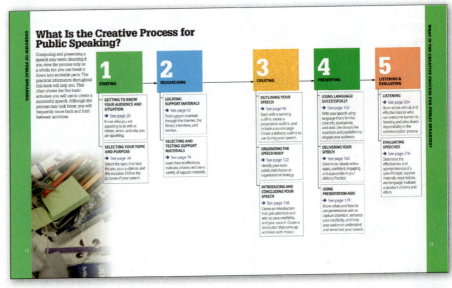

1

Designed for easy use and navigation: Color-coded parts, process charts, and blue cross-references help students quickly find answers to questions on any part of the speech process or type of speaking.

2

Presents concepts visually, supported by text: The pairing of visuals and detailed explanations allows students to get an overview at a glance and read on for specifics.

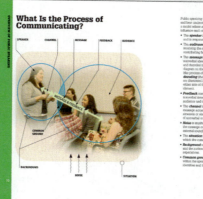

3

INCORRECT:	CORRECT:
Some believe basically that the radiation silently emitted from cell phones can cause cancer.	Cell phones emit tiny amounts of radiation, which scientists believe may be linked to certain types of brain cancer.

Driven by examples: Diverse examples—from student, community, business, historical, political, special occasion, and other speaking situations—are used extensively throughout and often annotated.

4

Emphasizes confidence-building: Starting with a section in the Overview chapter on overcoming apprehension, the text then features blue "Confidence Booster" sections throughout to help students deal with fears and be well prepared.

5

Emphasizes ethics at every stage: Building from the Overview material on ethics and avoiding plagiarism, "Practicing Ethics" sections are integrated into each part of the speech process.

CONFIDENCE BOOSTER

If giving a speech seems daunting to you, try to select a topic that is familiar and will be interesting to research. You can then keep your research focused, spend more time practicing, and use your nervous energy to feed your excitement.

PRACTICING ETHICS

- Avoid negative stereotypes.
- Understand that personal traits can change due to significant events, trends, and opportunities during a particular time in history.
- Respect diversity, all the time!

CHECKLIST for Time

❏ How much time will I have to speak?

❏ How early should I arrive?

❏ What day of the week and time of day will I speak? How might these influence my speech? Is either of these culturally significant for my audience?

❏ Where do I fall in the rotation of speakers? How might someone else's speech influence mine?

❏ Is there late-breaking news I should consider?

❏ Is this the first time this audience will hear me speak?

❏ What is my relationship with this audience? How can I improve my speech based on that relationship?

TIPS: Using Databases

- Search in the database as you would search with an Internet search engine.

- Use databases to help you narrow your topic.

- Start with a full-text search. You might find everything you need, not only information in abstract form.

- Put limits on your search by defining attributes.

- Search more than one database.

- Ask your librarian for help if you have questions or find using a database intimidating.

6

Includes Checklists and Tips for practical application: Extensive use of checklists gives students practical tools to help create and evaluate their speeches at each stage of the process. Boxed tips provide useful information and advice along the way.

7

Highlights a learning objective in each chapter heading: Chapter headings are in question-and-answer format—to ask common questions that beginning speakers have and to provide clear answers. Each chapter-opening contents section also serves as a list of learning objectives for that chapter.

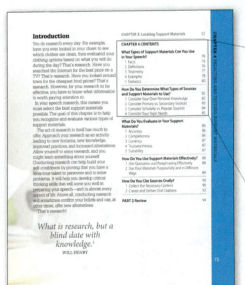

Introduction

You do research every day. For example, have you ever looked in your closet to see which clothes are clean, then evaluated your clothing options based on what you will do during the day? That's research. Have you searched the Internet for the best price on a TV? That's research. Have you looked around town for the cheapest food prices? That's research. However, for your research to be effective, you have to know what information is worth paying attention to.

In your research, this means you must select the best support materials possible. The goal of this chapter is to help you recognize and evaluate various types of support materials.

The act of research in itself has much to offer. Approach your research as an activity leading to new horizons, new knowledge, improved practices, and increased alternatives. Allow yourself to enjoy research, and you might learn something about yourself. Conducting research can help build your self-confidence by proving that you have a tenacious talent to persevere and to solve problems. It will help you develop critical thinking skills that will serve you well in preparing your speech—and in almost every aspect of life. Above all, conducting research will sometimes confirm your beliefs and can, at other times, offer new alternatives. That's research!

What is research, but a blind date with knowledge.[1]
WILL HENRY

CHAPTER 3: Locating Support Materials   52

CHAPTER 4 CONTENTS

What Types of Support Materials Can You Use in Your Speech?
1 Facts   76
2 Definitions   76
3 Testimony   77
4 Examples   78
5 Statistics   80

How Do You Determine What Types of Sources and Support Materials to Use?
1 Consider Your Own Personal Knowledge   82
2 Consider Primary vs. Secondary Sources   83
3 Consider Scholarly vs. Popular Sources   84
4 Consider Your Topic Needs   85

What Do You Evaluate in Your Support Materials?
1 Accuracy   86
2 Completeness   86
3 Currency   87
4 Trustworthiness   87
5 Suitability   87

How Do You Use Support Materials Effectively?   88
1 Use Quotation and Paraphrasing Effectively   88
2 Use Your Materials Purposefully and in Different Ways   88

How Do You Cite Sources Orally?   90
1 Collect the Necessary Content   90
2 Create and Deliver Oral Citations   92

PART 2 Review   94

CHAPTER 4: SELECTING AND TESTING SUPPORT MATERIALS

75

CHAPTER 4 CONTENTS

What Types of Support Materials Can You Use in Your Speech?
1 Facts   76
2 Definitions   76
3 Testimony   77
4 Examples   78
5 Statistics   80

How Do You Determine What Types of Sources and Support Materials to Use?
1 Consider Your Own Personal Knowledge   82
2 Consider Primary vs. Secondary Sources   83
3 Consider Scholarly vs. Popular Sources   84
4 Consider Your Topic Needs   85

8

Correlates with NCA learning outcomes:
Learning objectives are based on the outcomes described in Part One of "Speaking and Listening Competencies for College Students" by the National Communication Association. A guide in the back of the book points to where each outcome is addressed in the text.

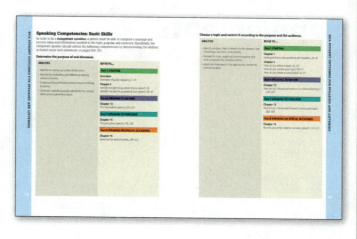

9

Based on how students do research: Chapter 3, "Locating Support Materials," and Chapter 4, "Selecting and Testing Support Materials," are designed around the astounding array of resources available to students today. Coverage emphasizes how to evaluate sources and how to cite them orally and in written form.

Supplements

FOR INSTRUCTORS

INSTRUCTOR'S MANUAL
Prepared by Maggie Sullivan, Loras College, this comprehensive, peer-reviewed resource offers a chapter-by-chapter guide to teaching with this innovative book! Each chapter features learning outcomes, a detailed lecture outline (based on the accompanying PowerPoint™ presentation package), discussion questions, activities, and content quizzes. There also are many suggestions for incorporating visual elements from the book and multimedia resources from MyCommunicationLab in your lectures and assignments.
Available at www.pearsonhighered.com/irc
(instructor login required); ISBN 0-205-90250-2

POWERPOINT™ PRESENTATION PACKAGE
Prepared by Christa Tess, Minneapolis Community & Technical College, this text-specific package provides a basis for your lecture with visually enhanced PowerPoint™ slides for each chapter of the book. In addition to providing key concepts and select art from the book, these presentations bring the book's exciting, visual presentation to life with pedagogically valuable animations as well as detailed instructor notes.
Available at www.pearsonhighered.com/irc
(instructor login required); ISBN 0-205-91293-1

PEARSON PUBLIC SPEAKING VIDEO LIBRARY
Pearson's Public Speaking Video Library contains a range of different types of speeches delivered on a multitude of different topics, allowing you to choose the speeches best suited for your students. Please contact your Pearson representative for details and a complete list of videos and their contents. Some restrictions apply.
Samples available at www.mycoursetoolbox.com

MYTEST COMPUTERIZED TEST BANK
This flexible, online test-generating program includes all questions found in the Test Bank, allowing instructors to create their own personalized exams. Instructors also can edit any of the existing test questions and even add new questions. Other special features include random generation of test questions, creation of alternate versions of the same test, scrambling of question sequence, and test preview before printing.
Available at www.pearsonmytest.com
(instructor login required); ISBN 0-205-91292-3

TEST BANK
The fully reviewed Test Bank, prepared by Janice Ralya Stuckey, Jefferson State Community College, contains multiple choice, true/false, completion, short answer, and traditional essay questions. Unlike any other public speaking test bank available, we also offer visual essay questions that require students to evaluate and discuss key visual elements from the book. Each question has a correct answer and is referenced by page, skill, and topic.
Available at www.pearsonhighered.com
(instructor login required); ISBN 0-205-90249-9

A GUIDE FOR NEW PUBLIC SPEAKING TEACHERS, 5/e
This handy guide helps new teachers prepare for and teach the introductory public speaking course more effectively. It covers such topics as preparing for the term, planning and structuring your course, evaluating speeches, utilizing the textbook, integrating technology into the classroom, and much more!
Available at www.pearsonhighered.com/irc
(instructor login required); ISBN 0-205-82810-8

FOR STUDENTS

FREE APP FOR APPLE iPHONES, iPADS, AND iPODS: "DKPS iCHECK"
This handy new app gives students quick and easy access to all 50 of the "checklists" from *DK Guide to Public Speaking* FREE of charge. Students can download iCheck directly on to their iPhone, iPad, or iPod Touch from the Apple iTunes App Store with no restrictions, fees, or pass codes.

PEARSON PUBLIC SPEAKING STUDY SITE
This open-access student Web resource features practice tests, learning objectives, and Web links organized around the major topics typically covered in the Introduction to Public Speaking course.
Available at www.pearsonpublicspeaking.com

STUDY CARD FOR PUBLIC SPEAKING
Colorful, affordable, and packed with useful information, the Pearson Study Cards make studying easier, more efficient, and more enjoyable. Course information is distilled down to the basics, helping students quickly master the fundamentals, review a subject for understanding, or prepare for an exam.
Available for purchase; ISBN 0-205-44126-2

MyCommunicationLab®

www.mycommunicationlab.com

Our MyLab products have been designed and refined with a single purpose in mind—to help educators create that moment of understanding with their students.

MyCommunicationLab delivers proven results in helping individual students succeed. Its automatically graded assessments, personalized study plan, and interactive eText provide engaging experiences that personalize, stimulate, and measure learning for each student. And, it comes from a trusted partner with educational expertise and a deep commitment to helping students, instructors, and departments achieve their goals.

- A **personalized study plan** guides students to focus directly on what they need to know, helping them succeed in the course and beyond.
- **Assessment** tied to videos, applications, and chapter content enables both instructors and students to track progress and get immediate feedback—and helps instructors to find the best resources with which to help students.
- The **Pearson eText** lets students access their textbook anytime, anywhere, and any way they want—including listening online or downloading to an iPad®.
- **Videos and Video Quizzes**: Sample student and professional speeches offer students models of the types of speeches they are learning to design and deliver. Many interactive videos include short, assignable quizzes that report to the instructor's gradebook.
- **MySearchLab**: Pearson's MySearchLab™ is the easiest way for students to start a research assignment or speech. Complete with extensive help on the research process and four databases of credible and reliable source material, MySearchLab™ helps students quickly and efficiently make the most of their research time.

- **MediaShare**: A comprehensive file upload tool that allows students to post speeches, outlines, visual aids, video assignments, role plays, group projects, and more in a variety of formats including video, Word, PowerPoint, and Excel. Structured much like a social networking site, MediaShare helps promote a sense of community among students. Uploaded files are available for viewing, commenting, and grading by instructors and class members in face-to-face and online course settings. Integrated video capture functionality allows students to record video directly from a webcam to their assignments, and allows instructors to record videos via webcam, in class or in a lab, and attach them directly to a specific student and/or assignment. In addition, instructors can upload files as assignments for students to view and respond to directly in MediaShare. Grades can be imported into most learning management systems, and robust privacy settings ensure a secure learning environment for instructors and students.
- **Class Preparation Tool:** Finding, organizing, and presenting your instructor resources is fast and easy with Pearson's class preparation tool. This fully searchable database contains hundreds of resources such as lecture launchers, discussion topics, activities, assignments, and video clips. Instructors can search or browse by topic and sort the results by type. You can create personalized folders to organize and store what you like or download resources, as well as upload your own content.

A **MyCommunicationLab** access code is available at no additional cost when packaged with select Pearson Communication texts.
To get started, contact your local Pearson Representative at **www.pearsonhighered.com/replocator.**

Acknowledgments

This book was a labor of love for many people, and I was blessed to work with a great team and to have folks from my professional as well as personal lives offering support. Thanks go to everyone whose work, input, and contributions are reflected in this book, including: at Pearson and Dorling Kindersley, Karon Bowers (Editor-in-Chief, Communication), Brenda Hadenfeldt (Development Editor), Stuart Jackman (Design Director for DK Education), Laura Coaty (Director, Market Research and Development), Laurie Panu (Senior Publisher's Representative), Blair Tuckman (Senior Marketing Manager), Sophie Mitchell (Publishing Director for DK Education), and Megan Sweeney (Editorial Associate); Tharon Howard, Director of the Clemson University Usability Testing Facility, and his team, including Wendy Howard; undergraduate students at both Clemson University and Tri-County Technical College who participated in usability studies; Faculty Advisory Board members, focus group participants, and reviewers (listed on pages xv–xvii); student and research assistants Steven Dotson, Crystaldawn Howell, Charity J. Hunter, and Karissa Scott; Columbia College students Michelle E. Arnold, Jeff Barringer, Caitlin Jenkins Campbell, Andria Caruthers, Desiree Chong, Rachel Coleman, Tori Gehlert, Ashley Hardy, Candace Johnson, Katherine Mancuso, Milos Milosavljevic, Logan Park, Kylie E. Stephenson, Jessica Ucci, Christopher Vietti, and Rachel K. Wester; and speech contributors Dorinda K. Stayton, Kimberly Albrecht-Taylor, Brendan Chan (University of Texas at Austin), and the Rev. John Yonker (Columbia, Mo.).

Throughout this project, I have been fortunate to enjoy the support and assistance from many colleagues on the Columbia College campus. I wish to thank: President Gerald Brouder, Terry Smith, Mark Price, Lori Ewing, Terry Obermoeller, and the Humanities Department; the entire Columbia College Technology Services group, specifically Kevin Palmer, Stefanie McCollum, and B. J. Donaldson; Megan Pettegrew-Donely and Kaci Smart; Lucia D'Agostino, Janet Caruthers, Lynda Dunham and her staff, Danny Campbell, Johanna Denzin, Ann Schlemper, Lizbeth Metscher, Julie Estabrooks, Tim Ireland, and David Roebuck.

I would like to thank several exceptional educators who have influenced me both professionally and personally: C. Sue Davis, Harriet McNeal, Dan P. Millar, Elyse Pineau, Ron Pelias, David Worley, and Mary Carol Harris. I am sincerely indebted to Sheron J. Dailey for helping me proofread and for challenging my ideas. Only a true mentor and friend would read every page as if it were her own.

I am extremely grateful to the Ford and Brown families for all the support and understanding—especially Bruce Brown.

What an adventure this was, and I thank ALL of you.

Lisa Ford-Brown

FACULTY ADVISORY BOARD

DK Guide to Public Speaking and *DK Speaker*

Shae Adkins, Lone Star College–North Harris; **Allison Ainsworth,** Gainesville State College; **Mary Alexander,** Wharton County Junior College; **Julie Allee,** Indiana University South Bend; **Barbara Baron,** Brookdale Community College; **Kate Behr,** Concordia College; **Constance Berman,** Berkshire Community College; **Kimberly Berry,** Ozarks Technical College; **Kirk Brewer,** Tulsa Community College, West Campus; **Ferald Bryan,** Northern Illinois University; **Rebecca Carlton,** Indiana University Southeast; **Gary Carson,** Coastal Carolina University; **Wendy R. Coleman,** Alabama State University; **Diana Cooley,** Lone Star College–North Harris; **Karin Dahmann,** Blinn College; **Natalie Dorfeld,** Thiel College; **Kelly Driskell,** Trinity Valley Community College; **Robert D. Dunkerly,** College of Southern Nevada; **Steve Earnest,** Coastal Carolina University; **Katrina Eicher,** Elizabethtown Community and Technical College; **Kristina Galyen,** University of Cincinnati; **Jo Anna Grant,** California State University, San Bernardino; **Tressa Kelly,** University of West Florida; **Sherry Lewis,** University of Texas at El Paso; **Daniel Leyes,** Brookdale Community College; **Terri Main,** Reedley College; **Anne McIntosh,** Central Piedmont Community College; **James McNamara,** Alverno College; **Donna Munde,** Mercer County Community College; **John Nash,** Moraine Valley Community College; **William Neff,** College of Southern Nevada; **Karen Otto,** Florida State College at Jacksonville; **Maria Parnell,** Brevard Community College, Melbourne; **Katherine Rigsby,** University of South Alabama; **Kristi Schaller,** University of Georgia; **Michael Shannon,** Moraine Valley Community College; **Pam Speights,** Wharton County Junior College; **Janice Stuckey,** Jefferson State Community College; **Christa Tess,** Minneapolis Community and Technical College; **Jane Varmecky,** Tulsa Community College, Southeast Campus; **Jenny Warren,** Collin County Community College, Spring Creek; **Rebecca Weldon,** Savannah College of Art and Design; **Susan Wieczorek,** University of Pittsburgh at Johnstown; **Susan Winters,** University of Cincinnati; **Brandon Wood,** Central Texas College; and **Quentin Wright,** Mountain View College.

FOCUS GROUP PARTICIPANTS

DK Guide to Public Speaking and *DK Speaker*

Carolyn Babcock, Savannah College of Art and Design; **Cameron Basquiat,** College of Southern Nevada; **Shirene Bell,** Salt Lake Community College; **Linda Brown,** El Paso Community College, Transmountain Campus; **Dawn Carusi,** Marietta College; **Helen Chester,** Milwaukee Area Technical College; **Russ Church,** Middle Tennessee State University; **Kathleen D. Clark,** University of Akron; **Janis Crawford,** Butler University; **Dale Davis,** University of Texas at San Antonio; **Ella Davis,** Wayne County Community College; **Shannon Doyle,** San Jose State University; **Jeanne Dunphy,** Los Angeles City College; **Jennifer Fairchild,** Eastern Kentucky University; **Jeff Farrar,** University of Connecticut; **Katie Frame,** Schoolcraft College; **Kathy Golden,** Edinboro University of Pennsylvania; **Don Govang,** Lincoln University; **Joy Hart,** University of Louisville; **James Heflin,** Cameron University; **Terry Helmick,** Johnson County Community College; **Wade Hescht,** Lone Star College–North Harris; **Heather Hundley,** California State University, San Bernardino; **Lynae Jacob,** Amarillo College; **Jim Kuypers,** Virginia Tech; **Libby McGlone,** Columbus State Community College; **Terri Moore,** Brevard Community College, Melbourne; **Tim Pierce,** Northern Illinois University; **Sherry Rhodes,** Collin County Community College, Courtyard Center; **Rebecca Robideaux,** Boise State University; **David Schneider,** Saginaw Valley University; **April DuPree Taylor,** University of South Alabama; **Paaige Turner,** Saint Louis University; **Julie Weishar,** Parkland College; and **Charla Windley,** University of Idaho.

ACKNOWLEDGMENTS

REVIEWERS
DK Guide to Public Speaking and *DK Speaker*

Donald Abel, Amarillo College; **Helen Acosta,** Bakersfield College; **Brent Adrian,** Central Community College, Grand Island; **Bob Alexander,** Bossier Parish Community College; **Krista Appelquist,** Moraine Valley Community College; **Brenda Armentrout,** Central Piedmont Community College; **Ann Atkinson,** Keene State College; Jackie Augustine, Victor Valley College; **Kevin Backstrom,** University of Wisconsin Oshkosh; **Cynthia L. Bahti,** Saddleback College and Orange Coast Colleges; Elise Banfield, Genesee Community College; **Kristin Barton,** Dalton State College; **Jennifer Huss Basquiat,** College of Southern Nevada; **Polly Begley,** Fresno City College; **Tim Behme,** University of Minnesota, Twin Cities; Belinda Bernum, Mansfield University; **Denise Besson-Silvia,** Gavilan College; **Melanie Lea Birck,** Bossier Parish Community College; **Mardia Bishop,** University of Illinois; **Carol Bliss,** California State Polytechnic University; **Tonya Blivens,** Tarrant County College, Southeast Campus; **Robert Boller,** University of Hawaii at Manoa; **Beverly McClay Borawski,** Pasco-Hernando Community College; **Jeffrey Brand,** Millikin University; **LeAnn Brazeal,** Kansas State University; **Heather Brecht,** Ithaca College; **Michele Bresso,** Bakersfield College; **Stefne Lenzmeier Broz,** Wittenberg University; **Barbara Ruth Burke,** University of Minnesota; **Donna Burnside,** University of Texas at Brownsville; **Nicholas Butler,** Arizona State University; **Dennis Cali,** University of Texas at Tyler; **Marybeth Callison,** University of Georgia; **Mary Carver,** University of Central Oklahoma; **Connie Caskey,** Jefferson State Community College; **Jennifer Chakroff,** Kent State University; **Angela Cherry,** Laney College; **Robert Christie,** DeVry College; **Carolyn Clark,** Salt Lake Community College; **Benjamin J. Cline,** Western New Mexico University; **Cindy Cochran,** Kirkwood Community College; **Jodi Cohen,** Ithaca College; **Teresa Collard,** University of Tennessee at Martin; **Leslie Collins,** Modesto Junior College; **Ron Compton,** McHenry County College; **Linda Carvalho Cooley,** Reedley College; **Jim Cunningham,** Embry Riddle Aeronautical University; **Andrea Davis,** University of South Carolina Upstate; **Quinton D. Davis,** University of Texas at San Antonio; **Tasha Davis,** Austin Community College, Round Rock; **Isabel del Pino-Allen,** Miami Dade College; **Susan Dobie,** Humboldt State University; **Natalie Dudchock,** Jefferson State Community College; **Ann Duncan,** McLennan Community College; **Janine W. Dunlap,** Freed-Hardeman University; **Kristen Eichhorn,** SUNY Oswego; **Marty Ennes,** West Hills College Lemoore; **Heather Erickson,** Emerson College; **Diane Ferrero-Paluzzi,** Iona College; James M. Floss, Humboldt State University; **Jeffrey Fox,** Northern Kentucky University; **Rebecca Franko,** California State Polytechnic University; **Barbara Franzen,** Central Community College; **Stacy Freed,** University of Tennessee at Martin; **Todd S. Frobish,** Fayetteville State University; **Mark S. Gallup,** Lansing Community College; **Joseph M. Ganakos,** Lee College; **Laura Garcia,** Washington State Community College; **Kevin M. Gillen,** Indiana University South Bend; **Donna Goodwin,** Tulsa Community College; **Donna Gotch,** California State University, San Bernardino; **Robert Greenstreet,** East Central University; **Howard Grower,** University of Tennessee; **Angela Grupas,** St. Louis Community College, Meramec; **Karen Hamburg,** Camden County College; **Carla Harrell,** Old Dominion University; **Richard Harrison,** Kilgore College; **Vickie Harvey,** California State University, Stanislaus; **Linda Heil,** Harford Community College; **Anne Helms,** Alamance Community College; **Linda Hensley,** Southwestern College; **Lisa Katrina Hill,** Harrisburg Area Community College, Gettysburg; **Tim Horne,** University of North Carolina at Charlotte; **Allison Horrell,** Spartanburg Community College; **Marcia W. Hotchkiss,** Tennessee State University; **Christopher Howerton,** Woodland Community College; **Teresa Humphrey,** University of South Carolina Aiken; **Mary Hurley,** St. Louis Community College at Forest Park; **Nancy Jennings,** Cuyamaca College; **Robert Kagan,** Manchester Community College; **Pamela Kaylor,** Ohio University Lancaster; **Rebecca M. Kennerly,** Georgia Southern University; **Peter Kerr,** Asbury University; **Susan Kilgard,** Anne Arundel Community College; **Ray Killebrew,** Missouri Baptist University; **Sandra King,** Anne Arundel Community College; **Loretta Kissell,** Mesa Community College; **Brian Kline,** Gainesville State College; **Krista Kozel,** Dona Ana Community College; **Staci Kuntzman,** University of North Carolina at Charlotte; **Kristina Langseth,** Minneapolis Community and Technical College; **Cindy Larson-Casselton,** Concordia College; **Jeffrey Lawrence,** Ivy Tech Community College, Columbus/Franklin; **Michael Lee,** College of Charleston;

Robert Leonard, Sinclair Community College; Charles E. Lester, Palm Beach Atlantic University; John Levine, University of California, Berkeley; Derrick Lindstrom, Minneapolis Community and Technical College; Darren Linvill, Clemson University; Karen Lollar, Metropolitan State College of Denver; Steve Madden, Coastal Carolina University; Kristen Majocha, University of Pittsburgh at Johnstown; Reed Markham, Daytona State College, DeLand; Ginger K. Martin, Guilford Technical Community College; Sujanet Mason, Luzerne County Community College; Leola McClure, MiraCosta College; James R. McCoy, College of Southern Nevada; Dee Ann McFarlin, North Central Texas College; Deborah Socha McGee, College of Charleston; Miriam McMullen-Pastrick, Penn State Erie, The Behrend College; James McNamara, Alverno College; Delois Medhin, Milwaukee Area Technical College; Shellie Michael, Volunteer State Community College; Josh Miller, Los Angeles Valley College; Barbara Montgomery, Colorado State University, Pueblo; Eric Moreau, College of Southern Nevada; Lynnette Mullins, University of Minnesota, Crookston; Heidi Murphy, Central New Mexico Community College; Thomas Murray, Fitchburg State University; W. Benjamin Myers, University of South Carolina Upstate; Alexa Naramore, University of Cincinnati; Kay E. Neal, University of Wisconsin Oshkosh; Mary T. Newman, Wharton County Junior College; Rebecca Nordyke, Wichita State University; Christine North, Ohio Northern University; Erin Obermueller, Concordia College–New York; Elizabeth Reeves O'Connor, Rochester Institute of Technology; Tami Olds, Northern Virginia Community College; Mary Oulvey, Southwestern Illinois College; Mariusz Ozminkowski, California Polytechnic State University, Pomona; Deborah Panzer, Nassau Community College; Daniel Paulnock, Saint Paul College; Jean Perry, Glendale Community College; Charlotte Petty, University of Missouri at St. Louis; Shirlee Pledger, Fullerton College; Mihaela Popescu, California State University, San Bernardino; Mike Posey, Franklin University; Shelly Presnell, Shasta College; Ann Preston, St. Ambrose University; C. Thomas Preston, Gainesville State College; Marlene M. Preston, Virginia Tech; Shannon Proctor, Highline Community College; Brandi Quesenberry, Virginia Tech; Rita Rahoi-Gilchrest, Winona State University; Michele Ramsey, Penn State Berks; Rasha Ramzy, Georgia State University; Paul R. Raptis, Gainesville State College; Jessica Reeher, SUNY Oswego; Catherine Reilly, Dominican College; Elizabeth Richard, Saint Louis University; Maryanna Richardson, Forsyth Technical Community College; William Richter, Lenoir-Rhyne University; Heather Ricker-Gilbert, Manchester Community College; B. Hannah Rockwell, Loyola University Chicago; Terry Rogers, Casper College; Estrella Romero, Riverside City College/Riverside Campus; Douglas Rosentrater, Bucks County Community College; Kimberly Ross-Brown, Bluegrass Community and Technical College; Chip Rouse, Stevenson University; Tracy Routsong, Washburn University; Noreen M. Schaefer-Faix, Defiance College; Lisa Schroeder, Southwestern Oklahoma State University; Sydney Scott, Pace University; Jeff Shires, Purdue University North Central; James R. Shoopman, Embry Riddle Aeronautical University; Kate Simcox, Messiah College; June Smith, Angelo State University; Shelley Larson Soleimani, Oakland Community College; Kalisa Spalding, Elizabethtown Community and Technical College; Denise Sperruzza, St. Louis Community College, Meramec; Ruth Stokes, Trident Technical College; Wendell Stone, University of West Georgia; Jacob Stutzman, Oklahoma City University; Robert L. Strain, Florida Memorial University; Erik Stroner, Iowa Central Community College; Tammy Swenson-Lepper, Winona State University; Judy Szabo, Northeastern Junior College; Ann Taylor, Northern Kentucky University; Michael Tew, Eastern Michigan University; Miki Thiessen, Rock Valley College; Ryan Thompson, McLennan Community College; Greg Toney, Tri County Technical College; Jill Trites, University of Minnesota; Judi Truitt, Volunteer State Community College; Suzanne Uhl, Mt. San Jacinto College; Shannon VanHorn, Valley City State University; Lauren Velasco, Foothill College; Rob Walsh, Valley City State University; Pamela S. Wegner, Black Hills State University; Deborah Wertanen, Minneapolis Community and Technical College; Patty Wharton-Michael, University of Pittsburgh at Johnstown; Charlene Widener, Hutchinson Community College; Robert L. Williams, Moberly Area Community College; Tyrell Williams, St. Phillip's College; Mark J. P. Wolf, Concordia University Wisconsin; Justin Young, Trine University; and Tony Zupancic, Notre Dame College.

PART 1
Starting

OVERVIEW OF PUBLIC SPEAKING   2

CHAPTER 1
Getting to Know Your Audience
and Situation   20

CHAPTER 2
Selecting Your Topic and Purpose   34

OVERVIEW OF PUBLIC SPEAKING

How Will Public Speaking Help You?

When Jenna and Sergei enrolled in a public speaking class, both saw it as a waste of time and dreaded it more than anything. Jenna worried that she wouldn't find anything interesting to say. Sergei was nervous and thought he would never want or need to use public speaking skills beyond class.

Before their class ended, Sergei and Jenna felt differently. Jenna realized that a speech about Ramen noodles could be interesting if she used dynamic language and delivery as well as unique support materials. She discovered that this popular college snack helped fight hunger in Japan after World War II. Jenna developed confidence in speaking and went on to own a consulting firm inspiring small business owners.

Sergei learned that his nervousness could be an asset and he could give a good speech. He still got nervous but knew how to positively channel his anxiety. Sergei joined the Mock Trial Club—something he would have passed up before the class. Even more astounding, he found he enjoyed it and changed his major to pre-law.

You may not yet see the benefit of learning to speak effectively, either. The extraordinary events that might happen in our lives, requiring us to step to the lectern, are hard to predict. But no matter what career you pursue, the influence that effective speaking will have on your life is significant. You will find yourself needing to defend a decision, promote your business, protect your family, or take a stance. These events require that you move beyond everyday skills and develop competent public speaking skills. This book will help you step up to those challenges.

OVERVIEW OF PUBLIC SPEAKING CONTENTS

How Can You Be a Successful Public Speaker? 4
1 Be Audience Centered 4
2 Be Knowledgeable, Creative, and Organized 5
3 Use Appropriate Presentation Techniques 5

How Can You Overcome a Fear of Public Speaking? 6
1 Face Your Fear Head On 6
2 Learn Techniques That Work for You 6
3 Practice, Practice, Practice 7

How Can You Be an Ethical Public Speaker? 8
1 Understand Ethics 8
2 Respect Diversity 8
3 Cite Sources to Avoid Plagiarism 9
4 Use Reliable Evidence, Logic, and Reasoning 9
5 Support and Endorse Freedom of Expression 9

What Is the Process of Communicating? 10

What Is the Creative Process for Public Speaking? 12

Using the Steps in This Book 19

CHAPTER 1: Getting to Know Your Audience and Situation 20
CHAPTER 2: Selecting Your Topic and Purpose 34
PART 1 Review 50

How Can You Be a Successful Public Speaker?

1 Be Audience Centered

2 Be Knowledgeable, Creative, and Organized

3 Use Appropriate Presentation Techniques

1

Be Audience Centered

Have you ever heard someone say, "You can't understand me until you have walked in my shoes?" This phrase symbolizes theorist and philosopher Kenneth Burke's notion of identification, as discussed in his book *A Rhetoric of Motives*. **Identification** (also called *empathy*) is the human need and willingness to understand as much as possible the feelings, thoughts, motives, interests, attitudes, and lives of others. Identification is at the core of being audience centered. As human beings, we are born separate but spend much of our lives looking for what we share with others. Being audience centered will guide you in selecting appropriate topics and help you in creating ways for your audience to connect with you and your topic.

→ See Chapters 1 and 2 for how to analyze your audience and select a topic.

2
Be Knowledgeable, Creative, and Organized

When the great artist Michelangelo was 88 years old, he allegedly wrote, "I am still learning." To be a successful speaker, you must be diligent and know as much as possible about your topic, audience, occasion, language, and methods of delivery right up to the moment the speech ends.

Bring your knowledge to life by being creative. Individuality, uniqueness, imagination, resourcefulness, and vision are all qualities of creativity. Imagine if Martin Luther King, Jr., had said "I have a hope" rather than "I have a dream." Imagine if Michael Jackson hadn't envisioned the video for "Thriller." We might not have one of the greatest speeches of all time, or music videos as we now know them might never have existed. Think outside the box and take chances that will set you apart from others.

Be organized. King and Jackson both contributed something unique by being creative and resourceful yet organized in an audience-centered manner. Successful speakers effectively organize their speeches to focus and engage their audiences.

→ Parts 1–5 will help you develop your knowledge, use your creativity, and organize your speech.

3
Use Appropriate Presentation Techniques

Think about how you talk to your best friend compared with how you speak to someone like your mother or grandfather. Most likely, you do not use the same language and speaking style with your friend that you do with an older relative. The same goes for speaking effectively in public. Speakers must think about the topic, audience, situation, and intent of their speeches when they select their verbal and nonverbal behavior and their delivery style. For example, reading from a manuscript about your trip to the state fair will seem strange and too formal.

Most of the speeches you will give in a class or your everyday life will use an *extemporaneous* style. Speaking extemporaneously requires you to logically organize the speech, practice sufficiently, and use minimal notes while giving the speech. Practicing is especially important to a successful speech. It helps you hone your skills, locate issues that are not working within the speech, and develop confidence.

→ See Chapters 8 and 9 for guidance on appropriate behavior and delivery styles.

TIP: Speech Anxiety
Remember that nervousness is normal—even important—and can help energize you!

How Can You Overcome a Fear of Public Speaking?

1 Face Your Fear Head On

2 Learn Techniques That Work for You

3 Practice, Practice, Practice

1

Face Your Fear Head On

Communication apprehension (also known as *speech anxiety*) is a term scholars give to the fears you may have about giving a speech. These fears can be so intense that you avoid situations where you must speak in front of a group, and they can manifest into physical distress such as nausea or panic attacks. Clearly, physical distress at this level is something you need to control, but some apprehension is good. The physical and psychological responses you have before a date, a big game, or a speech are normal; they can help you succeed at the task at hand, and they can be controlled.

2

Learn Techniques That Work for You

The process of controlling your anxiety begins with recognizing exactly what you fear and noting how your body and mind react to stress. Often, just naming what we are afraid of will help us see how unfounded our fears might be. Throughout this book, "Confidence Booster" boxes (such as the one to the right) offer insights that may help you respond to your physical and psychological reactions. Note that they are labeled "Confidence Booster," not "Anxiety Eliminator." A certain amount of intense reaction energizes you and prepares you for the event.

➔ See Chapter 9 for more on effective delivery practices, and use the Confidence Booster boxes throughout the book to help conquer stage fright.

3
Practice, Practice, Practice

Often your instinct is to stay away from situations that cause you stress. In the case of speech anxiety, if you really want to overcome it, you have to put yourself in speaking situations. The more you practice your speeches, and the more often you speak in front of an audience, the easier public speaking becomes. Ignoring anxiety makes that monster bigger and stronger.

CONFIDENCE BOOSTER

Training your body to adjust *before* you experience speech anxiety will help you control that inner demon. Many psychologists and communication practitioners suggest training your body to breathe deeply and to visualize happy, stress-free images. Remember, the key to training is practicing these techniques before you need them so that your body learns how it feels in a truly stress-free situation. These two techniques find their true power as a daily form of meditation and not just a quick fix for intense stress. The steps below are based on exercises from the University of Maryland Medical Center.

Deep Breathing

Deep breathing is a great way to relax the body.

1 Sit straight or lie on your back.

2 Slowly relax your body.

3 Begin to inhale slowly through your nose. Fill the lower part of your chest first, then the middle and top part of your chest and lungs. Be sure to do this slowly, over 8 to 10 seconds.

4 Hold your breath for a second or two.

5 Then quietly and easily relax and let the air out.

6 Wait a few seconds and repeat this cycle. If you become dizzy, slow down or stop.

Guided Imagery

In this technique, the goal is to visualize yourself in a peaceful setting.

1 Get comfortable and close your eyes or focus on a particular spot.

2 Imagine yourself in a place that makes you happy, such as on the beach or in a hammock.

3 Take yourself there mentally. Feel the sun and air on your skin, listen to the peaceful sounds, smell the flowers or ocean.

Practicing these techniques daily can have major stress-relieving effects on your body and will train it to understand what it feels like to relax.

A few deep breaths or taking yourself to your happy place just before a speech can refocus your mind on a body with less anxiety. Try to make it a habit to do one of these techniques four to five times daily, especially during potentially stressful times.

How Can You Be an Ethical Public Speaker?

1 Understand Ethics

2 Respect Diversity

3 Cite Sources to Avoid Plagiarism

4 Use Reliable Evidence, Logic, and Reasoning

5 Support and Endorse Freedom of Expression

Understand Ethics

Being ethical means much more than just following the rules. Rules are part of the equation, but ethics grows out of our need to develop social relationships with others and our responsibilities within those relationships. For you to construct and maintain good relationships, others must view you as trustworthy, competent, objective, and passionate about what you do and support.

Ethics should become a part of every decision you make as you create your speech. Use the "Practicing Ethics" boxes throughout this book to help you every step of the way.

Respect Diversity

As an ethical speaker, you must work at recognizing every member of your audience and respect his or her needs and motives. Avoid **ethnocentrism**, or the assumption that your own group or culture is better than all others. Create a sense of inclusion, not exclusion. Be respectful and helpful.

Be aware of your language choices and their power. Offensive language directed at someone's race, ethnicity, religion, gender, or culture is inappropriate at the very least and can be the fuel for hate groups at its worst. Use language for the good of others.

➔ See Chapter 1 to help you get to know your audience.

➔ See Chapter 8 for how to use language respectfully and ethically.

3
Cite Sources to Avoid Plagiarism

When you intentionally or accidentally use all or a portion of the words, ideas, or illustrations created by someone else without giving proper credit, you commit the unethical and potentially harmful act of *plagiarism*. There are two types:

- *Blatant plagiarism* can occur either when speakers take an entire speech or document and present it as their own or when a speaker takes parts of information from other sources and links the parts together, creating an entire speech out of someone else's words.

- *No-citation plagiarism* occurs when speakers fail to give source credit to a specific part of their speech that has been taken from another source.

Be sure to cite all of your sources.

→ See Part 2 for how to cite sources.

PRACTICING ETHICS:
How to Avoid Plagiarism

- Read and make sure you understand your institution's and instructor's plagiarism policies.
- Do your research early so that you have enough time to properly prepare.
- Keep detailed notes on any sources you use.
- Use your own words, sentence structure, and organizational structure.
- Utilize a variety of sources.
- Make sure that you cite sources of quotations, paraphrased material, facts, definitions, and statistics.
- Cite the sources of illustrations, graphs, photos, and other visual items if you did not create them yourself.
- Follow the class assignment rules for citing sources.

4
Use Reliable Evidence, Logic, and Reasoning

To be ethical, you must dedicate yourself to using reliable evidence, tight organization, and careful reasoning (avoiding fallacies). Be aware that overly emotional language can cloud your audience's ability to reason.

When speaking publicly, you have the opportunity to alter people's lives. Be careful with that responsibility. As Aristotle wrote in "De Caleo" ("On the Heavens"), "The least initial deviation from the truth is multiplied later a thousandfold."

→ See Chapter 4 for how to select evidence.
→ See Part 3 for help with organizing a speech.
→ See Chapter 8 for how to use language effectively and ethically.
→ See Chapter 14 for how to create sensible reasoning and avoid fallacies.

5
Support and Endorse Freedom of Expression

The *First Amendment* of the U.S. Constitution (adopted in 1791) states, "Congress shall make no law...abridging the freedom of speech, or the press..." As a public speaker, you are morally and legally obligated to comply with laws that protect others. Practicing the previous guidelines will help you protect the rights of others. Keep the following practices in mind as well:

- Be careful to debate ideas rather than to attack people.
- Keep your feelings in check.
- Above all, remember that the First Amendment is a form of protection and empowerment.

What Is the Process of Communicating?

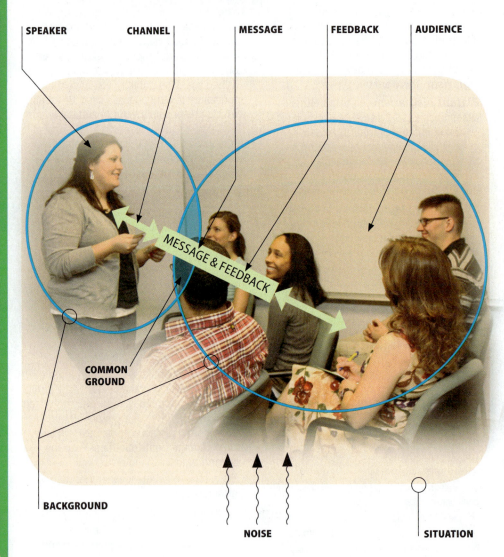

SPEAKER CHANNEL MESSAGE FEEDBACK AUDIENCE

MESSAGE & FEEDBACK

COMMON GROUND

BACKGROUND

NOISE

SITUATION

Public speaking is a communication process and best understood when represented as a model where several parts interact and influence each other.

- The **speaker** is the person who initiates and is responsible for most of the message.
- The **audience** is the person or persons receiving the speaker's message and contributing feedback.
- The **message** consists of the verbal and nonverbal ideas encoded by the speaker and decoded by the audience. In the diagram on the previous page, **encoding** (the process of conveying) and **decoding** (the process of interpreting) are illustrated by the double arrows on either side of the "Message & Feedback" element.
- **Feedback** consists of the verbal or nonverbal messages encoded by the audience and decoded by the speaker.
- The **channel** is the means of getting the message across, such as a voice over the airwaves or visual messages in the form of nonverbal or visual aids.
- **Noise** is anything that interferes with the message or feedback, such as external sounds or internal fear or illness.
- The **situation** is the location and time in which the communication takes place.
- **Background** refers to the speaker's and the audience's identities and life experiences.
- **Common ground** refers to the overlap within the speaker's and audience's identities and life experiences.

If you have the ability to carry on an ordinary conversation, you have the ability to speak publicly. The difference between public speaking and everyday conversation is that public speaking requires a more formal structure, use of language, and delivery style.

For years, we considered the process of communicating like a one-way street—information flowed from the sender to the receiver, but not the other way around. Then we viewed it as a two-way street with information traveling separately on each respective side of the street but not at the same time—to and from, back and forth. Today, we view communication as a much more complex process that is transactional. It is a **transactional process** because:

- The people involved in the act of communicating are actively and simultaneously sending as well as receiving information.
- Participants view their communication as intentional.
- The transfer of information between them takes place within a particular situation bound by relationship and culture.

You should view the speaker and the audience as co-communicators in the process, giving them almost equal responsibility and power to create as well as understand the message.

What Is the Creative Process for Public Speaking?

Composing and presenting a speech may seem daunting if you view the process only as a whole, but you can break it down into workable parts. The practical information throughout this book will help you. This chart shows the five basic activities you will use to create a successful speech. Although the process may look linear, you will frequently move back and forth between activities.

1 STARTING

GETTING TO KNOW YOUR AUDIENCE AND SITUATION

→ See page 20

Know who you are speaking to as well as where, when, and why you are speaking.

SELECTING YOUR TOPIC AND PURPOSE

→ See page 34

Select the topic that best fits you, your audience, and the occasion. Define the purpose of your speech.

2 RESEARCHING

LOCATING SUPPORT MATERIALS

→ See page 52

Find support materials through the Internet, the library, interviews, and surveys.

SELECTING AND TESTING SUPPORT MATERIALS

→ See page 74

Learn how to effectively evaluate, choose, and use a variety of support materials.

3 CREATING

OUTLINING YOUR SPEECH

➜ See page 96

Start with a working outline, create a preparation outline, and include a source page. Create a delivery outline to use during your speech.

ORGANIZING THE SPEECH BODY

➜ See page 122

Identify your main points and choose an organizational strategy.

INTRODUCING AND CONCLUDING YOUR SPEECH

➜ See page 136

Create an introduction that gets attention and sets up your credibility and your speech. Create a conclusion that sums up and ends with impact.

4 PRESENTING

USING LANGUAGE SUCCESSFULLY

➜ See page 152

Write your speech using language that is familiar, concrete, appropriate, and vivid. Use devices like repetition and parallelism to engage your audience.

DELIVERING YOUR SPEECH

➜ See page 162

Strive to be natural, enthusiastic, confident, engaging, and appropriate in your delivery. Practice!

USING PRESENTATION AIDS

➜ See page 178

Know when and how to use presentation aids to capture attention, enhance your credibility, and help your audience understand and remember your speech.

5 LISTENING & EVALUATING

LISTENING

➜ See page 204

Be an active, ethical, and effective listener who can overcome barriers to listening and who shares responsibility in the communication process.

EVALUATING SPEECHES

➜ See page 216

Determine the effectiveness and appropriateness of a speech's topic, support materials, organization, and language. Evaluate a speaker's delivery and ethics.

1 STARTING

GETTING TO KNOW YOUR AUDIENCE AND SITUATION

Knowing who you will be speaking to, as well as where, when, and why you are speaking, is fundamental to creating a speech.

All of your decisions during the speech-making process need to consider these factors.

- Who will be in the audience? What are the audience's beliefs, values, attitudes, or personal, social, or other traits?
- Where will the speech take place? What are the specific characteristics of the location that could affect your speech?
- What time of day will your speech take place? Will there be other speeches? What will happen before and after?
- Why is the audience gathered? Is it a special occasion?

➔ Chapter 1 shows you how to get to know your audience and situation.

SELECTING YOUR TOPIC AND PURPOSE

Your speech topic and purpose must interest you and should be appropriate to your audience and the occasion.

Here are some suggestions to help you in the selection process.

- Evaluate your speech assignment or speech invitation for hints about a topic or the type of speech you need to give.
- Create a list of possible topics by:
  - Brainstorming, or free-associating, about possible ideas
  - Exploring topic ideas related to the type of speech you are giving (to inform, to persuade, or to accentuate an event)
  - Searching the Internet, newspapers, or other media for ideas
- Review your list and select the topic that best fits you, your audience, and the occasion.
- Narrow your topic by writing a single, complete sentence about your topic and what you want to cover in the speech.
  - Do some preliminary research to see if you can locate enough appropriate and current information on the topic.
  - Think of three to five main points you might make about your topic, and create a working outline to guide your research.

➔ Chapter 2 shows you how to select an appropriate topic.

2 RESEARCHING

LOCATING SUPPORT MATERIALS

With the advent of the Internet, locating and collecting support materials has never been so easy or exciting. However, you can locate great materials in many places.

- **Start with your own personal knowledge and possessions.**
  Personal materials should primarily be used at the beginning of your research and should not be the only type of sources you consult.

- **Search the Internet.**
  Use search engines to locate Web sites, online references, virtual libraries and archives, and blogs.

- **Check out the library, either online or in person.**
  The library offers books, special collections, periodicals, government documents, reference material, online databases, and interlibrary loans.

- **Conduct interviews or surveys related to your topic.**

- **Take good research notes.**
  Prepare before you begin your research, take detailed notes, and refer to the appropriate style manual for your course to be sure you collect all the citation information you need.

→ Chapter 3 shows you how to locate support materials.

SELECTING AND TESTING SUPPORT MATERIALS

Support materials are the substance that fills the content of your speech. You should always:

- **Use a variety of materials** (examples, facts, definitions, statistics, or testimony).

- **Evaluate the materials:**
  - Are the materials accurate?
  - Are the materials complete?
  - Are the materials current?
  - Are the materials trustworthy?
  - Are the materials suitable?

- **Use the materials in an effective manner:**
  - Do you quote and paraphrase effectively?
  - Do the materials have a purpose?
  - Are you presenting the materials in a variety of ways?
  - Do you correctly and effectively cite the sources of the materials?

→ Chapter 4 discusses support materials in detail.

3 CREATING

OUTLINING YOUR SPEECH

You need to lead your audience through your speech, and outlining helps you create a logical structure.

All preparation outlines should adhere to formal outline rules, and citations should follow a style manual, such as MLA or APA. Your preparation outline should include:

- An introduction and a conclusion
- A body containing main points and support materials
- Links between each part
- Citations within the outline and a source page

Create a delivery outline, out of key words and phrases, to use during your actual presentation.

➜ Chapter 5 shows you how to create outlines.

ORGANIZING THE SPEECH BODY

Using an appropriate organizational strategy for the body of your speech is essential.

You choose a strategy by:

- Considering your speech goal (to inform, to persuade, to accentuate)
- Considering what your audience knows or needs to know about your topic
- Identifying your main points

Organizational strategies include chronological, topical, spatial, causal, comparative, problem–solution, and Monroe's motivated sequence.

➜ Chapter 6 explains the organizational strategies and shows you how to use them.

INTRODUCING AND CONCLUDING YOUR SPEECH

Your introduction and conclusion are the first and last opportunities you have to dazzle your audience, so dedicate time to crafting effective ones.

Your introduction should launch your speech by using this format:

- Attention-getter: Begin with material that grabs your audience's attention.
- Credibility material: Build your credibility by stating why you should give this speech.
- Relevance to audience: Build the audience's interest in you and your topic.
- Preview of speech: Introduce the topic and preview your main points.

Your conclusion should wrap up your speech with impact. Use this format:

- Summary statement: Briefly recap the speech's main ideas.
- Audience response statement: Tell your audience how you want them to respond to the speech.
- WOW statement: Provide closure with a memorable "wow" ending.

➜ Chapter 7 shows you how to create effective introductions and conclusions.

PRESENTING

USING LANGUAGE SUCCESSFULLY

Language is powerful, and you need to use it effectively.

Your speech should:

- Use language that is familiar, concrete, precise, and accurate.
- Use vivid language for emotional appeal.
- Use repetition and parallelism to help your audience remember points.
- Use language that is appropriate for you, your audience, and the occasion.

→ Chapter 8 shows you how to make effective language choices.

DELIVERING YOUR SPEECH

Successful delivery takes practice.

You should aim to:

- Be natural.
- Be enthusiastic.
- Be confident.
- Be engaging verbally and nonverbally.
- Be appropriate.

Remember to use your voice and body effectively. Vary your voice in rate, pitch, volume, and other characteristics. Be sure your appearance is appropriate, make eye contact, and use facial expressions and gestures to emphasize points in your speech.

Above all, practice, practice, and practice your speech some more!

→ Chapter 9 offers guidance on effective delivery techniques.

USING PRESENTATION AIDS

Not all speeches require presentation aids, but when you do use them, they can be beneficial.

Effective presentation aids can:

- Capture your audience's attention.
- Enhance your credibility if they are well made.
- Increase your audience's understanding of complex ideas or statistics.
- Improve your audience's ability to remember parts of your speech.

You can use audio or video clips, items, models, maps, graphs, charts, and/or pictures to enhance your speech.

To be effective, presentation aids should be:

- Easy to see.
- Kept simple.
- Appropriate for you, your audience, and the occasion.
- Well made.

→ Chapter 10 helps you determine if you need presentation aids and shows you how to craft them.

5 LISTENING & EVALUATING

LISTENING

As a college student, you spend most of your day listening. As a speaker, you need to help your audience listen successfully. Listening effectively is an ethical responsibility—as well as a necessity for gaining information and critically evaluating the communication of others. Our ability to listen influences our personal, professional, and public lives.

Effective listening faces several barriers that we must continually overcome:

- Environmental barriers, such as a siren
- Physiological barriers, such as a headache or hearing impairment
- Psychological barriers that occur in our heads, such as racism or sexism
- Linguistic barriers or verbal and nonverbal issues, such as not understanding slang or an unfamiliar nonverbal symbol

To overcome these barriers:

You must understand what listening is and accept your share of the responsibility in the communication process. As a speaker, help your audience listen more effectively by knowing who they are, grabbing their attention, creating a message that is interesting and easy to follow, controlling the environment, and paying attention to audience feedback. As an audience member, actively listen (concentrate by focusing on the verbal and nonverbal) and listen critically (assess the message, reserve your personal reactions, and be open minded).

EVALUATING SPEECHES

Learning to give evaluations of your own and others' speeches, and to accept other people's evaluations of your speeches, begins with viewing the process as a *good* thing. An evaluation is a form of assessment, an act of appreciation, or a means of self-improvement.

When you are evaluated or you evaluate someone else, you should consider:

- Is the topic appropriate?
- Did the speech use effective support materials?
- Was the speech organized effectively?
- Was the speaker's delivery effective?
- Were the language choices appropriate and effective?
- Was the speaker ethical?

Effective evaluation begins with being truthful, specific, sensitive, helpful, and positive.

→ Chapter 11 explains the listening process and shows you how to be a better listener.

→ Chapter 12 shows you how to use feedback to improve and how to be a constructive evaluator.

Using the Steps in This Book

Creating a speech is a lot like running a race, solving a puzzle, or playing a video game. You evaluate the other players and the situation; you research your options; you organize your strategy; and you plan an effective attack or move. You select a path to take, and you follow it, one step at a time, to the finish line. In the first five parts of this book, you will encounter the tools and activities to help you along the path of creating the best communicative events you can. In the last three parts, you will see those tools and activities put into practice when creating an informative, persuasive, or special occasion speech.

As American civil rights activist Jesse Jackson once said,

> *"If my mind can conceive it, and my heart can believe it, I know I can achieve it."* [1]

Use the steps in this book to conceive a great speech and to believe in your heart of hearts that you can deliver it. Take a deep breath, stand tall, walk to the lectern, and believe in yourself. You can achieve success and confidence in speaking!

1
GETTING TO KNOW YOUR AUDIENCE AND SITUATION

Introduction

Think about how you feel when someone cannot remember your name. Or gives you advice without learning who you are, what your needs are, or what motivates you. These behaviors can make you feel like you are not important or that what you believe does not matter.

Speaking to an audience that you have not taken the time to learn about creates similar feelings. It is a necessity and your ethical responsibility as a speaker to appreciate your audience if you want to succeed. Like a good friendship, a connection with your audience takes effort.

Audiences want you to do the work to grab and keep their attention. One way to do this is to recognize their **egocentrism**, or the tendency for your audience to be interested in things that relate and matter to them. Audiences want you to recognize that they are a unique group of individuals, not one mass without personality, which means crafting your speech to be **audience centered**. This approach begins the moment you start selecting your topic and continues to the moment you finish delivering your speech.

Speaking from an audience-centered standpoint begins with **audience analysis**—a systematic investigation of characteristics that make your audience unique. Audience analysis helps you answer:

- What ideas should be covered for this audience?

- How much information will they need?

- What language and support materials will work best for them?

- What could be potential audience expectations and reactions?

- What obstacles could affect the speech?

OVERVIEW OF PUBLIC SPEAKING   2

CHAPTER 1 CONTENTS

What Do You Need to Know About Your Audience?   22
1   Attitudes   22
2   Beliefs   23
3   Values   23

What Specific Traits Do You Need to Investigate?   24
1   Personal Traits   24
2   Psychological Traits   26
3   Social Traits   27

What Do You Need to Know About the Speaking Situation?   28
1   Place and Audience Size   28
2   Time   29
3   Occasion   29

How Do You Locate Audience and Situation Information?   30
1   Stop, Think, and Brainstorm   30
2   Research   30
3   Interview   31
4   Survey   31

How Can You Adapt to Your Audience During the Speech?   32
1   Adapt to External Noise   33
2   Adapt to Internal Noise   33

CHAPTER 2: Selecting Your Topic and Purpose   34
PART 1 Review   50

What Do You Need to Know About Your Audience?

1 Attitudes
2 Beliefs
3 Values

1

Attitudes

Attitudes are persistent psychological responses, predispositions, or inclinations to act one way or feel a particular way—usually positive or negative—toward something. For instance, you might like New York City better than Chicago, you may not trust anything found on the Internet, or you may like to date men that are tall and have dark hair. The longer someone holds an attitude, the more information he or she usually has to support it—and the harder it is to change.

CONFIDENCE BOOSTER

Analyzing your audience to know their point of view—and to see them as individuals instead of a mass of people—has the added benefit of helping you feel more comfortable in front of them. Spend the time necessary to get to know your audience.

2
Beliefs

Beliefs are those things a person accepts as plausible based on interpretation and judgment, such as believing in a religion or philosophy. For example, you may believe it is the responsibility of humans to take care of the planet, Internet bullying is harmful, the earth's seasons are caused by its tilting on its axis, or the United States has a responsibility to help other countries in times of disaster. Some beliefs may be easily accepted with only a little knowledge, whereas others take time to accept or may be very controversial.

3
Values

Values relate to worth or what a person sees as right or wrong, important or unimportant, desirable or undesirable. Values are our principles, such as cherishing family over professional success. Other examples of values held by many in the United States are independence, progress, freedom of speech, life, good health, honesty, wealth, and education. When you are from or belong to a country, culture, or religion, you may be expected to hold and share common values with the other members.

Beliefs, values, and attitudes make up the audience's **identity.** Of course, you will never fully know your audience's specific beliefs, values, and attitudes about every issue in your speech, but knowing as much as possible about them will help you make your speech more meaningful and you more confident.

What Specific Traits Do You Need to Investigate?

1 Personal Traits
2 Psychological Traits
3 Social Traits

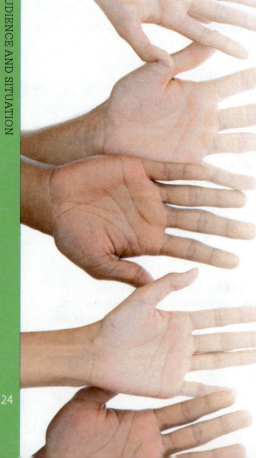

1

Personal Traits

Personal traits (sometimes referred to as *demographics*) include age, gender, sexual orientation, household type, education, occupation, income, and disabilities. Each characteristic can potentially provide insight into what's important to your audience, how they will feel about given issues, and what they accept as true.

The key to using personal traits effectively is to make yourself aware of potential traits present in your audience but not to compartmentalize or stereotype the audience. **Stereotyping** is false or oversimplified generalizing applied to individuals based on group characteristics. Allow the traits to guide but not dictate your interactions.

Although the potential personal traits you might need to consider are almost endless, a few to consider are listed in the checklist below and on the next page.

CHECKLIST for Personal Traits

❏ What's the age range of my audience? What's the average age?

❏ What's the gender ratio?

❏ Who are the audience members specifically? What do I know about their occupations? Education? Households? Disabilities?

❏ What's the average income or socioeconomic level?

❏ What might the audience already know about my potential topics?

NOTE: Not all of these questions will apply to every speaking event, but you should do your best to know as much as possible about the audience.

Remember to:

- Be respectful of gender and sexual orientation. No matter whether your audience is predominately male or female, or gay or straight, being insensitive will hurt your reputation and perpetuates negative stereotypes.

- Recognize that you may have few "traditional" household members in your audience. According to the Population Reference Bureau, only 7 percent of all U.S. households in 2002 were "traditional."

- Remember that high levels of education do not always equate with intelligence. College graduates are not smart about everything, and some very intelligent people are self-taught.

- Be cautious about connecting income levels and occupations.

- Consider that you may have audience members with disabilities. They often have unique insights and may have certain communicative challenges.

GENERATIONAL TRENDS

This table, adapted from *When Generations Collide* by Lynne Lancaster and David Stillman, describes some generational trends you can consider to help you understand how age might influence your audience.

Born before 1945 *(Traditionalists)*	Defining word: **loyal** Marry once, "save for a rainy day," little formal education, conservative, respect authority and America, not easily persuaded.
Born 1946–1964 *(Baby Boomers)*	Defining word: **optimistic** More educated, committed to belonging, political, very competitive, spend rather than save, divorce and remarry, cynical of and challenge authority.
Born 1965–1980 *(Generation X)*	Defining word: **skepticism** Product of divorce, single parents, or blended homes; independent; count on peers and friends more than family; influenced by media; struggle with money.
Born 1981–1999 *(Millennials or Generation Y)*	Defining word: **realistic** Smart, confident, practical, techno-savvy, concerned about personal safety, influenced by friends and media, appreciate diversity, can be very biased.

PRACTICING ETHICS

- Avoid negative stereotypes.
- Understand that personal traits can change due to significant events, trends, and opportunities during a particular time in history.
- Respect diversity, all the time!

2
Psychological Traits

The **psychological traits** of your audience pertain to their needs and motivations. In *Motivation and Personality*, psychologist Abraham Maslow outlined a classic theory demonstrating how people's needs motivate them to respond in certain ways. For example, if buying or doing something will help people satisfy a need, they will more likely make that purchase or do that activity. Maslow fine-tuned his theory by identifying five levels of needs, which are *hierarchical*. In other words, you must fulfill some of the basic needs before the other needs become crucial. **Maslow's hierarchy of needs** is best represented as a pyramid, with basic needs at the bottom, giving support to the higher levels.

Physiological needs are related to continued existence, such as food, water, general comfort, and sex. These are the most pure and most necessary for a person to continue to live. A speech on "How to Eat Healthy on a Budget" highlights this level of need.

Safety needs relate to what we need to feel secure, such as a roof over our heads and safety in our own homes. A speech demonstrating how to be ready in times of disaster evokes this type of need.

Social needs are those feelings we have about belonging. Most of us want to give and receive love, be close to others, and be supported. We have a strong need to feel a part of groups, such as family, friends, or religion. Pep rallies and speeches given during new student orientations on college campuses strive to fulfill this need.

Self-esteem needs relate to our strong need for respect from others we view as important, much as you may have felt when you were a teenager and wanted your parents to trust you and be proud of you. Pride, prestige, self-respect, accomplishment, recognition, and the need for success are aspects of this need. Speeches given at graduations usually focus heavily on this need.

Self-actualization needs relate to the need to feel achievement connected to personal identity, independence, happiness, and potential. An example of a self-actualization speech would be seven-time winner of the Tour de France and cancer survivor Lance Armstrong giving a motivational speech to a group of young cancer survivors. His LiveSTRONG motto characterizes this need.

CHECKLIST for Psychological Traits
❑ What needs might my audience have?
❑ Is there a level of needs where my audience has significant concerns?
❑ Because of their needs, will my audience be positive, apathetic, or negative toward my potential speech topics?
❑ How might I use their needs to show relevance to my topic or to persuade them?

3

Social Traits

Your audience's **social traits** relate to how they are affected by or identify with other groups of people. Two types of groups can influence your audience—those by choice and those by birth.

SOCIAL TRAITS BY CHOICE

The "by choice" group are people your audience members choose to connect with, like political parties, hobby communities, athletic teams, and religious, professional, social, or civic organizations. Studying these group connections can give you obvious but significant insights into how your audience will relate to you and your topic. For example, avid hunters may react negatively to a speech arguing for new hunting regulations unless they see a benefit to hunters or the animal population.

SOCIAL TRAITS BY BIRTH

The second group includes those relationships your audience members have with others by birth and by growing up within certain societies—specifically race, ethnicity, and culture.

Race is the biological differences of humankind, based on physical markers such as color and texture of hair, color of skin and eyes, shape of facial features, bodily build, and proportions.

Ethnicity stems from our national and religious affiliations.

Culture is the system that teaches a set of objectives and rules that help us survive and gain societal acceptance within our community. Individuals learn, share, and convey culture from generation to generation.

Race, ethnicity, and culture mold a person's identity and, therefore, will directly influence how he or she responds to issues.

As a speaker, you must be aware of and sensitive to diverse points of view. For example, U.S. "minorities" tend to consider issues such as equal opportunity and immigration laws more carefully than people in the "majority."

As another example, a *collectivist* culture like Taiwan stands for the group, so a collectivist audience may respond to an emphasis on community and duty. An *individualist* culture like the United States stands for self, and such audiences may respond to an emphasis on personal reward.

Consider diversity an opportunity rather than an obstacle, with ethical appreciation in every stage of your speech process.

CHECKLIST for Social Traits

- ❏ What organizations will sponsor the speaking event?
- ❏ What organizations might be represented at the event?
- ❏ What other social affiliations might influence my speech (such as hobbies or athletic teams)?
- ❏ What professions might be represented?
- ❏ What religions might be represented?
- ❏ What cultures, ethnicities, and races might be represented?

What Do You Need to Know About the Speaking Situation?

1 Place and Audience Size
2 Time
3 Occasion

CHECKLIST for Place and Audience Size

❏ Will I be giving the speech inside or outside?

❏ If outside, what are the plans if there is bad weather?

❏ What are the stage arrangements? Is there a lectern or table if I need one?

❏ How large will the audience be? In what arrangement? If the room is too small, can I move?

❏ Will I need to make any adjustments to be visible to the whole audience?

❏ Are there issues to consider for audience members with disabilities?

❏ Will I have the equipment I need? What are my backup plans? Can I practice with the equipment?

❏ Can I control the heating, lighting, and sound? Will they be a problem?

❏ Whom do I contact for help with any logistics?

❏ Does this place have significance for the audience?

1 Place and Audience Size

Imagine this scene: You are a shorter-than-average person about to give a commencement address from behind a solid wooden lectern, on a stage that is three feet above the floor where the first few rows of your audience are sitting. These audience members will see only the top of your head, if they can see you at all.

Or: Imagine giving a speech outdoors on a windy day—from loose manuscript pages.

Both of these examples highlight how important it is to consider the environment where you will be speaking and to plan ahead. A simple, short platform for the first speaker prevents embarrassment. A manuscript printed on heavy paper and attached in a binder prevents the second speaker's need to run after flying pages.

You may be in a public speaking class and know that your classroom is where you will give the speech. But such familiarity is a luxury you rarely have, and even in the classroom, you need to prepare. What if someone has taken the lectern to another room? You should always try to visit the space prior to your speech so that you can make changes if necessary and possible.

Think about any equipment you need and make sure it will be there. Make a backup plan if the equipment does not show up or is not working. Also, find out how large the audience will be. Audience size could influence how formal (for larger audiences) or informal (for smaller ones) your style can be. For a large audience, you may need more equipment, such as a microphone. Use the checklist at left to help you prepare.

2
Time

Time has two factors. The first are general elements related to the time of day, day of the week, rotation of speakers, events before the speaking event, and length of speaking time. Each element has the potential to influence your speech positively or negatively. For instance, holding audience attention during an after-dinner speech can be challenging because the audience has just eaten and may be tired.

The second factor is time's influence on your relationship with the audience. For example, if this is the first time the group hears you speak, you will likely be careful to build your credibility (also called ethos). If they have heard you speak many times and have responded favorably, you might be a bit less formal. Think about how your professor or your boss related to you when you first met. How does she or he relate to you now? Is there a difference? Has your relationship evolved over time?

Use the checklist below to see how time will affect your speech.

3
Occasion

Think about *why* your audience is gathered to hear your speech. How might the occasion influence their feelings about you and your topic? Are they a captive audience, required to be there, who do not feel like they can leave? Or are they a voluntary audience who made the choice to hear your speech?

Audiences required to attend an event, such as students at graduation or employees at a job-required meeting, can be apathetic, negative, or impatient. You might even experience some of these reactions in your classroom, as your audience has to be there regularly and must listen to many speeches. Captive audiences are not impossible to reach, but you must be more dynamic and interesting to gain their attention.

Mood is another consideration. Is the situation celebratory? Somber? Businesslike? Your speech should reflect and respect the appropriate mood.

Use the checklist below to assess your occasion.

CHECKLIST for Time

❏ How much time will I have to speak?

❏ How early should I arrive?

❏ What day of the week and time of day will I speak? How might these influence my speech? Is either of these culturally significant for my audience?

❏ Where do I fall in the rotation of speakers? How might someone else's speech influence mine?

❏ Is there late-breaking news I should consider?

❏ Is this the first time this audience will hear me speak?

❏ What is my relationship with this audience? How can I improve my speech based on that relationship?

CHECKLIST for Occasion

❏ What does the audience expect out of this event?

❏ What will be the mood of the day?

❏ Why is the audience here?

❏ How will they respond to the topic?

❏ Is this a special occasion? What is the relationship of any other speakers to the occasion?

❏ Does this audience have any social norms or expectations I should know about?

❏ Who's in charge of the event, and what is their relationship with the audience?

How Do You Locate Audience and Situation Information?

1 Stop, Think, and Brainstorm
2 Research
3 Interview
4 Survey

Adapting to your audience and situation begins immediately after you receive a public speaking assignment or engagement. The more you can predict about your audience early in the speech-making process, the better you can prepare. If you don't know your audience, you could choose an inappropriate topic or select the wrong source materials. There are several methods for collecting necessary information.

1
Stop, Think, and Brainstorm

As a speaker, you should start your audience analysis by thinking about what you already know, followed by brainstorming with others about the audience and situation. Simply taking the time to be mindful of what you (or someone close to you) might know could save valuable time. Turn to friends, relatives, teachers, or peers, and ask them what feelings or knowledge they might have about the audience and your potential speech ideas. Sometimes fresh eyes can see connections and issues that we cannot when we are so involved in the process.

2
Research

Simple detective work can be a great way to analyze your audience, especially if they are part of a larger group or organization. Often groups and organizations publish information about their membership, goals, activities, and accomplishments. The information might be on a group's Web site or in brochures, press releases, news articles, or annual reports. Opinion polls, census data, almanacs, local government archives, and historical societies are good sources as well, especially for general data about a population. You may find some of these sources through your library or online at sites such as gallup.com, pewresearch.org, census.gov, firstgov.gov, and infoplease.com.

3
Interview

Interview someone connected with the speaking event, a person familiar with the audience membership, or members of the audience. The interview can be in person, over the phone, by e-mail, or by regular mail.

- Consider what you need to know about the audience and situation. What will help you select or develop your topic? What will help you relate to the audience?

- Plan your questions to get the best responses.

  Open-ended questions allow the interviewee to give a detailed response and often will give you valuable information that you had not anticipated.

  EXAMPLE:
  What's it like living in the new student apartment complex?

  Closed-ended questions are used when you want general, quantifiable information. They can often be answered with a simple yes or no.

  EXAMPLE:
  Do you prefer living in a traditional residence hall rather than one with an apartment layout?

- Be willing to add questions that come to mind as you conduct the interview, but make sure you are conscious of how long the interview is running.

- End the interview by asking if you have missed anything important that would help you understand your audience better.

→ See Chapter 3 for more on how to conduct an interview.

4
Survey

Written surveys or questionnaires are helpful for gathering information from a large pool of people—and often from your audience. Surveys may contain open- and closed-ended questions but should tend toward the closed-ended. Use familiar language and a clean, consistent structure for your questionnaire. Other guidelines:

- Ask necessary demographic questions. ("What is your age?")

- Ask only one thing in each question.

- Make no assumptions about your respondents. Try to accommodate all possible answers. ("Other/please specify: ____")

- Use neutral responses for your participants to choose from. Don't be biased or leading.

→ See Chapter 3 for a detailed discussion on question construction for surveys.

How Can You Adapt to Your Audience During the Speech?

1 Adapt to External Noise
2 Adapt to Internal Noise

No matter how much you prepare for your audience, you cannot think of everything ahead of time. The communication process has too many variables that can change the outcome.

In the Overview, we reviewed the transactional process of communication. If you look back at it, you will notice that "noise" pushes into the process. This noise may interrupt the audience's ability to listen and your ability to communicate.

Chapter 11 will talk more about the importance of listening—for both the speaker and the audience—as well as how noise becomes a barrier to active listening. For now, you should realize that effective listening can only happen when the speaker and audience members are willing to work at it, by identifying and eliminating the noise.

➜ See Chapter 11 for more on how speakers and audience members can effectively listen to one another.

1
Adapt to External Noise

External noise occurs or originates outside of the mind or body and can be classified into two categories.

Environmental barriers:
sounds, movement, light, darkness, heat, cold, hard seats

Linguistic barriers:
misread verbal and nonverbal messages, such as slang, jargon, technical words, body language that differs across cultures

Anything from a loud lawn mower outside the window, to a computer that will not connect to the Internet, to a campus emergency the morning before your speech can change the best-laid plan, making it difficult for you to listen to your audience and for them to listen to you. Just remember:

- Stay calm.
- Pay attention to the noises affecting you and your audience.
- Be willing to adjust (such as pausing for the noisy lawn mower to pass or eliminating the noise if possible).

2
Adapt to Internal Noise

Internal noise occurs or originates inside of the mind or body and can be classified into two categories.

Physiological barriers:
hunger, sickness, disabilities, pain

Psychological barriers:
negative thoughts about the topic, distraction outside of the situation (such as a fight with a partner), fear, egocentrism, racism

Adapting to internal noise may require more work than adjusting to external noise. Points to keep in mind:

- If your audience's attention is wandering, call on members, move around the room, or vary your delivery to prompt them to listen.

→ See Chapter 9 for more on delivery.

- Be a creative, dynamic speaker and your audience will want to listen.
- Pay attention to the nonverbal behavior of your audience. The way people are sitting or their facial expressions are great feedback on how to adapt to the moment. For instance, if listeners seem confused, slow down and offer more examples to help them understand.
- Anticipate a potentially negative response and lessen the effect.

→ See Part 7 for more on how to influence your audience's responses.

- Ultimately, realize your audience is ethically responsible for listening to you.

In most cases, the audience will view you as a better speaker for being in enough control to handle problems—and to pull them back into the speech.

2
SELECTING
YOUR TOPIC
AND PURPOSE

Introduction

The key to any good speech is a first-rate topic. If you are using this book in a beginning speech class, selecting a good speech topic may seem like a challenge. Unless your instructor limits you, your topic could be almost anything. Any topic that is suitable for you, your audience, and the classroom situation is appropriate—which may seem overwhelming.

However, outside of your speech class, most of your public speaking opportunities will be professional or social. Your expertise may limit your topic choices, or someone else may tell you what your topic should be. Even so, you will still need to define carefully your purpose and central idea to help keep you on track when building your speech. In either case, starting your topic selection process early is crucial to your success. Speech topics can reach a dead end when they are not appropriate, or when you cannot locate enough information in a timely fashion. Also, allowing your brain to "chew" on your topic early will help you generate ideas, making the speech easier to prepare.

Imagine that you are planning a vacation. For weeks before the trip, you think constantly about what you will do, where you will eat, and what you will take. You make reservations and arrangements. By the time the vacation comes around, you are so prepared and excited that packing will seem easy and you will be ready to go. Giving your speech that same amount of time and excitement will result in a better, more enjoyable speech and will give you enormous confidence.

OVERVIEW OF PUBLIC SPEAKING   2

CHAPTER 1: Getting to Know Your Audience and Situation   20

CHAPTER 2 CONTENTS

How Do You Select a Topic?   36
1 Identify the General Purpose of Your Speech   36
2 Create an Idea Bank   37
3 Select Your Topic   39

How Do You Narrow Your Topic?   40

How Do You Create a Central Idea?   42
1 Identify the Specific Purpose of Your Speech   42
2 Identify the Central Idea of Your Speech   44
3 Evaluate Your Central Idea   46

How Do You Construct a Working Outline?   48

PART 1 Review   50

How Do You Select a Topic?

1 Identify the General Purpose of Your Speech

2 Create an Idea Bank

3 Select Your Topic

TIP: General Purpose

You can have only one general purpose—to inform, to persuade, or to accentuate (entertain, celebrate, etc.). Using an entertaining delivery style does not necessarily make your purpose to entertain. Your general purpose is your overriding goal for the whole speech.

1 Identify the General Purpose of Your Speech

Identifying the general purpose of your speech will help you narrow your topic options. The **general purpose** is the unrestricted aim of your speech, which can fall into three different categories.

To inform. The giving of information is the aim of this general purpose. Speeches focusing on topics such as "How to Make a Kite," "The History of Hershey's Chocolate," and "The Life and Career of Gilda Radner" are examples of speeches to inform.

To persuade. When your goal is *to reinforce*, *to change*, or *to influence* the attitudes, values, beliefs, or actions of your audience, you aim to persuade. Speeches arguing for health care reform or rallying members of the Republican party to support a candidate are examples of speeches to persuade.

To accentuate a special occasion. *To entertain*, *to celebrate*, or *to commemorate* is the aim of a special occasion speech. A wedding toast, a graduation speech, or a speech given by a breast cancer survivor to women recently diagnosed with breast cancer each has the aim to accentuate a special occasion.

If you are giving a speech for class, the assignment likely tells you the general purpose. When you are invited to speak, the audience or the occasion may dictate your general purpose. In some cases, you may have the flexibility to choose. For a commencement speech, for example, unless the invitation indicates your purpose, you can choose to inform, persuade, inspire, or entertain.

2

Create an Idea Bank

An **idea bank** is a list of general words and phrases that could be potential speech topics for you. Here's how to create an idea bank.

- Evaluate your speech assignment, the audience, and the speaking situation. Often this will help you limit your potential topics.

→ See Chapter 1 for how to evaluate your audience and situation.

- Write down your idea bank by hand. Using paper rather than a computer allows your mind to see connections and to jump more quickly from idea to idea.

- Make a list of potential topics by brainstorming, searching, or exploring your general purpose. Include as many ideas as you can that you find interesting.

BRAINSTORMING

Brainstorming is when you "free associate," or jump from one word or concept to another. The best way to start brainstorming is to take a personal inventory of your hobbies, interests, experiences, abilities, talents, values, attitudes, or beliefs. If you have trouble getting started, working with another person who knows you well may help. Record these concepts in your idea bank.

CONFIDENCE BOOSTER

If giving a speech seems daunting to you, try to select a topic that is familiar and will be interesting to research. You can then keep your research focused, spend more time practicing, and use your nervous energy to feed your excitement.

SEARCHING FOR TOPIC IDEAS

Another way to create an idea bank is *searching*, when you browse print publications, reference works, Web sites, or other media and materials for subject ideas.

For example, you can look through acceptable newspapers or magazines you already have access to at home or in a library, such as the Sunday paper in your area, *Time, Newsweek, The Week,* or *Smithsonian.*

You can also watch a news broadcast, search an academic database at the library, or browse the Internet. A few places you might look include About.com, Ask.com, Librarians' Internet Index, or Yahoo! Directory. The idea bank shown on this page is one example created by searching the Librarians' Internet Index.

IDEA BANK

Ideas from Librarians' Internet Index

Bubbles – How to make tools & solution

Fortune-telling

Kites

Pioneer life

Digital vs. film cameras

Women photographers

Juggling

Political memorabilia (19th & 20th centuries)

EXPLORING YOUR GENERAL PURPOSE

Using a third method to make an idea bank, *exploring your general purpose*, you can create columns for the different types of speeches and topic categories that fit your purpose. The following table offers some categories you can use to generate ideas.

→ See Parts 6, 7, and 8 for step-by-step discussions of how to create the types of speeches related to each general purpose.

If Your General Purpose Is...	Your Potential Topic Categories Are...
To inform: To describe	Object, person, animal, place, or event
To explain	Concept or issue
To demonstrate	Process

If Your General Purpose Is...	Your Potential Topic Categories Are...
To persuade:	Attitudes, beliefs, values, behaviors/actions, or policies
	(For topics under any of these categories, think about reinforcing, changing, or creating new attitudes, beliefs, etc.)

If Your General Purpose Is...	Your Potential Topic Categories Are...
To accentuate a special occasion:	Entertainment, celebration, commemoration
	(These categories are not as straightforward and will depend on the goal of the speech. You must adapt to the occasion as well as the audience. Most special occasion speeches take place at events like weddings, graduations, christenings, retirement parties, funerals, award ceremonies, inaugurals, dinners, holiday celebrations, fund-raisers, campaign banquets, conferences or conventions, and so on.)

Below is one example of an idea bank created by exploring a general purpose.

	IDEA BANK	
Places	*To inform*	*Animals/Insects*
Island of Anguilla	*To describe*	*Canaries*
Gettysburg		*Golden Retrievers*
Mississippi Headwaters		*Butterflies*
San Diego Zoo		*Bobcats in Missouri*

3
Select Your Topic

Ask yourself a series of focus questions to help identify topics that will work well and eliminate topics that will not.

- Which topics in my idea bank will work for my general purpose?
- Which topics fit the speech assignment or request?
- Which topics are most familiar to me?
- Which topics am I most comfortable speaking about?
- Which topics have positive aspects for the audience, occasion, speaking event, or timing of the event? Which topics might cause a negative reaction from the audience or are not appropriate?
- Which topics are new or unique to this audience?
- Which topics are worth the audience's time and attention?

For example, suppose you are volunteering at the local Historical Society and you create an idea bank (see above right) because the society wants you to give an informative talk. You ask yourself the focus questions and cross out topics, such as "kites," that do not relate to the society's exhibits because those topics may not interest visitors. You reason that visitors might like to hear a talk related to the recreated pioneer village on the property. Connecting this thought to your hobby of woodworking, you think that investigating how the pioneers built their homes will be a good topic. It passes the test created by the focus questions.

Idea Bank for Historical Society

~~Bubbles — How to make tools & solution~~

~~Fortune-telling~~

~~Kites~~

Pioneer life

Building homes   Pony Express

~~Digital vs. film cameras~~

~~Women photographers~~

~~Juggling~~   ghost towns

~~Political memorabilia (19th & 20th century)~~

Do some preliminary research to see if you can locate current, quality materials on the topic. As you research, ask these questions:

- Are there enough materials to create a speech that fits into my allotted speech time?
- Is there a variety of quality materials for the topic?
- Will I be able to locate and review the materials in time to prepare effectively for my speech?

If you are having trouble finding support materials, you may want to return to your idea bank for a new topic.

➜ Part 2 explains how to do research and evaluate support materials.

PRACTICING ETHICS
Your topic should not be harmful to you or your audience, and it should not break any laws or rules.

How Do You Narrow Your Topic?

Narrowing your topic may not seem all that difficult or important, but the scope of your topic can make or break your speech.

A well-defined, specific topic will help you:

- Achieve the general purpose of your speech. A topic that is too broad will not be thorough enough to be informative, persuasive, or celebratory.

- Reduce the time you spend researching and writing the speech.

- Increase your confidence for giving the speech. If you feel you are trying to cover too much material in a few minutes or you cannot remember all of the speech, your nervousness will increase. A narrow topic allows you to focus on an appropriate amount of material and to feel confident that your speech is not overloaded.

- Effectively deliver your speech at a comfortable rate. A speech that tries to cover too much will run long or seem rushed because you will talk too fast. A narrow topic helps keep the length down and allows you to speak at an understandable rate.

- Keep your audience focused on your topic. A well-defined topic will help audience members follow your speech and can prevent their minds from wandering.

Although you can narrow your topic in different ways, the main result of any method you use should be a focused, effectively written *central idea* (thesis statement). Your instructor may prefer a certain method, or the following steps can help you create a focused speech topic.

IDENTIFY THE SPECIFIC PURPOSE OF YOUR SPEECH	The *specific purpose* of your speech is a single statement that combines your general purpose, your audience, and your objective. The *objective* is the outcome or behavior you want your audience to experience or adopt after hearing your speech. → See pages 42–43.
IDENTIFY THE CENTRAL IDEA OF THE SPEECH	The *central idea* (also called a thesis statement, theme, or subject sentence) is a concise, single sentence summarizing and/or previewing what you will say in your speech. → See pages 44–45.
EVALUATE YOUR CENTRAL IDEA	Once you have created an initial central idea, you need to evaluate it. An effective central idea is vital to a successful speech because everything you say in your speech should relate back to this one complete statement. → See pages 46–47.
CONSTRUCT A WORKING OUTLINE	A *working outline* is a brief sketch of the body of your speech. The working outline will contain what you have composed so far—your topic, general purpose, specific purpose, and central idea—plus working main points to guide your research. → See pages 48–49.

How Do You Create a Central Idea?

1 **Identify the Specific Purpose of Your Speech**

2 **Identify the Central Idea of the Speech**

3 **Evaluate Your Central Idea**

1

Identify the Specific Purpose of Your Speech

Identifying your specific purpose is the first step in creating a focused central idea. The ***specific purpose*** of your speech is a single statement that combines your general purpose, your audience, and your objective. The ***objective*** of the specific purpose describes the outcome or behavior you want your audience to experience or adopt. Notice how the specific purpose examples at the top of the next page identify what the speakers want their audiences to take away from the speeches.

CHECKLIST for Evaluating a Specific Purpose

❑ Does my specific purpose contain my general purpose, my audience reference, and my objective for the speech?

❑ Is my specific purpose an infinitive statement (to inform, to convince, to motivate, to inspire)?

❑ Am I using clear, concise language?

❑ Does my specific purpose identify exactly what I want to discuss?

❑ Does my specific purpose focus on only one speech topic?

❑ Does my specific purpose relate to the audience? Does it work with the occasion and time? Is it appropriate for me?

❑ Am I trying to do too much? Will it fit the time?

EXAMPLES OF SPECIFIC PURPOSES

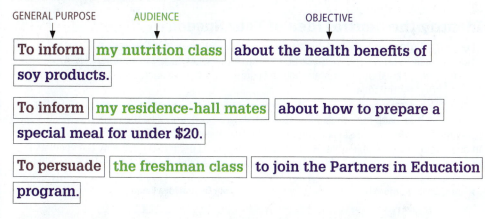

GENERAL PURPOSE · AUDIENCE · OBJECTIVE

To inform | my nutrition class | about the health benefits of soy products.

To inform | my residence-hall mates | about how to prepare a special meal for under $20.

To persuade | the freshman class | to join the Partners in Education program.

The above examples follow these guidelines for composing a specific purpose:

- Begin with an infinitive form ("To…") that reflects the general purpose, such as "To inform," "To persuade," or "To commemorate."
- Specify the audience. In the first example, the audience is "my nutrition class."
- State the objective. In the first example, the objective is to give the audience information "about the health benefits of soy products."
- Use clear, concise language. Avoid filler words or technical or long descriptions. For instance, the first example does not say, "the *awesome* health benefits of products *made with the fermented juice of a native Asian bean.*"
- Focus on only one speech topic. "The health benefits *and manufacturing* of soy products" would be two distinctly different speech topics.

Returning to your pioneer homes speech, you could construct a specific purpose this way:

GENERAL PURPOSE · AUDIENCE · OBJECTIVE

To inform | Historical Society visitors | about how pioneers built homes.

Your specific purpose should contain the key information and be concise, as the pioneer example shows. Once you have constructed a specific purpose, always evaluate it using the checklist to the left.

If you have a sound specific purpose, you are ready to identify and compose your central idea.

2

Identify the Central Idea of Your Speech

The **central idea** (also called a *thesis statement, theme,* or *subject sentence*) is a concise, single sentence summarizing and/or previewing what you will say in your speech. Any decision you make about your main points or support materials should connect back to the theme of this central idea.

How the central idea differs from the specific purpose can seem confusing, but the difference lies in how each functions. First, the specific purpose identifies the objective of your speech. Then, the central idea summarizes and/or previews the ideas your speech will cover in order to achieve its objective. Here are a few examples demonstrating how the specific purpose relates to the central idea. The objective of each specific purpose is shown in blue.

If Your Specific Purpose Is...	Your Central Idea Could Be...
To inform my nutrition class about the health benefits of soy products.	Today's market offers several soy products that are beneficial to our health.
To inform my residence-hall mates how to prepare a special meal for under $20.	You can prepare a special home-cooked meal with a few basic utensils, an eye for a bargain at the supermarket, and your residence-hall kitchenette.
To persuade the freshman class to join the Partners in Education program.	As college students, we need to give back to the community by joining the Partners in Education Program, which pairs our college with a local elementary school.

Notice how the second central idea example—preparing a special meal—previews the speech's possible main points (utensils, supermarket bargains, and kitchenette). Some instructors may require you to preview your main points in this way as a standard part of your central idea.

WHAT DOES AN EFFECTIVE CENTRAL IDEA INCLUDE?

Let's compose a central idea for the speech on pioneer home building. Start by looking at your specific purpose and identifying your objective.

SPECIFIC PURPOSE

To inform **Historical Society visitors** **about how pioneers built homes.**

OBJECTIVE

Your central idea will then summarize and/or preview what you will cover in your speech to achieve your objective. Here is one possible central idea:

CENTRAL IDEA

Pioneers moving westward built homes using available materials, basic hand tools, and general construction skills.

Notice how this example:

- Considers what your audience—the Historical Society visitors identified in your specific purpose—will need or want to know.
- Previews what your speech will include: in this case, the "available materials, basic hand tools, and general construction skills" pioneers used to build homes. This information comes from your preliminary knowledge and research.
- Focuses on only one speech topic: how pioneers built their homes.
- Uses simple, clear language that is not figurative or ambiguous. In the pioneer example, you could list the types of materials and tools, but if these types are no longer common, including them here could be confusing.
- Is a complete sentence, with a noun phrase and a verb phrase.
- Is a declarative statement, not a question.

These are all qualities your central idea should have in order to be effective.

→ The next two pages show you how to evaluate a central idea for these qualities.

3

Evaluate Your Central Idea

To evaluate your central idea for effectiveness, study it from two perspectives. First, check the mechanics; that is, make sure your central idea is written correctly with the proper parts, construction, and focus. Secondly, assess your central idea as it relates to your speech event and audience. Use the following guidelines and the checklist on the next page to help you evaluate.

MECHANICALLY SOUND

To be mechanically sound, your central idea should meet all four of the following criteria.

- **Your central idea should be a complete sentence.** A complete sentence contains a noun phrase and a verb phrase and can stand alone.

INCORRECT:

Positive aspects of the low-impact Kickbike, a bicycle-scooter hybrid.

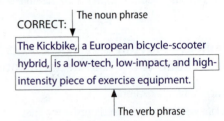

CORRECT: The noun phrase

The Kickbike, a European bicycle-scooter hybrid, is a low-tech, low-impact, and high-intensity piece of exercise equipment.

The verb phrase

Although the incorrect example ends with a period, it is only a noun phrase; without a verb phrase, it is not a complete sentence. The correct version contains both noun and verb phrases and can stand alone.

- **Your central idea should be written as a statement, not a question.**

INCORRECT:

How safe is the radiation emitted by your cell phone?

CORRECT:

Cell phones emit tiny amounts of radiation, which scientists believe may be linked to certain types of brain cancer.

Asking a question—as in the incorrect example—can help you think about your speech, but your central idea needs to be a declarative sentence, as in the correct example.

TIP: Refining Your Central Idea

Keep in mind that your central idea might change slightly as you do research and organize the speech. Be open to refining it as you move through the creative process.

- **Your central idea should use clear, specific, and direct language.** To be clear, use language familiar to the audience and words that are concrete. Avoid vague or filler language and qualifying phrases that can lessen the impact of your central idea.

INCORRECT:

Some believe basically that the radiation silently emitted from cell phones can cause cancer.

CORRECT:

Cell phones emit tiny amounts of radiation, which scientists believe may be linked to certain types of brain cancer.

In the incorrect example, "some believe" is vague—who are the "some"? "Basically" is a filler word that serves no purpose, and "silently" is unnecessary because all radiation is silent. The correct example drops the filler words and specifies "scientists believe" as well as what types of cancer may be caused by the radiation.

- **Your central idea should focus on only one speech topic.**

INCORRECT:

Kickbikes and elliptical trainers are low-impact, high-intensity pieces of exercise equipment.

Two nouns connected with a conjunction ("and") may indicate you have more than one speech topic.

CORRECT:

The Kickbike, a European bicycle-scooter hybrid, is a low-tech, low-impact, and high-intensity piece of exercise equipment.

CORRECT:

An elliptical trainer is a low-impact and high-intensity piece of exercise equipment.

In the incorrect example, "Kickbikes" and "elliptical trainers" are two equal topics that could each get a speech-length treatment. Notice how each of the correct examples previews possible points ("low-tech," low-impact," etc.) while focusing on a single speech topic.

APPROPRIATE FOR THE EVENT AND AUDIENCE

Because your central idea is a culmination of your broad topic, general purpose, and specific purpose, your central idea should, at this stage, be appropriate and focused enough for the event. However, you need to continue to assess if the topic is still narrow enough for the time allotted, interesting enough to grab your audience's attention, unique enough to not waste their time with something they already know, and accessible enough to not be too technical or confusing for them.

CHECKLIST for Evaluating a Central Idea

❏ Is the central idea written as one complete sentence?

❏ Is the central idea written as a statement (not a question)?

❏ Does the statement use clear, simple, and direct language?

❏ Does the central idea focus on only one speech topic?

❏ Can I cover this central idea in the time allotted for my speech?

❏ Is the central idea worth my audience's time and attention?

How Do You Construct a Working Outline?

The construction of a speech is a creative process, with many ways you can approach it. Some beginning students and their instructors find that creating a working outline at this point helps them focus and transition into the research phase of creating a speech.

A **working outline** is a brief (usually handwritten) sketch of the body of your speech. This outline will help you stay on track while researching your speech and give you direction on what to look for. The working outline will contain what you have composed so far—your topic, general purpose, specific purpose, and central idea—plus working main points to guide your research. The working main points may or may not be the main points you use in your final outline, but they serve the same purpose. Main points, which you will learn more about in Chapter 5, are the skeletal structure, or backbone, that makes up the body of your speech; they are the two to five most important ideas to know about your topic. **Working main points** are early drafts of your main points. They may be awkward in format and can change significantly as you research your topic.

→ Chapter 6 explains how to finalize your main points as you compose your speech.

CHECKLIST for Evaluating Working Main Points

❏ Does each main point cover *only one* key idea?

❏ Are my main points similarly constructed (are they parallel)?

❏ Am I roughly balancing the time spent on each point?

❏ Do my main points relate back to the central idea?

To construct your working main points:

1.

Turn to your central idea for categories. Write down your central idea and highlight its important issues. Evaluate the highlighted issues to see if you can discover two to five main categories with one distinct key idea per category.

CENTRAL IDEA:

Pioneers moving westward built homes using available materials, basic hand tools, and general construction skills.

CATEGORY	CATEGORY	CATEGORY
Basic hand tools	General construction skills	Available materials
KEY IDEA	**KEY IDEA**	**KEY IDEA**
What hand tools did pioneers use to build homes?	What were the general construction skills?	What materials were available for pioneers to use?

2.

Sum up each of your categories with a statement or question as shown in each key idea above. These are your working main points. Your final main points must be statements, but for now, questions may seem easier to formulate and may help focus your research. Write in complete sentences, make your points parallel in structure, and balance them so that you will spend roughly equal time on each.

> TOPIC: Pioneer life
>
> GENERAL PURPOSE: To inform
>
> SPECIFIC PURPOSE: To inform Historical Society visitors about how pioneers built homes.
>
> CENTRAL IDEA: Pioneers moving westward built homes using available materials, basic hand tools, and general construction skills.
>
> MAIN POINT #1: What materials were available for pioneers to use?
>
> MAIN POINT #2: What hand tools did pioneers use to build homes?
>
> MAIN POINT #3: What were the general construction skills?

The preliminary research you did when selecting your topic can help you compose working main points, which will continue to evolve as you prepare your speech. Use the checklist on the left to evaluate your working main points.

Part 1: Review

OVERVIEW REVIEW QUESTIONS

1. What makes a successful speaker? An ethical speaker?
2. How can you work at decreasing speech anxiety?
3. What is the transactional process of communication? Identify and explain each part.

CHAPTER 1 REVIEW QUESTIONS

1. What do you need to know and investigate about your audience?
2. What should you know about the speaking situation?
3. How do you locate audience and situation information?

CHAPTER 2 REVIEW QUESTIONS

1. What is the process for narrowing your topic?
2. What is a specific purpose? What questions should you ask when evaluating your specific purpose?
3. What is a central idea? What questions should you ask when evaluating your central idea?

TERMS TO REMEMBER

Overview

identification (4)
communication apprehension (6)
ethnocentrism (8)
plagiarism (9)
blatant plagiarism (9)
no-citation plagiarism (9)
First Amendment (9)
speaker (11)
audience (11)
message (11)
encoding (11)
decoding (11)
feedback (11)
channel (11)
noise (11)
situation (11)
background (11)
common ground (11)
transactional process (11)

Chapter 1

egocentrism (21)
audience centered (21)
audience analysis (21)
attitudes (22)
beliefs (23)
values (23)
identity (23)
personal traits (24)
stereotyping (24)
psychological traits (26)
Maslow's hierarchy of needs (26)
social traits (27)
race (27)
ethnicity (27)
culture (27)
external noise (33)
environmental barriers (33)
linguistic barriers (33)
internal noise (33)
physiological barriers (33)
psychological barriers (33)

Chapter 2

general purpose (36)
idea bank (37)
brainstorming (37)
specific purpose (42)
objective (42)
central idea (44)
working outline (48)
working main points (48)

PART 2
Researching

CHAPTER 3
Locating Support Materials 52

CHAPTER 4
Selecting and Testing Support Materials 74

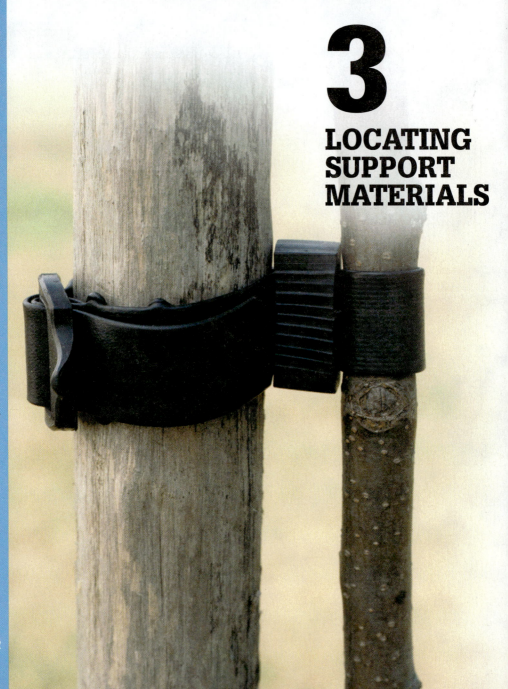

3
LOCATING SUPPORT MATERIALS

Introduction

Research is the act of investigating, evaluating, and summarizing information. The research activities in Chapters 3 and 4 will help you find effective **support materials** (or *evidence*)—information that explains, elaborates, or validates your speech topic. Support materials come from different types of **sources** (books, magazines, journals, blogs, Web sites, interviews, etc.).

For example, Logan is preparing a speech on basketball and wants to use some startling statistics about one of the best professional basketball players of all time. However, he also wants to choose a player not everyone in his class knows. Logan asked a librarian for help. She recommended first searching the Internet for a list of great players and then looking for a specific player from that list. Within minutes, Logan had the opening to his speech.

> According to NBA.com on August 9, 2011, which NBA star is the only player to average more than 50 points per game for an entire season? Who still has the best rebounding record of all time, with 23,924? Who was nicknamed the "Big Dipper"? If you answered Wilt Chamberlain, you are correct.

Because of the Internet and the quality of U.S. libraries, you (and Logan) have a vast amount of information at your fingertips, making research easier than ever.

TIP: Personal Sources

Don't forget to consider your own available personal sources. If your topic is something you are interested in, you may own books, objects, memorabilia, records of an event, video, pictures, or other related items. This is often a great place to start your research.

CHAPTER 3 CONTENTS

What Does the Internet Have to Offer You?	54
1 Search Engines	54
2 Commercial Web Sites	56
3 Nonprofit Organization Web Sites	56
4 Blogs	57
5 Personal Web Sites	57
How Can You Use the Internet to Access Libraries?	58
What Does the Library Have to Offer You?	60
1 The Catalog	61
2 Databases	62
3 Books	64
4 Newspapers	64
5 Magazines	65
6 Journals	65
What Can You Find Both on the Internet and in Libraries?	66
1 Government Resources	66
2 Reference Works	67
How Can You Gather Support Materials in an Interview?	68
1 Prepare for the Interview	68
2 Conduct the Interview	69
How Can You Gather Support Materials with a Survey?	70
1 Create the Survey	70
2 Conduct the Survey	71
How Do You Take Good Research Notes?	72
1 Prepare to Research	72
2 Know the Appropriate Style Manual	73
CHAPTER 4: Selecting and Testing Support Materials	74
PART 2 Review	94

What Does the Internet Have to Offer You?

1 Search Engines

2 Commercial Web Sites

3 Nonprofit Organization Web Sites

4 Blogs

5 Personal Web Sites

1

Search Engines

Search engines are the specific tools you use to search for information on the Web. You can access them through Web browsers (such as Internet Explorer or Mozilla Firefox). When you type search terms into an engine, it will then send back **hits**, or a list of Web pages, files, images, and other items related to the terms.

SOME GENERAL SEARCH ENGINES

Google	www.google.com
Yahoo!	www.yahoo.com
Bing	www.bing.com

SOME METASEARCH ENGINES

Metasearch engines search other engines and specialized sites.

A9	www.a9.com
Dogpile	www.dogpile.com
Excite	www.excite.com

SEARCHING THE INVISIBLE WEB

To search the invisible Web—information not accessible via general search engines—use sites like these:

Infomine	infomine.ucr.edu
Google Scholar	scholar.google.com
Alexa	www.alexa.com

TIPS: Search Terms

- Connect multiple search terms with *and, or,* or *not.*
- The first word in your search term gets the most emphasis.
- Use quotation marks around a phrase.

The following pages will show you how to locate and use types of Web sites and blogs in your research. **Web sites** usually consist of multiple, unified pages beginning with a home page. A Web site may be created and maintained by an individual, group, business, or organization. The contents of a Web site might include images, video, articles, facts, statistics, digital documents, and links to related Web sites.

The table below provides tips on how to evaluate online sources. Use common sense—don't believe everything you read on the Internet.

➜ See Chapter 4 for a detailed discussion on evaluating all sources.

WHAT SHOULD YOU EVALUATE?	HOW CAN YOU EVALUATE THIS INFORMATION?	TIPS
Accuracy: Does the information seem plausible?	• Check for citations. • Investigate the authors. • Verify content with other sources.	• Citations are usually located at the bottom of the page. • Look for an "About Us" link to find information or Google the authors. • Locate the same information in other sources.
Responsibility: Who is responsible for this Web site? What are their qualifications related to your topic?	• Look at the page header. • Study the site address (URL) for clues. • Scroll to the bottom of the home page for copyright information.	• Look for author information and research their qualifications. • A .org, .gov, or .edu extension may signify a more reliable source than .com or .net sites.
Impartiality: Could this site be biased? How are the site creators affiliated?	• Check for advertisements that may indicate a bias. • Check for a mission statement. • Consider whom the site is targeting as an audience.	• Some Web sites pay to be the top results in a search engine. They may be called sponsored links. • Look for a link such as "Our Mission," "FAQ," or "About Us" to find more information.
Currency: When was this site created? Is it important to your topic to have the most current information possible?	• Check for a copyright date or date of last update at the bottom of the home page. • Verify content with other sources.	• If a site has no copyright date, look for a date when material (such as an article or blog entry) was posted. • Look at citation dates for recent dates.

Specific types of sources, such as newspapers or magazines, also can be found using search engines.

➜ See pages 64–67 for more information on these types of sources.

2
Commercial Web Sites

Commercial Web sites are sites created and maintained by for-profit businesses or organizations. These Web sites are typically promotional sites but can include newspapers, television networks, and video and image services (e.g., YouTube or Google Maps).

WHEN TO USE

- To locate information about a company
- To gather support materials from sites of respected news organizations
- To find current or popular culture materials
- To find presentation aids (cite the sources)

ADVANTAGES

- Can offer information unavailable in print
- May be current (be sure to check dates)
- May be seen by your audience as reliable

DISADVANTAGES

- Are often biased toward the interests of the site owner or paid advertisers, if any
- May require verifying information with other sources or may not be verifiable
- May not credit all sources of information

TIPS ON LOCATING

- Use a search engine to find a specific site if you have one in mind, or search on your topic to locate related sites.

SAMPLE ORAL CITATION

"According to the feature story 'Monsanto Donates Corn and Vegetable Seeds to Haiti,' located on Monsanto.com on May 14, 2010, Monsanto has made efforts to help."

3
Nonprofit Organization Web Sites

Nonprofit organization Web sites are sites for local, national, and international not-for-profit organizations dedicated to issues or causes, such as UNICEF, MADD, the Special Olympics, or the Magic Johnson Foundation. Their URLs often end with ".org."

WHEN TO USE

- To locate detailed information about a particular issue or organization
- To locate emotional appeal examples

ADVANTAGES

- Can provide background and current information about a service or issue
- Are usually considered reliable sources
- Tend to use accessible language

DISADVANTAGES

- Have set goals or agendas, which may bias how information is presented
- May not include author credentials
- May accept paid advertisements, which may signal the site's information is biased

TIPS ON LOCATING

- Search online using the name of the organization or the issue it supports.

SAMPLE ORAL CITATION

"This graph, from the article 'Achieving Zero,' found June 1, 2010, on unicefusa.org, demonstrates the progress so far in reducing child deaths worldwide."

4
Blogs

A **blog** is a Web site or page that contains regular postings by its author(s) and may allow visitors to comment. When created by authorities, they can offer unique, credible information; but keep in mind that most blogs will represent specific opinions or points of view. Types of blogs include:

- Personal blogs (including Twitter)
- Corporate blogs (often for marketing)
- Subject blogs (politics, travel, fashion, etc.)
- Media blogs (comprised of videos, links, etc.)

WHEN TO USE
- To find examples of public opinion
- To find new developments about your topic (to verify with other sources)
- To gauge if a topic is controversial or of current general interest

ADVANTAGES
- Can provide current information
- Can be helpful in gauging public opinion
- Can offer unique material

DISADVANTAGES
- Are often biased toward the opinions of the blogger(s)
- May require verifying information with other sources
- May not credit all sources of information

TIPS ON LOCATING
- Use blog search engines (Google Blog Search, Blogarama, Bloglines, Technorati).

SAMPLE ORAL CITATION
"According to the White House blog on July 14, 2010, Air Force One totals 4,000 square feet of floor space on three levels."

5
Personal Web Sites

Personal Web sites are created by groups or individuals and focused on topics of personal interest. These sites, if created by a credible source, can offer personal or expert testimony. Much like blogs, personal Web sites can be created by anyone with the skills and equipment, and they may represent specific opinions.

WHEN TO USE
- To find material that humanizes your topic
- To find personal information about the site author(s)

ADVANTAGES
- Can be reliable support if author is a recognized expert on your topic
- Can offer unique material

DISADVANTAGES
- Can be written by anyone, regardless of his or her credentials (research the author's credibility)
- May require verifying information with other sources
- Are often promotional or biased toward the opinions of the author
- May not credit all sources of information

TIPS ON LOCATING
- Use the search engines discussed on page 54 to locate Web sites.

SAMPLE ORAL CITATION
"According to the official Web site of fiber artist Annette Kennedy, *Mountain Chapel* is an award-winning work from 2008."

How Can You Use the Internet to Access Libraries?

The facing page shows you an example of a library's online portal. Most libraries allow you to access at least some of their services online, and searching these portals is an effective way to do preliminary research on the library's holdings and resources, as well as to access online databases or reference material. Online access is also extremely helpful when you realize you need more information or you forget a citation and cannot get back to the physical library quickly. Most library portals allow you to:

- Search their catalogs and databases just as you would if you were sitting in the library (see the librarian for any special log-on requirements for databases).

- Utilize other services such as those noted on the library portal example on the next page. So explore your library portal and learn what it has to offer.

However, do not cut corners! Don't be afraid to go to the library. The reference librarian can save you time, as his or her job is to help you find information and resources. If researching is a relatively new process for you, begin with a face-to-face discussion with your librarian. He or she can help you learn how to use the resources designed to make your search faster and more effective. Whenever you ask a librarian for help, take the following items with you:

- Your speech assignment and any notes you have about it

- Your working outline

- Any research you have already completed

→ The next sections of this chapter will tell you more about the resources inside a library.

Stafford Library
Home

Ask a Librarian
About the Library
Library Catalog
MOBIUS Catalog
Journal/Newspaper Locator
Databases A-Z
Internet Links
Off-campus Access
Borrowing Laptops
Faculty Resources
Hours

Related Links
- APA/MLA Style Writing Help
- Math Center
- Career Center
- Directions to Campus
- Map of Campus

Find books...
- For Missouri campuses

  Stafford Library Catalog
  Find books, links to ebooks

  MOBIUS Catalog
  Search the collection
  may borrow books not

- For all campuses

  Search the Stafford Library

  Search libraries near you

Find articles...
For all campuses
Journal & Newspaper Locator
Search for a journal, newspaper
and/or through one of our online

Databases A - Z
An alphabetical listing of our

Find Articles by Subject
- Arts
- Business and Finance

Locate online writing help

You may find a list of Internet links related to your research needs or writing skills. For example, your library might have links to sites on evaluating Web material, writing essays, and avoiding plagiarism.

Contact a librarian

If you can't go to the library in person, you may be able to e-mail or chat with a librarian about a specific research question.

eBook search

Some library catalogs allow searches for eBooks.

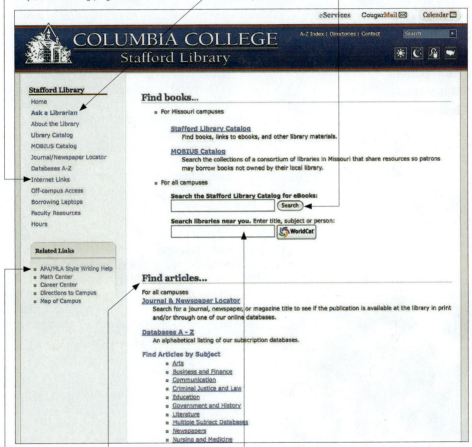

Style manual help

You can get help with creating citations and formatting your outline.

Article search

This section allows you to search for articles, journals, newspapers, and databases in its collection.

Search multiple libraries

Some campus libraries have reciprocity arrangements with other libraries, allowing you to borrow or consult a wider range of materials and saving you valuable time.

What Does the Library Have to Offer You?

1 The Catalog
2 Databases
3 Books
4 Newspapers
5 Magazines
6 Journals

You should always include the library in your research adventures. In most college towns, you have a library on or affiliated with your campus, as well as a public library. In some larger cities, you may find additional libraries dedicated to specialized topics. All of these libraries may have something to offer your speech topic.

The college library will have more academically oriented information, such as historical analysis and scientific research.

The public library will offer you access to more local history and statewide statistics, as well as popular books, newspapers, and magazines.

Special libraries are usually connected or related to a famous person (such as a presidential library), company, organization, government agency, or museum. You may need special permission to access the stacks in these libraries.

Many libraries also provide an interlibrary loan (ILL) service. ILL allows you to request items located at other libraries that will be delivered to your library. This service can give you access to much more material, but it can be time consuming (often more than a month for delivery) and can have associated fees.

TIP: Know Your Requirements
Most college speech assignments require that you use a certain amount of material from the library, rather than relying only on the Internet. Check your assignment and ask your instructor.

1

The Catalog

All libraries have a catalog system, typically an electronic search engine, designed to help you locate materials physically owned by the library. Items in the library's database are cataloged according to subjects and related subjects as assigned by the Library of Congress. Usually you can search for publications by title, author, or subject. The librarian can help you determine what search terms to use to target your research. You should always pay attention to the related subjects listed for other possible routes to take in your search. The tips given earlier for search engines are helpful here as well.

Contact a librarian: You can ask a librarian a question.

TIP: Visiting Other Libraries

If you want to use a library you are not affiliated with, check the library's Web site or call for its visiting patron policies. In many cases, a letter of introduction from the director of a library where you are already a patron will help you gain access.

Multifaceted search
This library lets you search all its collections and locations. You can also search items by format (print, audio, etc.) and other criteria.

Finding materials
You can locate books, articles, and other materials by searching catalogs and databases.

2
Databases

Although search engines like Google can help you find general information, they do not access everything, and you will usually need to do deeper research to find the highest quality support materials.

Most libraries subscribe to **databases**, or extensive collections of published works—such as magazine, newspaper, and journal articles—in electronic form, making them easy to search and locate. Databases contain descriptions and citation information about articles (title of article and publication, author, publication date, etc.), and they often include the full text of the articles. A database itself is not a source you will cite in your speech; it is a portal for finding a large amount of support materials from many different sources, all in one place.

Different databases may focus on different subject areas. For instance, ERIC (Education Resources Information Center) covers education research. Others specialize in arts, sciences, law, or business. Your reference librarian can tell you what databases are available at your library and what disciplines they cover, to help you choose the ones most relevant to your topic. Your library's Web site will likely include a link to these databases.

You search in databases much like you search in the library's catalog or with a search engine. A search screen from one common database (JSTOR) is shown on the next page. Just as with a search engine, you have options for basic and advanced searching. You may be able to limit your search by discipline or subject, to full-text articles only (rather than a description or abstract), to recent articles only, or by the language an article is written in.

Multiple-subject databases contain sources across a vast spectrum of disciplines and periodicals. Use these to research broadly and then to narrow your topic. Some common ones include:

- Academic Search Elite/EBSCOhost
- LexisNexis
- JSTOR
- Project MUSE

Specialized databases contain sources related to specific disciplines or topics. Use these to focus your research once you have your topic narrowed. Some common ones include:

- Bloom's Literary Reference Online (literary criticism and resources)
- CQ Weekly (coverage of acts of Congress)
- ERIC (education)
- OVID (science and health care)
- Standard & Poor's NetAdvantage (business)

TIPS: Using Databases

- Search in the database as you would search with an Internet search engine.
- Use databases to help you narrow your topic.
- Start with a full-text search. You might find everything you need, not only information in abstract form.
- Put limits on your search by defining attributes.
- Search more than one database.
- Ask your librarian for help if you have questions or find using a database intimidating.

Basic search
Enter key terms related to your topic.

Advanced search
Investigate how you can limit your search or do a detailed search.

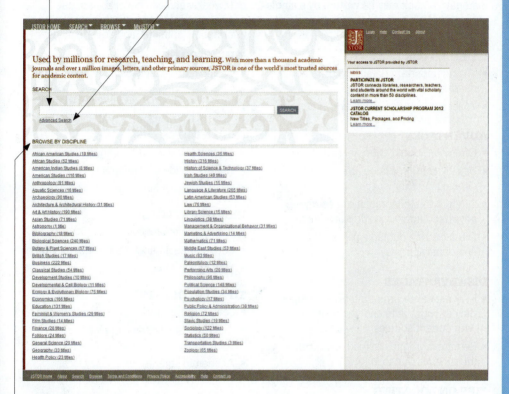

Discipline search
Some sites allow broad searching and browsing options, such as by academic discipline.

3
Books

You might use a variety of books for support materials. A book may be written by a single author, multiple authors, corporate authors, or government authors.

WHEN TO USE

- To find important detail and contextual information about your topic
- To locate facts, statistics, and examples

ADVANTAGES

- Often considered extremely reliable
- Usually contain a large amount of detailed information
- Often have bibliographies or source notes leading you to additional material
- Often contain quotable passages for emotional appeals

DISADVANTAGES

- May not have current information (check the copyright date and verify information with current sources)
- Require more time to read and glean information, due to length

TIPS ON LOCATING

- Search for your topic on sites like Amazon or Library of Congress (www.loc.gov) to identify books to seek at the library.
- Search the library catalog.

SAMPLE ORAL CITATION

"In her 2009 book *The Beginner's Guide to Preserving Food at Home*, Janet Chadwick offers several easy pickle recipes."

4
Newspapers

Newspapers are published daily, weekly, or biweekly and can be local, national, or international. They contain news, information, opinions, and advertisements.

WHEN TO USE

- To find current facts and statistics
- To locate extended examples
- To support current events or topics

ADVANTAGES

- Often viewed as current and reliable
- Feature condensed information
- Use accessible language

DISADVANTAGES

- Rarely cite references
- May require finding other in-depth sources
- May be outdated quickly

TIPS ON LOCATING

- Search the library databases.
- Public libraries often carry local and some national newspapers.
- Academic libraries often carry local, national, and international newspapers.
- Some newspapers are also online (note that online editions can be different).

SAMPLE ORAL CITATION

"A July 23 *Wall Street Journal* online article, 'BP Managers Named in Disaster Probe' by Ben Casselman and Russell Gold, said testimony in a federal investigation indicated several reasons to anticipate a major incident."

5
Magazines

Magazines are published on a regular schedule (weekly, monthly, or quarterly) and contain a range of articles, often related to a theme or focus. Magazines are generally financed by advertisements as well as a purchase or subscription price.

WHEN TO USE
- To find facts, statistics, and examples
- To support current events or topics

ADVANTAGES
- Often viewed as current and reliable
- Feature condensed information
- Use accessible language

DISADVANTAGES
- May not give background information
- May require finding other in-depth sources
- May be outdated quickly

TIPS ON LOCATING
- Search the library databases.
- Libraries often have many magazines and may archive old issues.
- Some magazines have Web sites, but they may differ from print versions or contain only old issues.

SAMPLE ORAL CITATION
"The king penguin is the second largest type of penguin. It can be as tall as three feet and weigh an average of 30 pounds, according to the September 2009 *National Geographic* article 'Every Bird a King' by Tom O'Neill."

6
Journals

Journals are academic and professional publications issued at regular intervals, such as quarterly. Journals are topic specific and exist in most major fields.

WHEN TO USE
- To find detailed facts and statistics
- To locate expert testimony
- When highly credible sources are needed
- With a highly educated audience

ADVANTAGES
- Have extremely high credibility
- Are written and peer reviewed by experts or specialists in the field
- Include extensive bibliographies where you may find further sources

DISADVANTAGES
- Are written in a formal style that may need to be adapted for your audience
- Use language specific to the field that may be difficult to understand

TIPS ON LOCATING
- Search the library databases.
- Academic libraries often carry selected scholarly/professional journals in print.

SAMPLE ORAL CITATION
"In her article, 'Geographies of Desire: Post-social Urban Space and Historical Revision in the Films of Martin Scorsese'—published in the Spring/Summer 2010 issue of the *Journal of Film and Video*—Professor Sabine Haenni argues that…"

What Can You Find Both on the Internet and in Libraries?

1 **Government Resources**
2 **Reference Works**

1 Government Resources

Government resources are information sources created by local, state, and federal governmental agencies. They can include books, reports, bills, pamphlets, maps, Web sites, or other documents.

WHEN TO USE
- To locate statistics and facts
- To locate policy information
- To locate practical information

ADVANTAGES
- Are often viewed as highly credible
- Are often very current
- Often contain information not available elsewhere
- Often have extensive bibliographies

DISADVANTAGES
- May not include citation information
- May be difficult to locate the specific publication you are looking for

TIPS ON LOCATING
- Search the Internet using the city or state name, or ask your librarian how to locate government holdings.
- Public libraries are often good sources.
- Go to www.usa.gov/directory/federal/index.shtml for a list of sites.
- The Government Printing Office Web site (www.gpoaccess.gov) offers information about federal government publications.

SAMPLE ORAL CITATION
"In 2010, the city's official Web site noted that more than 9,000 accidents occur yearly nation-wide due to drivers running lights."

2
Reference Works

A reference work is a compilation of information such as facts, data, and definitions arranged for easy access. Many printed reference works have a corresponding Web site.

Some examples are:

- Dictionaries (general and subject specific)
- Encyclopedias (general and subject specific)
- Thesauruses
- Yearbooks or annuals (e.g., *Statistical Abstracts, Facts on File Yearbook*)
- Atlases
- Grammar handbooks and style manuals
- Books of quotations
- Biographical reference books (e.g., *International Who's Who*)

WHEN TO USE

- To locate brief definitions or segments of information
- To locate statistics and facts
- To assist you in using language effectively
- To start your research and get a broad base of information to build upon

ADVANTAGES

- Are great places to begin your research
- Are useful places to get brief statistics, facts, and quotations
- Are helpful in constructing your outline

DISADVANTAGES

- May offer information that is too brief
- Can focus on obscure facts or definitions that are not popularly acceptable or used
- May be user-created sites, such as Wikipedia, which may not always be accurate and so are not viewed as credible. The source lists within these types of references may help you locate reliable primary sources, but always check with your instructor to see if using such user-created references is acceptable for your assignment.

TIPS ON LOCATING

- Check the reference section of your library or ask a reference librarian.
- Typing in a key word or phrase or asking a search engine a question will pull up many online references. Some commonly used Internet references are:

  Merriam-webster.com
  Infoplease.com
  Biography.com
  Refdesk.com
  The World Factbook

SAMPLE ORAL CITATION

"As defined in the *Longman Dictionary of American English,* dissonance is a lack of agreement between ideas, opinions, or facts."

CONFIDENCE BOOSTER

Allowing yourself to take the necessary time to effectively research your topic will not only help you compose a great speech but also increase your confidence. When you spend time building your knowledge about a topic, you become more comfortable talking about it.

How Can You Gather Support Materials in an Interview?

1 Prepare for the Interview
2 Conduct the Interview

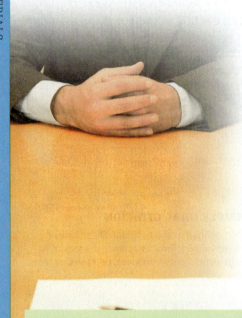

1

Prepare for the Interview

Interviews are information-gathering sessions where you (the *interviewer*) ask either one person or a group (the *interviewee/interviewees*) a series of prepared questions.

SET UP A TIME AND A LOCATION

- Set the time around your interviewee's schedule. Most interviews should last no longer than 30 to 60 minutes.
- Select a quiet and comfortable location.
- Reconfirm the time and place with your interviewee.

WRITE YOUR QUESTIONS

- Research the interviewee's background, and be sure your questions are appropriate to his or her expertise.
- Ask questions that help you gather the support materials you need.
- Use more open-ended questions than closed-ended questions. **Open-ended questions** encourage discussion or longer responses. This type of question may start with *who, what, where, when, why,* or *how*. **Closed-ended questions** prompt only "yes" or "no" answers.

DECIDE HOW TO RECORD THE INTERVIEW

- Note taking alone may work, or use an audio or video recorder as backup.
- As an ethical interviewer, you must have permission to audio or video record an interview. Some schools might require written permission.

2
Conduct the Interview

To conduct an interview, you should:

- Be well-groomed and dress appropriately.
- Make sure all equipment works.
- Arrive on time and begin on time.
- Thank the interviewee for his or her time.
- Explain your topic and speech goal.
- Give the interviewee time to respond.
- Allow yourself to think of *follow-up questions*, or new questions that occur to you based on the interviewee's answers so far. However, be aware of your time limit.
- Ask for clarification if necessary.
- Be an active listener.

→ See Chapter 11 for listening tips.

- Near the end of the interview, check your notes to see if you have the information you need.
- End your interview with a question like:
  Is there anything else I should know?
- End the interview on time.
- Take a few minutes immediately after the interview to make additional notes.
- Send the interviewee a thank-you note.

Use the checklist on this page to help prepare for and conduct your interview.

Sometimes meeting face-to-face for an interview is impossible. When necessary, you can use the telephone, e-mail, or instant messaging to conduct the interview. However, realize that these forms of information collection are not as effective as sitting face-to-face with the interviewee.

SAMPLE ORAL CITATION FOR INTERVIEW MATERIAL

"In a personal interview I conducted last month, local dentist Dr. Marvin Jones said that his office will donate supplies and a day of free checkups."

CHECKLIST for Interviewing

❏ Did I set up an appropriate time and place for the interview?

❏ Do my questions collect background information as well as necessary support materials?

❏ Are most of my questions open-ended?

❏ Do I have a means for recording the interview?

❏ On the day of the interview, am I well-groomed and dressed appropriately?

❏ Do I have everything I need to conduct the interview (questions, notebook, recorder, address, etc.)?

❏ After the interview, did I send a thank-you note?

PRACTICING ETHICS

When using information collected from an interview, you have an ethical responsibility to:

- Report the information as accurately as possible. Quote and paraphrase correctly and in context.

- Protect the interviewee from painful effects that might occur when you reveal something intimate or distressing about him or her to a larger audience. If an interviewee has requested anonymity or if you think you should protect his or her identity for any reason, use a pseudonym in your speech. During the speech, inform the audience that you have changed the name to protect the privacy of the individual.

How Can You Gather Support Materials with a Survey?

1 Create the Survey
2 Conduct the Survey

1
Create the Survey

Surveys are similar to interviews in that their purpose is to collect information. However, they help you collect quantifiable information from a large group of individuals known as the *population*. The responses given to survey questions are not as wide open as in an interview, and the survey is usually self-administered—requiring careful construction of the questions.

Most surveys are short. Unlike interviews, surveys benefit from using more closed-ended questions. Before you begin writing questions, take a few moments to focus on what specific information you want to collect, including demographic information important to your data and topic.

➔ See Chapter 1 for more information about demographics.

You can find many survey tools available online for free. Search using phrases such as "free survey tools" or "free survey maker."

CHECKLIST for Surveys

❏ Am I asking only one thing in each question?
❏ Am I using language that is clear and appropriate to my respondents?
❏ Did I use mostly closed-ended questions?
❏ Did I keep the questionnaire short and simple?

As you create your questions, use clear and appropriate language, ask about only one issue in each question, and try to accommodate all possible answers.

INEFFECTIVE:

> 1. Tell me why you shop at the farmers' market and what you buy.
>
> ....

This is really two open-ended questions in one that may take too long to answer.

EFFECTIVE:

> 1. Out of the following reasons, why do you shop the farmers' market? Please check all that apply.
>
> .... Value
>
> .... Quality of products
>
> .... Variety of organic products
>
> .... Other
>
> Please explain.
>
> ....
>
> ....

This question asks about only one issue and offers specific responses plus an option to add one not there.

2
Conduct the Survey

Once you have your survey written, you are ready to administer it. Most likely, you will only survey a **sample**, or portion, of the population you are researching.

The primary guidelines for selecting and determining the size of your survey sample are the following:

Select individuals who represent subgroups across the entire population.
Your sample should represent different genders, ages, races, religions, social statuses, and so on, if these are important to your survey. To help achieve the appropriate variety:

- Be sure you ask demographic questions in the survey so that you can see if you are getting a representative sample.
- Select individuals randomly.

Survey a large enough sample. "Large enough" means that you are reasonably confident that your sample represents the population and that your audience will find your results credible.

Factor in the location. For example, surveying students in the science building may mean that most of your respondents will be science majors.

SAMPLE ORAL CITATION FOR SURVEY MATERIAL

"In my February survey of 85 out of the 120 new employees here at the plant, more than two-thirds indicated a high level of satisfaction with their jobs."

How Do You Take Good Research Notes?

1 Prepare to Research

2 Know the Appropriate Style Manual

1

Prepare to Research

Before you begin your research, read Chapter 4 to guide you on the types of support materials you may find and how you might use each type. Use the checklist below to help you evaluate materials.

→ Chapter 4 helps you prepare to research.

Taking detailed notes is the key to good research, so establish a note-taking system. Most students use one of three basic methods:

- Take handwritten notes on note cards or sheets of paper.
- Photocopy or print pages containing support materials.
- Use a combination of written note taking and copying/printing.

Any of these methods can be effective, but handwritten notes (either alone or in combination with copying/printing) can work especially well when creating a speech. Remember, no matter what method you use, you will need to include specific citation information.

CHECKLIST for Evaluating Support Materials

❏ Is the information accurate?

❏ Is the information current and timely?

❏ Is the information complete? Am I missing anything?

❏ Will my audience view the information and the source as trustworthy?

❏ Is the information suitable for my audience?

2

Know the Appropriate Style Manual

Most beginning speech classes require students to use the style manual of either the *Modern Language Association (MLA)* or the *American Psychological Association (APA)* to cite sources properly in the written outline. Creating your speech outline and oral citations will be much easier if you adhere to your assigned style as you take your notes.

Beginning speakers often use books, Internet sources, and periodicals as their major sources. Here are a few examples for how to cite these sources using MLA and APA styles.

PRINTED BOOK

MLA STYLE:

Lear, Linda. *Rachel Carson: Witness for Nature*. New York: Holt, 1997. Print.

APA STYLE:

Lear, L. (1997). *Rachel Carson: Witness for nature*. New York, NY: Henry Holt.

FROM THE INTERNET

MLA STYLE:

Centers for Disease Control and Prevention. "2009 H1N1 Flu: Situation Update." *CDC.gov*. CDC, 2 Oct. 2009. Web. 3 Oct. 2009.

APA STYLE:

Centers for Disease Control and Prevention. (2009, October 2). 2009 H1N1 flu: Situation update. Retrieved from http://www.cdc.gov/h1n1flu/update.htm

PRINTED PERIODICAL (e.g., newspaper)

MLA STYLE:

Cailler, Daniel. "Mayor Favors Use Tax for Online Shoppers." *Columbia Daily Tribune*, 6 Oct. 2009: A12. Print.

APA STYLE:

Cailler, D. (2009, October 6). Mayor favors use tax for online shoppers. *Columbia Daily Tribune*, p. A12.

→ See Chapter 5 for a more detailed discussion of style formats.

REMEMBER

There are two types of plagiarism:

- **Blatant plagiarism**—occurs either when speakers take an entire speech or document and present it as their own or when speakers take parts of information from other sources and link them together, creating an entire speech of someone else's words.
- **No-citation plagiarism**—occurs when speakers fail to give source credit to a specific part of their speech.

4

SELECTING AND TESTING SUPPORT MATERIALS

Introduction

You do research every day. For example, have you ever looked in your closet to see which clothes are clean, then evaluated your clothing options based on what you will do during the day? That's research. Have you searched the Internet for the best price on a TV? That's research. Have you looked around town for the cheapest food prices? That's research. However, for your research to be effective, you have to know what information is worth paying attention to.

In your speech research, this means you must select the best support materials possible. The goal of this chapter is to help you recognize and evaluate various types of support materials.

The act of research in itself has much to offer. Approach your research as an activity leading to new horizons, new knowledge, improved practices, and increased alternatives. Allow yourself to enjoy research, and you might learn something about yourself. Conducting research can help build your self-confidence by proving that you have a tenacious talent to persevere and to solve problems. It will help you develop critical thinking skills that will serve you well in preparing your speech—and in almost every aspect of life. Above all, conducting research will sometimes confirm your beliefs and can, at other times, offer new alternatives.

That's research!

> *What is research, but a blind date with knowledge.*[1]
> WILL HENRY

CHAPTER 3: Locating Support Materials   52

CHAPTER 4 CONTENTS

What Types of Support Materials Can You Use in Your Speech?   76
  1 Facts   76
  2 Definitions   76
  3 Testimony   77
  4 Examples   78
  5 Statistics   80

How Do You Determine What Types of Sources and Support Materials to Use?   82
  1 Consider Your Own Personal Knowledge   82
  2 Consider Primary vs. Secondary Sources   83
  3 Consider Scholarly vs. Popular Sources   84
  4 Consider Your Topic Needs   85

What Do You Evaluate in Your Support Materials?   86
  1 Accuracy   86
  2 Completeness   86
  3 Currency   87
  4 Trustworthiness   87
  5 Suitability   87

How Do You Use Support Materials Effectively?   88
  1 Use Quotation and Paraphrasing Effectively   88
  2 Use Your Materials Purposefully and in Different Ways   89

How Do You Cite Sources Orally?   90
  1 Collect the Necessary Content   90
  2 Create and Deliver Oral Citations   92

PART 2 Review   94

What Types of Support Materials Can You Use in Your Speech?

1 Facts
2 Definitions
3 Testimony
4 Examples
5 Statistics

1

Facts

Facts are verifiable bits of information about people, events, places, dates, and times. Most audiences will accept a fact with minor support or a simple oral citation and will not require an extended logical argument to prove the fact. The fact must be typical and from a recent reliable source. For example:

> The Golden Gate Bridge opened to traffic on May 28, 1937.

> Hawaii and Alaska became U.S. states in 1959.

2

Definitions

For a classroom speech on digital piracy, Jonah used a definition to gain his audience's attention:

> When you hear the word piracy, do you think of *Pirates of the Caribbean*? Or do you think about bootlegged copies of DVDs or music? If you answered yes to the latter question, you know that such copying can constitute digital piracy. According to Judy Strauss and Raymond Frost, in their 2009 book *E-Marketing*, this form of "piracy" is "installing computer software or other copyrighted intellectual property (such as music or movies) that the individual did not purchase."

In general, **definitions** are brief explanations designed to inform your audience about something unfamiliar. As you can see in Jonah's speech, a definition can also be used as a language or persuasive device. How you define a word or phrase can persuade your audience to focus their attitudes or beliefs about that word or phrase in a particular way.

3

Testimony

Testimony is firsthand knowledge or opinions, either your own or from others. Testimony tends to be interpretive or judgmental.

Personal testimony is from your own personal experience or point of view. For example, Monica, a student, included her own story in an informative speech on adoption:

> Imagine you are six years old and your little sister is three, and the state takes you away from your birth parents. Imagine not knowing where you will live, where you will go to school, or if your little sister will go with you. That was my life when I was six. But my story has a happy ending: My sister and I were adopted by great people we now call Mom and Dad.

Monica's audience will probably view her expertise on this subject as high because she lived the experience. However, relying entirely on your own personal testimony can backfire. Supporting your knowledge with other forms of evidence is always important, even for many experts. Most speech assignments also require sources outside of your own personal experience.

Lay testimony (or *peer testimony*) occurs when an ordinary person other than the speaker bears witness to his or her own experiences and beliefs. When Senator John McCain included "Joe the Plumber's" comments in the October 15, 2008, presidential debate, he was using the testimony of an ordinary person in an effort to demonstrate problems with then-Senator Barack Obama's plan to solve the economic crisis.

Prestige testimony draws its effectiveness from the status of the person testifying, which often stems from his or her popularity, fame, attractiveness, high-profile activities, or age, if older. For example, advertisements and political statements that feature famous movie stars or sports figures are using prestige testimony. This testimony tends to be less credible logically but may appeal emotionally.

Expert testimony is testimony from a person the audience recognizes as an expert. The expert must be in a field related to your topic—a doctor for a medical topic, a teacher for an education topic, a scientist for a scientific topic, and so on. An expert's specialty can also be a factor; an eye doctor, for instance, is not an expert on heart surgery. Identifying your source's expertise to your audience is crucial:

> According to Kathleen Sebelius, the U.S. Secretary of Health and Human Services, the H1N1 flu virus does not seem to be as strong as anticipated. However, individuals should stay home if they are sick, and everyone should consider getting the vaccine—especially those at risk.

Identifying Sebelius's title lends credibility to her testimony—and to your speech.

CHECKLIST for Testimony

❏ If I am using personal testimony, do I support it with other sources?

❏ If I am using lay testimony, will my audience identify with the people giving the testimony and view them as credible?

❏ If I am using prestige testimony, will the audience view the person's reputation positively?

❏ If I am using expert testimony, do I tell my audience why the person is an expert?

❏ Are all the testimonies I use relevant to my topic?

❏ Is the person testifying free of bias?

4

Examples

Examples are specific instances or cases that embody or illustrate points in your speech. The content of the examples may embody or illustrate items, people, events, places, methods, actions, experiences, conditions, or other information. They act as samples, patterns, models, or standards that help your audience understand and accept your points. Effective examples bring life to your speech, making your topic vivid and concrete for your audience.

Examples fall into three categories: brief, extended, and hypothetical.

BRIEF EXAMPLES

Specific instances illustrating a single general notion are *brief examples*. You use this type of example to quickly illustrate something, and you can use several back-to-back to demonstrate frequency.

EXTENDED EXAMPLES

(also known as *stories, narratives, illustrations,* or *anecdotes*)

Extended examples are more detailed examples, allowing the audience to linger a bit longer on the vivid, concrete images the examples create. You can use a narrative or story in your introduction as an attention-getting device; in speeches with a general purpose to inspire; or as support material where you need to help your audience understand or make connections to your point or access their emotional responses. A good story must use language and imagery effectively to create—or transport the audience to—the world being described. The story has to fit together and be plausible in the eyes of the audience.

→ See Chapter 8 for more on effective language usage.

HYPOTHETICAL EXAMPLES

Examples based on the potential outcomes of imagined scenarios are *hypothetical examples*; they gain their power from future possibilities. An effective hypothetical example requires the speaker and the audience to have faith that the projected outcome *could* occur. In other words, the example is not real in the present but could happen in the future.

CHECKLIST for Examples

❏ Will the audience view my example as typical?

❏ Will the audience see the example as relevant?

❏ Will the audience find the example believable?

❏ Is the example representative of the larger group or category that it stands for?

❏ Do I have enough examples to support my point?

❏ Am I sure that no counterexamples can disprove my point?

A brief example in a speech about active senior citizens might look like this:

> Today's older adults are redefining what "older" means. George H. W. Bush, for example, celebrated his 85th birthday in June 2009 by skydiving from 10,500 feet over Maine.

Suppose you are preparing a persuasive speech on controlling the spread of HIV in South Africa. You find the article "Women, Inequality, and the Burden of HIV" in the February 17, 2005, issue of the *New England Journal of Medicine*. Editing a small portion of the article, you create an extended example:

> Thandi Dlamini grew up in a crowded four-room house with 13 family members. As the youngest girl, she was charged with cooking, cleaning, and caring for her elders. At age 19, she met her first boyfriend. From the perspective of Thandi and the other women in her community, he was quite a catch—he was older, unmarried, and financially stable. She dreamed that one day he would offer to pay her *lobola* (bride price) and she would have her own home. Several months after meeting, he and Thandi had sexual intercourse, and she says this was her first encounter.
>
> Nine months later, she gave birth to a daughter, Zama. The baby was sick from the beginning and by six months of age was seriously failing to thrive. After being tested for HIV, Thandi was given three tragic pieces of information: she had given her daughter HIV, no treatment was available, and Zama would not live long.
>
> *Ichilo*. Disgrace. *Amahloni*. Shame. This is how Thandi describes her feelings after leaving the hospital. Thandi's boyfriend left after he heard about the baby, and Zama died shortly after that.

For instance, a speech on emergency preparedness could use a hypothetical example about local risks:

> Cities like ours along the Mississippi River would experience great destruction if an earthquake erupted on the New Madrid Fault. One hundred years ago, when the fault last erupted, the force was so intense it changed the path of the Mississippi. That was before we settled the area and built many of our homes and businesses in the big cities near the fault. If a similar quake occurred today, we could have major destruction and fatalities. Recovery would take months. Would you have enough food and water for your entire family for a week? Do you have an emergency plan to react to a quake or to contact family members? Do you have necessary medical supplies? Are you prepared?

5

Statistics

Statistics are numerical facts or data that are summarized, organized, and tabulated to present significant information about a given population (people, items, ideas, etc.). When you use statistics correctly, your audience will view them as factual and objective. Statistics should not scare or confuse you or your audience.

Descriptive statistics aim to describe or summarize characteristics of a population or a large quantity of data. For example:

> Katie Smith, a WNBA Detroit Shock player and the 2008 MVP, has a career average of 15.8 points, 2.8 steals, 3.1 rebounds, and average playing time of 34.7 minutes per game as of August 3, 2009 (wnba.com).

The average (or *mean*, see the table on the next page) of Smith's statistics over her career gives the audience an idea of her talent in a brief snapshot. As another example, if you survey your entire speech class and calculate the percentage results of the survey, you are generating descriptive statistics.

Inferential statistics aim to draw conclusions about a larger population by making estimates based on a smaller sample of that population. For example:

> President Barack Obama's job approval rating, after hitting a low point of 52% in the middle of last week, has edged back up to 56% for the latest three-day period, July 31 through August 2 (Gallup.com).

This example says that 56% of all Americans approved of Obama's work. Yet the Gallup data, like most poll statistics in the news, are inferential. They come from only a portion of the population; if the poll is trustworthy, the portion is assumed to be representative of the whole.

As another example, if you poll only *one-third* of the students taking speech classes at your school and then make predictions about *all* students taking speech classes there, you are calculating inferential statistics.

USING STATISTICS

- Make sure your statistics are accurate. Check any calculations to confirm that they are correct.

- Verify important statistics from multiple sources for better validity.

- Do research to confirm that the collection, interpretation, and reporting methods for the statistics were ethical and valid and the sample is representative.

- If the statistics are based on a poll, any differences shown by the poll should be less than the poll's margin of error.

- Explain clearly to your audience what the numbers mean. Brief examples and visual aids often help make statistics understandable.

→ See Chapter 10 for help with creating presentation aids.

- Use statistics in moderation. Too many can make your audience stop listening.

- Inform your audience of any biases the source of the statistics may have.

- Report the statistics in a manner that does not twist their meaning.

- Comparing statistics can help explain them. Be sure to compare like things.

Different statistical data can make different measurements as well. A mean, a median, and a mode are some of the most common measurements used in speeches.

WHAT IS IT?	HOW DO YOU FIND IT?	EXAMPLES
A *mean* is an average of a set of numbers.	Add up all the numbers in a set and divide the sum by the number of items in the group.	Four speech scores: 88, 86, 81, 92 The sum: $88 + 86 + 81 + 92 = 347$ Divide sum by number of scores: $347 \div 4 = 86.75$ The mean: 86.75
A *median* is the "middle value" in your set of numbers after you have placed them in increasing order. The median separates the lower half of your sample from the upper half (e.g., those in the lower half of an income range and those in the upper).	When you have an *odd* amount of numbers, place your numbers in increasing order and simply locate the middle number.	Five speech scores: 88, 86, 81, 92, 84 Place in increasing order: 81, 84, 86, 88, 92 The median: 86
	When you have an *even* amount of numbers, place your numbers in increasing order and locate the two middle numbers; then add them together and divide by two.	Four speech scores: 89, 86, 81, 92 Place in increasing order: 81, 86, 89, 92 Locate the two middle numbers: 86, 89 Add them and divide by two: $86 + 89 = 175 \div 2 = 87.5$ The median: 87.5
A *mode* is the number that occurs the most in your set.	Place your numbers in increasing order and look for the number that repeats the most.	Set of speech scores: 84, 92, 75, 69, 84, 86, 91, 74, 84, 91 Place in increasing order: 69, 74, 75, 84, 84, 84, 86, 91, 91, 92 The mode: 84

CHECKLIST for Statistics

❏ Are my statistics accurate?

❏ Do I explain them clearly?

❏ Have I been careful not to use too many?

TIP: Modes

You may have more than one mode if multiple numbers occur with the same frequency, and you may not have a mode at all if each number in your set occurs only once.

How Do You Determine What Types of Sources and Support Materials to Use?

1 Consider Your Own Personal Knowledge

2 Consider Primary vs. Secondary Sources

3 Consider Scholarly vs. Popular Sources

4 Consider Your Topic Needs

1

Consider Your Own Personal Knowledge

Use your personal experience as an added value to your speech, but not for your *entire* speech. Even when you know a considerable amount about your topic, you need to demonstrate to your audience that your knowledge is credible. The best way to do that is to cite other material supporting your ideas or position.

WHEN CAN YOU USE YOUR OWN PERSONAL KNOWLEDGE?

Use your personal experience to build your own ethos (credibility) and to give a personal face to your topic. Your personal experience can be an excellent source of examples, definitions, facts, and emotional appeal. Again, use other sources for the bulk of your speech, to support your ideas and establish your credibility and reliability. Without support, your personal knowledge may be dismissed by your audience.

An *ineffective* use of personal experience would be giving a speech about your summer vacation to Africa with only a step-by-step account of your trip and your opinion of it. An *effective* use of personal experience would be' to use information from historical documents about places you visited, published travel guides, articles, and books on Africa for the bulk of the speech. Then you could add your personal experience throughout, giving life to the facts.

CONFIDENCE BOOSTER

Being proud of your speech goes a long way to building your confidence. If you know you have unique, interesting, accurate, current, and reliable materials, you can be proud of your speech and excited about giving it.

2

Consider Primary vs. Secondary Sources

One of the first source and support material considerations you need to make is whether to use primary or secondary sources or both. Each of these types of sources plays an important role in formal speech composing.

WHAT IS IT?	EXAMPLES
Primary sources are the original sources of the information. Primary source material is the closest to what is being reported on or studied; it is not being quoted by a second party.	Original research reports, photographs, graphics, videos, or documentaries; historical brochures or pamphlets; autobiographies; novels; poems; some speeches; letters; e-mails; diaries, blogs; some Web sites; eyewitness accounts
	Interviews, surveys, or field research you conduct about your topic
Secondary sources cite, review, or build upon other sources. Secondary sources quote or paraphrase primary sources.	Most newspaper and magazine articles; some journal articles; reviews; biographies; reprinted photographs or graphics; some Web sites quoting other sources
	Most speeches you give are themselves secondary sources. Rarely, if ever, should you give a speech where you do not use information from other primary and secondary sources to support your speech.

WHEN DO YOU USE PRIMARY OR SECONDARY SOURCES?

Both primary research and secondary sources will offer strong support materials for certain topics. Sometimes, one is better than the other, but you will usually use both.

For example, if you are giving a speech about parking needs on your campus or the potential need for an on-site day care at your corporate headquarters, you will need to do primary research to get a feel for the local needs. Using secondary research from other institutions or corporations who have positively implemented the program that you are arguing for will strengthen your argument even further.

In another speech, you might focus mostly on cancer statistics collected by physicians at major medical clinics to motivate your audience to stop smoking or to incorporate healthier eating habits. When you quote these statistics, you are using information from a secondary source. However, sprinkling personal narratives from real people you personally interview throughout those statistics humanizes the numbers and allows you to use primary source materials as well.

3

Consider Scholarly vs. Popular Sources

The basic differences between scholarly and popular sources are as follows.

WHAT IS IT?	CHARACTERISTICS	EXAMPLES
Scholarly sources are written for readers who are specialists in their academic or professional fields.	• Are written by authors with academic credentials related to your topic • Discuss and research topics at length • Use very technical language • Aim to educate specialists • Cite all sources supporting the research	Articles in journals, books, or research databases or on professional Web pages
Popular sources are written for general readers.	• Are often written by journalists • Tend to be short discussions • Use common language • Aim to educate and/or entertain the general public • Often cite no sources or give sources that are brief and incomplete	Articles in newspapers, magazines, newswires, or popular culture databases or on news-related Web pages

WHEN DO YOU USE SCHOLARLY OR POPULAR SOURCES?

Choosing to use scholarly or popular sources depends heavily on your topic and your audience, but you will always use at least one type and may use both. The main reason you would rely on one more than the other resides in the *credibility of the author* and the *reliability of the information.*

Most audience members will view scholarly research as more trustworthy and accurate than information from popular sources. However, some topics will not need that level of integrity or will relate more to popular culture than to academia. Even within these two categories, you will discover varying degrees of credibility and reliability. A well-regarded popular source that focuses on a particular subject is credible and reliable for a speech on that topic, such as *Fortune* magazine for finance issues, whereas you will be hard-pressed to find an audience that values information from the many tabloids on the market today.

4

Consider Your Topic Needs

Some topics demand special consideration when you are selecting your sources or support materials. The guidelines in this table are only suggestions, not steadfast requirements or limitations. Remember, always keep your relationship with the topic as well as your audience in mind as you make your decisions about support materials and sources.

TOPICS WITH SPECIAL DEMANDS	TYPES OF SUPPORT MATERIALS	TYPES OF SOURCES
Controversial or highly emotional topics	Statistics, examples, expert testimony, definitions, facts	Rely more on scholarly or highly respected or focused popular sources. Primary sources are a necessity.
Topics with a purpose to incite emotions or inspire	Examples (particular narratives), lay and expert testimonies	Popular sources tend to contain more emotionally evocative examples and lay testimony. Expert testimony will more often be found in scholarly sources or your own primary research (interviews and surveys).
Technical topics	Definitions, facts, brief examples, statistics	Rely more on scholarly or highly respected or focused popular sources. Primary sources are a necessity. If the audience is unfamiliar with the topic, include definitions of technical terms.
Abstract topics	Definitions, facts, brief examples (particular narratives)	Use more scholarly or focused popular sources.
Topics relating to current events	Statistics, examples, testimony, facts, definitions	Current events will require you to rely more on popular sources because the topics are too new to appear in scholarly sources. Scholarly sources may offer historical comparisons to the current topic.
Topics your audience knows well	Depends on the topic, but unique examples, statistics, facts, and testimony will help you inspire the audience to listen.	Depends on the topic, but the key here is finding unique information to keep your knowledgeable audience interested and learning.

What Do You Evaluate in Your Support Materials?

1 **Accuracy**
2 **Completeness**
3 **Currency**
4 **Trustworthiness**
5 **Suitability**

1
Accuracy

Accuracy is an ethical consideration for the original creators of the information and for you. Accurate support materials must meet two standards.

- First, the information should be verifiable from the original source as well as supported by multiple sources. You should use only materials that you can verify as accurate or are from an extremely reliable source.

- Second, you must use your support materials within their original context. Do not twist the information to fit an agenda that does not match the author's intent.

The accuracy of the information's creator or source is out of your control. However, you can attempt to verify information with other sources, evaluate your sources for accuracy, and always use sources that are extremely reliable.

2
Completeness

Particularly if you intend to inform or persuade your audience, you need a sufficient amount of comprehensive, detailed information to achieve your goal. Two or three examples are not enough to demonstrate or prove your central idea or even show a trend. To give complete information, you may need to summarize several types of examples or incorporate wide-ranging statistics. Persuasive speeches especially need complete information behind them to be ethical and influential.

3
Currency

Make sure you have the most current information possible about your topic, which is not as easy as it sounds. For instance, if you are researching online, always check the copyright date of a Web page or the last time it was updated.

If your topic is not one that is changing rapidly, a good general research rule to follow is to use information published or collected in the past five years.

You need to be as current as possible with your information right up to the moment you give your speech. Changes can happen quickly, especially if your topic is unpredictable or related to current events.

4
Trustworthiness

Your support materials' trustworthiness is similar to your ethos: it is measured by the opinion of your audience, not you.

- Select materials from trustworthy sources and provide the audience with the author's or creator's credentials.

- Select materials from unbiased sources. The creator of the materials should not have a hidden agenda—or if there is one, you need to inform your audience of that bias or not use the materials.

- Hold electronic sources to high standards of credibility. What is the purpose of the site? Who sponsors the site? Who contributes? Has the site been updated recently?

5
Suitability

Your support materials are suitable when your audience is able to view the materials as relevant to them, to the topic, and to the occasion. To demonstrate suitability:

- Use support materials with a purpose that is clear and concrete.

→ See the section "Use Your Materials Purposefully and in Different Ways" on page 89.

- Use materials that relate back to your central idea.

- Include information that shows your audience why the materials are relevant to them, to the topic, and to the occasion.

You never want to have a moment when your audience views your materials as awkward or inappropriate.

PRACTICING ETHICS

Manipulating your support materials to prevent your audience from being rational—or to make them overly emotional—is extremely unethical behavior. Remember these ethical guidelines:

- Present hypothetical examples as such—not as factual.
- Present prestige testimony honestly and not as expert testimony.
- Use statistics fairly and accurately.
- Use a variety of support materials and sources.
- Include and note primary sources orally during your speech.
- Research thoroughly for alternate points of view.
- Use and quote materials in their correct context.
- Use reliable, trustworthy sources.
- Give proper oral citations.
- Disclose any agendas or biases a source might have.

How Do You Use Support Materials Effectively?

1 Use Quotation and Paraphrasing Effectively

2 Use Your Materials Purposefully and in Different Ways

1

Use Quotation and Paraphrasing Effectively

The bulk of your speech should be your words and organization, but quoting your sources at key points can provide compelling additional support. Directly quoting from a source is generally more effective than paraphrasing. Quote precisely if the material is short and says something better than you can or is memorable. In your speech, signal a direct quotation orally by using a technique such as:

> Neil Shea writes in his March 2010 *National Geographic* article, "Dunga Nakuwa cups his face...."

Paraphrase when the section you wish to use is long, wordy, unclear, or awkward for you to say. **Paraphrasing** restates the content of the material in a simpler format and in your own words, using language appropriate for your audience. For example, here is a section of text from Aristotle's *Rhetoric:*

> The modes of persuasion are the only true constituents of the art: everything else is merely accessory. These writers, however, say nothing about enthymemes, which are the substance of rhetorical persuasion, but deal mainly with non-essentials.

Here is how a speaker might paraphrase this:

> According to the *Rhetoric*, Aristotle believed that logic was the only true method of persuasion and that everything else was merely ornamentation. Other (classical) scholars focused on less vital aspects of rhetoric and ignored the enthymeme (the classical logical argument).

Remember, when you summarize, quote, or paraphrase the work of others, you must cite the source orally and in your outline.

2

Use Your Materials Purposefully and in Different Ways

You will use most support materials for one of four purposes.

- To clarify unfamiliar or abstract information
- To hold your audience's attention
- To help your audience remember important aspects of your speech
- To prove a claim your speech makes

To achieve the purpose of each of your support materials, you can employ different approaches. Here are four common ones to try.

Direct: The easiest and most common way to use support materials is to be simple and straightforward. Here, you identify and use materials for what they are: examples, facts, definitions, testimony, or statistics.

For example, for a class speech on Argentine football (soccer) player Diego Maradona, Felipe creates this sentence:

In the 1986 World Cup quarter-final round, Diego Maradona scored two goals now known as the "Hand of God" and the "Goal of the Century."

This statement is a direct use of support materials—in this case, Felipe simply presents facts as facts.

Comparison: When you use support materials to point out similarities between two or more ideas, things, factors, or issues, you are using them as a **comparison**. For example, Felipe wants to assert that Maradona was as great a player as the famous Brazilian Pelé:

Diego Maradona and Pelé each made it to four FIFA World Cup finals.

Contrast: When you use support materials to point out differences between two or more ideas, things, factors, or issues, you are using them in **contrast**. Felipe tries this:

Pelé won three FIFA World Cups in his career, whereas Diego Maradona won only one.

Felipe's contrast of the players' World Cup successes is correct, but highlighting this contrast might suggest that Pelé was a better player than Maradona, not that they were equal.

Analogy: An **analogy** helps explain the unfamiliar by comparing and contrasting it to what is familiar. The key to using analogy is that your audience must be familiar with one of the two things being compared and contrasted. There are two types of analogies:

- **Literal analogy** compares and contrasts two like things.

Although Maradona and Pelé came from different playing backgrounds, their similar career successes make them the greatest footballers of all time.

Felipe can discuss Pelé and Maradona as two like things—successful players. You might use literal analogy if you are advocating once choice over another.

- **Figurative analogy** compares and contrasts two essentially different things.

Diego Maradona is like a god to many Argentines.

Felipe can use this analogy to highlight Maradona's popularity.

How Do You Cite Sources Orally?

1 Collect the Necessary Content
2 Create and Deliver Oral Citations

1 Collect the Necessary Content

You know that when you write a paper, you need to cite your sources. When you write and give a speech, you also need to use citations. **Citations** are the credits for the original sources of the support materials you are using.

As a speechwriter in a class, you will need to use both oral and written citations—oral during the speech and written ones on the outline. Chapter 5 will help you with written citations, and writing style manuals offer specific guidelines on how to format written in-text citations and source pages for your outlines.

Here we are concerned with the oral citations. During a speech, the oral citations you use must always be incorporated so that the audience clearly hears them because listeners do not have the outline or source page. Compared to a written paper, however, your oral citation is not as detailed. Your first citation of a source will be the most detailed, and any later reference to the same source needs just enough information to connect it back to the original.

For example, Nina is doing a presentation on actor and director Tom Hanks. Her speech focuses on his historical films. She needs to cite an article from *Time* Magazine.

> As Douglas Brinkley notes in his March 2010 *Time* article, "The World According to Tom," the only facts Hanks recalled from history lessons about World War II were that Japan bombed Pearl Harbor on December 7, 1941, and America retaliated on August 6, 1945, by dropping an A-bomb on Hiroshima.

This could be Nina's first oral citation for this source during her speech.

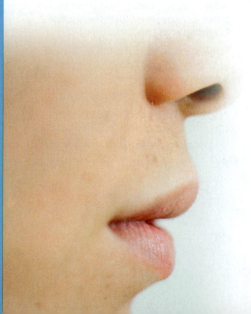

This table suggests the potential content of your first oral citations for different sources. Use it to help you collect the necessary information for your oral citations.

Your oral citation should include enough information that proper credit is given and that an audience member could locate the item being cited if he or she desires to do so.

CONTENTS OF ORAL CITATIONS

TYPE OF SOURCE	WHAT TO INCLUDE IN YOUR ORAL CITATION
Web site	Identify it as a Web site, title of Web page, site sponsor, and either the date of publication, last update, or when you accessed it; may include article title
Magazine or journal	Identify it as an article, name of magazine or journal, author and qualifications, and date of publication; may include article title
Newspaper	Identify it as an article, name of paper, author and qualifications, and date of issue; may include article title
Book	Identify it as a book, title, author and qualifications, and date of publication
Government document	Title, name of agency or branch of government publishing it, and date of publication
Brochure or pamphlet	Identify it as a brochure or pamphlet, title, who published it, and date of publication
Reference works	Title and date of publication
Videotape, DVD, or CD	Title of tape or disk and date
Television or radio	Title of the show, channel or network, and date of broadcast
Interview conducted by you	Identify yourself as the interviewer, name and identity of the person interviewed, and date of interview

If you need to create a written text of your speech (such as an outline) or a works cited or reference page, you will need more specific information.

➔ See Chapter 5 for more information on written citations and style manuals.

The next section will offer you examples and advice on how to construct and deliver your oral citations.

2

Create and Deliver Oral Citations

The main rule of oral citation is to make sure you cite everything you borrow from another source. This includes words, phrases, sentences, paragraphs, photos, diagrams, video and audio clips, graphs, and so on. If the item is not original to you, you must cite the source.

Your citations should not be too repetitive, misplaced, or boring. You want your audience to listen to them. Follow these suggestions:

Use variety when possible. Once you have given a detailed oral citation, subsequent citations for the same source can be shorter. For example, recall that Nina's first citation was very detailed:

> As Douglas Brinkley notes in his March 2010 *Time* article, "The World According to Tom," the only facts Hanks recalled from history lessons about World War II were that Japan bombed Pearl Harbor on December 7, 1941, and America retaliated on August 6, 1945, by dropping an A-bomb on Hiroshima.

Her second citation of this source might use the author's last name and the article title.

> Again, Brinkley, in his article "The World According to Tom," states that Hanks…

If Nina cites the same article again, she might only include:

> According to Brinkley,…

After you have cited a source three or four times, if the citations are close together, you can use a simple citation like Nina's last one.

Do not put every citation at the beginning or end of a quotation, summary, or para-phrase. Write them in different ways. Variety is the key to avoiding ineffective repetition and keeping your audience's attention.

Place your citations with the information being borrowed. A common error is to group all citations together at the beginning of a point or add them on to the end of the speech.

INEFFECTIVE:
The material from this section of my speech came from *Time* Magazine, April 19, 2010; Rachel Carson's book *Silent Spring;* and the spring 2010 *Nature Conservancy* Magazine.

The proper way to orally cite your sources is to cite each at the time you use it in the speech. If you have a lot of summarized information from one source, you might use this type of oral citation to begin the section:

> The information summarized in my next point comes from the 1999 book *Classical Rhetoric for the Modern Student* by Edward Corbett and Robert Conners.

If using visuals from another source, it is best to cite the source on your presentation aid and to orally note the citation during the speech.

CITATION ON A PRESENTATION AID:
Carl Zigrosser, *Prints and Drawings of Käthe Kollwitz.* New York: Dover, 1969. Print.

ORAL CITATION:
This 1927 self-portrait of Käthe, from the book *Prints and Drawings of Käthe Kollwitz,* depicts a solemn Käthe.

To draw your audience's attention to the written citation, you might gesture at its location on the aid. Placing the written citation in the same location on every aid will help guide your audience's eyes to it each time.

Be enthusiastic about your sources. Be proud of the research you did to support your speech. Speak clearly and maintain good volume as you cite sources. Use a variety of inflection that demonstrates your enthusiasm.

Practice saying your citations when you rehearse your speech. If you practice, you will remember better to include your citations; they will become more familiar; and you can further craft them to be effective. The table below shows the five types of support materials and gives sample beginnings for orally citing each type.

SAMPLE ORAL CITATIONS

TYPE OF SUPPORT MATERIALS	BEGINNING OF AN ORAL CITATION
Examples	"As Desdemona says in Shakespeare's *Othello*…"
	"Let me give you two examples of identity theft. The first comes from the May 10th issue of *Newsweek*…"
Facts	"As published in the July 2009 issue of the *Conservationist*, a lunar moth lives…"
Definitions	"*Time* Magazine—in its April 12, 2008, issue—defines…"
Testimony	"In an interview I conducted last October with Dr. James Wing in our history department, Dr. Wing said..."
	"As Chantal Smith, an eyewitness to the plane crash, said in January..."
Statistics	"According to the National Transportation Safety Board's Web site, accessed on May 6, 2010, the percentage of railroad accidents due to…"
	"In a June 2009 issue of *Lancet*, available online at…"

→ Chapter 5 on outlining and Chapter 9 on delivery will offer more examples and advice.

CHECKLIST for Oral Citations

❏ Does my citation include the necessary information?

❏ Am I citing everything borrowed from another source?

❏ Am I presenting my oral citations in a variety of formats?

❏ Are my citations properly placed?

❏ Have I practiced saying my citations within my speech, and do they seem to be a natural part of the speech?

Part 2: Review

CHAPTER 3 REVIEW QUESTIONS

1. How do you evaluate Internet sources? Why is evaluating online sources important?

2. What are the different types of Web sites available? Choose one type and explain how and why you might use it as a source.

3. What is a database and how can you use it in your research?

4. What are three guidelines to remember when determining a survey sample?

5. What are two important steps for taking good research notes? Explain.

CHAPTER 4 REVIEW QUESTIONS

1. What is testimony? Explain the four types.

2. How do the three types of examples differ from one another?

3. What is the difference between descriptive statistics and inferential statistics?

4. What are the five characteristics you should evaluate in your support materials? Explain each.

5. What are four purposes that support materials can be used for?

6. What is paraphrasing and when should you use it?

7. What are four suggestions for creating and delivering oral citations? Explain each.

TERMS TO REMEMBER

Chapter 3

support materials (53)
sources (53)
search engines (54)
hits (54)
Web sites (55)
blog (57)
databases (62)
interviews (68)
open-ended questions (68)
closed-ended questions (68)
follow-up questions (69)
surveys (70)
population (70)
sample (71)

Chapter 4

facts (76)
definitions (76)
testimony (77)
personal testimony (77)
lay testimony (77)
prestige testimony (77)
expert testimony (77)
examples (78)
brief examples (78)
extended examples (78)
hypothetical examples (78)
statistics (80)
descriptive statistics (80)
inferential statistics (80)
mean (81)
median (81)
mode (81)
primary sources (83)
secondary sources (83)
scholarly sources (84)
popular sources (84)
paraphrasing (88)
comparison (89)
contrast (89)
analogy (89)
literal analogy (89)
figurative analogy (89)
citations (90)

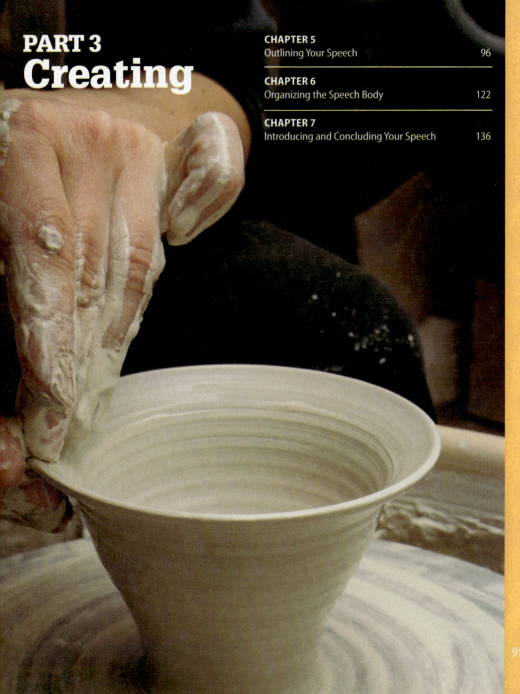

PART 3
Creating

CHAPTER 5
Outlining Your Speech   96

CHAPTER 6
Organizing the Speech Body   122

CHAPTER 7
Introducing and Concluding Your Speech   136

5
OUTLINING YOUR SPEECH

Why Do You Need an Outline?

"Why do I need an outline?" is possibly the question most frequently asked by beginning speakers. One of the best ways to see the value of an outline is to think of it as a piece of architecture.

Architects create a sound structure and use elements of design such as space, line, shape, texture, and color to design a safe, functional, and pleasing building. Without a plan, the building could be useless, unsightly, and likely to fall apart.

The same is true for a speech. Successful speeches contain distinctive features and components that are carefully structured for a particular function and pleasing effect.

You must be selective in what materials you use, and you must build them in a way that will hold your speech together and allow your audience to move easily through your information. Your outline is the blueprint you use to make sure everything is properly supported, in the right place, and easy to maneuver.

An outline helps you:

- Ensure that your main points relate to your central idea.
- Select the appropriate organizational strategy and keep it consistent.
- Make sure your subpoints are related and subordinate.
- Evenly distribute your support materials and investigate the quality of the material.
- Formulate links between parts of the speech.
- Design a speech your audience can follow and recall.

So, creating an outline is more than just busywork!

CHAPTER 5 CONTENTS

What Are the Parts of an Outline?	98
1 Introduction	99
2 Body of the Speech	99
3 Conclusion	99
4 Source Page	99
How Can You Create an Effective Outline?	100
1 Record the Topic, Specific Purpose, and Central Idea	100
2 Use Full Sentences	100
3 Cover Only One Issue at a Time	101
4 Develop the Introduction and Conclusion	101
5 Use Correct Outline Format	102
6 Use Balanced Main Points	104
7 Employ Subordination	104
8 Plan Out Formal Links	105
9 Use Proper Citations	105
What Are the Different Types of Outlines?	106
1 The Working Outline	106
2 The Preparation Outline	108
3 The Delivery Outline	112
What Can You Use to Link Your Speech Parts Together?	114
1 Transitions	114
2 Signposts	115
3 Internal Previews	115
4 Internal Reviews	115
How Do You Cite Sources in Your Outline?	116
How Do You Create a Source Page?	118
1 Follow the Overall Format Requirements	119
2 Create Proper Entries for Each Source	119
CHAPTER 6: Organizing the Speech Body	122
CHAPTER 7: Introducing and Concluding Your Speech	136
PART 3 Review	150

What Are the Parts of an Outline?

1 Introduction
2 Body of the Speech
3 Conclusion
4 Source Page

Creating a visual image in your mind of a basic outline will help you understand its parts and help you create an outline. Here is the basic blueprint for most outlines.

INTRODUCTION

SPEECH BODY

Link

I. First main point
  A. First subpoint of I
    1. First subpoint of A
      a. First subpoint of 1
      b. Second subpoint of 1
    2. Second subpoint of A
  B. Second subpoint of I
Link

II. Second main point
  A. First subpoint of II
  B. Second subpoint of II
    1. First subpoint of B
    2. Second subpoint of B
Link

III. Third main point
  A. First subpoint of III
  B. Second subpoint of III
Link

CONCLUSION

1
Introduction

The **introduction** opens the speech, grabs the audience's attention, and focuses it on the topic.

→ See Chapter 7 for how to create an introduction.

2
Body of the Speech

The **body** contains the central portion of the speech, including the main points, the multiple layers of subordinate points, and the links. It is, essentially, what you want to tell your audience about the topic.

Main points are the essential ideas you must cover or the main claims you wish to make, and they directly relate to your central idea. Most speeches will have two or three main points, but some speeches (usually process or persuasive) will have more— around five.

Subpoints (also called *subordinate points* or *supporting points*) offer information to support and relate back to the main point. You can have multiple layers of subpoints (e.g., your subpoints can have their own subpoints).

Links (also called *transitions*) act much like hyperlinks on your computer, which serve to make a logical jump between two places on your computer. Links in your speech will make logical connections between parts of your speech.

→ See "What Can You Use to Link Your Speech Parts Together?" on pages 114–115.

3
Conclusion

The **conclusion** ends your speech and takes one last moment to reinforce your main ideas as well as to "wow" your audience.

→ See Chapter 7 for how to create a conclusion.

4
Source Page

Many instructors will require a page at the end of your preparation outline that indicates the sources you used in your speech. You will create this page just as you do for a formal research paper, often using the style manual for the *Modern Language Association (MLA)* or the *American Psychological Association (APA)*. Style manuals are guides for writing and documenting research. Your instructor may require you to purchase a style manual, or you may just use the one located in your library's reference section. Make sure you have the correct style manual and that it is the most current. Certain software packages (including Word) can help you adhere to a style, although you should always check the citations and page format for accuracy.

→ See "How Do You Create a Source Page?" on pages 118–121.

CONFIDENCE BOOSTER

Knowing your material is the best way to lower your anxiety, and the best way to learn it is to be exceedingly meticulous, comprehensive, and systematic when creating the outline of your speech.

How Can You Create an Effective Outline?

1 Record the Topic, Specific Purpose, and Central Idea

2 Use Full Sentences

3 Cover Only One Issue at a Time

4 Develop the Introduction and Conclusion

5 Use Correct Outline Format

6 Use Balanced Main Points

7 Employ Subordination

8 Plan Out Formal Links

9 Use Proper Citations

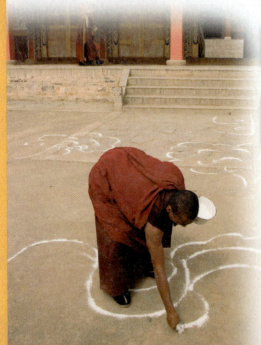

1
Record the Topic, Specific Purpose, and Central Idea

You should include the topic, specific purpose, and central idea at the top of the outline as a title framing the speech. Doing so will help you keep these elements of your speech in the forefront of your mind as you create the rest of the outline.

2
Use Full Sentences

Write each outline component in full sentences (but see Tip box below). This forces you to think in complete thoughts and will help you learn the speech as well as gauge its length. If you use only words or phrases in the preparation outline, you may struggle for the right words when giving the speech.

INCORRECT

> I. The beginning of football

CORRECT

> I. The game of football has come a long way since its beginnings.

TIP: Different Types of Outlines

Not every quality on pages 100–105 is necessary for different types of outlines. For example, you will include very few full sentences in your delivery outline. Full sentences are almost always required throughout your preparation outline. If you are not sure what your assignment requires, ask your instructor.

➜ See pages 106–113 for examples of complete outlines.

3

Cover Only One Issue at a Time

Covering only one issue at a time in each outline component will help you keep your speech simple enough for delivery and will keep you from writing the speech as a manuscript. The best method is to write only one sentence per component in the body of the speech.

INCORRECT

I. The City of Jackson needs to institute a plan to decrease the numbers of pigeons that infest it each year, breeding everywhere and roosting on buildings, because they spread diseases to humans and other animals and contaminate our waterways. The pigeons...

Avoid using words like **and**, **or**, **because**, or **but** to connect two independent issues in one sentence.

CORRECT

I. The City of Jackson needs to institute a plan to decrease the number of pigeons.
  A. Each year, thousands of pigeons flock to the city.
    1. They breed everywhere.
    2. They roost on many buildings.
  B. Pigeons spread disease.
    1. They carry germs that affect humans.
    2. They carry germs that affect animals.
    3. They can contaminate our waterways.

4

Develop the Introduction and Conclusion

Most instructors suggest creating your introduction and conclusion after you create the body of the speech (Chapter 7 will show you how). For now, recognize that they are an integral part of the preparation outline. Beginning speakers tend to cut corners in the development of a speech by deciding to improvise the introduction and conclusion as they speak. This practice sets you up for serious problems at critical moments in the speech. Speech anxiety is often the highest at the beginning, making the practice of "thinking on your feet" frustrating and often impossible. Therefore, you may forget crucial parts of the introduction and conclusion. Polish and practice them as you do the rest of the speech.

➜ See Chapter 7 for how to create effective introductions and conclusions.

5
Use Correct Outline Format

The format of an outline should be very systematic, helping you to logically structure your speech and aiding you in your delivery. You should always use correct outline formatting in the body of the speech. The following guidelines will help you.

DISTINGUISHING MAIN POINTS

Use Roman numerals to distinguish your main points.

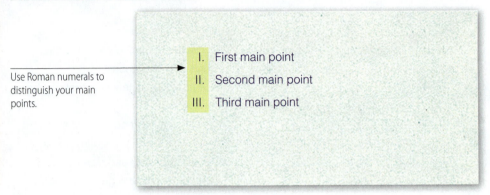

I. First main point

II. Second main point

III. Third main point

PATTERN OF SYMBOLS

Use a consistent pattern of symbols (e.g., uppercase letters, numbers, and lowercase letters).

Related points (indicated here with colors) should use the same type of symbol.

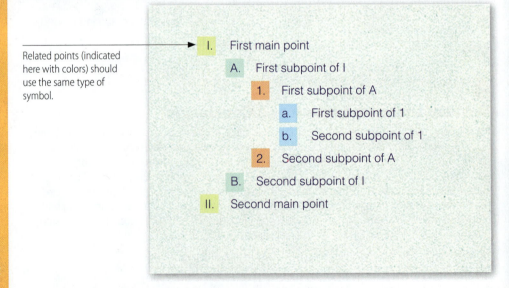

I. First main point

    A. First subpoint of I

        1. First subpoint of A

            a. First subpoint of 1

            b. Second subpoint of 1

        2. Second subpoint of A

    B. Second subpoint of I

II. Second main point

SUBPOINTS

Each subpoint must have at least two subdivisions if it has any. Think of it like cutting up an apple. If you cut up an apple, you have at least two pieces. You may end up with more pieces, but you cannot divide something without a result of at least two.

For example, subpoint A has two subdivisions, 1 and 2 (indicated here with colors).

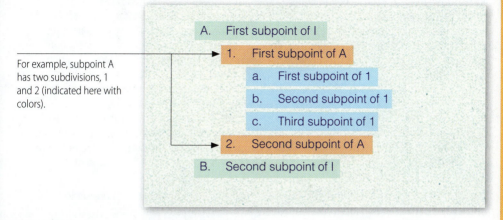

ALIGNMENT OF POINTS IN YOUR OUTLINE

Your main points should line up closest to the left margin of the page, and each subsequent subdivision should be indented further to the right.

Each main point should align left (align the periods), and each level of subpoints should be indented further to the right.

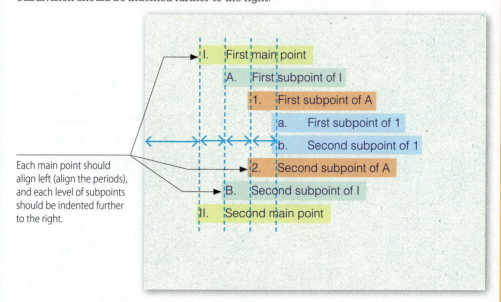

6

Use Balanced Main Points

Your main points should be equal in importance to each other. They will directly relate to the overall topic but should not overtly relate to each other. Each main point should coordinate with the others. For example, below are three relatively balanced main points:

> ▶ **Specific purpose:** To inform my audience about the National Football League (NFL).
>
> I. A brief history of the game of football explains the evolution of the NFL.
>
> II. The NFL has come a long way since its beginnings.
>
> III. Today, the NFL has a unique organizational setup.

Notice that each point is unique and relates back to the specific purpose.

Each of the above points is manageable in scope and should take roughly the same amount of time to present; the "brief history" in point 1 might be a bit shorter in duration.

➔ See Chapter 6 for details on how to logically organize your main points.

7

Employ Subordination

The components of your outline following each main point should be properly subordinate to the point above them. In other words, any statement that comes under a point must not be equal to or of greater importance than the point directly above it.

An easy test for this is to read the main point, mentally insert "because" or "for," and then read the subpoint. If doing so makes a logical connection between the main point and the subpoint, the subpoint is subordinate. For example, here is a main point followed by its first subpoint:

> I. The City of Jackson needs to institute a plan to decrease the number of pigeons.
>   A. Each year, thousands of pigeons flock to the city.

You can test the connection by mentally inserting "because":

| Main point I

The City of Jackson needs to institute a plan to decrease the number of pigeons **because** **each year, thousands of pigeons flock to the city.**

↑ Subpoint A

The test confirms that the main point and subpoint are logically connected and that the subpoint is subordinate.

8
Plan Out Formal Links

You should include links between major components of the speech. An effective speaker will lead the audience almost effortlessly from one point to another, and formal links will make this seem smooth, not jolting. For example:

> Now that we understand the formation of the National Football League, let's look at the structure of the NFL today.

→ See pages 114–115 for how to write effective links.

9
Use Proper Citations

Include in-text citations within the outline itself and a page with sources listed according to an acceptable style manual. In the outline, you can do your in-text citations one of two ways. Your first option is to follow your style manual. This example follows the MLA style of using *parenthetical citations*, or placing the citation information in parentheses at the end of a sentence:

> II. The NFL has come a long way since its beginnings.
>   A. Football is actually adaptations made to two different sports (Ominsky).

Alternatively, you could incorporate the citation into the outline text. This method is especially useful for beginning speakers. For example:

> II. The NFL has come a long way since its beginnings.
>   A. According to Dave Ominsky and P. J. Harari, in their 2008 book *Football Made Simple: A Spectator's Guide*, football is actually adaptations made to two different sports.

Before you decide how to cite your sources within the outline text, make sure you first check your instructor's requirements.

→ See pages 116–117 for more help with citations.

What Are the Different Types of Outlines?

1 The Working Outline
2 The Preparation Outline
3 The Delivery Outline

1

The Working Outline

Working outlines are usually handwritten attempts to organize your thoughts as you progress through the early stages of creating a speech—especially as you do research. For this type of outline, include your general purpose to help you keep it clearly in mind.

Working outlines will change often and will be a combination of complete thoughts, words, and phrases. Think of them as a way to record your thoughts, narrow in on your main points, and play around with organizational strategies. Your working outline is mostly for your eyes only. You should attempt to use correct outline form, but this is still a very free-flowing stage. For example, Steven is giving a classroom speech about fair trade chocolate. His topic, general purpose, specific purpose, central idea, and working outline are shown on the next page.

Steven remembered how important it is to formulate and record his topic, general purpose, specific purpose, and central idea as he created his working outline. Doing so helps him remain focused during his research. He plans to refer back to his specific purpose and central idea often so that he does not stray from his goal.

Topic: Fair Trade Chocolate

General purpose: To inform

Specific Purpose: To inform my audience about fair trade chocolate.

Central Idea: Fair trade chocolate is more than just expensive chocolate; it is responsible chocolate.

Like many beginning students, Steven found it helpful to create his potential main points as questions during this stage of the speech process. This can help Steven stay focused as he conducts research that answers each of the questions. Later, he will change his main points into declarative sentences.

I.   What is fair trade chocolate?

II. Why is chocolate an issue?
     A.   process of harvesting and where
     B.   chocolate is harvested by slaves

III. Where can you purchase fair trade chocolate locally?
     A.   stores
     B.   online
     C.   what's not fair trade

2

The Preparation Outline

Preparation outlines (also known as *formal* or *full-sentence outlines*) will be much longer and more detailed than working outlines. Designing a preparation outline allows you the opportunity to give the necessary time, effort, and thought to creating a successful speech.

The entire outline will adhere to correct outline form. The introduction, body, and conclusion will be clearly marked and connected with detailed links. The outline will end with a complete and correct source page, listing all the sources cited in the speech. You should follow your instructor's requirements for how to present the outline, but in most cases, it will be:

- Typed
- Double spaced
- Formatted in a specific and consistent way
- Handed in prior to or on the day you give your speech

The basic format of a preparation outline should look similar to the template at right. This template is the standard pattern you can use to create most speech outlines.

Student name	Class
Date	Instructor name

Topic
Specific purpose
Central idea

INTRODUCTION
    Attention-getter
    Credibility material
    Relevance to audience
    Preview of speech

(Link from introduction to first main point)

BODY
  I. First main point
    A. Subpoint
    B. Subpoint
      1. Subpoint of B
      2. Subpoint of B
      3. Subpoint of B

(Link between first and second main points)

  II. Second main point
    A. Subpoint
    B. Subpoint
      1. Subpoint of B
      2. Subpoint of B
    C. Subpoint

(Link between second and third main points)

  III. Third main point
    A. Subpoint
      1. Subpoint of A
        a. Subpoint of 1
        b. Subpoint of 1
      2. Subpoint of A
    B. Subpoint
    C. Subpoint

(Link to conclusion)

CONCLUSION
    Summary statement
    Audience response statement
    WOW statement

        Works Cited (or References)

Steven's preparation outline looked like this.

Steven Barker
October 22, 2010

COMM 110
Dr. Smith

Topic: The facts surrounding fair trade chocolate are astounding.
Specific purpose: To inform my audience about fair trade chocolate.
Central idea: Today, I want to share what fair trade chocolate is, why chocolate is an issue, and where you can purchase fair trade chocolate.

INTRODUCTION
Attention-getter: Raise your hand if you have had any chocolate today. Raise your hand if you have had any chocolate in the last week. How about the last month? Or the last year?
Relevance to audience: For those of you who raised your hands and even those of you who didn't, what you are about to hear will surely make you think twice before the next time you eat a chocolate candy bar.
Credibility material: As a member of the Christian Social Justice Committee, I have become concerned about fair trade chocolate.
Preview of speech: Fair trade chocolate is becoming a global concern in our culture today. To understand its impact, we have to answer the following three questions. What is fair trade chocolate? Why is chocolate an issue? Where can one buy fair trade chocolate?

(**Link:** First, what is fair trade chocolate?)

BODY
I. Fair trade, according to FairTradeFederation.org, is an economic partnership based on dialogue, transparency, and respect.
   A. Fair trade essentially is a combination of several ideals.
      1. It is set in place to provide safe work environments for industries.

      2. It allows for adequate levels of pay for all employees in industry.

      3. It prevents the practice of slavery in all associated industries.

      4. It ensures the rights of children.

  B. Fair trade chocolate is chocolate that is harvested and prepared by individuals who receive fair wages for the work that they do.

(**Link:** Second, why is chocolate such an issue?)

II. Chocolate harvested by slaves is such a big issue because of the limited product alternatives for consumption in the United States.

  A. It is estimated that there are more than 27 million modern-day slaves throughout the world (Batstone).

  B. The manner in which the chocolate-harvesting slaves are procured as well as how they are treated is horrendous.

      1. According to the 2001 documentary *Slavery*, these slaves are sometimes bought from parents for as little as $30.

      2. They are also taken from street corners in neighboring countries after being promised food and wealth.

  C. Ghana, Africa, grows cocoa for export.

      1. It is the world's largest exporter of cocoa beans.

      2. It is also the largest among the slave industry.

  D. The United States is the world's largest importer of cocoa beans.

(**Link:** Finally, where can one buy free trade chocolate?)

III. There are several places to purchase free trade chocolate.

  A. The Internet is the best place to purchase chocolate.

      1. Sweetearth.com deals specifically with fair trade.

      2. So does Divine Chocolate at divinechocolateusa.com.

  B. The Mustard Seed, which is located in downtown Columbia, is a fair trade–only store that sells Divine Chocolate.

  C. Kaldi's Coffee also sells fair trade chocolate. Their store is located in downtown Columbia right next to the Mustard Seed.

D. Some common chocolates are not fair trade.

    1. Hershey, Nestle, Mars, and Lindt chocolates make up more than 75 percent of the chocolate that most stores carry.

    2. These brands of chocolate are not slave free.

(**Link:** As you can see, free trade chocolate is available locally and via the Internet.)

CONCLUSION

Summary statement: Fair trade chocolate has become a big issue throughout the world today. Now you know what fair trade chocolate is, why chocolate has become an issue, and where you can purchase fair trade chocolate.

Audience response statement: You can now make an informed choice to eat responsible chocolate or not.

WOW statement: I will leave you today with a gift. This is a sample of Divine Chocolate. This is what chocolate should taste like because no little kid was forced to make it for you. This chocolate is slave free and guilt free. It is Divine!

Works Cited

"About Fair Trade." *FairTradeFederation.org*. Fair Trade Federation, 2007. Web. 19 Oct. 2009.

Batstone, David. *Not for Sale: The Return of the Global Slave Trade—and How We Can Fight It*. New York: Harper, 2007. Print.

Slavery. Dir. Kate Blewett and Brian Woods. Narr. Kate Blewett and Brian Woods. British Broadcasting Channel, 2001. Film.

3

The Delivery Outline

Delivery outlines will maintain the tight structure of the preparation outline but will eliminate much of the detail because you will know it by memory after writing the speech and doing some preliminary practicing. Create and use this outline as early as possible in the rehearsal stage of your speech. It is important that your "mind's eye" becomes familiar with the layout of this outline. You know you have become familiar enough with it when you can anticipate moving on to the next note card or page without looking down. This outline should assist you but not be a crutch. If you find that you want to read directly from it most of the time, it has too much detail. A delivery outline will also have delivery and presentation hints highlighted at key points during your speech. You should set up your delivery outline format with what you find the most useful and comfortable. The following is only one example, showing the note cards Steven used during his speech.

Intro.   *CARD # 1*

- Raise your hand if you have had any chocolate today. Raise your hand if you have had any chocolate in the last week. How about the last month? Or the last year?
- As a member of the Christian Social Justice Committee
- What fair trade chocolate is (slide)
- Why chocolate is an issue
- Where you can purchase fair trade chocolates

(Link: First, what is fair trade chocolate?)

CARD # 2

I. Fair trade, according to FairTradeFederation.org, is an economic partnership based on dialogue, transparency, and respect.
  A. Combination of several ideals (slide)
    1. Safe work environments for industries   *SLOW*
    2. Allows for adequate levels of pay for all   *DOWN*
    3. Prevents practice of slavery
    4. Ensures the rights of children
  B. Harvested and prepared by individuals that receive fair wages

(Link: Second, why is chocolate such an issue?)

CARD # 3

II. A big issue—limited product alternatives for consumption in the U.S.

   A. David Batstone, in *Not for Sale: The Return of the Global Slave Trade—and How We Can Fight It*, states more than 27 million modern-day slaves throughout the world

   B. Horrendous procurement and treatment (slide)

      1. According to a 2001 documentary titled *Slavery*, these slaves are sometimes bought from parents for as little as $30.

      2. Taken from street corners promised food and wealth

   C. Ghana, Africa (slide)

      1. World's largest exporter of cocoa beans

      2. Largest among the slave industry

   D. The U.S.—world's largest importer of cocoa beans

   (**Link**: Finally, where can one buy free trade chocolate?)

CARD # 4

III. There are several places to purchase free trade chocolate. (slide)

   A. The Internet

      1. SweetEarth.com

      2. DivineChocolateUSA.com

   B. Locally

      1. The Mustard Seed

      2. Kaldi's Coffee

   C. Common chocolates that are not fair trade.

      1. Hershey, Nestle, Mars, and Lindt chocolates make up more than 75 percent of the chocolate that most stores carry.

      2. These brands are not slave free.

CARD # 5

- Fair trade chocolate has become a big issue throughout the world today. Now, you know what fair trade chocolate is, why chocolate has become an issue, and where you can purchase fair trade chocolate.
- You can now make an informed choice to eat responsible chocolate or not.
- I will leave you today with a gift.

   (Begin to pass out candy.)

- This is a sample of Divine Chocolate. This is what chocolate should taste like because no little kid was forced to make it for you. This chocolate is slave free and guilt free. It is Divine!

What Can You Use to Link Your Speech Parts Together?

1 Transitions
2 Signposts
3 Internal Previews
4 Internal Reviews

1

Transitions

Transitions are words or phrases signaling movement from one point to another as well as how the points relate to each other. Transitions fall into the following categories.

TYPE OF TRANSITION	EXAMPLES
Time transitions are words and phrases that demonstrate a passing of time.	Let's move on to… Now that we have… We are now ready… In the future… Meanwhile… Later… Next…
Viewpoint transitions demonstrate a change in your view of a situation.	On the other hand… However… Conversely… Although… But…
Connective transitions simply unite related thoughts.	Also… Another… In addition… Moreover… Not only… but also…
Concluding transitions signal the end of a section within the speech or the ending of the entire speech.	Therefore… Thus… As a result… Finally… In conclusion… To summarize…

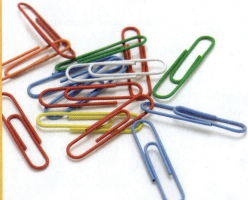

2
Signposts

Signposts are words or phrases that signal to the audience where they are with regard to related thoughts and/or what is important to remember. Some of the most common signposts are:

- First… Second… Third…
- My first reason… My second reason…
- Above all, remember…
- The most important aspects are…

For example:

> The first step in preparing a strawberry patch is to locate a well-drained, sunny location.

3
Internal Previews

As links, **internal previews** are like mini introductions and look like detailed signposts. These statements tell the audience what will be covered next in the speech. Here are two examples:

> Let's look at how the NFL consists of 32 teams, two conferences, and four divisions.

> There are many reasons why we need universal health care. However, I would like to focus on how a universal system would decrease the numbers of uninsured citizens, improve the access to proper care for those already insured, and help regulate the cost of care.

An internal preview is a great way to link your introduction and the body of your speech. It can act as the preview of your full speech, as in the last example above.

4
Internal Reviews

Internal reviews (also known as *internal summaries*) are like mini conclusions. They summarize what you have just covered in the previous section of your speech. Here are a few internal review examples:

> It is our responsibility to offer health care to every U.S. citizen, to improve access, and to lower care costs that force a need for a universal system.

> Knowledge, persistence, and charisma are what make a great salesperson.

> To review, you need a well-drained and sunny location, loamy soil, and certain nutrients to create the best strawberry patch.

Often you will combine internal previews and internal reviews with a transition, as these examples do:

> Now that you have selected the right location for the strawberry patch, prepared the soil, and purchased the correct plants for your climate, it is time to plant the strawberries properly.

> Now that we have discussed the evolution of football and the establishment of the NFL, we can move on to considering…

TIP: Effective Links

Creating your links ahead of time and placing them in the correct spots will help you remember to use them, and you won't struggle for words during the delivery of the speech. You should write out the links completely on the preparation outline. You might also use an abbreviated version of your links in your delivery outline so that you remember to include them.

How Do You Cite Sources in Your Outline?

As discussed in the Overview, citing your sources—in speeches and in writing—is an ethical responsibility and the only way to prevent plagiarism. Whenever you borrow words or concepts, directly quote something, or paraphrase, you need to cite the source. If what you are discussing is not common knowledge for most of your audience, you need a citation. When in doubt, cite a source.

Most speech instructors will ask you to follow your style manual. However, the instructor may offer instructions on how to handle citations unique to the public speaking forum. Be sure to check with your instructor.

Some general guidelines are:

- Cite your sources within the outline, followed by a source page at the end of the outline.
- Incorporate citations into the text of the outline, record them parenthetically, or use a combination of both.
- Unless the citation is part of the outline text, place it at the end of a sentence.
- The information within the citation should point to the source listed on the source page at the end of your outline.

Your style manual offers detailed discussions of how to cite effectively; however, the table at the right offers a few general rules and examples for citing sources within your outline.

→ See Chapter 4 for details on how to cite sources orally.

MLA CITATIONS
Use the author–page number method.

One author, parenthetical citation:
"…can help you save time and money" (Smith 345).

One author, in-text citation:
According to Smith's article in the November issue of… (345).

Two to three authors, parenthetical citation:
(Smith, Baker, and Jones 456)

Two to three authors, in-text citation:
According to Smith, Baker, and Jones, the people agreed with the candidate (456).

More than three authors:
(Wilson et al. 85)

No author identified:
Begin with the first few words of the source on the source page (usually the title).
"Only 10 percent polled agreed" ("Politics Today" 45).

Corporate or group authors:
The name of the group serves as the author.
(Food and Drug Administration 123)

No page number available:
(Food and Drug Administration)

APA CITATIONS
Use the author–publication date method.

One author, parenthetical citation:
"…can help you save time and money" (Smith, 2010).

One author, in-text citation:
According to Smith (2010), you can…

Two to six authors, parenthetical citation:
(Smith, Baker, & Jones, 2012)

Two to six authors, in-text citation:
Smith, Baker, and Jones (2012) found that the people agreed with the candidate.

More than six authors:
(Wilson et al., 2008)

No author identified:
Begin with the first few words of the source on the source page (usually the title).
"Only 10 percent polled agreed" ("Politics Today," 2012).

Corporate or group authors:
The name of the group serves as the author.
(Food and Drug Administration, 2009)

No date available:
(Food and Drug Administration, n.d.)

PRACTICING ETHICS
Using proper citations in your outline will help you remember to cite your sources orally, preventing you from plagiarizing portions of your speech.

REMEMBER
When citing Web pages, you may not know the author, or the material may have been created by corporate or group authors.

How Do You Create a Source Page?

1 Follow the Overall Format Requirements

2 Create Proper Entries for Each Source

As with citing sources within the text of your outline, your style manual will guide the creation of your source page. Again, you need to pay attention to any instructions given in class because an oral speech can have unique sources that your instructor may want included.

For example, APA style does not usually include personal communications (private letters, memos, e-mails, personal interviews, telephone conversations, etc.) on the source page. Many speech instructors, however, do want them cited formally on the outline and orally in the speech. In most cases, the speech instructor wants *all* sources included in your speech cited, including downloaded video, music, Internet documents, personal interviews, photos, and so on. In other public speaking situations, you may find that having a handout ready for distribution and including your source page will be helpful so that your audience can retain information better or do further investigation.

REMEMBER

Honesty about where you get your materials is the best policy and will build your credibility with your audience.

1
Follow the Overall Format Requirements

The following are general guidelines for creating the layout of the source page.

- Make sure you are using the most current and appropriate style manual for your class.

- If you are using MLA style, the source page uses the title "Works Cited," which is centered.

- If you are using APA style, the source page uses the title "References," which is centered.

- With either MLA or APA, your source page should:
  - be double spaced
  - use a hanging indent
  - list sources in alphabetical order
  - use the same font (style, color, and size) as the text of the outline
  - use standard one-inch margins

The table on the following pages shows you—at a quick glance—some differences between these two styles. Check your style manual for a more detailed description for creating a source page.

2
Create Proper Entries for Each Source

Each style manual gives detailed instructions on how to create the entries on the source page. You will want to refer often to your manual on how to create entries. The table on the following page outlines the most common sources used in a speech, according to MLA or APA. The key to a successful source page is to select a style and stay with it consistently. Remember to double-check for proper format if you are using software to create your source page. Software can make mistakes or be out of date.

CHECKLIST for Creating an Outline

❏ Did I include the topic, specific purpose, and central idea?

❏ Did I use full sentences?

❏ Do I have only one sentence for each outline component? Does each sentence cover only one idea?

❏ Did I create a complete introduction and conclusion?

❏ Am I using correct outline format?

　• Am I using Roman numerals for the main points, and are they closest to the left margin?

　• Am I using uppercase letters, numbers, and lowercase letters for the appropriate levels of subpoints?

　• Does each subpoint have at least two divisions?

❏ Are my main points equal in importance to each other?

❏ Do the components of my outline follow correct subordination?

❏ Did I include links?

❏ Did I include the in-text citations and a source page?

MLA AND APA AT A GLANCE

Book - MLA	Hurston, Zora Neale. *Their Eyes Were Watching God*. New York: Harper, 1990. Print.
Book - APA	Hurston, Z. N. (1990). *Their eyes were watching God*. New York, NY: Harper & Row.
Newspaper - MLA (Print and database)	Danielsen, Aarik. "Heritage in the Hand." *Columbia Daily Tribune* 18 Oct. 2009: C1+. Print. "Additional Fake Lipitor Recalled: Illinois Wholesaler Takes Action after FDA Issues Warning." *Kansas City Star* 18 June 2003: C1. *NewsBank*. Web. 28 Sept. 2009.
Newspaper - APA (Print and database)	Danielsen, A. (2009, October 18). Heritage in the hand. *Columbia Daily Tribune*, pp. C1, C2. Additional fake Lipitor recalled: Illinois wholesaler takes action after FDA issues warning. (2003, June 18). *The Kansas City Star*, p. C1. Retrieved from NewsBank.
Magazine - MLA (Print and database)	"Drug Safety: Partnership for Safe Medicines Arms Public against Counterfeit Drugs." *Biotech Business Week* 15 Dec. 2008: 54–56. Print. "Drug Safety: Partnership for Safe Medicines Arms Public against Counterfeit Drugs." *Biotech Business Week* 15 Dec. 2008: 1513. *LexisNexis*. Web. 28 Sept. 2009.
Magazine - APA (Print and database)	Drug safety: Partnership for safe medicines arms public against counterfeit drugs. (2008, December 15). *Biotech Business Week*, 54–55. Drug safety: Partnership for safe medicines arms public against counterfeit drugs. (2008, December 15). *Biotech Business Week*, 1513. Retrieved from LexisNexis Academic News Search.

Web page - MLA (With government author)	United States. Dept. of Health and Human Services. Food and Drug Administration. "Counterfeit Medicines—Filled with Empty Promise." *U.S. Food and Drug Administration*. Dept. of Health and Human Services, 1 Sept. 2009. Web. 3 Sept. 2009.
Web page - APA (With government author)	U.S. Department of Health and Human Services, U.S. Food and Drug Administration. (2009, September 1). *Counterfeit medicines—filled with empty promise*. Retrieved from http://www.fda.gov/Drugs/ ResourcesForYou/ucm079278.htm
Interview conducted by speaker - MLA	Jones, Timothy. Personal interview. 1 Nov. 2009. Jones, Timothy. Telephone interview. 1 Nov. 2009. Jones, Timothy. E-mail interview. 1 Nov. 2009.
Interview conducted by speaker* - APA	*APA normally does not recognize undocumented sources such as interviews. Because speakers often use interviews as source material, your instructor may ask you to include them as shown below.* Jones, T. (2009, November 1). Personal interview. Jones, T. (2009, November 1). Telephone interview. Jones, T. (2009, November 1). E-mail interview.

TIP: Examples of APA and MLA
Looking at correct source pages can help you visualize how to put one together. The sample on page 251 follows APA format and the samples on pages 111 and 303 follow MLA.

6

ORGANIZING THE SPEECH BODY

Introduction

The goal of Chapter 5 was to help you see the benefits of outlining, including how outlines can create the necessary structure for your speech to achieve its specific purpose. This chapter, however, will take you through more micro-level structuring by offering you ways (strategies) to organize your main points or the body of your speech.

A **strategy** is a plan designed to achieve a goal—in this case, your specific purpose. Strategy is concerned with the relationship and arrangement of your main points. In other words, your strategy is not about how you explain your main points (the content) but is about how your main points relate to and follow each other (the organization), to achieve your goal to inform, persuade, or accentuate a topic.

For example, if you are giving a demonstration speech in a chemistry class about a chemical reaction, the order of the steps is important to the outcome of the reaction and your audience's comprehension. If you complete steps out of order, the results could be disastrous.

In any speech, the strategy you use to order your main points can make or break an argument. The strategy you use can assist or hinder your audience's learning about or appreciation of a person, animal, place, event, object, concept, issue, or process. Helping you select the right strategy for you, your general purpose, your topic, and your audience is the goal of this chapter.

CHAPTER 5: Outlining Your Speech   96

CHAPTER 6 CONTENTS

What Organizational Strategies Can You Use in Your Speech?   124
- 1 Chronological   126
- 2 Topical   126
- 3 Spatial   127
- 4 Causal   127
- 5 Comparative   128
- 6 Problem–Solution   128
- 7 Monroe's Motivated Sequence   129

How Do You Make a Speech Out of a Strategy?   130
- 1 Select a Strategy   130
- 2 Discover Your Main Points   130
- 3 Create Your Main Points   132
- 4 Expand with Subpoints   134

CHAPTER 7: Introducing and Concluding Your Speech   136

PART 3 Review   150

What Organizational Strategies Can You Use in Your Speech?

1 Chronological

2 Topical

3 Spatial

4 Causal

5 Comparative

6 Problem–Solution

7 Monroe's Motivated Sequence

Most speakers choose from seven basic organizational strategies: chronological, topical, spatial, causal, comparative, problem–solution, and Monroe's motivated sequence.

Chapter 5 noted that there are three main parts to a speech: the introduction, the body, and the conclusion. The strategy you select will help you organize the body of your speech.

When you select a strategy, you will consider which one works best with your general purpose, the topic, and the audience. Because these three elements are constantly interacting with and reacting to each other, you may find that you can use more than one strategy effectively—and that is fine. Trust your instincts to select one that seems the best for your purpose, topic, and audience and for you as the speaker. The following pages will help you understand in greater detail how each strategy works.

ORGANIZATIONAL STRATEGIES FOR SPEECHES

STRATEGY	WHAT IS IT?	WHEN MIGHT YOU USE IT?	WHAT TYPES OF SPEECH USE IT?
Chronological	Strategy based on moving through time or sequential steps	Useful for speeches about a process or development over time or plan of action	Informative Persuasive Special occasion
Topical	Strategy highlighting the natural subtopics or divisions within a speech topic	Ideal when your topic has inherent subtopics	Informative Persuasive Special occasion
Spatial	Strategy describing the arrangement of space related to an event, place, or object	Useful when you need to walk your audience through a space or setting	Informative Special occasion
Causal	Strategy based on cause-to-effect or effect-to-cause	Effective for speeches focusing on causes or consequences of something already present or possible	Informative Persuasive Special occasion
Comparative	Strategy that explains or argues by comparing something to something else	Great when topics are abstract, technical, or difficult; beneficial for showing advantages	Informative Persuasive
Problem–solution	Strategy demonstrating a problem and then advocating or explaining a solution	Useful when trying to change attitudes or when calling for a particular solution	Informative Persuasive
Monroe's motivated sequence	A five-step strategy that motivates an audience to action based on their needs	Excellent strategy for a call to action speech	Persuasive

CONFIDENCE BOOSTER

Selecting the right strategy and sticking to it is a powerful confidence booster. The time you spend making sure you follow the strategy will help you become more familiar with the details of your speech. A major contributor to low confidence is not knowing what your next thought might be. Likewise, a well-organized speech will help you look and feel confident and trustworthy.

1 Chronological

You will use the **chronological strategy** when you need to move through steps in a process or develop a timeline. Depending on the topic and your general purpose, you might move forward or backward through the process or timeline for effect. This type of arrangement is especially helpful when stressing the history of an event, person, or thing or when demonstrating a process. For example:

Specific purpose: To inform my audience how to use a compost bin.

Central idea: Composting is an easy way to save space in our landfills while growing great vegetables or flowers.

 I. There are many types of composting bins, making it important to select the right one for your needs and budget.

 II. Where you position your composting bin can make composting either effortless or grueling.

 III. A few simple steps will help you maintain a sweet-smelling, productive compost pile.

 IV. Using the "black gold" from your pile will supply you with a bounty of produce or flowers.

Here, each main point walks the listener through the major steps of composting. The subpoints should do the same.

2 Topical

You will use the **topical strategy** (also called the *categorical*) when there is a strong inherent or traditional division of subtopics within the main topic. If you give a speech about chocolate, for example, a natural topic division could be white, milk, and dark. For a topic like taking a vacation to Orlando, you might divide the topic according to how people traditionally think about vacations— places to see, places to eat, and places to stay. Here's an example using the topical strategy to organize a speech on succeeding in school:

Specific purpose: To inform my audience about techniques to improve their schoolwork.

Central idea: To succeed in school, you need to organize your life, carefully manage your time, and focus mentally.

 I. Organization is the process of giving structure and order to your work.

 II. Time management is controlling or directing time into useful chunks.

 III. Mental focus is realizing what you have to do and concentrating hard on that single item.

Notice how each main point takes on a different subtopic—organization, time management, and mental focus. As individual subjects, these may seem unrelated, but in relation to the central idea and main topic, they are logically connected.

TIP: Demonstration Speeches

When you give a demonstration speech (a "how to do it" speech), you can use the chronological strategy to create a step-by-step organization.

3
Spatial

A *spatial strategy* recognizes space as a way to arrange the speech. This strategy is useful when you want to discuss your topic in relationship to a physical setting, a natural environment, or proximity. Examples might be speaking about your tour through the White House, room by room; telling the new freshman class about your campus, building by building; or speaking about historical sites like Gettysburg or Mount Vernon. A speaker can even arrange an informative speech about the human tooth spatially by beginning at the outermost part, the enamel, and working in to the soft center, or dental pulp. Here's another example:

Specific purpose: To inform my audience about the Grand Canyon.

Central idea: Carved by the Colorado River, more than 277 miles long, and more than a mile deep in places, the Grand Canyon National Park is like three parks in one when you visit the North Rim, the South Rim, and the Inner Canyon.

 I. The North Rim has a much higher elevation than the South, making it cooler with better views of the Canyon.

 II. The South Rim is more accessible and has several historical sites.

 III. The Inner Canyon is the unpredictable lifeline of the park.

The spatial strategy is often a useful way to deal with a setting as large as the Grand Canyon. It helps you divide the space (North Rim, South Rim, and Inner Rim) into more manageable parts.

4
Causal

You will use the *causal strategy* when you want your audience to understand the cause and effect or consequences of something. With this strategy, you can either trace the path that leads up to a certain result or backtrack from the effect to the cause. Which way you go depends on what is most important to your specific purpose.

For example, explaining the causes leading up to the economic crisis beginning in 2009 would be a great candidate for this type of arrangement.

Specific purpose: To inform my audience about the causes of the current economic crisis.

Central idea: The current economic crisis in the United States can be explained by examining the chain reaction created by the declining housing market and global financial ramifications.

 I. An unsustainable real estate boom brought prices the average family could not afford.

 II. Bank losses created a major loss of capital.

 III. The average person feels the effects of a recession.

Depending on your topic, you may have one cause leading to a single effect, a single cause leading to several effects, or several causes leading to one effect.

5
Comparative

The **comparative strategy** uses the practice of compare and contrast. In an informative speech, you might use this strategy with new, abstract, technical, or difficult-to-comprehend topics. Here, you compare your topic to something the audience knows. This strategy only works when the two things you are comparing are comparable or analogous. For example:

Specific purpose: To inform new students about college life.

Central idea: Comparing what college might be like to your high school experience will help you anticipate the next four years.

I. Your classroom experience will be unlike your high school class expectations.

II. Your social life will be different from what it was in high school.

III. Your everyday responsibilities will be different.

Notice how this example uses the comparative strategy for informative purposes. This approach helps the audience understand and follow the speech by comparing the unknown (college life) with the familiar (high school experience).

In a persuasive speech, this strategy can be used to convince an audience that one thing is better than another, by comparing the two. This is a common practice used by many salespersons and is often referred to as **comparative advantage.**

6
Problem–Solution

You will use the **problem–solution strategy** when you want to show your audience how to solve a problem, making it an arrangement suited for a persuasive speech. With this strategy, your speech will have two main sections dedicated to the "problem" and the "solution." For example:

Specific purpose: To convince my audience that artificial sweeteners are dangerous.

Central idea: Artificial sweeteners are an easy alternative for the calorie-conscious, but the toxic effects of these chemicals should prompt consumers to seek safer choices.

I. (problem): Artificial sweeteners like Splenda, sucralose, aspartame, and saccharin cause major side effects that can be potentially dangerous.

II. (solution): Gradually decreasing your intake of artificial sweeteners by drinking more water, unsweetened tea, or naturally flavored drinks is the solution to preventing future problems and improving your overall health.

Some persuasive speeches may need more than two main points, if the problem and/or solution is complex or if your audience might be unwilling to accept the problem and/or solution you propose.

PRACTICING ETHICS

Honesty and reliability are key traits of ethical persuasion. Don't mislead your audience into believing something is harmful or wrong if it isn't.

7

Monroe's Motivated Sequence

Developed by Alan Monroe of Purdue University in the 1930s, **Monroe's motivated sequence** is really a more detailed problem–solution strategy. Basing the speech on what motivates the audience, the speaker convinces the audience that the speaker has the solution to their needs. If you remember the discussion about audience needs and motivations in Chapter 1, you should see the benefit of this strategy, which has five stages:

- Attention—During this stage, you begin to direct your audience's attention toward your topic.

→ See Chapter 7 for ideas on creating attention-grabbing devices.

- Need—Here, you demonstrate for your audience that they need a change by suggesting that a problem exists and they need to solve it.

- Satisfaction—At this stage, you propose the solution to the problem and support it as the best one with the appropriate evidence. The audience must feel that your plan will work.

- Visualization—With the problem highlighted and the solution suggested, you now help the audience visualize how great the situation will be after they implement the plan. In other words, help them visualize the benefits.

- Action—Now, call them to action or tell them exactly what they must do to achieve the solution you have suggested.

The following example demonstrates how you would outline a speech using this strategy.

Specific purpose: To convince my audience that we need to save the mountain gorilla.

Central idea: The extinction of the mountain gorilla, who shares almost 98 percent of its genetic makeup with humans, could greatly cost humankind.

Introduction (attention stage): The mountain gorilla is one of the world's most endangered species with fewer than 740 remaining in Africa, and none has ever survived captivity (UC Davis).

  I. **(need stage):** The mountain gorilla shares almost 98 percent of its genetic makeup with humans, so many of the diseases, malnutrition, and habitat concerns afflicting the gorillas could affect the human population as well.

 II. **(satisfaction stage):** If this gorilla is to survive and the delicate balance of the ecosystem be maintained, we must safeguard the gorillas of Rwanda, Uganda, and the Democratic Republic of the Congo.

III. **(visualization stage):** During the past 10 years, the Mountain Gorilla Veterinary Project's medical program has helped increase the gorilla population by 17 percent, making the mountain gorilla the only great ape whose numbers are rising, not falling (UC Davis).

Conclusion (action stage): You can help save the mountain gorilla by supporting research and conservation efforts through donations to organizations like the African Wildlife Foundation or the Diane Fossey Gorilla Fund International or by spreading awareness of these issues.

How Do You Make a Speech Out of a Strategy?

1 Select a Strategy
2 Discover Your Main Points
3 Create Your Main Points
4 Expand with Subpoints

CHECKLIST for Selecting an Organizational Strategy

❑ Does the strategy work for my general purpose?

❑ Does my topic suggest a strategy?

❑ What does my audience need to know? What strategies support my goals for them?

1

Select a Strategy

Most speeches can use more than one strategy. Consider your general purpose, topic, and audience when selecting the best strategy for your speech.

First, be sure the strategy will work for your general purpose (to inform, persuade, or accentuate). Some of the strategies work for all types of speeches and some work only for informative or persuasive speeches.

Then, does your topic suggest a strategy? For example, a speech on the history of Mardi Gras calls for a strategy related to time (chronological).

Finally, what does your audience need to know or what are your goals for them? For example, if you are explaining a complex topic, the comparative strategy may help your audience understand the topic by comparing and contrasting it to something they are familiar with.

2

Discover Your Main Points

As noted in Chapter 5, your main points are the major themes or thoughts you want to discuss about your topic. Sometimes the strategy you select to use for the speech will suggest the focus of the main points. For example, with the problem–solution strategy, you know you will have at least one main point for the problem and one for a solution.

However, you may not be ready to select a strategy until you have discovered your main points. The best way to do this is to make a list of everything you want to convey in the speech. One common method is shown on the facing page.

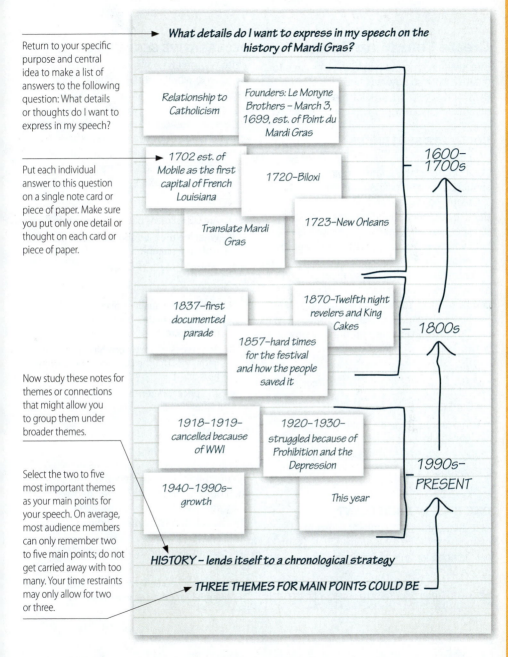

Return to your specific purpose and central idea to make a list of answers to the following question: What details or thoughts do I want to express in my speech?

Put each individual answer to this question on a single note card or piece of paper. Make sure you put only one detail or thought on each card or piece of paper.

Now study these notes for themes or connections that might allow you to group them under broader themes.

Select the two to five most important themes as your main points for your speech. On average, most audience members can only remember two to five main points; do not get carried away with too many. Your time restraints may only allow for two or three.

What details do I want to express in my speech on the history of Mardi Gras?

Relationship to Catholicism

Founders: Le Monyne Brothers – March 3, 1699, est. of Point du Mardi Gras

1702 est. of Mobile as the first capital of French Louisiana

1720–Biloxi

1723–New Orleans

Translate Mardi Gras

1837–first documented parade

1870–Twelfth night revelers and King Cakes

1857–hard times for the festival and how the people saved it

1918–1919–cancelled because of WWI

1920–1930–struggled because of Prohibition and the Depression

1940–1990s–growth

This year

1600–1700s

1800s

1990s–PRESENT

HISTORY – lends itself to a chronological strategy

THREE THEMES FOR MAIN POINTS COULD BE

3

Create Your Main Points

Effective main points will take some time to create. Doing so now will help you stay on track and save time. Aim for the following qualities to make your main points effective.

COMPLETE SENTENCES

Your main points should be complete thoughts, not only words or phrases. They should contain at least a noun and a verb.

Creating complete sentences will help you think in complete thoughts when you give the speech. Complete sentences will also help you be exact about what you want to say during each section of the speech.

For instance, the following incorrect example could be about anything related to candle making. You could be speaking about the history of candle making, the dangers of candle making, the mass production process, or the process of making candles at home.

INCORRECT:

I. Candle making

CORRECT:

I. The process of candle making is simple enough to do at home.

The correct example clarifies what you will speak about.

ONE IDEA IN EACH POINT

You should introduce only one idea in each main point. Watch for words like "and," "or," or "but" connecting two independent issues in one sentence.

➔ See Chapter 5 for how to cover only one issue at a time.

DECLARATIVE SENTENCES

Write your main points in declarative sentences, which should not be difficult because you tend to write most of your papers, letters, and notes this way. A declarative sentence simply states fact or argument and does not ask your audience to respond or take action. It states the main point you are making. Declarative sentences never end in a question mark.

INCORRECT:

I. Are LCD screens better than plasmas?

II. What are the pros and cons of an LCD and a plasma screen?

III. Which screen is cheaper?

CORRECT:

I. The positive qualities of current LCD screens make them better products than plasma screens.

II. Both types of televisions have potential negatives, but the LCD works best for most homes.

III. The price difference makes the LCD a better purchase.

COORDINATION

Your main points should adhere to coordination; that is, as much as possible, the main points are balanced or equal to each other in weight and level of ideas. They should not overtly relate to each other but should directly relate to your specific purpose.

For example, suppose your specific purpose is this:

To inform my audience about a few of the most influential American women painters.

In the following incorrect example, the main points relate back to the specific purpose, but they are unbalanced. You would spend most of the speech time on point one.

INCORRECT:

I. From the founding of this country through the mid-twentieth century, several American women painters influenced the art world.

II. Contemporary American women painters continue to set the new standard.

Instead, you might divide your main points into three significant periods of development. Doing so will allow you to coordinate and balance the amount of information to the artist highlighted. Plus, you will end with the most significant period of development for women painters. For example, few significant women artists in America were working prior to the 1800s, so your first main point could cover 1800–1874, marking the first significant period for female American painters. Your second main point could cover 1875–1974, and the last point could cover the new revolution of female painters from 1975 to the present.

CORRECT:

I. From 1800 to 1874, American women painters created genre art to appeal to the popular masses.

II. From 1875 to 1974, American women painters gained somewhat limited acceptance as professionals.

III. From 1975 to the present, American women painters have gained significant acceptance.

Within each main point, you would strive to select a similar number of influential painters to focus on and balance the information you have on each.

PARALLELISM

You use **parallelism** effectively when you arrange your words, phrases, or sentences in a similar pattern, which can help your main points stand out. For example, simply starting each main point with the same beginning pronoun can signal when you begin a new point and make it easier for your audience to remember the points.

I. Your classroom experience will be unlike your high school class expectations.

II. Your social life will be different from what it was in high school.

III. Your everyday responsibilities will be different.

→ See Chapter 8 for further discussion on using parallelism throughout your speech.

At this point, you should have the best strategy and main points for your topic and audience. Now you can begin to give body or substance to your speech.

CONFIDENCE BOOSTER

Parallelism, like repetition or mnemonic devices, can help you remember your speech. If you use the devices, you will spend less time looking at your notes and you will have more confidence in remembering the key issues.

4
Expand with Subpoints

The subpoints are the filling or content that give your speech substance. Subpoints elaborate on each of the main points. Their job is to clarify, emphasize, or provide detail for the main point they support. In the subpoints, you will use your support materials (statistics, facts, testimony, examples, etc.). You can have multiple layers of subpoints. Your subpoints can also have subpoints. The number of subpoints and layers will vary depending on how much materials you have to convey or need to use. Remember, adhering to proper outline format will help you see how your subpoints relate to the main points and to each other.

I. **First main point**

  A. **First subpoint of I**

    1. **First subpoint of A**

      a. **First subpoint of 1**

      b. **Second subpoint of 1**

    2. **Second subpoint of A**

  B. **Second subpoint of I**

II. **Second main point**

Related subpoints (indicated here by colors) should use consistent symbols and alignment.

➔ See Chapter 5 for a more detailed discussion on outline format.

Follow these suggestions when creating your subpoints.

- You should use full sentences.
- You should introduce only one idea in each subpoint.
- You should adhere to coordination and subordination. Each subpoint on the same level should coordinate or be equal with each other subpoint. Those subpoints directly below a main point or a subpoint should be subordinate, or secondary, to the point above them.

- Your subpoints do not need to follow the same organizational strategy you used for you main points. They can have a strategy of their own or be arranged as a formal argument.

➔ See Part 7 for more information on argumentation.

COMMON ORGANIZATIONAL PROBLEMS

If you follow the outlining and organizational suggestions in Chapter 5 and this chapter, you should not have many, if any, organizational problems. However, it is smart to watch out for the more common ones.

COMMON ORGANIZATIONAL PROBLEM	PREVENTION/SOLUTION
Your selected organizational strategy does not fit the topic or audience.	• Before you commit to a strategy, always consider what your audience needs to know (or do) about your topic. • While you consider the audience's needs, keep your general purpose, specific purpose, and central idea in mind. • Then select the strategy that helps you best fulfill the audience's needs as well as your goal for the speech.
You stop adhering to the arrangement of the strategy at some point during the speech.	• Refer to your textbook several times during the process of creating your outline to refresh your memory about the strategy you are using. • Set up an outline shell or template that mirrors the strategy before you start filling in support materials.
You have too many main points.	• Remember that most classroom speeches will only have time for two or three main points unless the strategy calls for more. • Longer speeches might make up to seven main points work, but your audience will have trouble remembering more than that. • If you feel like you need more main points, check your specific purpose. It may be too broad or you may have strayed from it.

You do not have enough time for the body of the speech.	• Check to see if you are spending too much time on the introduction or conclusion. The approximate formula for breaking down your speech time is:
	  Introduction: 15%
	  Body: 80%
	  Conclusion: 5%

You are spending too much time on one or two main points and cannot cover the rest efficiently.	• Try to keep each of your subpoints equal under a given main point. This is called a **standard of balance.** No one will be timing how long you stay on a point, but you do not want to shortchange a point.

7

INTRODUCING AND CONCLUDING YOUR SPEECH

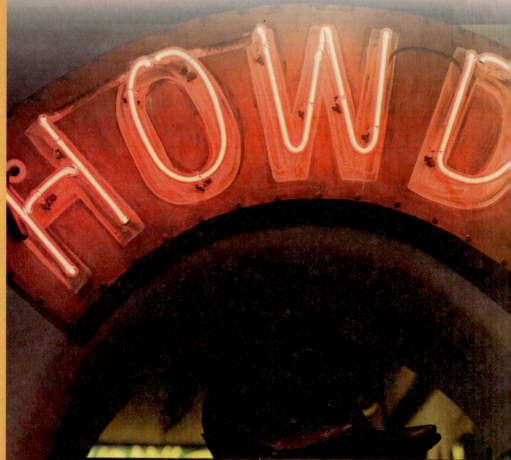

Introduction

Think about how the networks on television work to get you to watch a program. They give a tidbit just as the previous show ends, and then they try to draw you into staying with the program before they go to the first break. They never show the first commercial until you are laughing or in suspense so that you will want to "stay tuned." Likewise, if it is a weekly series, they will leave you at the end of the program excited and motivated to return, often with a "WOW" moment. You are hooked and will respond the way they want by returning to the show the following week.

The same is true for the introduction and conclusion of a good speech. The introduction must grab your audience's attention first and foremost. Your conclusion needs to let them down easy but offer a "WOW" moment. Your audience should be eager to respond to the topic as you intended. If you leave your audience breathless, speechless, or wanting to clap, you have given them a "WOW" moment and a powerful speech.

CHAPTER 5: Outlining Your Speech   96

CHAPTER 6: Organizing the Speech Body   122

CHAPTER 7 CONTENTS

What Should Your Introduction Do?   138
   1 Capture Your Audience's Attention   138
   2 Build Your Credibility Early   139
   3 Demonstrate Audience Relevance   139
   4 Introduce the Topic and Preview the Speech   139

What Are Effective Attention-Getters?   140
   1 Facts and Statistics   140
   2 Quotations   140
   3 Stories, Narratives, Illustrations, or Anecdotes   141
   4 Humor   141
   5 Questions   141

How Do You Organize an Introduction?   142

What Should Your Conclusion Do?   144
   1 Signal the Ending   145
   2 Summarize   145
   3 Elicit a Response   145
   4 Create an Impact One Last Time   145

What Can You Use as a "WOW" Statement?   146
   1 Quotations   146
   2 Stories, Narratives, Illustrations, or Anecdotes   146
   3 Humor   147
   4 Rhetorical Questions   147
   5 Challenges to the Audience   147
   6 References Back to the Introduction   147

How Do You Organize a Conclusion?   148

PART 3 Review   150

What Should Your Introduction Do?

1 Capture Your Audience's Attention

2 Build Your Credibility Early

3 Demonstrate Audience Relevance

4 Introduce the Topic and Preview the Speech

Many beginning speakers miss the importance of literally *launching* into their speech. The introduction should be one of the most exciting, moving, and interesting moments of the speech. Think of the emotional and physical feelings you have when you hear or say the word *launch*; that is exactly what your introduction should feel like.

1 Capture Your Audience's Attention

Think about the noise and distractions you hear as you enter a room of people, like a classroom. People are talking about the weather, recent events, family issues, or dating or work problems. They are moving chairs, shuffling papers, texting, or checking messages. Their minds and bodies are wandering, and you have to get them to focus on you and your topic. As people who love fishing or the Texas Longhorns would say, you have to "hook 'em," or capture their attention.

This function of the introduction may be the most important—you have to get the audience's attention before you can do anything else with your speech. Good speakers spend a lot of time crafting their attention-getters.

Take a look at the following attention-getter used by Andalee, a student, for her speech on laundry skills.

> Classes have been in session a few weeks now, and I bet the laundry monster is about to bust out of your closet. You may not have a clean pair of socks or, worse yet, a clean outfit for your date tomorrow night. Maybe you did a load and everything white came out pink because you missed sorting out a red sock. Add in special laundry care instructions or a stain, and your stress level over how to do your laundry hits the top of the chart. How much bleach do you really need to use? Does liquid fabric softener go in before the rinse cycle or during? Should you use enzymes? Heck, what are enzymes?

Andalee uses anecdotes, questions, and other attention-grabbing tactics.

→ See "What Are Effective Attention-Getters?" on pages 140–141 for more details.

2
Build Your Credibility Early

Your introduction should begin to reveal your credibility as a speaker with ethical consideration for your audience and a relationship with the topic. Aristotle referred to the speaker's credibility as *ethos*. The audience needs to perceive you as kind, competent, caring, honest, and excited about your topic and speech event. You can start establishing ethos in the introduction by:

- Being confident—practice your introduction until you are sure of it and your abilities

- Demonstrating your knowledge of the topic

- Pointing out what you have in common with the audience or topic

- Making it evident that you are sincere and concerned for the audience's well-being

Building your credibility in the introduction does not need to be complicated. In most speeches, employing an effective delivery style and using a simple sentence begin the process. You will continue to build credibility throughout the speech. In her laundry speech, Andalee drew on her experience:

> As a mother of a toddler and as a spouse, I wash laundry all the time! I have spent a lot of time researching the best and cheapest way to keep our clothes looking great.

3
Demonstrate Audience Relevance

Audiences want to know quickly why your speech is relevant to them. An early statement about what your topic has to offer can demonstrate that they have something to gain from listening to you. For example, Andalee highlighted relevance by adding this statement after establishing her credibility:

> As a college student like you, I have to use time wisely and keep the cost of replacing damaged clothes or purchasing expensive laundry aids to a minimum.

4
Introduce the Topic and Preview the Speech

After capturing your audience's attention, you need to give listeners a preview of what they can expect from your speech. This step moves the focus from you to the essence of your speech and usually consists of a single sentence or two, briefly outlining your speech. For example:

> Today, I want to help you see that doing the laundry doesn't have to be stressful or expensive. Actually, it can be quite easy if you take the time to properly sort your laundry, purchase a few basic cleaning items, and follow proper washer and dryer techniques.

In these two sentences, Andalee has given a quick preview of what her speech will cover.

TIP: Delivering the Introduction
Using an energetic delivery from the introduction of your speech onward can also build interest and get your audience excited about the topic.

What Are Effective Attention-Getters?

1 Facts and Statistics

2 Quotations

3 Stories, Narratives, Illustrations, or Anecdotes

4 Humor

5 Questions

An ***attention-getter*** is something you say, show, or do to get your audience to focus on you, your topic, and the goal of your speech. In most cases, it should be the first words spoken or the first images or actions shown.

Attention-getters have a big job, so spend time crafting them, trying them out on someone else, and practicing them. Generally, you will use one of five creative tactics.

1
Facts and Statistics

Facts and statistics can help you point to a remarkable situation or problem. They can be very vivid or shocking even though they are condensed. For example:

> According to the Centers for Disease Control and Prevention at cdc.gov, heart disease is the leading cause of death for women. In 2006, 315,930 women died from heart disease. That was more than one in every four, or 26%, of deaths. Heart disease is no longer a "man's disease."

2
Quotations

Quotations are words or passages written or said by someone else. For an attention-getter, you want a succinct and interesting quotation from someone who will raise your credibility. The quotation may come from a speech, novel, poem, play, TV or movie dialogue, or another similar source.

> "To stand at the edge of the sea, to sense the ebb and flow of the tides... is to have knowledge of things that are as nearly eternal as any earthly life can be," writes the famous environmental activist Rachel Carson, in her 1941 book *Under the Sea-Wind*.

3
Stories, Narratives, Illustrations, or Anecdotes

Stories, narratives, illustrations, or anecdotes are vivid accounts that can personalize your speech by helping the audience identify with the topic. The accounts should be interesting, evoking, and entertaining. You should not need to explain them. Be creative and selective. The accounts can be true or fictional, from your personal life or from broader arenas. Be careful if you are telling your own story because you may become too emotional or the audience may have such heightened empathy for you that it is hard for them to listen.

Here's a short example.

> Zohar is a nine-month-old boy. He does not have the comforts of growing up that you and I have. Zohar coughs violently. An IV pumps medicine into his shriveled arm—medicine that may soon run out. His ribs show clearly through his fragile skin. Zohar's parents hold his tiny hands and pray for his recovery, but Zohar has malaria and severe malnutrition. He is near death. Zohar is only one—one of thousands who will die, one of millions affected. Zohar was born in the region of Darfur, in a country called Sudan, on the continent of Africa, where children just like him are being forced out of their homes by violence as we speak. Journalist Emily Wax, in her June 2004 *Washington Post* article "In Sudan, Death and Denial," introduces us to Zohar and his family.

This example has just enough emotional appeal to draw the audience in.

4
Humor

Humor can build a positive relationship with your audience and lighten up a dry or complex topic. However, you must be careful when using humor if you want to be effective and ethical. Any use of humor should:

- Relate to your audience, topic, and/or occasion
- Be funny (try it out on someone else)
- Not be demeaning to a particular group of people
- Be understandable to your audience (be careful of using humor across cultures or subcultures that might not understand the joke)

5
Questions

You can use a question or a series of questions to direct your audience's attention to your topic. The questions can be asked in a manner to get a direct response or posed as *rhetorical questions* when you do not want a response but simply want to focus audience attention. Below are some examples.

Response-evoking question:

> By a show of hands, how many of you are not allowed by the university to bring a car to campus?

Rhetorical question:

> Are you tired of taking the bus to the mall or bumming a ride because the university won't allow you to bring a car to campus?

How Do You Organize an Introduction?

Most speech instructors suggest creating the body of the speech before you write either the introduction or conclusion. You need to know the tone and content of your speech before you can introduce or conclude it.

Once you are ready to write your introduction, its major parts should correspond to the four functions discussed earlier in this chapter. Your introduction should be no more than 15 percent of the total speech time, so you usually have under a minute to carry out these functions.

Any introduction should start with a good attention-getter, but you can present the other parts in just about any order. Beginning speakers often have the impulse to introduce themselves first. However, if you will be introduced or if the audience already knows you, this step is not necessary. Remember that the first thing you do or say should be designed to grab the audience's attention.

The template below and the example on the next page suggest the two most common arrangements for the parts of an introduction.

INTRODUCTION

Attention-getter: ....
....

Credibility material: ....
....

Relevance to audience: ....
....

Preview of speech: ....
....

Jameel is creating a speech on compulsive shopping for his class assignment. After many drafts and revisions, his introduction looks like this:

INTRODUCTION

Attention-getter: Shopping—it's the American pastime. It gives us a temporary high and a feeling of enjoyment we can't find quite the same way in other activities. As Robert Coombs suggests in his 2004 book, the *Handbook of Addictive Disorders*, "Almost all of us have purchased goods at some time to cheer ourselves up, and many see money and material possessions as tangible signs of personal success. We use consumption to improve our image, self-esteem, or relationship with others." But the questions are how far is too far, and how much is too much? And should you consider yourself or a loved one a compulsive shopper?

Relevance to audience: According to a 2006 survey by the Stanford University School of Medicine, 5.8 percent of the U.S. population—about 17 million people—are compulsive shoppers. That means two of us in this room might be considered compulsive shoppers.

Credibility material: Personally, I enjoy the many highs of shopping and have at times spent more than I should on one trip to the mall. But does that make me a compulsive shopper?

Preview of speech: In this speech, I will explore compulsive shopping as an addictive disorder, who tends to have the disorder, and how it can be treated.

Jameel has correctly included all four parts of an introduction. What attention-getter tactics can you identify? How has Jameel applied some of those tactics to other parts of his introduction?

CHECKLIST for Your Introduction

❏ Do I have an effective attention-getter?
❏ Do I begin to establish my credibility?
❏ Do I establish relevance between my audience and the topic?
❏ Do I preview the speech?

CONFIDENCE BOOSTER

Most beginning speakers experience their strongest communication apprehension in the first few minutes of a speech. A solid and creative introduction can help you feel more comfortable. Never plan to just "wing" or improvise your introduction. Be prepared; practice the introduction completely and multiple times. Doing so will help you feel more relaxed.

What Should Your Conclusion Do?

1 Signal the Ending

2 Summarize

3 Elicit a Response

4 Create an Impact One Last Time

The best way to think about a conclusion is to see it as almost the reverse of your introduction, or that they are very similar and frame your speech. You will use some of the same tactics in the conclusion that you did in the introduction. Although you usually will not need to demonstrate your credibility with the topic or show the relevance to the audience at this point in the speech, you do need to review what you have said, tell the audience what you want them to do, and "WOW" them one last time. Ultimately, your conclusion should provide closure, leaving your audience enlightened and satisfied.

Do not rush creating your conclusion or cut short the process because you think you can craft it as you give the speech. Your conclusion is the last moment you have to increase your audience's understanding and appreciation, persuade them, or entertain them. Take advantage of this significant moment.

The next few pages will help you harness the power of your conclusions.

1

Signal the Ending

Think of this function like the end of a good movie or book. Throughout, the viewer or reader has moved along a path that builds to one defining moment—the ending. In speeches, you need to signal that ending. The most common ways to signal that the end is near are:

- A vocal change, such as slowing down and beginning to lower your intensity
- A physical change, such as moving from behind the lectern (often accompanied by a vocal change)
- A language signal, such as "In conclusion…" or "Today, we have…"

Once you have signaled the conclusion, you should not bring up new information about your topic. Otherwise, you are taking your audience back to information that should be in the body of the speech, which is confusing.

2

Summarize

This is your last chance to tell your audience about your topic in a way that will help them remember it. This statement should effectively and concisely restate your speech's main points.

For example, a speech informing your audience about counterfeit medicines popping up for sale in places like the Internet could have a summary statement such as:

> We've learned a lot about counterfeit medicine today. However, what's important to remember is, first, counterfeit medicine is widespread; second, counterfeit medicine is difficult to contain; and third, there are steps you can take to protect yourself from counterfeits.

3

Elicit a Response

Ideally, you do not want your audience to come away from your speech as passive vessels—taking in your speech but doing nothing with it. Therefore, you need to elicit, or bring forth, the response you wish them to have in relation to your topic. In other words, tell the audience what you want them to do with the information you have just given them. For example:

> Now that you know that counterfeit medicines can be a problem, it is time for you to take action to protect yourself and your loved ones….

Or, as another example, at the end of a toast:

> Please join me in toasting our new mayor….

4

Create an Impact One Last Time

Finally, the very end of your speech should take one last moment to really make your speech memorable and leave your audience with an intense feeling. That feeling should almost compel them to clap enthusiastically. That is the "WOW" moment of a speech. Because this moment is important to the effectiveness of your conclusion, the next section of this book will help you craft an effective "WOW" statement.

What Can You Use as a "WOW" Statement?

1 **Quotations**

2 **Stories, Narratives, Illustrations, or Anecdotes**

3 **Humor**

4 **Rhetorical Questions**

5 **Challenges to the Audience**

6 **References Back to the Introduction**

1 Quotations

When using a quotation to end a speech, the quotation may have a direct relationship with the topic or may be somewhat metaphorical in capturing the essence of the topic.

For example, for a speech related to the Apollo 11 landing or a speech motivating the audience to volunteer, you could end with:

> As Neil Armstrong said, "That's one small step for man; one giant leap for mankind."

2 Stories, Narratives, Illustrations, or Anecdotes

These devices help humanize your topic and can appeal one last time to your audience's emotions. In a conclusion, keep them as short as possible and try not to read them directly, which would lower their impact.

For example:

> I would like to end with a story about my grandfather. During World War II, he….

Emotional power can be an effective way to help your audience remember your speech.

TIP: Use Attention-Getter Techniques
The best way to think about a "WOW" statement is to treat it like the attention-getter in the introduction. Many of the techniques you can use to grab your audience's attention can dazzle them at the conclusion of the speech as well.

3
Humor

Laughter is a positive experience for most individuals and can ease an audience out of your speech. Remember to make any use of humor relate to your audience, topic, and/or occasion; test the material to see if it is really funny; avoid demeaning humor; and make sure your audience will understand the joke.

For example, you might end a speech on reducing stress with this bumper-sticker saying:

> "Stress is when you wake up screaming and you realize you haven't fallen asleep yet."

4
Rhetorical Questions

A series of rhetorical questions can focus how you want your audience to think about your topic and the goal.

For example, in a speech to persuade college students to help in an afterschool program, these questions could end the speech:

> See these children? *(click to slide 5)* Do you want them to end up like other inner-city children? Do you want them to be another crime statistic?

This speaker pairs the rhetorical questions with an image to increase the effect.

5
Challenges to the Audience

Ending by challenging your audience to act in a certain way can focus their attention on that behavior.

For example, adding another question to the previous example challenges the audience to make a proposed response:

> See these children? *(click to slide 5)* Do you want them to end up like other inner-city children? Do you want them to be another crime statistic? Do you have 20 minutes a week that you could give toward changing the lives of these children? I do, and I hope you will join me in volunteering in the Glenwood afterschool program.

6
References Back to the Introduction

This type of "WOW" statement creates a frame for your speech by referring back to the attention-getter you used in your introduction.

For example, if you use the first few lines of a poem to start a speech, you might end with more of the poem. Or, if you tell a story at the beginning, returning to that moment of emotional appeal and finishing the story can nicely frame your speech.

→ See page 149 for an illustration of this technique.

PRACTICING ETHICS
Be ethical when using humor. Many jokes and humorous stories can be inappropriate or derogatory. Review the discussion about the ethical use of humor in attention-getters (page 141) if needed.

How Do You Organize a Conclusion?

Your conclusion should be approximately 5 percent of your speech time. This is not much time, and you do not want to leave your audience feeling either like you suddenly stopped speaking or you went on forever after you signaled the ending. So it is important to spend some time constructing your conclusion.

CONCLUSION

Summary statement: ....
....

Audience response statement: ....
....

WOW statement: ....
....

As in your introduction, the organization of your conclusion can vary; but generally, the above template and the example on the next page show the basic order. Remember to always end with a "WOW" statement.

END OF

ROUTE

CYCLISTS

DISMOUNT

For the end of his classroom speech about unrest in Darfur, Kyril crafted this succinct and moving conclusion.

CONCLUSION

Summary statement: I hope my speech today has offered you some insight into the Darfur issues. We have discussed the history of Darfur, why the violence in the region continues to worsen, and how we can make an effort to bring about peace.

Audience response statement: My purpose in giving this speech is to persuade you that even as citizens of the United States, we can take action to save lives.

WOW statement: Remember nine-month-old Zohar from the beginning of my speech? Zohar did not make it—and he became one of the thousands who died. To his parents, Zohar was their only child. To the world, Zohar is a statistic. Your actions could make Zohar, a child and someone's son, one of the last to be a statistic.

Kyril has correctly included all three parts of a conclusion. Notice how his "WOW" statement refers back to a story in his introduction and finishes that story to end on a note of emotional appeal.

CHECKLIST for Your Conclusion

❏ Do I signal the ending of the speech?
❏ Do I end the speech soon after signaling the conclusion?
❏ Do I restate my main points?
❏ Do I challenge the audience?
❏ Do I have the best possible "WOW" statement ending my speech?
❏ Do I have the necessary oral citations, if any are needed?

Part 3: Review

CHAPTER 5 REVIEW QUESTIONS

1. List and briefly explain the nine qualities of an effective outline.

2. What are the three different types of outlines, and why should you use each one?

3. Explain the four different types of links and give an example of each.

4. Using the appropriate style manual for your class, create a source page entry for this book.

CHAPTER 6 REVIEW QUESTIONS

1. Name three strategies you could use for an informative speech, and explain why each is an effective choice for informing.

2. Name three different strategies you might use for a persuasive speech, and explain why each is an effective choice for persuading.

3. How should you determine and select which strategy is the best for your speech?

4. What are the five main qualities you should adhere to when creating your main points? Briefly explain them.

CHAPTER 7 REVIEW QUESTIONS

1. What are the four functions of a speech introduction?

2. What are five types of attention-getters you can use? Write an example of one.

3. What are the four functions of a speech conclusion?

4. What are six types of "WOW" statements you can use? Write an example of one.

TERMS TO REMEMBER

Chapter 5
introduction (99)
body (99)
main points (99)
subpoints (99)
links (99)
conclusion (99)
working outlines (106)
preparation outlines (108)
delivery outlines (112)
transitions (114)
signposts (115)
internal previews (115)
internal reviews (115)

Chapter 6
strategy (123)
chronological strategy (126)
topical strategy (126)
spatial strategy (127)
causal strategy (127)
comparative strategy (128)
comparative advantage (128)
problem–solution strategy (128)
Monroe's motivated sequence (129)
parallelism (133)
standard of balance (135)

CHAPTER 7
attention-getter (140)
quotations (140)
rhetorical questions (141)

PART 4
Presenting

CHAPTER 8
Using Language Successfully   152

CHAPTER 9
Delivering Your Speech   162

CHAPTER 10
Using Presentation Aids   178

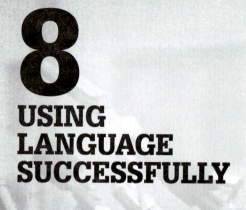

8
USING
LANGUAGE
SUCCESSFULLY

Introduction

These quotations from famous speeches throughout history demonstrate the power of language. You may recognize most of them and may even be able to quote one or two. King's evocative phrasing, Truth's use of a straightforward rhetorical question, and Henry's as well as Clinton's use of parallelism help etch these quotations into our minds. Like these speakers, you can learn to harness the power of language. This chapter will offer you advice, examples, and tools for using language to its fullest potential to help your speech be a success. You will learn why language is powerful, how to use it effectively, and how to boost your language's distinctiveness.

CHAPTER 8 CONTENTS

What Makes Language So Important?	154
1 Meaning	154
2 Culture	155
3 Power	155

How Can You Use Language Effectively?	156
1 Be Clear	156
2 Be Correct	157
3 Be Specific	158
4 Use Oral Style	158
5 Be Appropriate	159
6 Be Distinctive	160

CHAPTER 9: Delivering Your Speech	162
CHAPTER 10: Using Presentation Aids	178
PART 4 Review	202

"I have a dream that my four little children will one day live in a nation where they will not be judged by the color of their skin, but by the content of their character" [1]

MARTIN LUTHER KING, JR.

"Ain't I a woman?" [2]

SOJOURNER TRUTH

"I know not what course others may take; but as for me, give me liberty, or give me death!" [3]

PATRICK HENRY

"And let us heed the call so that we can create a world in which every woman is treated with respect and dignity, every boy and girl is loved and cared for equally, and every family has the hope of a strong and stable future." [4]

HILLARY RODHAM CLINTON

What Makes Language So Important?

1 Meaning
2 Culture
3 Power

1

Meaning

Language or, more precisely, *words* are symbols that you create, learn, and use to express your thoughts and feelings. Words are:

- **symbolic:** A word represents what it is referring to either by association, resemblance, or convention.

- **arbitrary:** The relationship between the word and what it stands for is random, subjective, or coincidental.

Think about the word *book*. Nothing about the letters that make up that word, or their arrangement, directly relates to the thing you are reading from right now. That relationship is understood only when you learn to associate the word (*book*) with pages bound between two covers.

In your mind, if a word is familiar, you have two meanings that help you then come up with a definition of the thing represented. They are the *denotative* and *connotative* meanings of a word.

The **denotative meaning** of a word is the accepted meaning and is the one found in the dictionary. Some words have more than one denotative meaning. For example, *bats* can be animals or sporting equipment.

The **connotative meaning** of a word is the emotional and personal reaction you might have to a word. Perhaps you're afraid of bats (the animals). Your reaction could be anywhere on a continuum from an emotional avalanche (a significant positive or negative response to a word) to an emotional famine (no real response at all).

As a speaker, you should always be aware that your audience may not have the same denotative or connotative meaning in mind for a word you use.

2
Culture

Language is one of the means individuals use constantly to create, share, and transmit their cultural identity.

Culture is learned patterns of beliefs, values, attitudes, norms, practices, customs, and behaviors shared by a large group of people. These patterns often change and are shared through symbolic interaction (i.e., language).

The online and social networking cultures you may belong to are examples of how connected language and culture are to each other. Since the Internet explosion of the past century, cyber-culture members have had to learn many new words, phrases, and grammatical conventions. Cyber-cultures tend to change almost daily, so their language is extremely dynamic. If you want to practice the proper norms, customs, and behavior, you have to stay on top of the current language—words and terms like *blogging, texting, tweeting, hashtag, skype,* and *apps*.

As a speaker, you are part of multiple cultures that influence your language choices. However, none is more important to the public speaker than the culture/cultures represented in the audience and connected to the speech topic. If you have the opportunity to give the same speech to different, diverse audiences, your language may be radically different.

PRACTICING ETHICS

The words you choose to use can create meaning and cultural identity, influence feelings and attitudes, move people to action, or empower or break down individuals and groups. Carefully selecting your words is one of your most important ethical practices when giving a speech.

3
Power

Do you know the children's rhyme "Sticks and stones may break my bones, but words will never hurt me"? Although its intent is to teach a child to view words as powerless, words are anything but powerless.

Language helps you understand and create meaning, and through language, you create, share, and transmit cultural identity—and that is powerful.

Language allows you to name experiences or things. Before Bill Wasik, senior editor for *Harper's Magazine,* staged the first "flash mob" in 2003, the term did not exist. You may now know that a flash mob is, as described by author Clay Shirky in *Here Comes Everybody,* "a group that engages in seemingly spontaneous but actually synchronized behavior" that is organized via e-mail, for example. You have language to describe the act—and that is powerful.

Language can bring people together for a common cause. For example, once you understood the meaning of the term *flash mob,* you could then participate in one. This ability to gather or mobilize is powerful.

Language can persuade you to act. Maybe you persuade a friend to join you in a flash mob. Persuasion is powerful.

Unfortunately, language has the power to create and maintain inequality, to control, to hurt, and to disempower. Much of Adolf Hitler's power came from his persuasive speeches. In this case, language is powerful in misleading and damaging ways.

Fortunately, language creates equality, frees, heals, and empowers as well—think of the language used by activists like Bono— and that is powerful.

How Can You Use Language Effectively?

1 **Be Clear**
2 **Be Correct**
3 **Be Specific**
4 **Use Oral Style**
5 **Be Appropriate**
6 **Be Distinctive**

1

Be Clear

In your speech, more so than in writing, it is imperative that you use language your audience will recognize and understand. Language clarity means that your audience immediately recognizes and understands your word choices. Keeping your language clear and familiar is highly contingent on knowing your audience.

➔ See Chapter 1 for details on getting to know your audience.

These guidelines will help you keep your language clear and familiar:

- Select a style and level of language appropriate to your audience.

- Be cautious with ***jargon***, or specialized or technical language, which might be confusing. If you use it, do so sparingly and define words that could be unfamiliar.

- Be cautious with abbreviations and acronyms, which can be confusing to a listener. An ***abbreviation*** is the shortening of a word to stand as the whole word. For example:

    bro = brother

    An ***acronym*** is a word formed from the initials or other parts of several words.

    NATO = North Atlantic Treaty Organization

    Use abbreviations and acronyms sparingly, if at all, and always explain them the first time you use them in a speech.

TIP: Intercultural Audiences
Jargon, abbreviations, and acronyms can be unfamiliar and confusing to intercultural audiences. Be especially sensitive to language with diverse audiences.

2

Be Correct

Your language should be free, as much as possible, of interpretation error and should adhere to certain standards. Using language incorrectly often leads to misunderstanding and low speaker ethos (credibility). When speakers use language incorrectly, they tend to use the wrong word, mispronounce words, and/or use incorrect grammar.

→ See Chapter 9 for more on pronunciation.

Although you can be a bit less formal with your grammar in an oral presentation, you still want to adhere to correct grammar rules. Do not equate informal with incorrect. Here are four common errors.

ERROR #1: MISPLACED MODIFIER

This error occurs when you place a modifier too far away from what it is modifying.

INCORRECT:
The man caught a bass wearing a purple hat.

CORRECT:
The man, wearing a purple hat, caught a bass.

ERROR #2: PRONOUNS

There are three common pronoun errors. First, make sure your pronouns are in agreement (plural vs. singular) with the nouns they refer to.

INCORRECT:
Everyone wants their own piece of the pie.

CORRECT:
Everyone wants his or her own piece of the pie.

Second, make sure you use the correct form of a pronoun for its function in the sentence. Use pronouns such as *I, she,* and *he* as subjects; use forms such as *me, her,* and *him* as objects.

INCORRECT:
Him and me are best friends.

CORRECT:
He and I are best friends.

He and *I* are subjects in the above examples. Below, *her* and *me* are objects, receiving the action of Mom's yelling.

INCORRECT:
Mom yelled at she and I.

CORRECT:
Mom yelled at her and me.

Third, if you are using the third-person singular pronouns (*he, she, one,* and *it*), use *doesn't, does not,* or *does.* For all other pronouns (*I, you, we,* and *they*), use *don't, do not,* or *do.*

INCORRECT:
She don't want to go.

CORRECT:
She doesn't want to go.

ERROR #3: *WENT* VERSUS *GONE*

When using a helping verb (like *has* or *have*), use the past participle form of a verb.

INCORRECT:
I should have went to the party.

CORRECT:
I should have gone to the party.

ERROR #4: SUBJECT/VERB AGREEMENT

A singular noun in the present tense uses a singular verb. Plural nouns use plural verbs. The following sentence refers to only one of many coats; the noun is singular and the verb should be, too.

INCORRECT:
One of these coats are mine.

CORRECT:
One of these coats is mine.

3
Be Specific

Getting your message across in a straight-forward manner is necessary in a speech. In an instant, your audience must interpret your message and formulate a response and/or commit it to memory. Here are some steps that will help you stay specific.

- Be concrete. Concrete words focus on a person, object, action, and/or behavior and help listeners create a complete and, hopefully, accurate image.

  ### ABSTRACT:
  Puck and Zelda are dogs.

  ### CONCRETE:
  Puck and Zelda are golden retrievers.

- Eliminate unnecessary words.

- Speak primarily in the active voice. In the active voice, the subject is doing the action stated in the verb. In the passive voice, the subject receives the action.

  ### ACTIVE:
  The dog caught the mole.

  ### PASSIVE:
  The mole was caught by the dog.

- Avoid clichés. **Clichés** are overused words or phrases that have lost their effect. Some examples:

  Before I knew it   Cut to the chase

- Avoid fillers. **Fillers** are sounds, words, or phrases that serve no purpose and do not help your audience understand the message. For example:

INSTEAD OF	SAY
a number of	several

  ### AVOID FILLERS SUCH AS
  ah, um, like, you know, or actually

4
Use Oral Style

If you have ever read a transcript of a verbal conversation, you know that the way people speak is different from the way they write.

When you give a speech, you want to use an oral, or verbal, style rather than a written style. In oral style, you use more everyday language, personal pronouns such as *we* or *you,* contractions, and shorter sentences that put the subjects and verbs closer together. Here are the major differences between written and oral styles:

CHARACTERISTICS OF ORAL STYLE	CHARACTERISTICS OF WRITTEN STYLE
Informal language	Formal language
Animated language	Technical language
Simple sentence structure	Complex sentence structure
Personally tailored messages	Impersonal messages
Repetition and restatement	Detailed and complex thoughts

For example, Makenna gave a speech to her class about counterfeit drugs, making the mistake of writing it like a paper. One of her sentences was as follows:

The next reason why the market for this form of counterfeiting is growing can be attributed to the Internet.

This same sentence might have been more effective if Makenna had used oral style:

The Internet is the next reason why we are seeing a growth in the counterfeit drug market.

5
Be Appropriate

The type of language you use should suit you, your audience, and the situation. Always remember that you are cocreating your message with your listeners. Their denotative and connotative definitions of a word may or may not be the same as yours. Your success depends on selecting appropriate language that is constructive, not destructive.

USE CULTURALLY APPROPRIATE AND UNBIASED LANGUAGE

- Avoid singling out personal traits or characteristics (such as age, disability, race, sex, sexual orientation, and so on) when they do not relate to the subject at hand. For example:

  INCORRECT:
  The gay student had coffee.

  The student's sexual orientation has nothing to do with the consumption of coffee.

- Use the name for an individual or group that they prefer, such as:

  African American or black; Asian or Asian American; American Indian or Native American; white or Caucasian; Hispanic, Latino, or Chicano

  Gay, lesbian, bisexual, or transgendered (avoid homosexual)

- Avoid language that promotes stereotypes. Some examples to avoid:

  woman driver, Mr. Mom, redneck

- Use gender-neutral language. The table below offers a few suggestions.

USE GENDER-NEUTRAL LANGUAGE

AVOID	USE INSTEAD
man and wife	husband and wife; couple; partners
chairman or chairwoman; fireman; congressman; councilwoman	chair or chairperson; firefighter; congressperson; councilmember
housewife	homemaker, parent, or caregiver
pronoun *he* to represent both male and female or *he* in situations generally viewed as masculine (such as sports) pronoun *she* in situations generally viewed as female	the plural *they*, or replace with *one*, *you*, or *he or she* You can also reword to avoid using pronouns: "On average, each nurse was disappointed with the raise." or "On average, nurses were disappointed with their raises."
girl or boy (over the age of 18)	woman or young woman; man or young man
Miss and Mrs.	Ms. to refer to married and unmarried women (as you would use Mr.)

6

Be Distinctive

Distinctive language is lively, vivid, attention grabbing, and memorable. You can boost your speech's distinctiveness by using language that appeals to your audience's senses, embellishing your words, or using speech devices.

APPEAL TO THE SENSES

Using language that appeals to one or more senses can bring an object to life, invoke passion, or entertain. Although not every sentence should use a sensory appeal, think about how you can turn an ordinary statement into a sensory image. Use the table below to help you.

SENSES	WHY MIGHT I APPEAL TO THIS PARTICULAR SENSE?	EXAMPLES
Sight (visual)	To make a visual comparison between things or to restore a visual image from memory	"The water on the floor glimmered in sunlight."
Sound (auditory)	To help the listener understand how something sounds or to evoke a sound memory	"As the wind blew, you could hear the cracking and splitting of the tree limbs."
Smell (olfactory)	To take a person back to a place, time, or feeling, as people often associate smell with memories	"My favorite memory is the cool leathery smell of the brand-new football my Dad gave me when I was eight."
Taste (gustatory)	To associate the taste of something with something known or to restore taste memory	"It tastes like chicken." "The sweet rolls were chewy and buttery."
Touch (tactile)	To create the feel of something or evoke a relationship/feeling between the person and the object touched	"Think about the last time you really played a video game and how the controller warmed to your intensity and vibrated softly as you fought your battle."

CHECKLIST for Using Language Effectively

❏ Is my language correct?
❏ Is my language clear? Do I avoid jargon?
❏ Is my language specific? Do I use concrete words and active voice?
❏ Is my language appropriate and unbiased?
❏ Do I use oral style?
❏ Is my language distinctive?

CONFIDENCE BOOSTER

Building your vocabulary will help you feel more comfortable when speaking. If you have a broad and varied vocabulary, you can be more powerful, creative, and interesting when developing your speech. You can build your vocabulary by reading more, looking up words when you don't know them, and working new words into your everyday speech.

EMBELLISH LANGUAGE

You can use techniques called **tropes** to embellish or enhance ordinary words. Adapted from Edward Corbett and Robert Connors, *Classical Rhetoric for the Modern Student*, the following table explains the most common tropes.

TROPE	WHAT IS IT?	EXAMPLES
Simile	An explicit comparison between two things, using *like* or *as*	busy as a bee, clear as a bell, cold as ice, common as dirt, crazy as a loon, cute as a button, eats like a bird
Metaphor	An implied comparison	"Every day is an uphill battle." "That outfit is a train wreck."
Personification	Giving human traits to an object, idea, or animal	"My computer hates me." "The camera loves you"
Oxymoron	Connecting two ordinarily contradictory words together	act naturally, Hell's Angels, jumbo shrimp, Led Zeppelin, Iron Butterfly, found missing, deafening silence, unbiased opinion
Rhetorical questions	Asking a question, but not for the purpose of receiving an answer	"[I]f you wrong us, shall we not revenge?" —William Shakespeare, *The Merchant of Venice*, 3:1

USE SPEECH DEVICES

The techniques of manipulating word order—or **schemes**—can help you create distinctive language. Adapted from Corbett and Conners, the table below explains a few common speech devices.

SCHEME	WHAT IS IT?	EXAMPLES
Repetition	Replicating the same words, phrases, or sentences for emphasis	"Harriett Tubman had one piece of advice... If you want a taste of freedom, **keep going**. Even in the darkest of moments, ordinary Americans have found the faith to **keep going**." —Hillary Rodham Clinton, 2008 DNC speech
Assonance	Repeating a similar vowel sound	"... the **odious apparatus** of Nazi rule." —Winston Churchill
Alliteration	Repetition of initial consonants in two or more words in close proximity	"Already American vessels have been **searched**, **seized**, and **sunk**." —John F. Kennedy, *Profiles in Courage*
Parallelism	Duplicating the same grammatical patterns more than once	**"Tell me and I forget. Teach me and I may remember. Involve me and I will learn."** —Benjamin Franklin

9
DELIVERING YOUR SPEECH

Introduction

Think about someone you consider a good speaker and the first time you saw him or her speak. Think about how the speaker's use of voice kept you interested in the topic and signaled what was important. Think about what the speaker did with his or her hands, arms, and face to create and reinforce a message. What did the speaker wear? Did the clothing seem appropriate to the speech and occasion? Do you think the speaker gave this speech without rehearsing it several times?

Because you found this speaker effective, he or she probably spent some time thinking about gestures, voice, use of space, clothing, and other delivery issues. Odds are, the speaker practiced that speech several times before giving it.

A public speech is a presentation that merges the written speech with the oral presentation, and both are open to interpretation. Your message and delivery work together to create the whole experience. Therefore, delivery is important. Effective delivery does not draw attention to itself and uses both verbal and nonverbal elements to assist the message on its way to the audience. Effective delivery is natural and engaging, and it demonstrates confidence. This chapter will help you employ a delivery style that can help your audience understand, appreciate, and enjoy your message.

> *We are what we repeatedly do; excellence, then, is not an act but a habit.*[1]
>
> WILL DURANT,
> summarizing Aristotle

CHAPTER 8: Using Language Successfully   152

CHAPTER 9 CONTENTS

What Are the Elements of Vocal Delivery?   164
1 Pitch   164
2 Rate   164
3 Volume   165
4 Pause   165
5 Variety   166
6 Pronunciation   166
7 Articulation   167
8 Dialect   167

What Are the Elements of Physical Delivery?   168
1 Appearance   168
2 Eye Contact   169
3 Facial Expression   170
4 Gestures   170
5 Movement   171
6 Posture   171

What Are the Methods of Delivery?   172
1 Extemporaneous Speaking   172
2 Manuscript Speaking   173
3 Memorized Speaking   173
4 Impromptu Speaking   173

How Do You Prepare for an Extemporaneous Speech?   174
1 Read Aloud the Preparation Outline   175
2 Prepare Your Delivery Outline   175
3 Prepare Your Presentation Aids   175
4 Practice Multiple Times   176
5 Do a Final "Dress Rehearsal"   176
6 Prepare for Questions   177
7 Prepare for the Day of the Speech   177

CHAPTER 10: Using Presentation Aids   178
PART 4 Review   202

What Are the Elements of Vocal Delivery?

1 Pitch

2 Rate

3 Volume

4 Pause

5 Variety

6 Pronunciation

7 Articulation

8 Dialect

1
Pitch

Pitch is how high and low your voice is in frequency and is determined by how fast or slow your vocal cords vibrate. The greater the number of vibrations per second your cords move, the higher the pitch.

One factor affecting pitch is how relaxed or stressed your body is. When you are excited, tense, or frightened, the muscles around your voice box (larynx) tighten, raising the pitch of your voice. Think of the difference between a calm statement, "The tree is falling," and a warning, "The tree is falling!"

Pitch is something you can work on if your voice is extremely high or low; and, as with many elements in your speech, variety in pitch is important. A constant pitch, known as **monotone**, is distracting and boring. Varying your pitch (**inflection**) will help you demonstrate enthusiasm, excitement, concern, and dedication to the topic.

2
Rate

Your vocal **rate** is the speed at which you speak. The average rate a person can speak is between 120 and 150 words per minute. You can manipulate your rate to add excitement, exhilaration, or urgency to your speech. The key to a good overall rate is to pay attention to your audience. If your audience seems bored, speeding up may help. If the topic is difficult and they appear confused, slowing down would be helpful. If you feel out of breath during your speech, that is a good indication that you are talking too fast. Slow down, let your audience catch up, and allow yourself to breathe.

3

Volume

Your vocal **volume** is how loud or soft your voice is. Some speech instructors would say the appropriate volume is just a bit louder than your normal speaking voice. However, you need to consider the size of the room and audience, the level of environmental noise, and whether you must project on your own or will be using a microphone.

Aim for a volume that can vary and still be heard in the back row of the audience when you are at your softest—and not hurt your vocal cords at your loudest. Pay attention to the cues your audience sends you about your volume. They may lean forward if you are too quiet and turn their heads slightly to hear you better. If you are too loud, they may lean back, lower their chins slightly, and frown.

TIPS: Using a Microphone

If a room or audience is too large, the acoustics are poor, or you are physically unable to project your voice, you will need to use a microphone.

- If possible, practice your complete speech with the sound system to uncover problems.
- Perform a second sound check 30 minutes or so before the event starts.
- Determine the type of microphone and how far or close you need to be to it.
- Beware of distracting vocal sounds (popping sharp consonants or heavy breathing) or nonverbal sounds (hitting the lectern) that might be amplified by the system.
- Be careful not to make side or private comments that might be heard over an open microphone. Always assume that the microphone is on until you are a safe distance from it.

4

Pause

A vocal **pause** can be used for more than just slowing down your speaking rate. Pauses can allow your audience to linger on a thought, in order to apply meaning or gauge significance. Also, pauses can be used as a tool for enhancing or emphasizing a point.

At the end of his inaugural address on January 20, 1961, former President John F. Kennedy used pauses to focus his audience's attention on the message and evoke a major reaction. Each line break below represents a pause (capitalization indicates increased volume); you can listen to the speech on YouTube.

> And so, my fellow Americans,
> ask NOT
> what your country can do for you;
> ask what you can do for your country.

REMOVING VOCAL FILLERS

Do not be afraid to use pauses to help avoid using vocal fillers. As you learned in Chapter 8, fillers are extraneous sounds and words like *ah, um, like,* or *you know.* Most pauses are not significant to the audience, but the fillers become distracting.

Removing vocal fillers is a process. The first step is to make a conscious effort to recognize that you are using fillers. Then, you must work to recognize when and why you use them. The next step is to preempt the usage, which takes time, dedication, and patience.

- Practice so you will recall what to say next. Speakers tend to use vocal fillers when struggling for their next word.
- Have someone signal you each time you use a filler during a rehearsal.
- Record your speech and listen for fillers.

5
Variety

You use vocal **variety** when you fluctuate, change, or adjust your volume, pitch, rate, and pauses. To do so brings your voice and, therefore, your words to life, filling them with expression and animation. To be an effective speaker, you must employ vocal variety.

To understand what vocal variety can do for your speech, locate a video clip (on AmericanRhetoric.com or YouTube) of former President Ronald Reagan's "tear down this wall" speech—remarks delivered in front of Brandenburg Gate in Germany on June 12, 1987.

As Reagan speaks the following words, his voice deepens, slows at times, and rises in volume to punch the ending. The below excerpt is written poetically to simulate Reagan's vocal variety. End-of-line breaks represent longer pauses, added spaces between words represent short pauses, and capitalization represents increased volume and intensity.

> General Secretary Gorbachev,
> if YOU seek peace,
> if you seek prosperity for the Soviet Union
> and Eastern Europe,
> if YOU seek liberalization:
> Come   here   to THIS gate!
> Mr. Gorbachev,
> open   THIS   gate! (*applause*)
> Mr. Gorbachev,
> MR. GORBACHEV,
> TEAR   DOWN   THIS   WALL!

His effective delivery inspired listeners. Listen to a recording and see if you, too, can feel the energy when he speaks.

6
Pronunciation

Correct **pronunciation** is the standard or commonly accepted way to make a word sound. For example, do you know someone who says the word *picture* like the word *pitcher*? The word *picture* should be pronounced "pik-tchure," and *pitcher* should be pronounced "pit-chure."

Poor pronunciation can, at the very least, slow down your audience's listening skills as they try to figure out what you intend or, in the worst case, cause complete misunderstanding.

Recognizing when you mispronounce a word can be difficult, as you may not know you are doing it. Ask your friends and family to pay attention and tell you when you mispronounce a word. If you are unsure of how to pronounce a new word, look it up or ask someone who should know. Many online dictionaries allow you to play sound recordings of correct pronunciations.

Not knowing how to correctly pronounce words can also significantly lower your ethos (credibility). Be diligent and find out the correct way to pronounce the words you plan to use in your speech.

TIP: Pronunciation
If you know you have trouble pronouncing a word and cannot break the habit, use an alternative word if possible.

7
Articulation

Articulation is how completely and clearly you utter a word—for example, saying "morning" instead of "mornin'." Closely linked, and often used synonymously with articulation, is **enunciation**, or the distinctiveness and clarity of linked whole words—for example, saying, "Did you eat yet?" instead of "Jeat yet?"

Speaking fast, mumbling, running words together, and dropping vowels or consonants (as in "drinkin'") are all considered poor articulation or enunciation—commonly referred to as "lazy speech." Audiences may view these habits as inappropriate for a public speech, which can harm your ethos.

Mumbling is a common problem for beginning speakers. If you have this habit, make a conscious effort to eliminate it. Warming up your mouth can help. Before entering the speech location, open your mouth wide several times, stretching your jaw muscles (be careful if you have medical issues with your jaw), then hum as you rapidly vibrate your lips together. Like an athlete stretches, you need to warm up your mouth's muscles.

8
Dialect

All cultures and subcultures have unique elements in their speech known as dialects. A **dialect** is how a particular group of people pronounces and uses language. Dialects can be regional (e.g., the South) or ethnic (e.g., Jewish English).

Dialects are important for establishing and maintaining cultural identity, so you do not automatically need to avoid using dialect. However, if your dialect is significantly different from that of your audience, it can distract them and decrease your effectiveness.

When a dialect interferes with communication, it is usually because grammar and vocabulary cause the misunderstanding. For example, in the Boston area, you might hear a water fountain called a bubbler or a rubber band called an elastic.

When speaking outside of your region or culture, use the more standard vocabulary. Doing so will help you prevent misunderstanding and distraction while maintaining your individual identity.

CHECKLIST for Vocal Delivery

❏ Am I using both low and high pitches? Do I need to regulate my natural pitch?

❏ Is my rate too fast or too slow?

❏ Is my volume appropriate for this space and the audience size? Do I need to use a microphone?

❏ Am I using pauses effectively?

❏ Do I use enough vocal variety?

❏ Am I pronouncing all my words correctly?

❏ Am I mumbling, running my words together too fast, or clipping consonants or vowels?

❏ Will my dialect distract the audience?

What Are the Elements of Physical Delivery?

1 Appearance
2 Eye Contact
3 Facial Expression
4 Gestures
5 Movement
6 Posture

1
Appearance

If you know of her, two things come to mind when you think of Lady Gaga—her music and her appearance. Although her appearance is not what makes her a good singer, it is part of the persona she wishes to create, helping her stand out and be memorable.

Similarly, you should not underestimate the influence your appearance can have on your speech. *Appearance* includes your dress and grooming choices. Once you walk into a room, the people around you begin to form first impressions about you. Unlike Lady Gaga, you should rarely, if ever, draw attention to your appearance because you want your audience to focus on your message. Your appearance should improve your ethos and support your message. Here are some guidelines:

- Always be well groomed.
- Dress for the occasion. You want to dress a bit better than what is expected for the occasion and the audience.
- Consider environmental issues. Wearing black on a hot, sunny day may make you sweat and appear more nervous.
- Use your appearance to support your topic. For example, wearing a suit for a speech on changing motor oil in a car will seem odd.
- Think about the mood, attitude, or image you want to project.
- Avoid wearing distracting items like flashy colors or jewelry.

2
Eye Contact

If there is one piece of advice effective speakers understand, it is to make eye contact. You must establish and maintain eye contact with your audience if you want them to stay focused on you and your message and view you as trustworthy. In addition, eye contact enables you to obtain feedback during the speech.

Although cultural norms differ, Western culture prefers **direct eye contact**, or briefly looking straight into the eyes of the other person. During a public speaking occasion, you can accommodate this cultural preference by randomly selecting several people in the audience to make direct eye contact with. Choosing those audience members who are actively listening to your speech and smiling will help boost your confidence as well.

The beginning speaker often uses ineffective eye contact. Familiarize yourself

Direct eye contact
Choose several audience members to make direct eye contact with. As an audience member, help the speaker by being an active listener and maintaining eye contact with him or her.

with the ineffective practices in the table below. If you recognize yourself in any of these categories, try to self-regulate the behavior or ask a friend to watch you during your speech.

INEFFECTIVE EYE CONTACT	WHAT IS IT?	EFFECTIVE SOLUTION
The Bobber	A speaker who bobs up and down rhythmically from notes to audience	Practice the speech so you don't rely on your notes so much, or shorten your delivery outline.
The Stargazer	A speaker who looks above and beyond the audience	Don't be afraid to look at your audience. Most audiences are friendly.
The Obsessor	A speaker who looks at only one or two audience members during the whole speech	Use more of the space in front of the audience, forcing you to look at more people, and practice including most of the audience.
The Obliterator	A speaker who tends to look at only one side of the audience and forgets the rest	Prior to the speech, familiarize yourself with the edges of the audience in all directions. Move around and use more of the space in front of the audience during the speech.

3

Facial Expression

Facial expressions are the use of facial muscles to convey your internal thoughts or feelings. Many animals use facial expressions, but humans seem to be the masters of this form of communication. Although you have thousands of different expressions, only six seem to be universal.

UNIVERSAL EXPRESSION	HOW DO YOU MAKE IT?
Happiness	Raise mouth corners into a smile
Fear	Raise brows, open eyes fully, and open mouth slightly
Surprise	Arch brows, open eyes wide to expose more white, and drop jaw open slightly
Disgust	Raise upper lip and wrinkle nose bridge (which raises cheeks)
Anger	Lower brows, press lips together firmly, and bulge eyes
Sadness	Lower mouth corners and raise inner portion of brows

Here are some keys to using effective facial expressions.

- Match your expressions to your verbal message.
- Keep your expressions natural. Avoid overdoing or exaggerating them.
- When speaking across cultures, consider the universality of your expressions.

4

Gestures

You use *gestures* when you use your body or parts of it (hands, arms, eyes, or head) to convey a message and feelings during your speech. The gestures used during a speech are usually either emblems or illustrators.

Emblems are speech-independent and culturally learned gestures that have a direct verbal translation. When you shrug your shoulders  to convey "I don't know" or form a circle with your thumb and index finger on the same hand to communicate a feeling of "OK," you are using emblems. Winking, nodding yes, waving hello, and rolling your eyes are emblems, too. An emblem may not mean the same thing in another culture, so be careful.

Illustrators are speech-dependent and closely linked to what is being said. They help you demonstrate words or messages in a  speech. For example, if you put up one finger as you say, "my first point," you are using an illustrator.

Effective gestures should:

- Vary, so that they do not become rhythmic and distracting
- Be appropriate to the speech, audience, and occasion
- Be purposefully used and add to your message

5
Movement

Movement refers to your use of motion and space during the speech. How to use space depends, as always, on your needs, the topic, the audience, and the occasion.

If the topic and the event are extremely formal, such as a graduation ceremony, standing to the side of the lectern or moving around on the stage is less acceptable. However, most speech events will allow some flexibility with movement and will be better if you use it. Standing completely still can make you seem rigid or unapproachable and can cause any nervous tension in your body to intensify.

Lecterns (especially with microphones) are useful tools but can be a barrier between you and your audience. If you want to build a friendlier and more approachable relationship, avoid using a lectern. If possible, stand to the side or move around periodically. You should avoid pacing, however. Just remember to make your movement purposeful, not distracting, and consistent with your verbal message. If a microphone is necessary, try to use a lapel or wireless one.

6
Posture

Posture is the position of your body during your speech and, like your facial expressions, can convey inner thoughts and feelings you have about yourself, your audience, the topic, and the situation. If you are nervous, your body might be rigid and straight. If you are very relaxed, depressed, or tired, your shoulders might droop or you might lean against the table or lectern. If you close off your body by hiding behind a lectern or crossing your arms, you appear less approachable.

Conversely, if you are somewhat at ease and excited about your speech, your body will be open (front of the body visible), mostly relaxed but energized, and straight but not stiff. This posture is more natural and inviting to the audience. It conveys that you are enthusiastic and comfortable with your audience, topic, and situation. Your posture can significantly influence your ethos.

Bad posture
Crossing your arms or leaning against the lectern

Good posture
More natural and inviting to the audience

CHECKLIST for Physical Delivery

❏ Is my appearance well groomed and appropriate?

❏ Am I employing good direct eye contact?

❏ Am I varying my facial expressions, gestures, and movements? Are they natural?

❏ Does my posture convey enthusiasm for my topic, the audience, and the occasion?

What Are the Methods of Delivery?

1 **Extemporaneous Speaking**
2 **Manuscript Speaking**
3 **Memorized Speaking**
4 **Impromptu Speaking**

1

Extemporaneous Speaking

Extemporaneous speaking is considered the most acceptable contemporary method of delivery. Here, you plan out, rehearse, and deliver the speech from a key-word/phrase outline.

WHEN SHOULD YOU USE IT?

This type of delivery is more audience centered than others because it is speaking "with" your audience and not "at" them. When your goal is to give an audience-centered speech, this is the method to use. In fact, you should try to use this method most of the time. Most classroom speeches require extemporaneous delivery.

DELIVERY TECHNIQUES

With the extemporaneous style, you will expand on the brief notes you have in front of you as you speak. You have rehearsed the speech so that you are not scrambling for something to say, which allows you to adapt to the audience and to sound more natural. Preparing the speech effectively and rehearsing it enough to become very comfortable with the topic are essential to this type of delivery.

→ See also "How Do You Prepare for an Extemporaneous Speech?" on pages 174–177.

2
Manuscript Speaking

Manuscript speaking occurs when you read directly from a word-for-word copy of the speech.

WHEN SHOULD YOU USE IT?
This form of delivery is used when you must present the speech exactly as planned, so that you do not omit important details or misstate critical information.

DELIVERY TECHNIQUES
Make as much eye contact as possible, keep your gestures high and not hidden by the lectern or prompter, and keep your voice dynamic. Rehearse until you are comfortable with your delivery and message. Mark delivery tips on the manuscript.

3
Memorized Speaking

Memorized speaking means you rehearse the speech so much that you commit the full text to memory.

WHEN SHOULD YOU USE IT?
Some speakers employ memorized delivery when accuracy and the appearance of spontaneity are equally important. This method works well for brief speeches, such as toasts.

DELIVERY TECHNIQUES
The key to an effective memorized speech is to rehearse it a lot and make it sound fresh. Keep your excitement high and use effective verbal and nonverbal delivery techniques.

4
Impromptu Speaking

Impromptu speaking is the only method of delivery that has very little, if any, preparation or rehearsal. If any outline is used, it is simply notes jotted down quickly.

WHEN SHOULD YOU USE IT?
Even though this is the least-prepared type of speech, often uses a very basic organizational strategy, lacks solid evidence, and uses simplistic language, impromptu speaking is the type of delivery we use the most in our everyday lives. You use this type of delivery when answering a question in a public forum (like the classroom), when you need to offer information or dispute an issue during a meeting, or when you are asked to address an audience at a moment's notice.

DELIVERY TECHNIQUES
The best technique is to always be prepared with appropriate knowledge and information. You will almost always be asked to respond about something you should or do know. These steps will help you put your thoughts together:

- Pay close attention during the event.
- If you have time, write down key words or ideas and think about a logical order.
- Limit your remarks to two or three points.
- Think about what evidence you can offer to support your points.

PRACTICING ETHICS
Sometimes impromptu speaking will make you feel like you are being "put on the spot" or asked to speak without preparation. Never make up information to sound good or to get through the moment.

How Do You Prepare for an Extemporaneous Speech?

1 **Read Aloud the Preparation Outline**

2 **Prepare Your Delivery Outline**

3 **Prepare Your Presentation Aids**

4 **Practice Multiple Times**

5 **Do a Final "Dress Rehearsal"**

6 **Prepare for Questions**

7 **Prepare for the Day of the Speech**

REHEARSAL NOTE

There is no magical formula for how many times you need to rehearse your speech for each of the following steps. The key is: as much as you need to move successfully to the next step. If you read your preparation outline aloud two times and feel you are ready to make the delivery outline, then do so. However, if you find yourself struggling to remember details when using the delivery outline, you need to back up a step. Check your logic, and read the preparation outline aloud several times. If you have not spent enough time with the details or if the logic is flawed, your speech will be hard to remember.

Rehearsing is an individual process that will be specific to you. Do not assume that if your friend can give a speech with only two rehearsals, so can you. Pay attention to what does or does not work for you, and adapt your rehearsals to your needs. Be willing to improve as you practice your speech. Even an excellent speech has room for improvement.

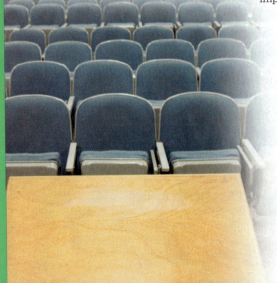

1

Read Aloud the Preparation Outline

At this step in the rehearsal process, you want to read aloud the preparation outline several times. Pay attention to the order of your points, how much support material you are using, and the order of the support materials. Include your links as well to see if they smoothly transition between points and parts of the speech. Read aloud the introduction and conclusion to see if they are interesting and flow well. Read the preparation outline one more time at a reasonable pace and time yourself. Make changes where necessary to correct issues or to adhere to the time limit. At this point, you should be under the time limit because you have not added verbal and nonverbal techniques or presentation aids that will take up time during your speech. Once you feel like you have a solid speech, move on to the next step.

2

Prepare Your Delivery Outline

Now, you want to reduce your preparation outline to only key words, phrases, and important quotations, statistics, or details. Try not to include too much of the introduction or the conclusion. You will tend to read it if you do, and direct eye contact is crucial.

Add delivery cues after you have what you think is the final delivery outline. Include any delivery cues you need at the moments you think you might need them. Remember to note cues for presentation aids.

➔ See Chapter 5 for more help creating a delivery outline.

3

Prepare Your Presentation Aids

Next, prepare the presentation aids exactly as you will use them in the speech event. Do not cut corners here. You want to practice with the finished aids to discover any problems and to make them seem a natural part of your speech.

➔ See Chapter 10 for more on using and creating presentation aids.

TIP: Preparation Outline
You should have your preparation outline done at least two days before the speech event or in the time frame required by your instructor. You cannot prepare your delivery outline or rehearse the speech effectively if your preparation outline is incomplete. Most speakers need to practice over the course of several days to make a speech sound conversational, so give yourself time to spend with your finished preparation outline.

TIP: Delivery Outline
If your hands tend to shake when you give a presentation, use stiff paper, note cards, or something like a file folder or clipboard to support your delivery outline. This will allow you to feel comfortable when picking up your notes or not using a lectern.

4
Practice Multiple Times

Now it is time to put your speech on its feet. Practice your speech exactly as you plan to give it. Here are some hints:

- At this stage, always practice from the delivery outline. If you discover that you are struggling with any part, read over the preparation outline and then return to practicing with the delivery outline.

- Practice a few times in front of a mirror and/or record your speech. Watch for distracting behavior. Is your posture appropriate, and are you using effective gestures? Audio or video recording a rehearsal is a helpful step. Doing so will allow you to focus on vocal quality. Video recording a rehearsal will also help you pay attention to your body language and eye-contact issues, which are hard to monitor while you practice.

- Time yourself several times while using your finished presentation aids and necessary equipment, if any. You want to get as close as possible to the time limit.

- Practice with a rehearsal audience. Ask family members, friends, or classmates to play the role of audience for you. Ask them to offer feedback on the content of the speech, your delivery, or your strengths and weaknesses.

- Evaluate what you have learned from the rehearsal audience and from watching and listening to yourself. Change the speech message or your delivery style when necessary. Rehearse the speech again, incorporating these changes.

→ See Chapter 12 for help with evaluating your speech.

5
Do a Final "Dress Rehearsal"

The last step in the rehearsal process is to do what actors call a "dress rehearsal." With this rehearsal, you want to simulate as closely as possible the exact event when you will give the speech. So it is important to:

- Rehearse in the space (or a close alternative) where you will give the speech.

- Use the exact delivery outline you will use during the speech. Make sure you number the pages or cards to prevent a mix-up the day of the speech.

- Use the exact presentation aids and necessary equipment.

- Try to rehearse at the exact time to consider potential issues with noise, lighting, temperature, and so on.

- Rehearse standing or sitting as you will during the speech.

- Wear the clothing you plan to wear to see if it is appropriate and makes you feel confident.

- Ask a friend or colleague to watch your dress rehearsal and offer comments.

- Rehearse until you are as comfortable as possible, but do not wear yourself out. You will need energy for your speech event.

CONFIDENCE BOOSTER

- The more you practice with your delivery outline and presentation aids, the lower your apprehension will be.
- During the speech, avoid apologizing or calling attention to your shortcomings. Your audience may have missed them. Don't dwell on them, or you'll lose your concentration and audience focus.

6
Prepare for Questions

Not all speaking situations will have an opportunity for an audience question-and-answer (Q and A) session. Like some impromptu speeches, a Q and A session may happen spontaneously, so be prepared:

- Anticipate questions you might get, and plan answers. Think about and consider questions you hope for—or dread.

- Practice your answers.

- If your topic is particularly complex, prepare a "Facts Sheet" with details that you can consult during the Q and A session.

- Remain calm, confident, and professional with aggressive or difficult questioners.

- Be honest if you do not know the answer. "I don't know" is an acceptable answer if you have demonstrated your knowledge in other ways. Offer to look for an answer and get back to the audience member if the situation allows you to do so.

- Give your speech to a practice audience and have them ask you questions.

7
Prepare for the Day of the Speech

THE DAY BEFORE THE SPEECH

- Avoid activities that will stress your voice, mind, or body. Get a good night's sleep (eight hours), eat right, keep hydrated, and limit your caffeine and alcohol consumption. Avoid taking drugs such as antihistamines or expectorants before you speak.

- Prepare what you will wear.

- Practice at least once so that you can go to sleep that night feeling confident.

THE DAY OF THE SPEECH

- Don't forget to eat. If your body doesn't have the fuel it needs, nervousness may intensify and your memory will decrease. If your speech is within an hour of a meal, avoid eating foods that can irritate your throat, such as ice cream, milk, and chocolate.

- Get to the speech event early so that you are not rushed.

- Check all necessary equipment and deal with any issues you discover.

- If you will be speaking for a long period of time, keep water handy.

- Try to be by yourself just before the speech and prepare yourself mentally. Do vocal or physical activities to warm up and lessen your apprehension.

- Look over your notes one more time to make sure they are in the right order.

- Finally, walk to the front of the room with confidence.

10
USING PRESENTATION AIDS

Introduction

Presentation aids are two- or three-dimensional visual items, video footage, audio recordings, and/or multimedia segments that support and enhance your speech. Presentation aids can:

- Make it easier for your audience to understand your topic. The aids can illustrate the concepts in your speech and provide condensed information and examples.

- Grab and maintain audience interest. The aids can make your information more vivid and usually more dramatic.

- Assist with retention. Your audience will retain more information if you not only *tell* them but also *show* them.

- Improve your credibility, or ethos. If your presentation aids are well made, used appropriately, and not distracting, they will bolster your ethos and professionalism.

- Help you cross a cultural divide by supplementing your words for a diverse audience. For example, pictures may help if your audience struggles with English.

- Convey emotion. Visual images and audio recordings are effective ways to create an emotional audience response.

- Help you maintain an extemporaneous delivery. Proper use of presentation aids forces you to know your speech well enough to venture away from your delivery outline to incorporate and explain the aid.

CHAPTER 8: Using Language Successfully   152
CHAPTER 9: Delivering Your Speech   162

CHAPTER 10 CONTENTS

What Are the Types of Presentation Aids?   180
   1 Actual Items   180
   2 Models   181
   3 Photographs   181
   4 Drawings   182
   5 Charts and Tables   182
   6 Graphs   183
   7 Media   185

How Do You Determine What Presentation Aids You Need to Use?   186
   1 Establish Their Purpose   186
   2 Select the Best Type   187
   3 Consider How to Display Them   187

What Are Common Methods for Displaying Aids?   188
   1 Chalkboards and Whiteboards   188
   2 Posters   189
   3 Handouts   189
   4 Flip Charts   190
   5 Advanced Technology   190

How Do You Craft an Effective Aid?   192
   1 Follow Good Design Principles   192
   2 Give Yourself Enough Time to Be Creative   195

How Can You Use Presentation Software?   196
   1 Create a Storyboard   197
   2 Begin with PowerPoint Basics   198

How Do You Use a Presentation Aid Successfully?   200

PART 4 Review   202

What Are the Types of Presentation Aids?

1 Actual Items

2 Models

3 Photographs

4 Drawings

5 Charts and Tables

6 Graphs

7 Media

1

Actual Items

You can use people, animals, or objects when they are the actual items you are talking about or relate to the topic of your speech and help relay your message. For example, if you are planning to give a demonstration speech on cake decorating, you might decorate cupcakes with different designs for easier transport and display.

Advantages

- Can get your audience's attention
- Can demonstrate, illustrate, exemplify, or emphasize your topic
- Can be simple to add to your speech when you do not need to create them
- Can help the audience visualize persuasive issues
- Can add humor

Disadvantages

- Can be scary or dangerous to your audience or inappropriate for the occasion or location of the speech (e.g., live spiders or snakes, guns, anything with a flame, cats if people are allergic, etc.)
- Can be too small to see or too large to bring
- Can distract the audience from the message

2

Models

Models are three-dimensional representations. Models are usually scaled to size—often smaller than the real thing, such as a model car, but sometimes larger, such as a model of a molecule.

Advantages
- Are great alternatives when you cannot bring the actual items
- Can get your audience's attention
- Can demonstrate, illustrate, exemplify, or emphasize your topic
- Can be simple to add to your speech when you do not need to create them
- Can help you visually compare and contrast

Disadvantages
- Can be hard to locate and expensive
- Can be too small for everyone to see
- Can be unpredictable if they have working parts
- Can distract the audience from the message

3

Photographs

Photographs are two-dimensional representations of places, concepts, people, animals, or objects. They can be original photographs, posters of photographic images, or other types of print display.

Advantages
- Can be as effective as an object or model
- Can condense a lot of material onto one aid
- Can create a sense of authenticity
- Can be easy to use
- Can help you compare and contrast
- Can appeal to the audience's emotions
- Can help you explain an abstract concept

Disadvantages
- Can be hard for the entire audience to see
- Can be less effective than an actual item or model
- Can be overused if they are stock photographs, making them less effective than photographs created for your speech

4

Drawings

Drawings are maps, sketches, diagrams, plans, or other nonphotographic representations of places, concepts, people, animals, or objects. They may show a whole or part of an area or dissect the parts or workings of something.

Advantages

- Can be very helpful when objects or models are not practical or available
- Can visually demonstrate how something works, operates, or is constructed
- Can sometimes be located ready-made
- Can show detail, processes, details, relationships, or arrangements
- Can be used to emphasize location, geography, or topography (especially maps)

Disadvantages

- Can be hard to locate or create
- Can be hard for the entire audience to see
- Can have too much detail
- Can lower your credibility if sloppy

5

Charts and Tables

Charts are visual summaries of complex or large quantities of information. Two common charts are flowcharts and organizational charts. *Flowcharts* (see example below) diagram step-by-step development through a procedure, relationship, or process. *Organizational charts* illustrate the structure or chain of command in an organization. *Tables* consist of numbers or words arranged in rows, columns, or lists.

Advantages

- Can make the complex understandable
- Can summarize a lot of information
- Can show relationships and potential cause-and-effect issues
- Can help an audience think through hypothetical situations (especially charts)
- Can help the audience understand exact numbers or information quickly

Disadvantages

- Can be less memorable than other visuals
- Can require a lot of time to explain
- Can be confusing if too detailed
- Can be hard for the entire audience to see

1 STARTING	2 RESEARCHING	3 CREATING	4 PRESENTING	5 LISTENING & EVALUATING
GETTING TO KNOW YOUR AUDIENCE AND SITUATION → See page 20 Know who you are speaking to as well as where, when, and why you are speaking.	**LOCATING SUPPORT MATERIALS** → See page 52 Find support materials through the Internet, the library, interviews, and surveys.	**OUTLINING YOUR SPEECH** → See page 96 Start with a working outline, create a preparation outline, and include a source page. Create a delivery outline to use during your speech.	**USING LANGUAGE SUCCESSFULLY** → See page 152 Write your speech using language that is familiar, concrete, appropriate, and vivid. Use devices like repetition and parallelism to engage your audience.	**LISTENING** → See page 204 Be an active, ethical, and effective listener who can overcome barriers to listening and who shares responsibility in the communication process.
SELECTING YOUR TOPIC AND PURPOSE → See page 34 Select the topic that best fits you, your audience, and the occasion. Define the purpose of your speech.	**SELECTING AND TESTING SUPPORT MATERIALS** → See page 74 Learn how to effectively evaluate, choose, and use a variety of support materials.	**ORGANIZING THE SPEECH BODY** → See page 122 Identify your main points and choose an organizational strategy.	**DELIVERING YOUR SPEECH** → See page 162 Strive to be natural, enthusiastic, confident, engaging, and appropriate in your delivery. Practice!	**EVALUATING SPEECHES** → See page 216 Determine the effectiveness and appropriateness of a speech's topic, support materials, organization, and language. Evaluate a speaker's delivery and ethics.
		INTRODUCING AND CONCLUDING YOUR SPEECH → See page 136 Create an introduction that gets attention and sets up your credibility and your speech. Create a conclusion that sums up and ends with impact.	**USING PRESENTATION AIDS** → See page 178 Know when and how to use presentation aids to capture attention, enhance your credibility, and help your audience understand and remember your speech.	

6
Graphs

Whereas charts and tables simply organize numbers and words, **graphs** are visual representations of numerical (statistical) information that demonstrate relationships or differences between two or more variables. There are four common types: line graphs, bar graphs, pictographs, and pie graphs.

LINE GRAPHS

Line graphs contain numerical points plotted on a horizontal axis for one variable and on the vertical axis for another; you then connect the points to make a line. Be sure to clearly label horizontal and vertical axes so that your audience can see and understand them. See an example below.

Advantages
- Can simplify complex statistical information
- Can be extremely easy to read if created effectively

Disadvantages
- Can be less effective if you have more than three lines to plot
- Can require a projector

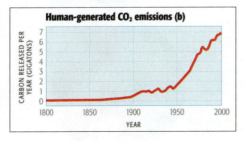

BAR GRAPHS

Bar graphs (also known as bar charts) are visuals consisting of vertical or horizontal bars that represent sets of data. Make sure your horizontal and vertical axes are clearly labeled.

Advantages
- Can be easy for your audience to interpret if created effectively
- Can demonstrate change over time at a glance

Disadvantages
- Can be less effective in black and white
- Can require a projector

TIP: Showing Time
When creating a line or bar graph and time is a variable, always put time on the horizontal axis.

PICTOGRAPHS

Pictographs (also known as pictograms) are bar graphs that use pictures instead of bars. Make sure to label the graph and assign a unit measure to the individual pictorial icons.

Advantages

- Can make statistical information more interesting
- Can be easy for your audience to interpret if created effectively

Disadvantages

- Can take time to locate appropriate pictures or icons to represent your data
- Can be unfamiliar to your audience
- Can be less effective in black and white
- Can require a projector

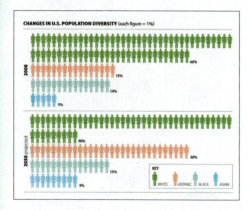

PIE GRAPHS

Pie graphs (also known as circle graphs or pie charts) are circular graphs with sections representing a percentage of a given quantity. Use a pie graph when comparing segments of a whole. It is best to limit your segments to seven or fewer; you can combine the smallest ones if you have more than seven. Always make sure your pie adds up to exactly 100 percent. Labels should be brief and outside the segments if needed.

Advantages

- Can help your audience quickly visualize the divisions of the whole item you are discussing
- Can effectively graph up to seven variables at once

Disadvantages

- Can be difficult to clearly and visibly label the segments
- Should be in color

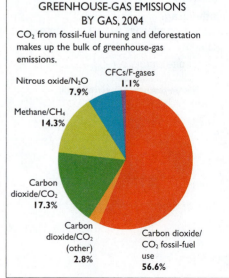

TIP: Finding Icons

These sites offer icons and graphics that might be helpful when creating a pictograph:

www.coolarchive.com
www.freegraphics.com
www.iconbazaar.com

7

Media

VIDEO AND AUDIO

Audio and video clips can be effective presentation aids. **Video clips** are any footage you use from television, movies, or any other type of video. **Audio clips** are recordings of sound only.

Advantages

- Can grab attention and make a speech memorable by appealing to your audience through sight, sound, and movement
- Can illustrate a point
- Can be linked to PowerPoint slides
- Can increase your ethos when used properly

Disadvantages

- Can require special production skills
- Can require special equipment
- Can require a lot of practice with the equipment to smoothly incorporate the video and audio into the speech
- Should only be used for short durations so that they do not become the speech or compete with the speaker
- Can increase the potential for errors, ineffective use, and equipment failure

MULTIMEDIA

Multimedia refers to the combination of multiple presentation aids (still images, graphs, text, sound, and video) into one choreographed production.

Advantages

- Can be very creative and appeals to almost all senses
- Can be very professional
- Can increase your ethos when used properly

Disadvantages

- Can be too flashy and distracting
- Can be costly and time-consuming to make
- Requires special equipment
- Can require special production skills
- Can be difficult to coordinate
- Should only be used for short durations so that the aids do not become the speech or compete with the speaker
- Can increase the potential for errors, ineffective use, and equipment failure

How Do You Determine What Presentation Aids You Need to Use?

1 Establish Their Purpose

2 Select the Best Type

3 Consider How to Display Them

To determine which presentation aids to use, establish a purpose for each aid; select the best types for you, your audience, and your topic; and consider what options you have to display or produce the aids. You should think about all these elements together, although one might take precedence over another. For example, if you will be speaking to a large audience, a handwritten list of numbers on a flip chart will not do much to support your speech, whereas professionally created graphs can be helpful.

1

Establish Their Purpose

You should never use a presentation aid just because you can or to be glitzy. The important parts of any speech are you and the speech message. Your presentation aids should assist, support, and facilitate your message, not detract from or outshine it. Each aid you use needs a distinct purpose. You can establish the purpose by returning to your preparation outline and considering where in the outline you need to use an aid to:

- Grab attention or maintain interest
- Reinforce understanding and promote clarity
- Appeal to your audience's emotions
- Help the audience remember key issues
- Aid in intercultural communication

TIP: Check Your Assignment

Consult the requirements for each of your class assignments. Some assignments may require presentation aids, and some may limit or not allow them. Follow the instructor's guidelines.

2
Select the Best Type

You should select the type of presentation aids you use by considering what is best for you, your topic, your audience, and the situation.

FOR YOU

When considering yourself as a factor, think about the answers to questions such as: What equipment am I comfortable with? What software do I need to create or present the aids? Am I familiar enough with that software to be effective? Which aids would I feel comfortable using? Which types will raise my credibility? Which presentation aids do I have time to create and practice with?

FOR YOUR TOPIC

When considering your topic, think about your speech goal: Is it informative or persuasive? If informative, how can your aids help the audience visualize your message, challenge what the audience already knows, or simplify information? If persuasive, think about how your aids can support an idea, evoke emotions, demonstrate fulfilling a need, call the audience to action, or show audience relevance. Ask yourself: How can each aid move through the speech to reach the conclusion?

FOR YOUR AUDIENCE

When considering your audience, reflect on their relationship with the topic and their ability to access the presentation aid. Ask yourself: What do they need to know about the topic, and which aids would be supportive? Will the information in the speech be difficult for the audience to understand? If so, which aids will best assist their understanding? Are there reasons why all or part of the audience would not be able to access a presentation aid? For example, are there factors that might prevent someone from reading or seeing visuals or hearing video/audio clips?

FOR THE SITUATION

Where, why, and when you are speaking could significantly influence which type of presentation aids you use. For example, many visual aids will not work outside, and even quality audio is challenging. Likewise, many special occasion speeches are given at events where certain presentation aids would seem strange. For example, a PowerPoint presentation might seem inappropriate during a eulogy or wedding toast. However, displaying an object or pictures that relate to the person being eulogized or raising your glass to signal the wedding toast would be acceptable.

3
Consider How to Display Them

Finally, you must consider how the aids will be presented for the audience. Various methods are available to most speakers. Your decision will be determined by what you are comfortable with, the size of the audience, the availability of equipment, what will work in the speech environment, cost, and effectiveness. The next section will explain some options for displaying your presentation aids. Whichever method you select, remember to practice multiple times with that method as you rehearse your speech.

What Are the Common Methods for Displaying Aids?

1 **Chalkboards and Whiteboards**
2 **Posters**
3 **Handouts**
4 **Flip Charts**
5 **Advanced Technology**

1
Chalkboards and Whiteboards

Chalkboards and whiteboards are usually available in classroom settings and provide impromptu surfaces for writing (with chalk or special markers).

Advantages

- Are usually free and easy to use
- Can be used spontaneously
- Can easily be edited or corrected by erasing
- Can have few potential problems
- Can supplement other aids

Disadvantages

- Can be considered low-tech and unprofessional
- Can do little to build ethos
- Can limit your eye contact with the audience
- Require good writing and spelling skills

When to Use Chalkboards and Whiteboards

- For impromptu explanations
- For brainstorming with the audience
- As a backup to other aids

Helpful Hints for Usage

- Use this type of aid sparingly.
- Locate an eraser, some chalk, or a working marker before starting the speech.
- Use upper- and lowercase letters and print legibly.

2
Posters

Posters are hand- or computer-created single-sheet visuals intended to be attached to a wall or displayed on an easel. They typically include text and visual elements but may be entirely visual or entirely textual.

Advantages

- Can grab attention
- Can be useful for condensing information
- Can be professionally prepared (although expensive to print)

Disadvantages

- Are less effective for large audiences
- Can look sloppy if created by hand
- Can be time-consuming and difficult to create

When to Use Posters

- When you do not have or do not trust electronic equipment
- To demonstrate a sequence or change over time by placing each step on a new poster.
- For small group presentations

Helpful Hints for Usage

- Keep your posters simple, neat, and professional.
- Make them large enough to be seen from the back of the room.
- Proofread your posters or have someone else do it.
- Discreetly number multiple posters to keep track of their order.
- Plan out how to display your posters; never hold them.
- Practice with your posters.

3
Handouts

Handouts are standard-size printed pages designed to help you distribute new information that will summarize or reinforce your speech message.

Advantages

- Can be easy to use and inexpensive
- Can contain large amounts of information

Disadvantages

- Can be extremely distracting
- Can be costly if long and/or for a very large audience

When to Use Handouts

- When details are too small for other aids
- When audience retention is crucial
- To reiterate or summarize
- To provide copies of your presentation
- As a backup to other aids

Helpful Hints for Usage

- Under most circumstances, give handouts after the speech to avoid distracting the audience.
- Only distribute handouts before giving the speech when it is absolutely necessary. Single-page handouts are best, if possible.
- Never distribute handouts during a speech.
- Include a title, the date, your name, and contact information.
- Make sure they look professionally made.
- Make about 10 percent more copies than you expect to hand out.

4
Flip Charts

Flip charts are large pads, usually of unlined or lined paper, displayed on a large freestanding or small tabletop easel.

Advantages
- Are convenient, easy to use, and inexpensive
- Do not require electricity

Disadvantages
- Do not work well for large groups (best for 10 or fewer audience members)
- Can be sloppy and time-consuming
- Require good writing and spelling skills

When to Use Flip Charts
- To appear spontaneous and involve the audience
- For small group presentations

Helpful Hints for Usage
- Practice writing on and using the chart.
- Prepare the pages in advance or pre-write in light pencil.
- The first page should be blank or contain a title.
- Leave every other page blank so the next aid doesn't show through.
- Use no more than five words across and five lines down.
- Write only on the top two-thirds of the page.
- Print legibly; write letters at least three inches tall, and use upper- and lowercase.
- Use black and blue for text and strong primary colors for emphasis.

5
Advanced Technology
CONTEMPORARY MEDIA

Along with the ability to easily transfer information, current media options offer you the ability to display information in ways that were unimaginable to an average person a few decades ago.

The LCD (liquid crystal display) projector often replaces the television or small monitor and can project large images, from computers or DVD or VCR players, for numerous audience members to all see at once. Document cameras are contemporary overhead projectors with the ability to project opaque pages and objects. Digital media players give you easy access to audio or video clips. Even software packages, like Microsoft's PowerPoint, make presentation aids more polished and integrated into your speech.

Advantages
- Can be very professional-looking
- Can build speaker ethos
- Can often include Internet access
- Can appeal to multiple senses of the audience members
- Can be seen and heard by larger audiences

Disadvantages
- Can be less effective when you want to create an intimate approach
- Can upstage you
- Can be time-consuming to create the aids
- Can require special knowledge to create or run the aids

TRADITIONAL MEDIA

Although considered less effective and out of date, traditional media devices such as standalone CD players, DVD players, VCRs, overhead projectors, and slide projectors are helpful in some situations. They may be all you have available; the best solution for the size of audience (if it is small); best for the environment; or valuable as a backup plan.

Advantages

- Can be relatively easy to learn to use
- Can back up contemporary media devices
- Can have fewer problems than more contemporary technologies
- Can be less expensive and, therefore, more commonly available

Disadvantages

- Can be viewed as less-advanced technologies and are therefore not as strong at building ethos
- Can be awkward and more difficult to integrate into a speech than are computer-aided and computer-generated aids

When to Use Advanced Technologies

- When you want aids that are more effective than other printed or handmade display options
- When you are comfortable enough to create an effective aid and can easily present it
- If the equipment is available

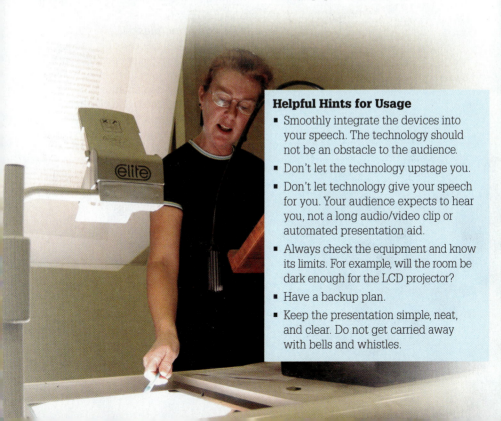

Helpful Hints for Usage

- Smoothly integrate the devices into your speech. The technology should not be an obstacle to the audience.
- Don't let the technology upstage you.
- Don't let technology give your speech for you. Your audience expects to hear you, not a long audio/video clip or automated presentation aid.
- Always check the equipment and know its limits. For example, will the room be dark enough for the LCD projector?
- Have a backup plan.
- Keep the presentation simple, neat, and clear. Do not get carried away with bells and whistles.

How Do You Craft an Effective Aid?

1 Follow Good Design Principles

2 Give Yourself Enough Time to Be Creative

1

Follow Good Design Principles

In *Slide:ology: The Art and Science of Creating Great Presentations,* Nancy Duarte writes, "To succeed as a presenter, you must think like a designer."

Communication educators might add that to be a good designer, you must think like an audience-centered communicator, always mindful of your audience. Every decision you make about a presentation aid's design should relay your message better and focus on the audience's needs for understanding that message.

To meet this goal, you must follow good design principles and give yourself enough time to be creative.

Design principles relate to the arrangement and placement of various elements (color, text, line, images, space, etc.) for optimum effect. When you create two-dimensional presentation aids, think about the arrangement and placement of visual elements on the page, poster, or slide. Likewise, when you think about the relationship of all of your aids within a given speech, you need to consider arrangement and placement to allow the aids to nourish your verbal message. There are five design principles you should consider.

TIP: Plan Your Time

Plan your time carefully. You are better off starting early and having time left over to rehearse more—or to relax and feel confident about your preparation—than scrambling at the last minute and creating poor presentation aids.

UNITY

The principle of unity recognizes the need for the elements you use to relate to each other. If you use multiple aids, they should fit together as a unified whole to support your speech. For example, here are some aids for a speech about Greece.

Source: Dorling Kindersley

Color unity
Make sure colors work well together and are complementary (opposite on the color wheel), analogous (colors that touch each other on the wheel), or monochromatic (variations of one color, as shown here).

Color harmony
Make sure your color palette is in harmony with the tone of your speech. Here, the blues suggest the waters surrounding Greece.

Image unity
Images should relate to the text shown with them and to your verbal message at that moment.

PATTERN

The pattern principle recommends that you create a design format and use it consistently. Reusing patterns will help your audience quickly digest the material because the layout is familiar and not distracting. Keep your pattern simple.

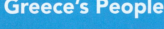

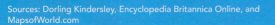

Sources: Dorling Kindersley, Encyclopedia Britannica Online, and MapsofWorld.com

Backgrounds
Use consistent colors, textures, or images for background.

Fonts
Use the same types, colors, and sizes of fonts with related elements (e.g., format all titles the same).

Content
Try to feature similar content for each main point if possible.

Symbols
Use the same symbols (bullets, checkmarks, etc.) to establish related patterns.

BALANCE

Balance deals with the feeling of equilibrium—a feeling of stability, symmetry, and calm. Balance in your aids will enhance your audience's feeling that your speech is balanced and organized.

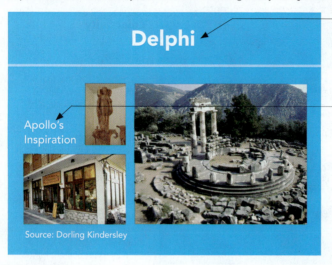

Delphi

Apollo's Inspiration

Source: Dorling Kindersley

Balanced fonts
Choose easy-to-read sans serif fonts (such as Tahoma or Arial), and use only one or two. Avoid using all caps.

Readable font size
Use a large enough font size to be seen by everyone in the room—44 point for titles and 24 point to 32 point for other text is one general guideline.

Effective balance
Balance the elements with each other and with the blank space.

EMPHASIS

You can use design elements to emphasize what is most important. Also, your complete arsenal of presentation aids for a speech should adhere to the principle of emphasis. Use only aids that stress the important aspects of your verbal message.

Currency

- Greece's official currency is the euro (symbol €).

- 1 euro equals 100 cents.

- On August 2, 2010, the exchange rate was 1.00 USD – 0.79 EUR.

Sources: Worldtravelguide.net and Alamy.com

Titles
Use titles for things like lists, graphs, or areas of a poster. Titles emphasize and foreshadow your speech content.

Emphasizing text
Light text against a dark background projects the best.

Emphasizing elements
Bullets, color, images, text size, text structures (underline, bold, or italic), and music are ways to draw the eye or ear to what is important.

RHYTHM

Rhythm has to do with a real or imagined sense of movement. Just as you can create a sense of rhythm with your vocal quality, you can create a visual sense of rhythm by emphasizing movement. Also, the pacing of your presentation aids throughout the speech can establish a rhythmic flow.

Added animation and sound can create rhythm, but be careful that they do not distract from or compete with your speech message. Limit these and use them consistently—and for a meaningful purpose, not simply because they are available. Some easier ways for beginning speakers to use rhythm in aids are text placement and images that contain or suggest movement.

- **Text placement:** Using text or spacing that relates to each other, such as placing titles and source lines in the same position on each aid, creates one type of rhythm. For example, note how the titles and source lines in the Greece presentation aids are placed similarly throughout the series.

- **Movement**: Images that contain movement or move across or around the background can create a sense of rhythm. For example, look at the Currency slide on the previous page. The photo of the euro "sliding" across the Greek flag suggests movement.

2
Give Yourself Enough Time to Be Creative

The time needed to be creative is difficult to predict because of so many variables. For example, can you easily come up with interesting ideas? Are you familiar with how to research and collect ideas? Are you comfortable with the method for producing your aid? The answers to these questions can drastically affect the time it takes to create your aids. For a general idea, Nancy Duarte offers a time frame for creating an hour-long presentation with 30 slides. If you adapt her recommendations to an eight-minute speech with four to six slides, your creation time might be similar to the following timeline:

- **1 to 2 hours** for researching and collecting ideas/information

- **1 hour** to evaluate audience needs and to outline your ideas

- **2+ hours** to create the presentation aids

- **30 minutes to 1 hour** to rehearse with aids

4.5 to 6+ hours total

Keep in mind that this is an estimate and you are the only one who can predict how long it will take. Be honest with yourself. If you don't know how to use the software or tend to spend a lot of time on details, you will need more time. Likewise, if it only takes you 30 minutes to create four slides, are you being creative and supporting your speech the best way you can?

How Can You Use Presentation Software?

1 Create a Storyboard

2 Begin with PowerPoint Basics

Many presentation software packages are available that can help you create an extremely professional presentation aid incorporating text, images, charts, graphs, sound, and/or video into one presentation. The most common is PowerPoint, which you can use to make posters and handouts as well. Although software packages have revolutionized the ability to create professional presentations for almost anyone, they have downsides as well.

- They are overused and often used poorly.
- They can steal the show so much that your speech, which is your main focus, is ignored.
- They can turn the listeners off or destroy your credibility as a speaker.

Learn how to take advantage of presentation software without letting it have power over your speech. Creating computer-generated presentation aids takes time and knowledge. If you have not used such software before, you will need extra time to learn it and use it.

TIP: Software Tutorials

Investing in a good tutorial might be wise if presentation software is something you will use often. Here are some potentially helpful PowerPoint sites.

office.microsoft.com/en-us/powerpoint-help

office.microsoft.com/en-us/powerpoint/HA101942821033.aspx (This page has a link to a demo on creating a presentation.)

www.iupui.edu/~webtrain/tutorials/powerpoint2000_basics.html#getting_started

www.csun.edu/it/training/guides/#powerpoint (Under "Software/Applications," click on "Microsoft.")

1

Create a Storyboard

Storyboarding is similar to outlining a speech and is the act of sketching out the content and arranging the sequence of your slides. Storyboarding before you open your software is valuable for determining how many slides you will need and their order. A slide's purpose should be to help the audience understand your message better. Your slides should not be just talking points for you to read off of during the speech.

STEPS FOR STORYBOARDING

1. Create each slide by hand on a separate sheet of paper.

2. Include a title slide or an introduction slide. Decide if what you put on that slide reveals or only hints at your topic. Sometimes, mystery is an attention-getter.

3. Think about your main points and try to limit yourself to one slide per main point. You can count slides that build up as one, but limit this type of animation. Do not put your delivery outline on the slides. Give your audience time to read and absorb each slide.

4. Use a slide for the conclusion if helpful or to intensify your WOW statement.

5. Remember to place blank/blackout slides when you need to draw the focus back to you. This form of "white space" will give your audience a break from the visuals and will help them focus on your verbal message.

6. Adhere to effective design principles.

PRACTICING ETHICS

You must observe copyright laws. Students and educators may use original work by another person for a class presentation, but they must follow these rules.

- You may use a very small amount (under a minute) of copyrighted film, video, or animation without permission.

- You may use less than 30 seconds of music or lyrics from one musical piece without permission.

- You can use an entire photograph or illustration, but only a small portion of images from a collection (less than 10 percent of the collection).

- You cannot post that presentation material back to the Web without permission.

- You must display and mention the source, author/creator, title, and date of the material.

- You must display the copyright symbol (©) when necessary.

- Cite all sources of the material in your presentation aids and on your source page.

These rules apply to materials legally downloaded from the Internet or obtained by other legal means. Illegally downloaded materials are never fair use. (See http://copyright.lib.utexas.edu/copypol2.html for more fair-use information.)

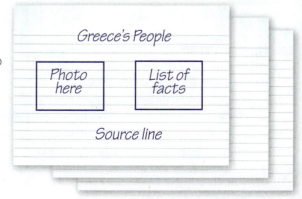

197

2

Begin with PowerPoint Basics

Although giving a complete tutorial on PowerPoint here is not possible, the following discussion highlights some of the basics you might need to know. Make sure you learn the features of the version of PowerPoint you have on your computer. The examples here are shown in PowerPoint 2008 on a Mac.

Tools
The tabs along the toolbar will allow you to do tasks such as cut and paste, change fonts, add bullets, insert text and images, select a design, check spelling, and view your slide show.

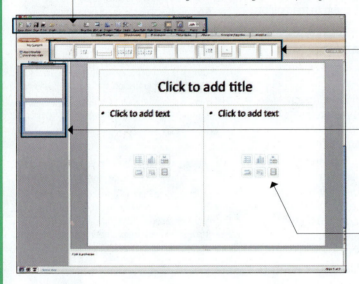

Slide layout
This function includes built-in slide layouts as well as a blank slide if you want to build one from the ground up.

Slide thumbnails
Here you can scroll through mini versions of your slides. Click and drag slides to change order. Click between slides to add one.

Placeholders
Unless you select a blank slide, dotted borders will outline the preset placeholders for inserting images or text.

GETTING STARTED

- Start with a new slide. You may find it easiest to create a title slide first, before moving on to content slides, to practice with the software's features.

- Select or create a slide theme. The program has several built-in designs, each offering a unified theme of colors, fonts, and graphic options. Don't pick one that is too busy.

- Select or create a slide layout. Remember to keep it as simple as possible.

- Using the insert functions, begin inserting your text and/or images.

- Don't forget to periodically save your slide show.

DESIGNING SLIDES

As you create your slides, follow the design principles outlined on pages 192–195. PowerPoint offers many ways to incorporate text, visuals, video, audio, and animation, but the simpler you keep your aids, the more effective they can be.

Color

Limit your use of color and maintain consistency throughout. Ideally, use one background color or slide theme and two to three font colors, at the most, for titles, text, and emphasis. Medium colors are usually better than very dark ones.

Space

Using the preset slide layouts will show you how arranging and grouping together similar information and leaving space free of images or text can help you adhere to effective design principles. You do not want your audience to be overwhelmed visually or to feel the slides are out of balance (for example, top- or bottom-heavy).

Text

Clearly, text will be an important part of your slides. You should use titles and, in some cases, you may include several lines of text in the main part of the slide. Keep text brief and organized so that your audience can read it quickly. Lists and bulleted items work well.

Select fonts that are easy to read. Limit your fonts to no more than two different ones on a single aid, and be consistent throughout the slides. Remember to avoid using all capitals (use both upper- and lowercase). Use italics, underlining, different-colored text, and boldface sparingly and for emphasis only. Titles and text should be in large sizes, such as 36 points or larger for titles and 24 points or larger for text.

Images and Sound

PowerPoint gives you several options for inserting visuals, audio, and video. The first rule for deciding what and if to use inserts in your slides is to ask: How does this item help illustrate, support, or clarify my topic? If you don't have a solid answer to that question, you don't need the image, sound, or video. If the insert passes that test, it also must be:

- Large and clear enough to be seen
- A high-enough resolution to be projected on a large screen
- Clearly related to your topic and ethically appropriate
- Displayed with a title and, if needed, source information
- Smoothly integrated into the presentation

Keep in mind that simpler is often better.

TIPS: Presenting the Slides

- Have a backup plan in case the system fails.
- Check the order of your slides against your delivery outline.
- Know how to display the slides in slide-show view, not the normal view you used as you created them.
- Learn slide-show commands. (For example, when in slide-show mode, press the B key for black out and the W key to return to the visual. This will help you display slides only when you are referring to them in your speech.)
- Rehearse using the slide show (in the speech-event space if possible).
- Make sure you have saved all of the slides, sound clips, and video for transportation to the event.
- Check the equipment the day of the speech.

How Do You Use a Presentation Aid Successfully?

PROOFREAD, PREVIEW, AND PRACTICE

Always proofread your aids for spelling or other errors. Having someone else proofread them is often a good idea to catch details that you might miss.

Preview any computer-generated aids in the room where you will give the speech, at or close to the time you will speak, and with the exact equipment if possible. Sunlight can wash out projected images, and some LCD projectors are not very bright. If you encounter such issues, you may need to change color schemes. Make sure the system will accept the medium (flash drive, CD, etc.) your presentation is stored on. Be sure to save all of the files associated with the presentation in the same folder on the medium you will take to the speaking event; a common error is to forget audio or video files. The software you use to create the presentation should be the same version as the one you will use to deliver the presentation.

Practice with all aids you plan to use, including people, objects, models, computer-generated aids, and others. Not knowing how to use an aid or fumbling with it—or the equipment used to project it—will lower your ethos and increase your communication apprehension. You should be comfortable with your aid and any equipment related to it.

CHECK THE EQUIPMENT

Always check that the equipment is present, working, and set how you want it. You do not want to be surprised by discovering that you did not turn on the equipment. You will need to pause or talk over the booting-up process, making you seem unprepared. Check the sound level of audio equipment. Even check for chalk, markers, and erasers, if there is any possibility you will need them.

KNOW WHEN TO DISPLAY AIDS

Display your aids as you need them, and then remove them from sight. The element of surprise helps draw your audience's attention to your topic as you display items and pulls attention back to you as you remove them. Turning the aid around or over, removing it from sight, or going to a blank slide/screen are all simple ways to achieve this.

DON'T PASS THE AIDS AROUND

If you have objects, items, pictures, or handouts, don't pass them around. This is distracting, and it is highly unlikely that everyone will get to see passed-around aids within the time frame of your speech. All of your audience needs to see the aid at the time you are speaking about it. If possible, give out all handouts after your speech. If you think the handouts will help listeners understand as you go, give them to the audience before you begin and incorporate them into the speech. Focus the audience on where you are on the handout.

USE THE TOUCH, TURN, TALK METHOD

The "Touch, Turn, Talk Method" refers to how you should relate to your presentation aid and the audience. The "Touch" stage happens as you point to, direct your eyes toward, move toward, and/or literally touch the aid you are using, drawing the focus completely to the aid. The "Turn" stage happens as you turn from the aid and regain eye contact with the audience. Then you move into "Talk," where you explain the aid. The process should be a fluid back and forth between you, the aid, and the audience. You need to acknowledge the aid, return to the audience, and explain the content of the aid. Just displaying an aid or talking directly to the aid, instead of looking at the audience, is not effective.

PREPARE A BACKUP PLAN

Always have a backup plan. Be prepared for it to rain or snow the day of your speech, and have a way to keep your aids dry. Be prepared for equipment to be missing or to fail. If you have a plan, you will not be as stressed when something does go wrong, and you will still be able to give your speech effectively.

CHECKLIST for Presentation Aids

❏ Do my aids look professional?

❏ Do they support and enhance my speech?

❏ Are my aids appropriate for the topic, audience, and situation?

❏ Am I ethically representing information with my aids?

❏ Are my aids clear, simple, and understandable?

❏ Did I effectively design the aids?

❏ Do I cite sources in the speech and on the visuals?

❏ Do I effectively incorporate the aids in the speech?

❏ Do I use lead-in and transition devices where necessary?

❏ Do I balance my aids throughout the speech?

CONFIDENCE BOOSTER

Presentation aids can boost your confidence by:

- Helping you internalize your information as you create the aids
- Helping you organize your thoughts
- Serving as a way for you to present your message more professionally
- Giving you the opportunity to change your visual focus and/or physically move during the speech
- Offering you the opportunity to redirect your audience's eyes to something besides you

Part 4: Review

CHAPTER 8 REVIEW QUESTIONS

1. Why is language so important to the public speaker?
2. What are six guidelines for using language effectively? Give an example of each.
3. What are the differences between oral style and written style?
4. What are some ways you can make your language distinctive? Explain.

CHAPTER 9 REVIEW QUESTIONS

1. What elements should you consider in your vocal delivery? Briefly explain each.
2. What elements should you consider in your physical delivery? Briefly explain each.
3. What is the difference between each of the four methods of delivery?
4. What are the main steps for preparing for an extemporaneous speech?

CHAPTER 10 REVIEW QUESTIONS

1. What are the seven types of presentation aids?
2. What should you consider when determining what aids you need to use? Explain.
3. What are the common methods for displaying an aid?
4. What design principles should you employ when creating an aid?

TERMS TO REMEMBER

Chapter 8
symbolic (154)
arbitrary (154)
denotative meaning (154)
connotative meaning (154)
culture (155)
jargon (156)
abbreviation (156)
acronym (156)
clichés (158)
fillers (158)
tropes (161)
schemes (161)

Chapter 9
pitch (164)
monotone (164)
inflection (164)
rate (164)
volume (165)
pause (165)
variety (166)
pronunciation (166)
articulation (167)
enunciation (167)
dialect (167)
appearance (168)
direct eye contact (169)
facial expressions (170)
gestures (170)
emblems (170)
illustrators (170)
movement (171)
posture (171)
extemporaneous speaking (172)
manuscript speaking (173)
memorized speaking (173)
impromptu speaking (173)

Chapter 10
presentation aids (179)
models (181)
photographs (181)
drawings (182)
charts (182)
flowcharts (182)
organizational charts (182)
tables (182)
graphs (183)
line graphs (183)
bar graphs (183)
pictographs (184)
pie graphs (184)
video clips (185)
audio clips (185)
multimedia (185)
design principles (192)

PART 5
Listening & Evaluating

CHAPTER 11
Listening   204

CHAPTER 12
Evaluating Speeches   216

11
LISTENING

Introduction

"Can you hear me now?"

This memorable slogan from a 2002 Verizon commercial emphasizes, in its simplicity, the importance of being heard. If a speaker cannot be heard, the audience cannot listen and the communication process cannot take place.

Effective listening helps you:

- Increase your knowledge. It allows you to take in, process, and use information; it helps you develop your expertise and skills.

- Build and maintain healthy relationships with your family, significant other, friends, and coworkers. Listening gives you clues to their identities and shows them that you care.

- Fulfill your communicative responsibility. In the Overview, you learned that communication is transactional because the audience actively participates. The act of listening completes the transaction between the speaker and the audience.

This chapter focuses on the listening process and how you can help others and yourself become better listeners.

> *The most basic and powerful way to connect to another person is to listen. Just listen. Perhaps the most important thing we ever give each other is our attention.*[1]
>
> RACHEL NAOMI REMEN, M.D.

CHAPTER 11 CONTENTS

What Is the Process of Listening?	206
What Are the Types of Listening?	208
1 Appreciative Listening	208
2 Empathic Listening	208
3 Informative Listening	209
4 Critical Listening	209
What Can Prevent Effective Listening?	210
1 Internal Noise	211
2 External Noise	211
How Can You Help Your Audience Listen More Effectively?	212
As an Audience Member, How Can You Listen More Effectively?	214
1 Listen Actively	214
2 Listen Critically	215
CHAPTER 12: Evaluating Speeches	216
PART 5 Review	226

What Is the Process of Listening?

Understanding the listening process begins with grasping the difference between hearing and listening. As this diagram suggests, **hearing** happens when sound waves strike the eardrum and spark a chain reaction that ends with the brain registering the sound. **_Listening_** is the conscious learned act of paying attention and assigning meaning to an acoustic message. Hearing is the first step in listening. Unless you are hearing impaired physically or by some artificial means, it is impossible not to hear. In contrast, you must _choose to_ listen.

Next, it is important to realize that listening is a process. A process, at its basic level, is the act of inputting something into a series of phases that results in a particular output. To complete the listening process, you must go through at least three phases and up to as many as five. The first three necessary steps are receiving, attending, and understanding. From there, a listener decides to respond and/or commit the message to memory.

HEARING
is the physiological process of receiving sound.

ATTENDING
UNDERSTANDING
RESPONDING
REMEMBERING

LISTENING
is the act of paying attention and assigning meaning.

RECEIVING SOUND

Receiving is the physiological process of hearing. The outer ear collects the sound waves, sending them to the inner ear, where the ear converts the sound and transmits it to the brain.

Attending is the phase where you make your brain pay attention to a given sound. For example, stop and listen to the sounds around you now. You may be able to hear birds outside, music, people talking next door, or the soft whoosh of air coming from the air conditioner or heater. Now, imagine a person speaking in the middle of this symphony of sound, and pay attention to his or her words. If you are able to do so, you will no longer pay attention to some of those other sounds. It is as if you are not hearing them. The sounds do not go away; you are still hearing them but not attending to them. You have chosen to concentrate (mentally focus) on one sound (the person's voice) and exclude others.

Understanding occurs when you apply meaning to a sound and is where communication really begins. You may hear a message and attend to it, but if you do not understand it, the communication was unsuccessful. If you enter a room where two students from Russia are speaking in their national language, you will hear it, if nothing prevents you from doing so. You may attend to their conversation if they are your friends and you are interested in what they may be discussing. But the understanding will not take place unless you know Russian.

Responding is the phase where you give a formal response to the sounds you have processed. Some communication scholars end the listening process with understanding because communication was either successful or not. However, the communication process is transactional, and most listeners offer one of three different responses or some combination of them.

- *Verbal responses* are spoken or written feedback. Your verbal response might paraphrase the speaker's message, ask for further explanation, or simply answer a speaker's question.

- *Nonverbal responses* are visual cues offered by the listener (such as nodding yes or frowning when confused). They can be effective in their brevity but leave great room for misinterpretation.

- *Silence,* or no perceptible response, can also be a response. The listener may choose not to respond because that seems appropriate, or silence can suggest a problem between the speaker, listener, and/or message. Silence can also signal concentration. You often need other nonverbal cues to interpret silence properly.

Remembering, or retaining what you hear, is the final stage. Good listening skills often make use of a person's short-term and long-term memories. In the short term, you listen carefully for details to help you follow the speech's strategy and/or argument. The memory of those details helps you make sense of the speech in the moment but not necessarily remember it later. In the long term, you may commit a broad understanding of the speech to memory as a means of retaining valuable information or maintaining a change in your attitudes, values, or beliefs.

What Are the Types of Listening?

1 Appreciative Listening
2 Empathic Listening
3 Informative Listening
4 Critical Listening

When you engage in the process of listening, you do so to achieve a goal. The four listening goals are to appreciate, empathize, comprehend, and be critical. You will always have one of these goals as your overarching reason for listening. However, listeners often use a combination to achieve that main goal. For example, you may be listening for information but at the same time evaluating it critically for believability. Each of these goals corresponds to a type of listening.

1
Appreciative Listening

Appreciative listening happens when you listen for recreation or enjoyment. Examples of appreciative listening are:

- Listening to a comedy show
- Listening to your favorite band
- Listening to water flowing in a stream and birds singing

Speeches designed with a goal to entertain require this type of listening as well.

2
Empathic Listening

Empathic listening occurs when your purpose is to give the speaker emotional support. Examples here could be:

- A religious leader listening to a congregation member
- A counselor listening to a patient
- A friend listening to another friend in need

This type of listening emphasizes carefully attending to the speaker; supporting the speaker by listening more than responding; and empathizing, or feeling as the other person feels.

3
Informative Listening

You engage in *informative listening* when you want to gain insight or comprehension. This approach to listening emphasizes concentrating on language, ideas, and details as well as remembering the knowledge.

In classes, you use informative listening when you pay attention to your professors. Other places where you might engage in informative listening could be:

- When a friend gives you directions to his new apartment
- At the hardware store as a sales associate tells you how to install tile
- When a doctor gives you medical instructions

In all of these examples, you listen for clarification of the language, you concentrate on the necessary details, and you engage in some sort of activity to help you remember (e.g., taking notes or memorizing).

4
Critical Listening

Critical listening takes place when you listen carefully to a message in order to judge it as acceptable or not. This is the type of listening behavior you use when listening to:

- A presidential debate
- A salesperson trying to sell you a new stereo
- A friend when you are trying to decide if she is telling you the truth

Critical listening is the root of critical thinking. Theorists Brooke Moore and Richard Parker, in their book *Critical Thinking*, define **critical thinking** as "the careful, deliberate determination of whether one should accept, reject, or suspend judgment about a claim [or information] and the degree of confidence with which one accepts or rejects it." Astronomer Carl Sagan called this your "baloney-detection kit." Sagan's suggestion was to "equip yourself with a baloney-detection kit…and be able to tell what is baloney and what is not."

You currently live in a time when informative and persuasive acts bombard you from all sides. They come at you from radio, television, the Internet, T-shirts, and even cereal boxes. You must be able and willing to ask questions such as: Why? Where did that information come from? How old is it? Who benefits from it? Who will get hurt?

PRACTICING ETHICS

Critical listening and critical thinking are such important parts of the communication process that you should almost always engage in a certain level of critical listening and thinking. For example, your main goal for listening to a speaker may be to gather information, but you should never assume information is correct simply because the speaker says so.

What Can Prevent Effective Listening?

1 Internal Noise
2 External Noise

Most people would define noise as unpleasant sounds that might be loud, startling, irritating, or unwelcome. In the process of communicating, **noise** refers to the unwanted barriers that prevent you from listening effectively to the speaker. They can be pleasant or unpleasant things.

For example, you might find the deep, melodious voices of actors James Earl Jones and Morgan Freeman so pleasing that you focus more on the beauty of their voices than their messages. Or you might feel that the harsh, nasal voices of actors Fran Drescher (in character in *The Nanny*) and Gilbert Gottfried (comedian and the original voice of the AFLAC duck) are so annoying that you stop listening to the words spoken. Either of these vocal qualities could become a barrier and, therefore, noise preventing you from attending to what is important about the message.

Noise is not always connected to the speaker; it can be something like a clock ticking, someone tapping a pencil, distracting thoughts, or hunger. Understanding what can become noise is the first step to preventing it from distracting you. There are two general categories of noise influencing communication.

1
Internal Noise

Internal noise is any barrier to effective listening that originates within the body or mind of the listener. Internal noise can be either a physiological or a psychological barrier.

- *Physiological barriers* are bodily conditions that prevent or constrain your ability to process information.

- *Psychological barriers* are emotional conditions that prevent you from focusing on and absorbing a message. For example, your communication anxiety may prevent you from listening to the speech given just before yours, or your fear of a boss could prevent you from listening to his or her comments. A fight with your best friend or worries over how to make a car payment may preoccupy you. Perspective differences (seeing the message from different points of view) between a teenager and a parent can prevent listening when they do not share the same attitudes, values, beliefs, or expectations.

2
External Noise

External noise is any barrier to effective listening that originates outside of the listener's body and mind. External noise can be either an environmental or a linguistic barrier.

- *Environmental barriers* occur when something within the room or area where the speech is given interrupts your ability to concentrate.

- *Linguistic barriers* happen when the verbal and/or nonverbal messages from the speaker are unfamiliar or misunderstood by the listener.

INTERNAL NOISE		EXTERNAL NOISE	
Physiological Barriers	**Psychological Barriers**	**Environmental Barriers**	**Linguistic Barriers**
Examples	*Examples*	*Examples*	*Examples*
Headache	Boredom	Environmental sounds	Jargon
Lack of sleep	Fear	Smells	Awkward sentence structure
Pain	Don't-care attitude	Disruptions	Difficult vocabulary
Illness	Preoccupation	Bad ventilation	Unfamiliar or distracting nonverbal delivery
Hearing or visual impairments	Anger	Room temperature	Poor organization
	Anxiety	Uncomfortable seats	
	Frustration	Lighting	
	Prejudice	Sight issues	
	Perspective differences		

How Can You Help Your Audience Listen More Effectively?

Know your audience. Be aware of barriers they might have toward you, your topic, or the speaking situation. If you know your audience will have a negative response to your topic or might have physiological or psychological issues preventing effective listening, recognizing and addressing these issues up front may help lessen their effects.

→ See Chapter 1 on getting to know your audience.

Create an effective message. Using an effective attention-getter, appropriate language, a sound organizational strategy, and exceptional supporting materials will help your audience stay connected to your speech. Difficult or obscure language will frustrate them. A poor organizational strategy will confuse them and they will stop trying to follow you; good organization is key. Also, presenting compelling information about your topic is one of the best ways to keep your audience listening.

Be confident. Some audience members have trouble listening to messages delivered with low confidence because their empathy for the speaker overrides their focus on the content. Others may not give much weight to a speech when the speaker lacks confidence. Know your message well, and be self-assured and bold when you speak.

Control the environment. When you enter the speaking environment, change aspects that might reduce listening, if you can. For example, adjust temperature and lighting or remove any distracting noises.

Listen to your audience. As you speak, be attentive and responsive to verbal or nonverbal audience behavior that suggests they are confused, bored, or distracted.

Lend a helping hand across cultures. In our increasingly global society, you will likely speak to an audience including individuals from cultures different from yours. Take the time to learn what you can about their cultures. This table offers some suggestions for helping the cross-cultural audience member listen to and understand your speech. However, they can be helpful in any communicative situation.

HOW CAN YOU INCREASE EFFECTIVE LISTENING?	EXPLANATION
Get to know other cultures.	Try to know what cultures are in your audience and learn about them. Study and interact with other cultures regularly so that you are always sensitive to them. For example, some people from other cultures will nod in agreement to be polite when they do not understand.
Use a comprehensible oral delivery style.	Slow down, articulate and pronounce carefully, and use repetition and rephrasing.
Use nonverbal cues.	In the United States, smiling demonstrates your enthusiasm, and gesturing could highlight important points. Be careful not to use culturally specific nonverbal cues that might be misread.
Use presentation aids.	Presentation aids can help summarize or repeat information that might be difficult to remember or understand through oral delivery alone.
Be realistic and thorough in your message.	Take a little longer to discuss complex issues, and do not use idioms, jokes, sarcasm, or exaggerations that might be confusing.
Listen to the audience's verbal and nonverbal feedback.	Watch for looks of confusion or blank expressions, side discussions that seem to be asking for clarification, shuffling through papers about the speech as if looking for clarification, or significant use of a translation dictionary device as you speak. These are signals that someone is struggling with your message.

CONFIDENCE BOOSTER

- Dress for the occasion. Clothes make a difference.
- Stand tall.
- Try to minimize nervous behavior. If your hands shake, gesture with them.
- Captivate your audience with effective volume, tone, and articulation.
- Maintain eye contact with audience members.

CHECKLIST for Helping Your Audience Listen

❑ What do I know about my audience that might interfere with their ability to listen?
❑ Am I using the best means possible to grab and keep this audience's attention with this topic?
❑ How can my delivery and confidence level help?
❑ How can I control the environment better?
❑ What cues are the audience members sending me?

As an Audience Member, How Can You Listen More Effectively?

1 Listen Actively
2 Listen Critically

1

Listen Actively

Listening is a full-time job. The sheer quantity of information you receive each day makes listening a tiresome activity but an even more important one if you are to be an effective consumer of information. A few simple steps will help you be an active participant in the transaction between you and a speaker.

- Give your full attention. Do not watch the cars out the window, daydream, or think about the fight you had with someone before the speech. Help the speaker focus your attention on the topic at hand.

- Listen for the main points.

- Take notes to help you remember.

- Respond to the speech. Giving feedback will help the speaker tailor the message to you and the other audience members. Nonverbal responses, like nodding when you understand or looking confused when you do not, are always helpful. In some cases, the speaker or the situation will signal that you can be more verbally interactive, such as raising your hand or just speaking up to ask a question. Pay attention to what is appropriate.

- Do not fake paying attention.

- Participate in the question-and-answer session after the speech, if one is conducted.

- If you are a cross-cultural listener, work at building your vocabulary and knowledge of idioms/informal expressions. Pay attention to the speaker's body language (posture, gestures, intonation, expression, etc.). Let the speaker know when issues prevent understanding.

2

Listen Critically

As human beings, our ability to think critically is one of the differences that distinguishes us from our furry and feathered friends as well as from machines. When you listen to a speech in a public forum, listening critically is important. Being an effective critical listener takes time and practice. Employing the following tactics will help you develop this skill.

SIGNS YOU ARE A CRITICAL LISTENER/THINKER

- You listen carefully.
- You ask questions—especially the question "Why?" (either mentally asking yourself or, if and when appropriate, directly asking the speaker).
- You explore alternatives.
- You maintain a sense of childlike curiosity—everything is interesting or possible.
- You suspend judgment until more of the details are given.
- You define criteria for making judgments but not at the expense of alternatives.
- You are willing to adjust.
- You are willing to keep an open mind.

You will find active and critical listening easier if you put yourself in the shoes of the person speaking. Just like an effective speaker must consider the audience's traits, an effective listener needs to empathize and identify with the speaker's feelings, thoughts, motives, interests, or attitudes. This act of empathizing and identifying is what theorist and philosopher Kenneth Burke called *identification* in his book *A Rhetoric of Motives*. Identification will prevent you from prematurely judging the speaker or topic, keep you from being resistant to new ideas or speaking styles, and prevent you from overreacting to "hot-button" issues—all of which can be barriers to effective listening and critical thinking. Speaker and listener are co-participants, equals, in the process of communication.

CHECKLIST for Listening More Effectively

❏ Am I giving the speaker my full attention?
❏ Am I actively trying to comprehend the message?
❏ Am I signaling the speaker with the appropriate feedback?
❏ Am I critically listening?

TIP: Taking Good Notes

- If possible, familiarize yourself with the topic before the speech.
- Develop a note-taking shorthand, using symbols or abbreviations such as: i.e. (that is, in other words), & (and), # (number), @ (at), ! (important), ** (remember).
- Prepare your space for note taking.
- Listen for and record main points and pertinent subpoints.
- Use indentations and other similar outlining strategies to distinguish points.
- Use margins for questions or comments you have.
- As soon as possible after the speech, go over your notes and fill in further or summarize.

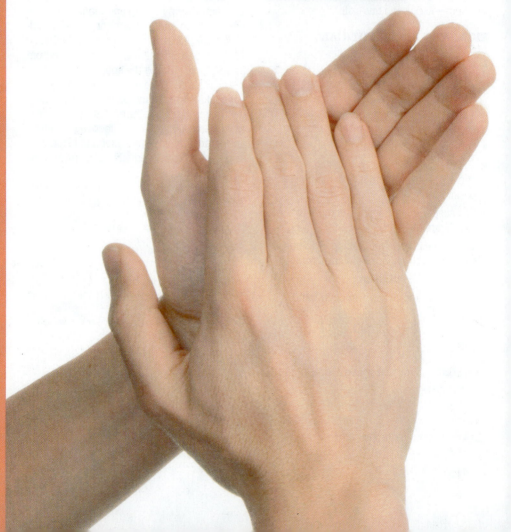

12
EVALUATING
SPEECHES

Introduction

For a beginning speaker, using critiques constructively is hard to do. This chapter will help you become an effective participant in the process of evaluating public speaking.

Whether you are sitting beside a pond talking to a friend or speaking in an auditorium to 300 people, your communicative act is scripted for that audience and framed in a certain context or culture, with participants motivated by different needs, all creating their own meanings. Once two or more people engage in a communicative act, their need to make meaning of the message also requires them to engage in evaluation, as both speaker and audience. This process begins with effective listening (see Chapter 11) and has its heart in the assessment of the communicative act.

Whether we are communicating interpersonally or publicly, rules, standards, language, and culture guide us if we are to make sense. Our job as speakers is to welcome and grow with evaluation. Our job as listeners is to offer constructive criticism to help with that growth.

Oral evaluations are brief overviews, delivered in oral form, describing what the evaluator saw and felt about the speech. Oral evaluations may come either after each individual speech or at the end of a session of speeches. Formal oral evaluation of a speech in a public forum is rare.

Written evaluations are assessments given in written form, which tend to contain more detailed descriptions and suggestions. The speaker may receive the evaluation just minutes after the speech or days later, depending on how the evaluator creates the written evaluation or how detailed it may be.

→ See page 223 for one example of a checklist that could be used as a written evaluation.

CHAPTER 11: Listening   204

CHAPTER 12 CONTENTS

Why Is Evaluation Important to a Speech?   218
  1 Evaluation Is a "Good Thing"   218
  2 Evaluation Teaches Critical Thinking Skills   220
  3 Evaluation Builds Your Confidence   221
  4 Evaluation Makes You a Better Communicator   221

**What Should You Consider When
Evaluating Speeches?**   222
  1 The Speech Message   222
  2 The Speaker's Presentation   222

Who Evaluates Your Speech?   224
  1 You   224
  2 The Audience   224
  3 The Instructor   224
  4 Your Classroom Peers   225

PART 5 Review   226

Why Is Evaluation Important to a Speech?

1 Evaluation Is a "Good Thing"

2 Evaluation Teaches Critical Thinking Skills

3 Evaluation Builds Your Confidence

4 Evaluation Makes You a Better Communicator

1
Evaluation Is a "Good Thing"

Evaluation is a good thing!
Evaluation is a good thing!

Keep repeating this as your new mantra. Because, believe it or not, this statement is true, and the earlier you adopt it as your mantra for most things you do in life, the better you will do those things.

You may be skeptical of this simple sentence because you view criticism or evaluation as a demoralizing, negative experience. You may see it as finding fault, censuring, or disapproving. But constructive evaluation can be a very positive experience.

Do you remember the discussion in Chapter 8 demonstrating how language helps us denotatively and connotatively create and give meaning to our lives and experiences? That works with evaluation as well. So, changing a negative connotation of evaluation allows a positive connotation to develop.

CHECKLIST for Effective Evaluation

❏ Did I describe for the speaker what I saw and heard?

❏ Did I offer an evaluation of whether the speech was effective or not?

❏ Did I explain my personal feeling on why it was effective or not?

❏ Did I support the evaluation with a rationale or related norm?

At its basic level, **evaluation** is description grounded in a justified judgment. In other words, evaluation is simply someone telling what he or she saw and heard, grounded in "why."

In their book *Performance Studies: The Interpretation of Aesthetic Texts*, Ron Pelias and Tracy Stephenson Shaffer break down the process of evaluation as *description*, *judgment*, *justification*, and *rationale*. Pelias and Shaffer are performance-studies scholars, and their discussion focuses on the evaluation of staged artistic performances; but because public speaking is a public event, their discussion applies here as well. Pelias and Shaffer argue that effective evaluation involves accurately describing a speech, fairly judging its worth, and logically justifying your view of it based on rational norms and reasons. For example:

DESCRIPTION

"When your attention-getting device took us to the edge of the canyon and described the air ..."

Description answers: What did I see and hear?

JUDGMENT

"I really liked that."

Judgment answers: Was it good or not?

JUSTIFICATION

"The moment was so real, it gave me goose bumps. I was pulled into the speech, and I felt like I was there by the canyon."

Justification answers: Why was it good or not?

RATIONALE

"One of the major functions of the introduction is to grab the audience's attention and pull them into the speech. You achieved that goal by using emotive language and a great extended narrative."

Rationale answers: What is the logic or norm behind my justification?

Note that nothing in the examples above talks about fault, censorship, or disapproval. Evaluation is about describing what you see, making a judgment about how you feel about it, and then offering a sensible justification for what works or needs improvement. (Use the checklist on page 218 as a reminder.) Improvement does not mean tearing down or destroying; it means elevating to the next level of worth. If something about your speech is not quite working, then the message you intend to send may be misinterpreted or not received at all. Evaluation can help you adjust your speeches so that your messages are successful.

Nothing we do is perfect, and we can always strive to improve. When given appropriately and constructively, evaluation fosters growth and progress along the lifelong path to developing the great speaker and thinker who resides within you. View your speech as a diamond in the rough and evaluation as helping you carve a way to the beauty. Embrace evaluation; do not fear it. Evaluation is a good thing!

2

Evaluation Teaches Critical Thinking Skills

Think a moment about these questions.

- Are you being too trusting?
- Is that really the best buy?
- Can you learn from history?
- Are you thinking creatively?
- Can you think outside of the box?

These are all questions that force us to think about our mindset and that of others. Such questions are designed to make us creators and participants in our own lives rather than passive vessels.

Imagine if Alexander Graham Bell had not wondered if there was a way to send our voices across vast spaces or if he had given up after the first experiments failed. You might still be sending messages only by mail or telegraph, and cell phones would not even be in our vocabulary, much less in our pockets. Imagine if your grandmother had never played around with her recipes to make them better. You would not have those special cookies or cakes to eat.

Critical thinking is important in our lives, and we must always strive to be better thinkers. Chapter 11 first introduced you to critical thinking as it relates to critical listening; here you should note that critical thinking is the mechanism for evaluation.

As the detective Sherlock Holmes says in *The Hound of the Baskervilles*, "The world is full of obvious things which nobody by any chance ever observes." Holmes understands that chance observation teaches nothing and often passes by us. When you evaluate another speaker, your own speech, or a listener's evaluation of your speech, you are engaging and honing your critical thinking skills—observing detail and making a reasoned judgment about that detail.

Critical thinkers are always, like Holmes, seeking the answers to these questions: Who? What? When? Where? Why? To whom?

Imagine if Macy, a student, gives a speech arguing that an electric toothbrush is better than a regular brush and she says:

Research shows that you will get better dental checkups if you use an electric toothbrush.

This statement may be true, but you as the listener should ask questions like:

Who conducted and funded the research? Who is reporting the research Macy quotes? Are there any studies refuting this?

Asking these questions allows you to seek alternative viewpoints and may give you reason to change your own.

PRACTICING ETHICS

A good critical thinker should also be an honorable one. Don't use your critical thinking skills to mislead, exploit, deceive, confuse, confound, aggravate, discourage, or harm. Great critical thinkers practice their skills with civility.

CONFIDENCE BOOSTER

Beginning speakers tend to focus their listening on what they consider "negative comments." Listen carefully to the whole evaluation. Assess what is important for you to work on in your next speech, and celebrate what was a success. Realize that striving for excellence in public speaking is an exciting, continually evolving process.

3
Evaluation Builds Your Confidence

Effective evaluation will build your confidence if you let it. Effective evaluation is not only about what needs to be improved; it also focuses on the successes.

As individuals, we are often hardest on ourselves and see only the negative. If evaluators listen carefully and do their job completely, they will describe the complete picture of your speech. Their evaluations will enrich your speech experience so that your next speech will be better and your confidence higher. Knowing what worked and what needs to be improved, and then taking the steps to work on those issues, will build your view of yourself as a good speaker. For example, Macy might respond negatively if someone gave her this response:

> Your evidence and logic were great. However, you need to work on keeping my attention during the detailed explanations and watch moving around aimlessly too much.

Yet this is really a nice comment if she listens carefully to it. First, having solid evidence and logic is one of the hardest things to do, and this listener has just stated that Macy excelled in those areas. She should be very proud of that. Secondly, using language and delivery techniques to keep the audience's attention during detailed explanations might take a little work to fix, but these are areas even the beginning speaker can improve on quickly. Some of the new delivery techniques employed to keep the audience's attention might even keep Macy from moving around so much.

4
Evaluation Makes You a Better Communicator

No matter whether you are the one receiving the evaluation or giving it, participating in the act of evaluating will make you a better communicator. Most people learn better by watching and doing. The more you watch other speakers to learn where they succeed or need improvement—and then apply that knowledge to your own speeches—the more you will elevate your own skills.

So watch and listen to other speeches for ideas. As you observe a speech, ask yourself questions like these:

- What type of support materials stood out as the most effective in this speech?
- What language choices worked well?
- What about this person's delivery was effective?
- What made the speaker appear extremely confident?
- How did the speaker use space?
- How did the speaker incorporate audience feedback?
- What "tricks of the trade" did the speaker use to keep listeners' attention?

The list of questions you could ask is almost endless, and the skills and concepts you are learning throughout this book will guide you to what to look for in a successful speech. As you grow as a speaker as well as an audience member, you will ask better, more detailed questions. You will notice the nuances of great communication.

What Should You Consider When Evaluating Speeches?

1 The Speech Message
2 The Speaker's Presentation

Unless you are competing or debating with someone else, most evaluators base their evaluations on established standards (often called a *criterion-based evaluation*). This form of evaluation assesses speakers' abilities to meet set standards and does not compare them to others.

In the classroom, your instructor will explain the standards she or he deems important to the class objectives or the assignment. You can categorize most, if not all, of those standards under one of two headings: the speech message or the speaker's presentation.

1
The Speech Message

Evaluation standards related to the speech message focus on the effectiveness of the topic selection, research, and the creation of the message. These standards correspond to the discussions in Parts 1 through 3 of this book and to the first four sections (topic, introduction, body, and conclusion) in the brief listing of potential standards on the next page.

2
The Speaker's Presentation

Evaluation standards related to the speaker's presentation spotlight successful uses of language, delivery techniques, and presentation aids. These standards correspond to the discussion in Part 4 and to the last section (presentation) of the list on the next page.

Remember, this form is only one sample; your instructor will use an evaluation that corresponds to your assignments.

TOPIC

- ❑ Speech accomplished purpose (to inform, to persuade, or to accentuate) ◄──── The speech message
- ❑ Topic appropriate to speaker, audience, and occasion
- ❑ Interesting topic

INTRODUCTION

- ❑ Gained attention and interest
- ❑ Established credibility
- ❑ Indicated relevance to audience
- ❑ Declared central idea
- ❑ Previewed speech

BODY

- ❑ Main points clear and obvious to the audience
- ❑ Points followed an appropriate organizational strategy
- ❑ Main points appropriately researched and supported
- ❑ Main points supported with appropriate presentation aids when necessary
- ❑ Oral citations included throughout speech
- ❑ Linked parts of speech

CONCLUSION

- ❑ Contained a summary statement
- ❑ Offered an audience response statement
- ❑ Effectively came to closure (WOW statement)

PRESENTATION

- ❑ Language was clear, concise, and appropriate
- ❑ Gestures/body movements were effective ◄──── The speaker's presentation
- ❑ Consistent and effective eye contact
- ❑ Used vocal variety/emphasis/volume/rate
- ❑ Used appropriate delivery style
- ❑ Spoke with enthusiasm
- ❑ Spoke with conviction and sincerity
- ❑ Good use of delivery outline
- ❑ Presentation aids appropriate to speech topic (if applicable)
- ❑ Used presentation aids throughout entire speech (if applicable)
- ❑ Used professional presentation aids (if applicable)
- ❑ Speech met time requirements

Who Evaluates Your Speech?

1 You
2 The Audience
3 The Instructor
4 Your Classroom Peers

1 You

Good evaluation begins with you, and you are already doing it as you create your speech. Be reflexive *after* the speech as well. In other words, how did your actions or discussion in the speech affect the speech event, and how did the speech event affect your actions? What were the positive outcomes? What can be improved?

Always self-evaluate your performance. Your instructor may also require you to turn in a written self-evaluation as part of the class experience.

2 The Audience

When an audience actively participates in your speech, they offer you feedback that can help you adjust your speech. They nod their heads in agreement; they lean forward; they ask questions for clarification. These nonverbal and verbal responses are all clues to how effective you are being as the speaker. In formal or public settings, you may also get written evaluation forms that the audience fills out after the speech.

3 The Instructor

In a public speaking class, evaluation is an essential part of the learning process. Most instructors use both oral and written evaluations to reinforce learning and the main principles taught in the class. When and how they evaluate, as well as the format they choose, can vary. Use each evaluation as a tool for improving your next speech.

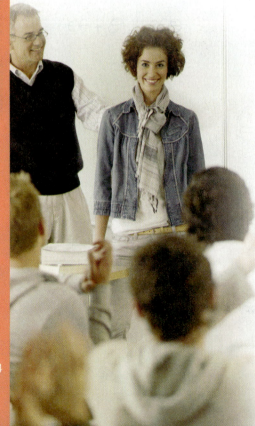

4
Your Classroom Peers

In the public speaking classroom, students will often evaluate speeches given by others in the class. Depending on your instructor's teaching practices, peer evaluation can be oral and/or written. Some guidelines for providing useful feedback are shown in the table below.

HOW CAN YOU EVALUATE A SPEECH?	EXPLANATION	EXAMPLES
Offer constructive feedback.	Instead of just offering a quick, unexplained response, include specifics. Answer the question "Why?"	INCORRECT: "It was good." CORRECT: "It was a good persuasive speech. The range of supporting evidence and reliability was really convincing."
Be positive first.	Look for positive elements and offer them first to frame your evaluation in an encouraging way. If you listen effectively, you will note something positive about the speech.	INCORRECT: "You had more than 45 'ums' in your speech." CORRECT: "Wow, this was a unique topic. I've read about victory gardens but didn't realize how important they were during the war. To improve your effectiveness, you might want to work on eliminating the vocal filler 'um.' You had a lot of these, and they became distracting."
Always offer improvement tips.	No speech is perfect. Always give speakers advice on what they might do to be even better next time.	"I loved your use of presentation aids during the first half of the speech. It might be nice to carry that throughout the full speech by adding a few aids in the second half."
Avoid demeaning comments and attacks.	Humiliating the speaker or giving blunt negative responses about the speech is not helpful. Remember to describe, judge, justify, and rationalize your response.	INCORRECT: "This was a dumb topic for this audience." CORRECT: "As a college student, I had a bit of trouble staying with your topic of banning school uniforms in high schools because I am older. Is there a way to make this topic more appropriate to this audience?"
Be objective.	Personal feelings can cloud the goal. If you have issues with the topic or speaker or think either is "cool," do not base your evaluation on unrelated or superficial feelings.	INCORRECT: "You're so funny!" CORRECT: "This speech was very funny, and I loved it. I was really entertained. However, the purpose was to persuade me. I got caught up in the funny parts and forgot what you wanted me to do."

Part 5: Review

CHAPTER 11 REVIEW QUESTIONS

1. Why is effective listening important?
2. Explain the listening process. Include in your answer the steps of the process and how listening differs from hearing.
3. What are the four types of listening? Briefly explain each.
4. What is noise? Include in your answer a brief explanation of the types and barriers.
5. What can you do to help your audience be more effective listeners?
6. What can you do to be a more effective listener?

CHAPTER 12 REVIEW QUESTIONS

1. Why is evaluation important to you and your speech?
2. Explain and give a brief example of an evaluation as it moves through the evaluation process (description, judgment, justification, rationale).
3. What should you consider when evaluating a speech?

TERMS TO REMEMBER

Chapter 11
hearing (206)
listening (206)
receiving (207)
attending (207)
understanding (207)
responding (207)
remembering (207)
appreciative listening (208)
empathic listening (208)
informative listening (209)
critical listening (209)
critical thinking (209)
noise (210)
internal noise (211)
physiological barriers (211)
psychological barriers (211)
external noise (211)
environmental barriers (211)
linguistic barriers (211)

Chapter 12
oral evaluations (217)
written evaluations (217)
evaluation (219)
description (219)
judgment (219)
justification (219)
rationale (219)

13

THE INFORMATIVE SPEECH

Introduction

From the interpersonal to the public, informative speaking permeates our daily lives. Throughout the course of your life, you will give numerous informative speeches of all types.

For example, you might need to tell a friend how to fix the carburetor on an old John Deere tractor, how to groom a dog, or how to plant a garden. You might need to explain the components of a computer or digital camera. If you have children in your life, you will need to teach them things like how to tie their shoes, brush their teeth, fold their shirts, safely use a stove, or understand the importance of family traditions.

In your public and professional lives, you will need to understand how to pass on information effectively if you want to be successful. No matter if you are an auto mechanic, truck driver, doctor, teacher, accountant, forensic scientist, or nanny, you will need to use your informative skills daily.

Through informative speaking, we pass on knowledge, create our cultures, and survive. The better we are at informative communication, the better our lives will be.

The first five parts in this book outline the steps in the process of creating a successful speech. The next three will help you see how to use this process or parts of it for specific types of speeches and speaking situations.

In this chapter, you will use the public speaking process to build an informative speech.

CHAPTER 13 CONTENTS

What Is the Creative Process for Informative Speaking? 230

What Is Informative Speaking? 232

How Do You Choose and Research an Informative Topic? 234
1 Get to Know the Audience and Situation 234
2 Create an Informative Idea Bank 235
3 Select and Narrow Your Informative Topic 235
4 Determine the Best Type of Informative Speech 236
5 Identify Your Specific Purpose 236
6 Identify Your Central Idea 237
7 Create a Working Outline 238
8 Conduct Your Research 239

How Do You Construct the Informative Outline? 240

How Do You Organize an Informative Speech? 242
1 Recognize Your Organizational Strategy 242
2 Commit to a Strategy 242
3 Construct Main Points 244
4 Organize Support Materials 244
5 Compose Your Introduction and Conclusion 245

How Should You Prepare to Present or Evaluate an Informative Speech? 252
1 Put Your Speech on Its Feet 252
2 Evaluate the Message and Presentation 253

PART 6 Review 254

What Is the Creative Process for Informative Speaking?

Passing information on to other individuals through speech requires you to be logical and purposeful. This chart briefly outlines the five basic activities you will use to create an effective informative speech. Allow yourself to move creatively back and forth between each activity as you fashion your speech to pass on information.

1 STARTING

2 RESEARCHING

HOW DO YOU CHOOSE AND RESEARCH AN INFORMATIVE TOPIC?
→ See page 234

Know who you are speaking to as well as where, when, and why you are speaking.

Select the informative topic that best fits you, your audience, and the occasion.

Craft a central idea that defines exactly what you want your audience to learn.

Understand how to evaluate, choose, and use a variety of support materials. Good informative materials must be accurate, current, complete, and suitable.

Find support materials through the Internet, the library, interviews, and surveys.

3
CREATING

HOW DO YOU CONSTRUCT THE INFORMATIVE OUTLINE?
➔ See page 240

Start with a working outline, create a preparation outline, and include a source page. Create a delivery outline to use during your speech.

HOW DO YOU ORGANIZE AN INFORMATIVE SPEECH?
➔ See page 242

Identify your main points. Use an organizational strategy appropriate for an informative speech.

Create an introduction to gain attention and set up your speech. Create a conclusion to sum up, tell your audience how to respond, and end with impact.

4
PRESENTING

5
LISTENING & EVALUATING

HOW SHOULD YOU PREPARE TO PRESENT OR EVALUATE AN INFORMATIVE SPEECH?
➔ See page 252

Use language that is familiar, concrete, and appropriate.

Practice your delivery so that you are natural, enthusiastic, confident, and engaging.

Consider using presentation aids to help your audience understand and learn.

Be an active and effective listener engaged in the informative process.

Determine the effectiveness and appropriateness of the speech's topic, support materials, organization, and language. Evaluate the speaker's delivery and ethics.

Be a critical thinker.

CONFIDENCE BOOSTER
Parts 1 through 5 have prepared you for this process. This chapter will take you step by step through the process as it relates to the informative speech. Remember the Jesse Jackson quotation from the Overview. You can conceive a great speech a step at a time. You can believe in yourself. You can achieve it. Relax and be confident that you can create a successful informative speech.

What Is Informative Speaking?

At its essence, speaking to inform is the act of *giving*. **Informative speaking** gives your audience *completely new* knowledge, skills, or understanding about your topic or increases their *current* knowledge, skills, or understanding.

The gift you give can range from a topic that seems indefinable, like the origin of life, to a practical topic like changing a tire. Whether you are the CEO of a large corporation, a local automotive salesperson, or a parent involved in the community's educational system, informative speaking is the bread and butter of our daily communication. We are constantly asked to describe, explain, demonstrate, or report on almost every aspect of our lives.

PRACTICING ETHICS

The main benchmarks of great informative speaking are accuracy, unity, and inclusiveness. Ethically, these benchmarks translate into being:

- Truthful and reliable when selecting support materials
- Complete in your coverage of the topic, not simply relying on personal knowledge
- Organized enough to demonstrate how things "fit together" in the speech
- Evenhanded and unbiased when offering information
- Responsible in selecting an appropriate and legal topic for you, your audience, and the situation

You can categorize most informative speeches as speeches to describe, explain, or instruct. Normally, the topic—or what your audience needs to know about the topic—determines the type.

- A **speech to describe** usually describes an object, a person, an animal, a place, or an event.
- A **speech to explain** clarifies a concept or issue.
- A **speech to instruct** teaches or demonstrates a process.
- In some speaking situations, you might be required to give an informative **speech to report**, which is an oral report or briefing. You will most often give this type of speech when you are part of a group or organization, including the workplace, and need to report on the progress of something.

The following table lists each type of informative speech, its corresponding topic labels, and examples of a speech topic for each.

TYPE OF INFORMATIVE SPEECH	TOPIC LABEL	SAMPLE SPEECH TOPICS
TO DESCRIBE	Object	To describe the features of an iPod Touch
	Person	To describe the life and music of Odetta
	Animal	To describe the life cycle of the butterfly
	Place	To describe the Great Barrier Reef
	Event	To describe what happens at the opening of the Olympics
TO EXPLAIN	Concept	To explain basic principles of Islam
	Issue	To explain current concerns surrounding same-sex marriage
TO INSTRUCT	Process	To instruct about (demonstrate) creative ways to wrap a gift
TO REPORT	Oral report or briefing	To report recent findings related to student parking needs on campus

How Do You Choose and Research an Informative Topic?

1 Get to Know the Audience and Situation

2 Create an Informative Idea Bank

3 Select and Narrow Your Informative Topic

4 Determine the Best Type of Informative Speech

5 Identify Your Specific Purpose

6 Identify Your Central Idea

7 Create a Working Outline

8 Conduct Your Research

1

Get to Know the Audience and Situation

If your topic is not appropriate to your audience and situation, you face an uphill struggle to engage your audience. Take time to learn about your audience and situation. Doing so will also help you determine what type of informative speech (to describe, explain, instruct, or report) to create.

For example, if you work for a research lab and must present findings to the company funding your research, you would give a *speech to report*. However, you might give the same information in a *speech to explain* at a conference of experts in your field; your speech's content, language, and delivery would change.

Use the review checklist below to help you analyze your audience and situation.

→ Chapter 1 discusses in detail how to analyze your audience and the situation.

REVIEW CHECKLIST for Audience and Situation Analysis

❏ What are the personal traits (age, race, gender, etc.) of my audience? Are there additional characteristics to consider, such as nationality or disabilities?

❏ What are my audience's needs and knowledge level?

❏ What might they know about potential topics?

❏ Why is the audience here?

❏ What is my relationship with the event?

❏ How much time will I have to speak?

❏ What are the details (location, time, other speakers, occasion, etc.) of the event?

❏ What are the audience's expectations because of the occasion?

❏ How do these factors influence my topic or type of informative speech?

2

Create an Informative Idea Bank

Using the idea bank method from Chapter 2, make a list of potential topics that lean toward a specific purpose to inform—any topic you can explain, describe, or demonstrate. Your assignment may not allow you to do all three, but you can delete topics later if they do not work. Below is one example of an informative idea bank. Remember to consider anything a potential topic at this point. Look around and let your mind free-associate.

If you have trouble getting started, read through magazines or local papers, browse the Internet for ideas, or just look around your room or house. For example, what's the history of the Coke bottle shape? How was bubble gum invented? How can you make a pie out of the breakfast drink Tang?

3

Select and Narrow Your Informative Topic

You can now focus in on the broad topic that best fits you, your audience, and the situation. Use the process from Chapter 2 to narrow your idea bank. For an informative speech, especially consider these questions:

- Which topics might give completely new knowledge to your audience?
- Which topics would listeners like to know more about?

Suppose you created the idea bank below for class and are narrowing your selections. You focus on national parks, as many people like to travel, but "parks" is too broad. You've already begun narrowing the topic with free associations of Boundary Waters, Ansel Adams, and Yosemite. As your college is near the Boundary Waters and Ansel Adams is only peripherally related to parks, you choose Yosemite.

This topic is still broad, but you can narrow it further later. For now, do some preliminary research to see if you can find quality information on the topic. If researching it seems difficult, you may want to revisit your idea bank for another topic or change the angle of this one.

→ See Chapter 2 if you need more help selecting and narrowing a topic.

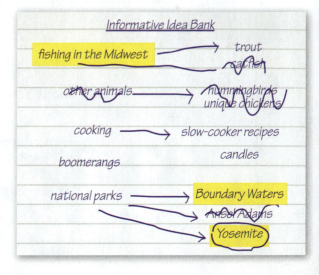

Informative Idea Bank

fishing in the Midwest → trout / catfish

other animals → hummingbirds / unique chickens

cooking → slow-cooker recipes

boomerangs   candles

national parks → Boundary Waters
→ Ansel Adams
→ Yosemite

4

Determine the Best Type of Informative Speech

Earlier in this chapter, you learned that there are different types of informative speeches. Sometimes, simply labeling your topic as an object, person, animal, place, event, concept, issue, or process is enough to determine the type of speech you will create. For example, your Yosemite topic clearly fits as a speech to describe.

If you do not yet have an angle for your topic, consider what your audience needs to know. For example, if your topic is baseball gloves and your audience consists of players, they probably know how to take care of a glove. So a process speech on cleaning a glove might not interest them unless you have unique information. However, they may not know how a glove is made (a different process topic) or the history of the glove (an object topic).

Use the table on page 233 to help determine the appropriate type of informative speech for your topic. Correctly identifying your type of informative speech will help you settle on a suitable organizational strategy later.

5

Identify Your Specific Purpose

A good specific purpose begins to shape your speech topic into a more manageable size. The specific purpose is a single statement merging together your general purpose, your audience, and your objective for the speech. For your Yosemite topic, you know your general purpose is to inform. Merging your general purpose with your audience and objective, your specific purpose would look like this:

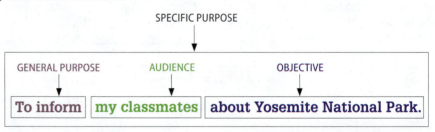

SPECIFIC PURPOSE

GENERAL PURPOSE	AUDIENCE	OBJECTIVE
To inform	my classmates	about Yosemite National Park.

This specific purpose will help you keep your general purpose (to inform) and your audience (college students) connected to the objective of your speech (telling about Yosemite National Park).

→ See Chapter 2 if you need more help identifying your specific purpose.

REVIEW CHECKLIST for Evaluating an Informative Specific Purpose

❏ Does my specific purpose contain my general purpose, my audience reference, and my objective?

❏ Does my specific purpose begin with "to inform"?

❏ Is it a statement, not a question?

❏ Is it clear and concise, with only one speech topic?

6
Identify Your Central Idea

Now you are ready to formulate your central idea (also called a thesis statement), or the concise one-sentence summary or preview of exactly what you want to say in your informative speech. This is the course you will take to achieve the objective of your specific purpose.

Below are two possible examples of how the specific purpose of your Yosemite speech can become a central idea. The objective of the specific purpose is shown in blue.

If Your Specific Purpose Is...

To inform my classmates about Yosemite National Park.

Your Central Idea Could Be...

Yosemite National Park is more than a park; it is an experience that can change people.

or

Yosemite National Park is more than a park; it is an experience that can change people through its adventures, its waterfalls, and the great Half Dome.

Both could be acceptable. Some speech instructors like the simpler form of the first, and others like the central idea to reflect your main points, as the second example does. For some speeches, it might be difficult to establish the exact main ideas prior to doing research. You can always refine that part of the central idea as you begin to create your preparation outline.

→ See Chapter 2 if you need more help formulating your central idea.

TIP: Build on Your Central Idea

As you build your speech, you should always return to your central idea and use it as a test for how appropriate your support materials are to the speech. Always ask: Does this material directly relate to my speech objective? Will my audience see my reason for including this material as support for a main point? How can I clearly show them?

REVIEW CHECKLIST for Evaluating an Informative Central Idea

❑ Is my central idea informative in nature?
❑ Is my central idea written as a complete sentence?
❑ Is it a statement, not a question?
❑ Does the statement use clear and concise language?
❑ Does my central idea focus on one speech topic?
❑ Can I cover this central idea in the time allotted?
❑ Is this informative central idea worth my audience's time?

7

Create a Working Outline

At this stage, you should take a few minutes to map out a working outline to guide your research. A working outline is a rough (often handwritten) outline or road map for your final speech. This process will help you see connections and develop your goal. As you collect support materials for your speech, add what you find to this working outline. This will help you see where you need more information or when you need to change something.

Your working main points might be questions you think need to be answered or simply phrases that relate to subtopics. As with your central idea, your main points will continue to evolve and become more defined as you create your speech. They may change significantly because, in the preparation outline stage of creating your speech, you want your main points to be concise and complete declarative sentences, not questions.

→ Chapter 5 explains the benefits of a working outline and the elements of a preparation outline.

TOPIC: Yosemite National Park

GENERAL PURPOSE: To inform

SPECIFIC PURPOSE: To inform my classmates about Yosemite National Park.

CENTRAL IDEA: Yosemite National Park is more than a park; it is an experience that can change people through its adventures, its waterfalls, and the great Half Dome.

I. What adventures are available at Yosemite?
II. What is important to know about the waterfalls?
III. What is important to know about Half Dome?

Remember, you may use questions for the main points in your working outline, but you should use declarative sentences in your preparation outline.

REVIEW CHECKLIST for Working Main Points

❑ Does each main point cover only one key idea?
❑ Are my main points similarly constructed (are they parallel)?
❑ Am I roughly balancing the time spent on each point?
❑ Do my main points relate back to my central idea?

8
Conduct Your Research

The key to any good speech is a variety of acceptable support materials. Keep your eyes open for different possibilities, and do not rely on only one research tool (for example, only the Internet). Think about your audience and their relationship with your topic to help you select appropriate materials.

Most informative speeches will rely heavily on facts, definitions, testimony, and examples. Although you might use statistics, they should be used only to explain or describe, not to persuade.

When you are researching an informative speech, you want to find materials that will make your audience want to listen and learn. The best ways to do that are:

- Select materials that have a language level appropriate for your audience.

- Find materials that will interest your audience because they are relevant, unique, current, and easy to understand.

- If the topic is complex, make sure you use materials from multiple perspectives and means. Everyone learns differently.

Web sites, books, newspapers, magazines, newsletters, journals, government resources, reference works, and firsthand personal knowledge are all effective sources of support materials for an informative speech. The Internet, library, interviews, and even surveys can offer a wealth of information. Government pamphlets and Web sites are often a good resource for speech topics that demonstrate or instruct.

If your topic directly relates to a local business, the staff there might be able to supply materials. For example, even if you do not live in the area of Yosemite National Park, most cities have travel agencies that will have information on Yosemite. If a national park is located near you, someone there might be able to help you locate information. You could also search newspapers near Yosemite or contact the park directly via phone or e-mail. Be creative when considering possible locations for quality support materials.

→ See Part 2 if you need help with research.

REMEMBER

To test your support materials, you should make sure they are:

- Accurate
- Current
- Complete
- Trustworthy
- Suitable

REVIEW CHECKLIST for Informative Support Materials

❏ Will my support materials make my audience want to listen and learn?

❏ Will my support materials help my audience learn something new?

❏ If my topic is difficult, do I have multiple ways of approaching the topic?

❏ Are the support materials unique for my audience?

❏ Do I have a variety of types from various sources?

❏ Are the materials current and complete?

❏ Are the sources credible?

❏ Did I take good notes so that my information is correct with complete citation information?

How Do You Construct the Informative Outline?

Next, you need to organize your thoughts. For an informative speech, sound organization is critical if you want your audience to learn and remember. Outlining is the only way to tighten up your organization.

Most instructors will ask you to complete a preparation outline (also called a full-sentence or formal outline). This outline is highly structured, includes complete sentences, and typically ends with a source page. Your instructor may ask you to turn in a copy of the preparation outline as a valuable diagnostic tool. Later in this chapter, you will create your delivery outline for rehearsal and for presenting the speech.

Preparation outlines should adhere to several traits, which are discussed in Chapter 5, but you can use the review checklist below and the template on the next page to help you create your outline. Be sure to link parts of your speech together with a transition, a signpost, an internal preview, or an internal review.

The following section on organizing the speech will help you further develop your preparation outline. Remember, this process is not linear and referring back and forth between sections in this chapter will help you achieve your goal.

→ See Chapter 5 if you need more help with outlining or with creating links.

REVIEW CHECKLIST for Creating an Outline

❑ Am I using full sentences?

❑ Am I introducing only one point per outline symbol?

❑ Are my main points parallel and do they coordinate?

❑ Do my main points relate to my central idea?

❑ Do my subpoints relate to the point they follow?

Follow either the format shown below or one that your instructor suggests.

Student name Date	Class Instructor name

Topic: Yosemite National Park
Specific purpose: To inform my classmates about Yosemite National Park.
Central idea: Yosemite National Park is more than a park; it is an
                  experience that can change people through its
                  adventures, its waterfalls, and the great Half Dome.

This example shows how you would begin to use the template to create your Yosemite speech.

INTRODUCTION
    Attention-getter
    Credibility material
    Relevance to audience
    Preview of speech

(Link from introduction to first main point)

BODY
    I.   Yosemite's adventures are for all ages and cultures with varied interests.
       A. Subpoint
       B. Subpoint
          1. Subpoint of B
          2. Subpoint of B
          3. Subpoint of B

Begin filling in main points as you have them written. Use only one sentence per each outline symbol, whether it is a main point or a subpoint. You must have two or more subpoints.

(Link between first and second main points)

    II. Second main point
       A. Subpoint
       B. Subpoint
          1. Subpoint of B
          2. Subpoint of B
       C. Subpoint

(Link: If you continue your hike past the Vernal and Nevada Falls, you will reach what is possibly the most photographed place in the park—Half Dome.)

Be sure to formally write out your links. In an informative speech, the links help your audience group information for better understanding and retention.

    III. Third main point

       A. Subpoint
          1. Subpoint of A
             a. Subpoint of 1
              b. Subpoint of 1
          2. Subpoint of A
       B. Subpoint
       C. Subpoint

(Link to conclusion)

CONCLUSION
    Summary statement
    Audience response statement
    WOW statement

The introduction and conclusion are extremely important to the effectiveness of your speech. Spend time on them. A section later in this chapter will help you.

Works Cited (or References)

How Do You Organize an Informative Speech?

1 **Recognize Your Organizational Strategy**

2 **Commit to a Strategy**

3 **Construct Main Points**

4 **Organize Support Materials**

5 **Compose Your Introduction and Conclusion**

1

Recognize Your Organizational Strategy

Informative speeches can utilize a chronological, topical, spatial, comparative, problem–solution, or causal strategy. Knowing which types of informative speech these strategies fit with most comfortably should begin to help you recognize which strategy you want. Use the table on the next page as a guide.

For example, in your Yosemite speech, you want to talk about park adventures, the waterfalls, and Half Dome. These are natural subtopics, which lend themselves well to the topical strategy.

2

Commit to a Strategy

The lines between objects, people, animals, places, events, concepts, issues, and processes can blur. Often it is difficult to speak about a process without defining some objects or to speak about people without placing them at events. Who could talk about the 1960s singer Janis Joplin without placing her at the Monterey Jazz Festival or Woodstock? To understand her and her music, you must talk about those events in music history. Therefore, many topics can fit into one or more strategies. The important thing is that you select one and stay with it.

→ See Chapter 6 if you need help selecting an organizational strategy.

The best way to stay committed to a strategy is to choose one as you begin to construct your main points and think about what you need to tell your audience. Again, this process is not linear. You cannot finalize main points before selecting the strategy; and some strategies will not work for certain speech goals because you cannot create or support the main points necessary to use that strategy.

STRATEGY	WHAT TYPES OF INFORMATIVE SPEECH DOES IT FIT?	WHEN MIGHT YOU USE IT?	SAMPLE SPEECH TOPICS
Chronological	To describe To instruct	When giving a speech related to time or history or when you need to teach a sequence/process	• To describe the history of Savannah, Georgia • To instruct on the proper way to wax skis
Topical	To describe To explain	With any informative speech that has natural, inherent subtopics	• To describe different types of butterflies in the West • To explain basic principles of color theory
Spatial	To describe	To describe a place, event, or object based on its relationship to space	• To describe a film festival based on the different venues around town • To describe the human tooth from the inside out
Comparative	To describe To explain	To compare a complex topic to something your audience knows better	• To explain Islam by comparing it to Christianity
Problem–solution	To explain To report	When a solution has been implemented and you need to explain why	• To explain next year's tuition increase
Causal	To describe To explain	To describe or explain something based on how it is caused (or the reverse)	• To explain how second-hand smoke causes asthma

TIP: Informing
- Don't assume that the audience has knowledge of your topic. Explain terms and concepts.
- Use clear, concrete language that your audience will understand.
- Be interesting and logical.
- Appeal to different learning styles.

3
Construct Main Points

If you return to your working outline, you can see the basis of your main points in the questions you wrote. However, final main points cannot be questions, so these need some work.

> I. What adventures are available at Yosemite?
> II. What is important to know about the waterfalls?
> III. What is important to know about Half Dome?

Form is incorrect for a preparation outline

Main points need to be complete declarative sentences, written in a parallel structure, and balanced with each other. The working main points above could be rewritten as:

I. Yosemite's adventures are for all ages and cultures with varied interests.

II. Yosemite has several magnificent waterfalls, many of which are America's tallest.

III. Yosemite's most famous icon is Half Dome.

➔ See Chapter 6 if you need help with constructing main points.

4
Organize Support Materials

Proper outlining requires you to demonstrate how your subpoints containing the support materials are subordinate to your main points and to any subpoints that precede them. For example, if you have your first main point of the Yosemite speech and have located appropriate support materials, you will be able to add the next level of the outline.

I. Yosemite's adventures are for all ages and cultures with varied interests.

A. You can take it easy watching for wildlife like the black bear, bobcat, white-headed woodpecker, or mountain goat.

B. Physical activities you could engage in include hiking, rock climbing, swimming, horseback riding, camping, and white-water rafting.

C. Nightlife activities include stargazing at a vast, open sky or even having a cocktail at the Iron Door Saloon.

As you add the next level of support material detail, your outline will start to fill out even more.

➔ See pages 246–251 for a complete outline.

How you organize the material under each point or subpoint depends on the strategy you are using. For example, the Yosemite speech can use a topical strategy at all levels of the outline, so it is really up to you to decide which point comes first.

5

Compose Your Introduction and Conclusion

The introduction and conclusion of your speech can make or break its success. See some excerpts below and the complete text on pages 246–251.

An introduction for an informative speech should "pitch" your speech to your audience. It should tell them why they need to learn more about your topic or at least amuse them in some creative way about the topic.

INTRODUCTION

This should be one of the "wow" moments in your speech	**ATTENTION-GETTER:** Several years ago, when I was about to embark on a serious life change and move half a world away from where I had lived since 18, I went to a place, a location, a mystical spot that had a healing and peaceful effect on me. I had to say "good-bye and thank you." Michele, my friend, and I had made it to the top of Half Dome in Yosemite National Park, and I felt like I was on top of the world! I was near heaven—almost close enough to reach out and touch it...
State why you should give this speech	**CREDIBILITY MATERIAL:** When I moved to Atwater, California, my grandmother told me that I must visit Yosemite. "It is awesome," she said. My teenage mind thought, "Yeah, right! As if nature could be all that exciting." In the end, I became a regular customer of this adventure, peacefulness, and beauty...
Give them a reason to listen	**RELEVANCE TO AUDIENCE:** Yosemite has a similar effect on almost all visitors. Conservationist and Sierra Club founder John Muir stated it well in *Our National Parks* when he said, "Climb the mountains and get their good tidings..."
Give them a road map to your speech	**PREVIEW OF SPEECH:** Although my words and pictures could not do Yosemite justice, I hope to give you an idea of how wonderful it is by taking a glimpse at some general adventures the park has to offer, its waterfalls, and the awe-inspiring Half Dome.

The informative speech conclusion should leave your audience hungry for more knowledge about your topic. Your goal is to inspire them to pursue more information on their own.

CONCLUSION

What should your audience remember?	**SUMMARY STATEMENT:** Sadly, my speech has only given you a small piece of Yosemite, and it is ever changing with the seasons. In the winter, it is a vast wonderland of white beauty that is just indescribable. In the fall, the colors explode all around you. It is no wonder that John Muir spent so many years there...
What do you want them to do?	**AUDIENCE RESPONSE STATEMENT:** If you think national parks are only for family vacations and retirement visits, then you are seriously mistaken and will miss out on so much that you could experience and benefit from. Yosemite is a place to visit when you are young and healthy and can do all the physical adventures it has to offer.
Dazzle them one more time	**WOW STATEMENT:** Yosemite healed my soul. It taught me what is important in life and that we can miss so much beauty. Until I did the research for this speech, I didn't realize that I was feeling the same motivations as John Muir and Ansel Adams a century before me. Don't you want to experience the same?

→ See Chapter 7 for more details on writing introductions and conclusions.

PREPARATION OUTLINE FOR AN INFORMATIVE SPEECH

Your name   Class

Date   Instructor's name

Topic: Yosemite National Park

Specific purpose: To inform my classmates about Yosemite National Park.

Central idea: Yosemite National Park is more than a park; it is an experience that can change people through its adventures, its waterfalls, and the great Half Dome.

INTRODUCTION

Attention-getter: Several years ago, when I was about to embark on a serious life change and move half a world away from where I had lived since 18, I went to a place, a location, a mystical spot that had a healing and peaceful effect on me. I had to say "good-bye and thank you." Michele, my friend, and I had made it to the top of Half Dome in Yosemite National Park, and I felt like I was on top of the world! I was near heaven—almost close enough to reach out and touch it. I knew I would never forget this moment as a strange but oddly familiar feeling came over me. I had never felt so independent and free, nor had as much confidence in myself. I knew from then on that if I put my mind to it and had faith in myself, I could achieve anything.

Credibility material: When I moved to Atwater, California, my grandmother told me that I must visit Yosemite. "It is awesome," she said. My teenage mind thought, "Yeah, right! As if nature could be all that exciting." In the end, I became a regular customer of this adventure, peacefulness, and beauty, making the 45-minute drive to Yosemite often.

This outline is only one example. Be sure to follow your instructor's guidelines.

Using descriptive language and emotional appeal can grab your listeners' interest.

Relevance to audience: Yosemite has a similar effect on almost all visitors. Conservationist and Sierra Club founder John Muir stated it well in *Our National Parks* when he said, "Climb the mountains and get their good tidings. Nature's peace will flow into you as sunshine flows into trees. The winds will blow their own freshness into you, and the storms their energy, while cares will drop off like autumn leaves."

Preview of speech: Although my words and pictures could not do Yosemite justice, I hope to give you an idea of how wonderful it is by taking a glimpse at some general adventures the park has to offer, its waterfalls, and the awe-inspiring Half Dome.

(**Link:** Let's begin with some general attractions at the park.)

BODY

I. Yosemite's adventures are for all ages and cultures with varied interests.
    A. You can take it easy watching for wildlife like the black bear, bobcat, white-headed woodpecker, or mountain goat.
        1. According to the National Park Service's Web page for Yosemite, there are more than 250 species of animals in Yosemite.
        2. The wide range of species is mostly due to the diverse habitats that have not been degraded by human activity.
        3. John William Uhler, on the Web page "Yosemite National Park," states that Yosemite embraces nearly 1,200 square miles and ranges from 2,000 feet in altitude to over 13,000 feet above sea level.
    B. Physical activities you could engage in include hiking, rock climbing, swimming, horseback riding, camping, and white-water rafting.
        1. White-water rafting takes place on the ferocious Merced River during the spring and early summer months, when snow from atop the mountains is melting into the river.

An engaging quotation can provide expert testimony and effective emotive language, to help build your ethos (credibility).

Including your oral citations on the outline will help you remember them during the speech and prevent you from committing plagiarism.

2. Although the waters are ferocious, there are rafting trips available for beginners and advanced levels.

C. Nightlife activities include stargazing at a vast, open sky or even having a cocktail at the Iron Door Saloon.

(**Link:** When you are exhausted, you can relax and take in the breathtaking beauty of the world-famous waterfalls.)

II. Yosemite has several magnificent waterfalls, many of which are America's tallest.

A. May and June are the best months to visit most of the falls.

B. There are hundreds of waterfalls in the park, but they begin to disappear in July as the last of the snow melts from atop the mountains.

C. The most popular are Yosemite Falls, Bridalveil Fall, Vernal Fall, and Nevada Fall.

1. The roaring and crashing of the water is so loud when you get close that you can't hear someone talking right next to you.

2. It is overwhelming and makes you feel small.

3. It made me realize that my problems were even smaller.

4. As Paul Whitfield states in *The Rough Guide to Yosemite National Park,* Yosemite Falls is the highest in North America at 2,425 feet.

a. Yosemite Falls is actually two falls—Upper Yosemite Fall and Lower Yosemite Fall.

b. A steady breeze blows from the base of the lower fall due to the force of the air drawn down with the water and creates a steady spray.

c. During a full moon in the spring and early summer, the spray creates "moonbows" at the base of the falls.

Interesting detailed facts and statistics support the main point about waterfalls.

5. The Bridalveil Fall is a mere 620 feet, notes Whitfield.
   a. The National Park Service's Web page states that this is "often the first waterfall visitors see when entering the valley."
   b. In the spring, it is huge, but the rest of the year, it has its characteristic light, swaying flow that gives it its name.
   c. You can walk to the base up a steep trail.
6. Vernal Fall is 317 feet, according to Whitfield.
   a. This fall is still active in September and October, with peak flow in late May.
   b. This fall is not visible from the main valley, but you can see it from the Happy Isles Trail.
   c. The National Park Service notes that when the road is open, a wheelchair-accessible trail is available.
7. Nevada Fall is 594 feet.
   a. This fall is active in September and October as well, with peak flow in late May.
   b. This fall is not visible from the main valley, but you can see it from the Happy Isles Trail.
   c. When the road is open, a wheelchair-accessible trail is available, according to the National Park Service.

(**Link:** If you continue your hike past the Vernal and Nevada Falls, you will reach what is possibly the most photographed place in the park—Half Dome.)

III. Yosemite's most famous icon is Half Dome.
   A. According to the National Park Service, Half Dome rises to 5,000 feet above the Yosemite Valley and 8,800 feet above sea level.

Include your links in the outline, and use them where you need to guide your audience to the next thought (usually between parts of the speech and the main points).

B. Getting to the top of Half Dome is a 17-mile hike that takes nine to 12 hours to complete, round trip.

    1. You must complete the trip in one day.

    2. You do not still want to be on the mountain after dark.

C. The last 400 vertical feet is at an angle of 60 degrees that requires the use of steel cables and wooden two-by-fours to reach the summit.

D. If you have forgotten gloves, which we did, there are usually some stuffed under a rock at the base of the cables, left by fellow hikers and rangers.

E. Before climbing this last leg, be sure to heed the warning engraved on the steel sign that's embedded into the side of the granite mountain: "DO NOT ASCEND TO THE TOP OF HALF DOME IF THUNDERCLOUDS ARE VISIBLE ANYWHERE IN THE SKY. HALF DOME HAS BEEN STRUCK BY LIGHTNING IN EVERY MONTH OF THE YEAR."

    1. When we began to climb, the sky was a beautiful crystal-clear blue.

    2. After 15 minutes on top, in the midst of taking in the magnificence and feeling on top of the world, black clouds rolled in from out of nowhere.

    3. The 20 or so people on top of Half Dome were then all trying to get down at once and in a hurry, because both the peak and the steel cables attract lightning.

    4. We made it down fine by staying calm, but we were sad that we had to cut the summit visit so short after that long journey.

CONCLUSION

Summary statement: Sadly, my speech has only given you a small piece of Yosemite, and it is ever changing with the seasons. In the winter, it is

> Personal testimony with a hint of emotional drama can build up to your conclusion.

> Signal the conclusion with language and vocal delivery.

a vast wonderland of white beauty that is just indescribable. In the fall, the colors explode all around you. It is no wonder that John Muir spent so many years there and worked so hard to protect and defend it. And it is no wonder that Ansel Adams, the world-famous photographer, spent many years there photographing landscapes.

Audience response statement: If you think national parks are only for family vacations and retirement visits, then you are seriously mistaken and will miss out on so much that you could experience and benefit from. Yosemite is a place to visit when you are young and healthy and can do all the physical adventures it has to offer.

WOW statement: Yosemite healed my soul. It taught me what is important in life and that we can miss so much beauty. Until I did the research for this speech, I didn't realize that I was feeling the same motivations as John Muir and Ansel Adams a century before me. Don't you want to experience the same?

Evoke or give expert testimony whenever you can to build ethos.

References

DNC Parks & Resorts at Yosemite, Inc. (2010, June 3). Yosemite National Park. Retrieved from http://yosemitepark.com

Muir, J. (1901). *Our national parks*. New York, NY: Houghton Mifflin.

Uhler, J. W. (2007). Yosemite National Park. Retrieved from http://yosemite.national-park.com

U.S. Department of the Interior, National Park Service. (2008, December 8). Yosemite National Park. Retrieved from http://www.nps.gov/yose

Whitfield, P. (2008). *The rough guide to Yosemite National Park* (3rd ed.). New York, NY: Rough Guides.

Yosemite Association. (2010, April). Visit Yosemite National Park and the Sierra Nevada. Retrieved from http://yosemite.org

Include only sources cited in the speech and format them according to an acceptable style manual (APA style is shown).

How Should You Prepare to Present or Evaluate an Informative Speech?

1 Put Your Speech on Its Feet

2 Evaluate the Message and Presentation

Put Your Speech on Its Feet

You have finally made it to where you can put your speech on its feet. As you move to the delivery stage, you need to pay special attention to the final language choices you make. Effective language in an informative speech will assist in the learning process by being simple and clear, yet unique enough to be educational.

➜ See Chapter 8 for detailed help with using effective language.

Rehearse the speech several times to make it sound natural and conversational. First, practice the speech a few times from the preparation outline. Think about parts you know well, and cut them to create your delivery outline. Then practice and eliminate more until you only have words, phrases, and quotations you need to read for accuracy. Put this resulting outline on note cards or other easy-to-handle materials to use during your speech. Practice several more times with the delivery outline.

➜ See Chapter 5 for help creating a delivery outline and Chapter 9 for help with your delivery.

Presentation aids are not necessary in every speech, but they can be very beneficial to an informative speech by helping to:

- Build redundancy, which will help your audience remember information.
- Gain and keep your audience's attention.
- Summarize large portions of information.
- Build your credibility.

➜ See Chapter 10 for help with presentation aids.

Evaluate the Message and Presentation

Listening is crucial if the information in a speech is to be relayed effectively, and evaluating yourself and other speakers will help you improve your own techniques. If you are the speaker, think about how you can help your audience understand and retain information. If you are an audience member, listen critically. Evaluate the message for clarity, accuracy, and organization. Does the speech meet its informative goal? Assess the delivery. Keep a critical eye out for what works and what does not.

➔ See Part 5 if you need help with listening critically to and evaluating speeches.

Use this checklist, or guidelines provided by your instructor, to evaluate informative speeches. This list can also help guide you as you create and practice a speech.

CHECKLIST FOR EVALUATING THE INFORMATIVE SPEECH

TOPIC
...... Speech accomplished purpose to inform
...... Topic appropriate to speaker, audience, and occasion
...... Interesting topic

INTRODUCTION
...... Gained attention and interest
...... Established credibility
...... Indicated relevance to audience
...... Declared central idea
...... Previewed speech

BODY
...... Main points clear and obvious to the audience
...... Points followed an appropriate organizational strategy
...... Main points appropriately researched and supported
...... Main points supported with appropriate presentation aids when necessary
...... Oral citations included throughout speech
...... Linked parts of speech

CONCLUSION
...... Contained a summary statement
...... Offered an audience response statement
...... Effectively came to closure (WOW statement)

PRESENTATION
...... Language was clear, concise, and appropriate
...... Gestures/body movements were effective
...... Consistent and effective eye contact
...... Used vocal variety/emphasis/volume/rate
...... Used appropriate delivery style
...... Spoke with enthusiasm
...... Spoke with conviction and sincerity
...... Good use of delivery outline
...... Presentation aids appropriate to speech topic (if applicable)
...... Used presentation aids throughout entire speech (if applicable)
...... Used professional presentation aids (if applicable)
...... Speech met time requirements

Part 6: Review

CHAPTER 13 REVIEW QUESTIONS

1. What is informative speaking?

2. What are the four types of informative speeches? Explain each.

3. How do you determine the best type of informative speech to use?

4. Write three effective informative central ideas for your speech class. Explain why they are effective.

5. When conducting research for an informative speech, what should you consider when selecting effective support materials?

6. What organizational strategies work well with informative speaking?

7. Give examples of informative speeches using problem–solution and causal strategies. How would they differ from a persuasive speech using these strategies?

TERMS TO REMEMBER

Chapter 13
informative speaking (232)
speech to describe (233)
speech to explain (233)
speech to instruct (233)
speech to report (233)

PART 7
Speaking to Persuade

CHAPTER 14
Tools for Persuading   256

CHAPTER 15
The Persuasive Speech   278

14
TOOLS FOR PERSUADING

Introduction

Persuasion is a deliberate attempt by the speaker to create, reinforce, or change the attitudes, beliefs, values, and/or behaviors of the listener.

A DELIBERATE ATTEMPT...

If you remember the communication model in the Overview (see pages 10–11), you know that the act of communication grounds its beginning in the speaker and the speaker's deliberate attempt to send a message to the audience. For a communicative act to be persuasive, the speaker's intent or general purpose must be to persuade.

... TO CREATE, REINFORCE, OR CHANGE ATTITUDES, BELIEFS, VALUES, AND/OR BEHAVIORS

As Chapter 1 noted, *attitudes, beliefs*, and *values* make up your audience's identity.

➔ Review pages 22–23 in Chapter 1 on attitudes, beliefs, and values.

In addition, *behaviors* are unconcealed actions or reactions people have, often in response to some sort of stimuli. These audience attributes are what you deliberately plan to create, reinforce, or change when you persuade.

When an audience does not have the knowledge to hold a set attitude, belief, or value, or to understand why to behave a particular way, you persuade the audience to create or adopt the attitude, belief, value, or behavior you are advocating.

If the audience already agrees with you, you reinforce that attitude, belief, value, or behavior. At other times, you help your audience change existing attitudes, beliefs, values, and behaviors. Values are often the hardest to change.

CHAPTER 14 CONTENTS

What Should a Persuasive Speech Do? 258
1 Narrow Listeners' Options 258
2 Seek a Response 258
3 Support a Proposition of Fact, Value, or Policy 259
4 Rely on Varied and Valid Support Materials 260
5 Use Highly Structured Organization 260
6 Use Different Types of Appeals 260
7 Highlight Emotive and Stylistic Language 261
8 Emphasize Powerful and Direct Delivery 261
9 Acknowledge the Audience's Freedom to Decide 261

What Are the Traditional Appeals Used to Persuade? 262
1 Appeal to Pathos 262
2 Appeal to Mythos 263
3 Appeal to Ethos 264
4 Appeal to Logos 265

What Are the Modern Appeals Used to Persuade? 266
1 Appeal to Need 266
2 Appeal to Harmony 268
3 Appeal to Gain 269
4 Appeal to Commitment 269

What Are the Parts of an Argument? 270
1 Claim 270
2 Evidence 270
3 Warrants 271

What Are the Different Types of Arguments? 272
1 Argument by Deduction 272
2 Argument by Induction 274
3 Argument by Analogy 275
4 Argument by Cause 275
5 Argument by Authority 275

What Are Faulty Arguments? 276

CHAPTER 15: The Persuasive Speech 278
PART 7 Review 306

What Should a Persuasive Speech Do?

1 Narrow Listeners' Options

2 Seek a Response

3 Support a Proposition of Fact, Value, or Policy

4 Rely on Varied and Valid Support Materials

5 Use Highly Structured Organization

6 Use Different Types of Appeals

7 Highlight Emotive and Stylistic Language

8 Emphasize Powerful and Direct Delivery

9 Acknowledge the Audience's Freedom to Decide

1

Narrow Listeners' Options

Chapter 13 shows you that informative speaking is like giving a gift to your listeners. Persuasive speaking is like offering guidance to your listeners when they have several options to choose from and need your help to determine which is the best one. The job of the ethical persuasive speaker is to determine the best and safest option, support that decision logically, and offer information to the audience in a manner that allows them to make a wise decision. Persuasive speaking helps an audience limit their options and make sound choices.

2

Seek a Response

In the persuasive speech, you have an audience response in mind. That audience response determines which of the three types of persuasive speeches you will give.

- When you want to create a new or change an existing attitude, belief, value, or behavior for your audience, you are creating a persuasive speech to *convince*.

- When you overcome apathy in your audience or reinforce an existing attitude, belief, value, or behavior, you are creating a persuasive speech to *stimulate*.

- When you ask your audience to take action, you are giving a speech to *actuate*.

3

Support a Proposition of Fact, Value, or Policy

When you create a persuasive speech, you have an overarching argument (the body of the speech) that supports the assertion you are making in your central idea. The assertion you are making in your central idea is a proposition of fact, value, or policy.

For example, if your central idea is:

Foods marked organic are not necessarily healthier than conventional foods.

The proposition you are supporting with this central idea is:

Organic foods are not healthier than conventional foods.

And once you have identified your proposition, you can determine if it is a proposition of fact, value, or policy. Let's look at each category:

- *Proposition of fact:* Answers "What is accurate or not?" For example:

  SUVs are safe.

  Lee Harvey Oswald was part of a conspiracy to assassinate President John F. Kennedy.

  Genetically altered vegetables are not healthy.

- *Proposition of value:* Answers "What has worth or importance? What is good, wise, ethical, or beautiful?" For example:

  Funding NASA programs is a good use of tax dollars.

  Downloading or sharing music without payment or permission from the copyright holder is unethical.

  It is irresponsible to text message while driving.

- *Proposition of policy:* Answers "What procedures, plans, or courses of action need to be terminated and/or implemented?" This type of proposition can ask the audience to immediately act (To persuade my audience to volunteer to clean the city) or to simply agree (To persuade my audience that the city should outlaw smoking in public buildings). Other propositions of policy include:

  All homeowners should be required to recycle.

  The City of Jonestown should not implement a tax on pet owners.

  The recreation center should be open 24 hours a day.

  The state needs stiffer laws related to child abuse crimes.

In your organic foods speech, your proposition looks at the *accuracy* of the assertion that organic foods are not necessarily healthier than conventional foods. Therefore, your central idea seeks to support a *proposition of fact*.

Knowing the type of proposition your central idea supports will help you select an organizational strategy for creating the body of the speech, which will be made up of smaller arguments. These arguments will ultimately sustain your central idea—for instance, that organic is not necessarily healthier than conventional.

PRACTICING ETHICS

Persuasion is a complex process and a powerful practice that you must not take lightly. You must use the highest ethical standards when your intent is to persuade someone to think or act in a proposed way.

4
Rely on Varied and Valid Support Materials

Think about the last time someone misled you, either accidentally or intentionally, into thinking or doing something that you might not have if you had known all the facts. Most of the time when a deception of this type occurs, it is because someone did not make sure you were given accurate, complete, current, or trustworthy information. The outcome of this act could at worst be dangerous and at least negatively influence your relationship with the deceptive person for a very long time.

As the person crafting a persuasive message, you have a responsibility and a duty to prevent either accidental or intentional deception, and just "saying so" does not prove a point. You must use quality material such as testimony (mostly expert), statistics, comparisons, brief and detailed examples, and narration to support your points. Valid support materials are accurate, current, complete, trustworthy, suitable, and from ethical sources.

➔ See Part 2 for how to find and test support materials.

CONFIDENCE BOOSTER

A variety of quality, persuasive support materials is a must for effective persuasion. Knowing you have quality support materials will help you have confidence in your speech as well.

5
Use Highly Structured Organization

Your audience needs to follow every detail of the argument you are presenting, so your organization must be appropriate to the topic and precise down to the smallest detail. There are organizational strategies that are only appropriate for persuasive speaking, and some strategies will be better for certain topics. Once you have the overarching strategy for the speech (such as a problem–solution strategy), you need to think about how to arrange your arguments. If you want to have a successful persuasive speech, you must choose your organizational strategy carefully and arrange your support materials into effective arguments for the entire speech.

➔ See Chapters 5 and 6 for detailed discussion on how to organize your speech.

➔ See "What Are the Different Types of Arguments?" on pages 272–275 for how to arrange your arguments effectively.

6
Use Different Types of Appeals

Appeals (also called *proofs*) are the means by which you prove or establish the argument you are making. Because human beings often rationalize before they act or change, you must use a variety of appeals to persuade them. Appeals can be categorized as either *traditional* or *modern*.

➔ See "What Are the Traditional Appeals Used to Persuade?" and "What Are the Modern Appeals Used to Persuade?" on pages 262–269 for an extended discussion of appeals.

7
Highlight Emotive and Stylistic Language

As with all speeches, selecting the most effective language for a persuasive speech is very important. In persuasive speeches, using emotive and stylistic language helps your audience members follow your arguments, remember them, and be emotionally moved. Good persuasive speakers are extremely careful to follow the guidelines for language usage common to all speeches. For example, think about how you might use language devices like "therefore" and "as a result of" to signal clearly the bridge between two steps in an argument or how you can use language ethically to stir the emotions of your audience.

→ See Chapter 8 for how to use language successfully.

8
Emphasize Powerful and Direct Delivery

If you want to persuade an audience to agree with you, your delivery must be powerful and direct. Your voice and body language should suggest a high level of confidence and trust. You want an enthusiastic and varying vocal quality as well as good eye contact. Your posture should be lively and energetic. Your voice and body should be saying, "I believe what I am saying with my heart and soul. Isn't this exciting!"

→ See Chapter 9 for help with your speech delivery.

9
Acknowledge the Audience's Freedom to Decide

Imagine if you were forced to hold a belief you knew was not plausible, support a value that you did not agree with, or act in a way that went against everything you stand for. Good and ethical persuasion is a democracy. In other words, when a speaker engages in a good and ethical persuasive act, she or he allows and recognizes that anyone involved in that act is a free and equal participant in the decision-making process.

As the saying goes, "Life is full of choices," and your audience has the ultimate right to make whatever choices they wish. Forcing a choice or disrespecting someone for not selecting the choice you care about is not appropriate or ethical. Your job as a persuasive speaker is to present the best arguments possible so that the audience can make the best decision possible.

PRACTICING ETHICS
Persuasion is not coercion! **Coercion** is forcing somebody, via threats or intimidation, to do something against his or her will. Persuasion gives the person the necessary knowledge to change or act differently via her or his own free will.

261

What Are the Traditional Appeals Used to Persuade?

1 Appeal to Pathos
2 Appeal to Mythos
3 Appeal to Ethos
4 Appeal to Logos

In the fourth century BCE, Aristotle wrote in his *Rhetoric* about persuasion. Aristotle determined that you persuade others by three main appeals (pathos, ethos, and logos), and even a fourth one (mythos) under certain circumstances. Aristotle was so insightful when he came up with this system for understanding persuasion that it still applies today. Although he favored logos, Aristotle realized that the best persuasive speech uses some combination of the four.

1

Appeal to Pathos

An appeal to **pathos** deals with the listener's emotions. In other words, you can use your audience's sympathy and imagination to affect their attitudes, values, beliefs, or behaviors.

Eliciting your audience's emotions is a conjuring process and not a command! You must use vivid description and emotive language to stir your audience's sense of emotions such as fear, sympathy, empathy, happiness, or anger.

You see this type of appeal often in the media. The January 12, 2010, earthquake that devastated Haiti offered many opportunities for the news media and relief organizations to appeal to the world's emotions through video and photos of the people of Haiti. In the months after the quake, many news stories and appeals for money included pictures of women, men, and children covered in dust, being pulled from the rubble, or waiting in long lines for food and water.

Appeal to human emotion is often an effective way to advance a cause. Vivid description, especially by trusted experts who have firsthand knowledge, can be very moving.

PRACTICING ETHICS
Appeals to emotions should always be used in conjunction with a variety of other types of appeals. For the best effect, pair appeals of pathos with logos.

Imagine giving a speech to persuade your audience to donate to Haitian relief and using this quotation from the Web site for the International Committee of the Red Cross (www.icrc.org), immediately before calling for an audience response.

> According to Riccardo Conti, the ICRC's head of the delegation in Haiti, "Amid the crying and wailing, people are spending the night outside. People are trying to comfort each other. What you are hearing in the street are the prayers of thanks of those who surivived." These Haitians survived the quake, and now it is time for us to help them survive the aftermath.

Although it may seem unethical to play with your audience's emotions, philosophers and rhetoricians from Aristotle to George Campbell and Richard Whately have argued that logic alone may not be enough to get people to act. Appeals to emotions should never be used alone; but depending on the topic and your audience's relationship with that topic, you may need emotional appeals to put your audience in the right mood to accept your logical argument, or you might need the logical argument to frame the appeal to their emotions.

Examples and narratives (stories) are often the most effective support materials for appealing emotionally. When you give speeches to persuade your audience to donate time or money to help a cause, you can humanize the cause for the audience members by using extended examples (ministories) about the people they will help.

2
Appeal to Mythos

The appeal to mythos is often fueled by emotion and not always viewed as a noteworthy appeal. **Mythos** relates to a sense of one's history in the larger culture and the need to be a member of that culture. For example, our sense of what it means to be a woman or man evolves from a community-accepted understanding of what is valued in women and men.

Other aspects of our cultural identity have a mythic appeal as well. In the United States, patriotism, nationalism, faith, pride, and valor are strong traditions and values. For example, you could appeal to mythos in a speech advocating buying American:

> In conclusion, we have seen that American-made products tend to be safer because we have stricter regulations and that buying them keeps our people employed and puts money back into local economies. So, be an American—buy American!

Most cultures create and perpetuate their mythic identity in the stories they weave into legends, folktales, music, and poetry. When you appeal to mythos in a speech, you often use narratives (stories) to create a strong sense of cultural identity, which, in turn, moves your audience to a change in belief, attitude, value, or behavior. For instance, you might use mythos in a speech about increasing taxes to fund local schools:

> Determination and knowledge are what built this great country, and we need to support our country by supporting our schools.

A downside to mythos is that it can promote **ethnocentrism**, or the notion that one's culture or viewpoint is superior to that of others.

3

Appeal to Ethos

Ethos is the credibility inspired by the speaker's character, or what Aristotle called *moral character*. You can have a strong argument and emotional appeal, but if the audience questions your character, you will have trouble persuading them.

The key to using your credibility effectively is to realize that it resides in *how your audience views you* and not in how you view yourself. You may have the best of intentions, but if your audience doesn't trust you, your credibility and persuasive ability will be low. Aristotle claimed that the speaker's credibility evolved from *competency* and *character*. In modern times, a third trait, *charisma*, has been recognized.

- *Competency* is the audience's perception of how knowledgeable you are about your topic. The more knowledgeable you appear, the greater the likelihood of persuading your audience. Mentioning your related experience/education, citing a variety of support materials from credible sources, and presenting a polished speech will help demonstrate your competency.

- *Character* is the audience's perception of your intentions and of the concern you have for the audience. Do they see you as trustworthy, objective, honest, and similar to them? Finding ways to connect with the audience, demonstrating that you have investigated alternatives and oppositions to your positions, and emphasizing your concern for the audience rather than just for yourself will build your character.

- *Charisma* is the audience's perception of your personality. Do they see you as energetic, friendly, approachable, and vocally as well as physically pleasing? Be confident and assertive in a positive manner. Use language and gestures to demonstrate your dynamic personality and excitement about the topic.

Your ethos progresses through three levels:

- The *initial level* of ethos is the credibility your audience perceives in you before your speech starts. The audience may have preconceived feelings about you that give you either high or low credibility. They may not know you at all, which might make them apathetic, or they may assign you a level of credibility by how you are introduced, who introduces you, or the reason for the speaking event.

- The *derived level* of ethos is the credibility your audience assigns you during your speech based on the content and effectiveness of the speech.

- The *terminal level* of ethos is your credibility with your audience after you have finished your speech. Your ability to handle questions after the speech, your exiting behavior, and any follow-up comments you make after the end of your speech can influence the level of credibility your audience assigns you.

The appeal to ethos also includes the ethos of your sources. You audience must view your sources within the speech as accurate, recent, and without bias. You must identify your sources and demonstrate why they are trustworthy.

→ See Part 2 for discussion of source credibility and citations.

4

Appeal to Logos

The human ability to use logic can be a powerful persuasive tool. When you appeal to logic, or ***logos***, in a speech, you appeal to the listener's ability to reason through statistics, facts, and expert testimony to reach a conclusion. Therefore, you engage in *reasoning*—the rational thinking humans do to reach conclusions or to justify beliefs or acts. You build arguments to influence your audience's beliefs, values, attitudes, and behaviors. The rest of this chapter will explain arguments in more detail, but here is the basic format of an argument:

1. Make a statement.
2. Offer support materials related to the statement as evidence.
3. Draw your conclusion.

For example, Katie is a student in a state that is considering a ban on cell phone use while driving. Katie, whose best friend died in a crash while using her phone, will argue in her speech for supporting the ban. She creates her first argument using this basic format.

STATEMENT:	Cell phone use while driving is pervasive.
EVIDENCE:	As of October 2008, 266 million people in the United States subscribed to some form of wireless communication, including cell phones. This is up from 4.3 million in 1990 (Insurance Information Institute, 2008).
EVIDENCE:	In 2006, a study reported that at any moment during the day, 8 percent of all drivers are on their cell phones (Siegel).
CONCLUSION:	Given the number of people subscribing to cell phones and the number of drivers using them, it would be difficult to drive anywhere and not meet someone using a cell phone.

Katie's next argument uses this same format and continues to support her overall purpose.

STATEMENT:	Cell phone use while driving is dangerous.
EVIDENCE:	A National Highway Traffic Safety Administration study showed that 80 percent of crashes and 65 percent of near crashes involve driver inattention three seconds before the event, with the most common distraction being cell phones (Insurance Information Institute, 2008).
EVIDENCE:	Conversations using a cell phone demand greater continuous concentration from the driver, diverting attention away from the road (Insurance Information Institute, 2008).
EVIDENCE:	A 2005 Australian study showed that crashes were four times more likely while drivers were talking on cell phones and for 10 minutes after the phone call than when a cell phone was not used (Healy, 2008).
CONCLUSION:	Numerous studies suggest that cell phone usage while driving is dangerous.

This material is only a part of Katie's speech, but you can begin to see how she logically leads her audience to the same conclusions she has reached.

What Are the Modern Appeals Used to Persuade?

1 Appeal to Need
2 Appeal to Harmony
3 Appeal to Gain
4 Appeal to Commitment

Although much of how you persuade relies on the classical appeals of logic, credibility, emotions, and cultural identity, the modern speaker can use other types of motivational appeals. Modern theorists argue that motivation to change can be grounded less in the logical and more in the psychological. In other words, people are motivated by such psychological appeals as meeting their needs, creating a sense of harmony, gaining something, or acting out of commitment.

1

Appeal to Need

This modern method of persuasion recognizes that your audience members have needs they see as important and necessary to fulfill. Demonstrating, when possible, how your topic will help your audience fulfill a need can be an effective motivator.

In Chapter 1, you learned about Abraham Maslow's *hierarchy of needs* theory, which states that humans have a set of needs that must be met. These fit into five hierarchical categories, beginning with *physiological needs* and then progressing up to *safety, social, self-esteem*, and *self-actualization needs*. They are hierarchical in that you must meet the lower, more basic needs before you can progress up to the higher ones.

Appealing to your audience's needs makes for an effective persuasive speech. With this type of appeal, you collect and arrange support materials to demonstrate that what you are suggesting in your speech fulfills a need of the audience members.

Described by Alan Monroe in *Principles and Types of Speech*, Monroe's motivated sequence is a classic organizational strategy using an appeal to need (see Chapter 6, page 129). In the second, third, and fourth stages of the sequence (highlighted on the next page), you thoughtfully and intentionally demonstrate to your audience that they have a need; propose a solution to them that will satisfy the need; and then help them visualize the benefits. This appeal relies on you knowing the audience's needs and paying attention to the hierarchy. For example, trying to convince a group of recently unemployed autoworkers to contribute to a 401K retirement fund will not be effective, because they have other important financial needs.

THE HIERARCHY OF NEEDS

Self-actualization needs relate to the need to reach your highest goal or potential.

Self-esteem needs relate to the need for respect or being viewed by others as important, which leads to feeling good about oneself.

Social needs relate to the need to belong or to be in lasting relationships, such as intimate partnerships, friendships, families, and social groups.

Safety needs are needs for overall security and protection, such as a sense of safety in your home, relationships, or shelter.

Physiological needs are needs for food, water, air, general comfort, and sex.

(Pyramid diagram)

- SELF-ACTUALIZATION NEEDS
- SELF-ESTEEM NEEDS
- SOCIAL NEEDS
- SAFETY NEEDS
- PHYSIOLOGICAL NEEDS

MONROE'S MOTIVATED SEQUENCE

ATTENTION STAGE
You direct your audience's attention toward you and your topic.

NEED STAGE
You demonstrate to your audience that they have one of the needs in the hierarchy.

SATISFACTION STAGE
You propose a solution to meet the need.

VISUALIZATION STAGE
You help the audience visualize the benefits of the solution.

ACTION STAGE
You tell the audience what they must do to adopt the solution and achieve satisfaction.

→ See Chapters 6 and 15 for more on using Monroe's motivated sequence to structure a persuasive speech.

2 Appeal to Harmony

In his book *A Theory of Cognitive Dissonance*, Leon Festinger introduced **Cognitive Dissonance Theory**, which emphasizes the human need to be in a harmonious state (consonant state). However, sometimes, there are conflicting attitudes, values, beliefs, ideas, or behaviors that cause an inharmonious feeling (dissonant state).

For example, think about how you feel when you eat really good pizza or chocolate cake. Part of your mind is happy with the taste of the food and eating it all, but another part of your conscience is reminding you that eating a lot of pizza or cake is not healthy. You end up feeling guilty, or in a dissonant state of wanting more of the good food but torn about the amount of calories and/or fat. Once there, you rationalize your way to a harmonious state by either convincing yourself that eating a lot of pizza or cake is okay because you will diet tomorrow or stopping because your healthy side wins out.

People are driven to reduce a dissonant feeling, and as a speaker, you can use that drive to motivate your audience to agree with you. For example, if you are giving a speech to an audience you know believes in the greenhouse effect, you might convince them to reduce their carbon footprint by creating a dissonant feeling in them. One way to do that would be to show them how big their carbon footprint is and how it directly relates to environmental destruction.

Creating an uncomfortable feeling in your audience can be unpredictable, especially if their beliefs in what you are discussing are deeply seated. Just because you create dissonance does not mean your audience will automatically accept your solution. They may find a way to discredit you or your sources, they may stop listening, or they may simply hear what they want to hear by tuning in only to parts of your message. When an audience has deeply held feelings about your topic, you might choose not to create dissonance for them.

PRACTICING ETHICS

As with any form of appeal, the appeal to harmony should be used with care. Do not take advantage of your audience's need for a harmonious state. It is your ethical responsibility to avoid creating unnecessary dissonance that might cloud your audience's judgment or ability to reason.

3
Appeal to Gain

When you appeal to gain, you are recognizing that most people weigh or evaluate their actions based on what the actions might cost them. In *Belief, Attitude, Intention, and Behavior*, Martin Fishbein and Icek Ajzen formulated a theory that helps you understand how this appeal works. Their theory, the **Expectancy-Outcome Values Theory**, suggests that people will evaluate the cost, benefit, or value related to making a change in an attitude, value, belief, or behavior to decide if it is worthwhile or not. People in a situation like this will ask questions such as:

- Is this a good or bad idea?
- Will my family, friends, or colleagues approve or disapprove?
- If they disapprove, what are the ramifications?
- Are those ramifications worth it?
- Will my family, friends, or colleagues think better of me if I do this?

People will try to determine what they will gain or lose by changing. During a persuasive speech, if you can demonstrate to your audience that what you are asking to change or do will be a gain and not a loss, you may be able to motivate them to agree.

For example, if you are trying to convince a group of college students that they should engage in community service or sign up for an internship because future potential employers like to see these activities on résumés, you are appealing to the students' need to gain more than the time it will take to participate in the service or internship.

4
Appeal to Commitment

Another appeal recognizes how audience members might react to your message depending upon their relationship with the topic. The **Elaboration Likelihood Model**, presented by Richard Petty and John Cacioppo in *Communication and Persuasion*, suggests that people process persuasive messages based on their commitment or involvement. The model argues that people will process your message by one of two ways: central processing or peripheral processing.

Audience members who are motivated and want to think critically about your topic are engaging in *central processing*. Those who see your message as irrelevant, uninteresting, or too complex will not pay close enough attention to be critical and are engaging in *peripheral processing*.

Think about how you listen in a class you do not find interesting. Then think about how you listen in your favorite class. Your level of commitment and involvement makes you process those courses differently. In the less interesting course, your listening may be shallow—just enough to get the facts to pass the test. In your favorite course, you may take notes, read before class, and participate in discussion. You are excited about the course.

As a speaker, you can use this knowledge to create a message relevant to the majority of your audience's interests. The challenge with this type of appeal is that you need to know your audience and what they will process centrally. This heightens the significance of conducting effective audience analysis.

→ See Chapter 1 for more information about audience analysis.

What Are the Parts of an Argument?

1 Claim

2 Evidence

3 Warrants

An *argument* is a reason or a series of reasons you give to support an assertion. Arguments have three parts: a claim, evidence, and warrants.

1 Claim

Earlier you learned that all persuasive speeches support a proposition of fact, value, or policy and that your central idea summarizes or previews what you specifically want to assert. When you make a smaller argument within the body of the speech, you will have a claim that acts just as your central idea does for the whole speech. The *claim* of an argument is the assertion you are making and will be a claim of fact, value, or policy. Each claim should be a single, concise sentence. For example:

CLAIM OF FACT: People who wear seat belts tend to take better care of their health.

CLAIM OF VALUE: Owning a gun is wrong.

CLAIM OF POLICY: All public buildings should be smoke-free.

Rarely, if ever, can you prove that a claim is 100 percent correct. Claims can be qualified as "possible," "probable," or "beyond doubt."

2 Evidence

The support materials you have gathered become *evidence*, or the information that proves your claim. Evidence comes in the form of examples, facts, definitions, testimony, and statistics. Let's say your speech is on the following:

CLAIM OF POLICY: The city should change the current city ordinance to allow citizens to own a small flock of hens within the city limits.

To support your claim, you consult books for evidence such as the fact that naturally raised chickens and eggs have a better nutrient value than factory-farmed chickens.

3

Warrants

Just presenting evidence will not necessarily demonstrate that your claim is accurate. British philosopher Stephen Toulmin, in his book *The Uses of Argument*, suggests that you also need **warrants**, or assumptions that act as links between the evidence and the claim. This step is where you help your audience draw a conclusion about your claim and the evidence provided.

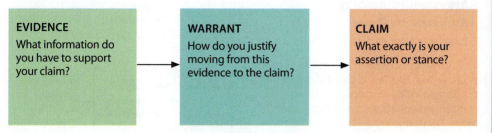

EVIDENCE
What information do you have to support your claim?

WARRANT
How do you justify moving from this evidence to the claim?

CLAIM
What exactly is your assertion or stance?

Staying with your topic about urban chickens, if you take two bits of information—one about the health benefits of chicken in general and one that naturally raised chickens tend to be more nutritious than chickens raised on factory farms—you could support your claim like this:

EVIDENCE
Chicken is a great source of protein. Naturally raised chickens have a better nutrient value than those raised on factory farms.

WARRANT
Anyone raising his or her own chickens has access to a more nutrient-enriched form of protein.

CLAIM
Local citizens should be allowed to raise chickens.

There are three types of warrants that can link the evidence to the claim:

- *Authoritative warrants* assume that the claim is accurate based on the credibility of the source of the support materials.

- *Motivational warrants* are based on the speaker's and audience's needs and values.

- *Substantive warrants* are based on the reliability of the support materials.

In the urban chickens example above, the warrant is motivational, based on the value of healthy eating—that naturally raised chickens are a desirable nutrient-rich source of protein.

Warrants can be expressed or unexpressed, but in order for your argument to work, your audience must either intuitively understand or be shown the connection.

What Are the Different Types of Arguments?

1 Argument by Deduction
2 Argument by Induction
3 Argument by Analogy
4 Argument by Cause
5 Argument by Authority

The differences between types of arguments relate to how they are constructed after you create your claim. Remember, a claim is a concise sentence stating what you want to prove. For example:

> All dolphins, whales, and porpoises are mammals.

Once you know what you want your audience to accept, you need to decide what type of argument you want to construct. There are five types of arguments.

1
Argument by Deduction

Argument by deduction constructs a series of general statements (known as *premises*) that together prove the claim/conclusion correct.

When arguing by deduction, you can use one of two formats: a *syllogism* or an *enthymeme*. The **syllogism** is the classical form of deductive reasoning with this structure.

MAJOR PREMISE
All mammals feed their young milk via mammary glands located on the female of the species.

Includes a generally accepted statement

MINOR PREMISE
All female dolphins, whales, and porpoises feed their young milk produced by mammary glands on the female.

Includes a specific observation

CONCLUSION
Therefore, all dolphins, whales, and porpoises are mammals.

Includes a statement that ties the major and minor premises together

When you use deductive arguments in a speech, you will not usually be so methodical in how you phrase the argument. This same syllogism might be presented as:

According to scientists, there are several characteristics that define mammals, but the most significant is how they feed their young. All mammals have the ability to feed their young through mammary glands located on the body of the female of the species. Dolphins, whales, and porpoises all have this unique ability to allow their offspring to suckle. We consider dolphins, whales, and porpoises to be marine mammals.

MAJOR PREMISE

MINOR PREMISE

CONCLUSION

Sometimes, one of your premises will be obvious or common knowledge and you will not need to state it; this type of truncated syllogism is an **enthymeme**. In the example below, you would drop the obvious minor premise—that Fred is a human—and jump to the conclusion.

MAJOR PREMISE
All humans are mortal.

CONCLUSION
Therefore, Fred is mortal.

Deductive reasoning must present a sound argument. To be sound, the major and minor premises as well as the conclusion must be factual; if they are not, the result is a *faulty syllogism*. For example:

MAJOR PREMISE
All environmentalists are vegetarians.

MINOR PREMISE
Yeon is an environmentalist.

CONCLUSION
Therefore, Yeon is a vegetarian.

FAULTY SYLLOGISM

The major premise here is false because many environmentalists are not vegetarians. Yeon may be an environmentalist, but that does not necessarily mean Yeon is a vegetarian. Likewise, Yeon may be an environmentalist and a vegetarian, but being a vegetarian may have nothing to do with being an environmentalist. To make a sound deductive argument, you want to ask: "Can I prove the major and minor premises are true? Is the conclusion reasonable, given the two premises?"

2

Argument by Induction

Whereas deduction deals with certainty, induction predicts probability. When you construct an **argument by induction**, you will argue from specific cases to a general statement suggesting something to be likely based on the specific cases. We often use this type of reasoning in our everyday lives.

For example, if you buy a box of assorted chocolates and you eat three or four pieces in the box only to discover they are stale, you do not keep eating and assume the next one will not be stale. Instead, you reason that if the first three or four pieces (the specific) are stale, the whole box (the general) is stale. If you check out gas prices at 9 or 10 gas stations in your city and they are all $2.79, you reason that gas in your town will probably cost $2.79 everywhere.

The reliability of these claims resides in the quantity and quality of the specific cases. The same is true for a speech using argument by induction. The induction can be based on examples, statistics, facts, or testimony.

This diagram demonstrates how you might reason through specific cases to support the claim "ZZtravel.com is the cheapest and best place to book spring-break trips."

SPECIFIC CASE #1
Student A purchased airline tickets and hotel reservations to Cancun from ZZtravel.com because the service was the cheapest.

SPECIFIC CASE #2
Student B rented a car and made hotel reservations for a trip to Orlando from the same online service because it was the cheapest she could locate.

SPECIFIC CASE #3
Student C purchased airline tickets to make a trip back home to Oregon from the same online service because it was the cheapest.

SPECIFIC CASE #4
Student D purchased airline tickets and a Eurail pass for a trip to Germany from the same online service because it was the cheapest he found.

CLAIM
ZZtravel.com has the best rates for a variety of travel needs and destinations.

TIP: Inductive Arguments

Inductive arguments are useful when you know your audience is against what you are about to claim.

3

Argument by Analogy

When you create an **argument by analogy**, you conclude that something will be accurate for one case if it is true for another similar case. In other words, if it is true for A, it is true for B because they are so similar.

For example, many people who argue for a universal health care plan in the United States do so by making a comparison to Canada. Their claim based on an argument of analogy might be something like this:

> Because the United States and Canada are so similar and a universal plan works in Canada, then universal health care will work in the United States.

As in this example, you will most often use an argument by analogy when giving a persuasive speech on a proposition of policy.

As discussed in Chapter 4, there are two types of analogies: literal and figurative. An argument based on literal analogies (the comparison of two similar things) works the best. Rarely will a figurative analogy (a metaphorical comparison of dissimilar things) prove a claim, and most of the time, a figurative analogy ends in faulty reasoning.

CHECKLIST for Creating an Argument
- ❏ Is my claim a concise, declarative sentence?
- ❏ Do I have enough quality evidence to support my claim?
- ❏ What are my warrants or justifications for moving from the evidence to the claim?
- ❏ Which type of argument will fit best with the claim I want my audience to accept?
- ❏ Have I followed the guidelines for correctly constructing this type of argument?

4

Argument by Cause

Argument by cause attempts to demonstrate a relationship between two events or factors in which one of the events or factors causes the other. This form of reasoning may take an effect-to-cause or cause-to-effect form. Here are two claims suggesting this type of argument.

The increase in violence in our public schools is the effect of increased violence in the entertainment world.	EFFECT-TO-CAUSE
Procrastinating on your assignments will cause you to get lower grades.	CAUSE-TO-EFFECT

5

Argument by Authority

Argument by authority locates its power in the ethos of the testimony of others you might use to support your claim. When you use this type of argument, you collect testimony from individuals the audience will perceive as experts on the topic.

Argument by authority works only if the audience perceives the experts as credible and unbiased. For example, if you wanted to support the claim that stoplight cameras decrease accidents and save lives, you might consider quoting the chiefs of police in towns and cities already using these devices. For maximum effect, you should quote your sources directly, and you should always give their credentials.

What Are Faulty Arguments?

When a speaker creates an argument, she or he can unintentionally or intentionally create a faulty argument or error in logic known as a **fallacy**. Fallacies occur when evidence is used incorrectly or the interpretation of the evidence is incorrect.

As a speaker and as an audience member, it is important for you to be able to recognize when an argument falls apart or does not make sense, making it a bad argument. When you create a speech, always double-check that you are correctly using and interpreting your evidence for each argument.

There are numerous types of faulty arguments, but the fallacies in the table on the next page are some of the most common. Edward Corbett and Robert Connors in *Classical Rhetoric for the Modern Student* and Steven Toulmin, Richard Rieke, and Allan Janik in *An Introduction to Reasoning* offer more detailed discussions of these and additional fallacies.

PRACTICING ETHICS

Using a fallacy to persuade is unethical. You should never do so intentionally, and you should work to prevent fallacies from occurring in your speech by mistake.

FALLACY	WHAT IS IT?	EXAMPLE	HOW CAN YOU AVOID IT?
Hasty generalization	Drawing a general conclusion without sufficient support materials	"I have had major problems with my car. This brand of car is worthless."	Use a significant number of current and quality cases to argue from the specific to the general.
Faulty use of authority	Using testimony from someone who is not an authority on the subject	Celebrities endorsing a product that they are not experts on	Make sure the person is a recognized expert related to your topic.
Post hoc ergo propter hoc	Assuming that because one event comes after another, the first causes the second	"Eating black-eyed peas on New Year's Day brings good luck during the year."	Verify with valid support materials that one event causes the other.
Ad hominem	Attacking the person instead of challenging an argument	"How can you question my education policy? You don't have children in our schools."	Focus your arguments on issues, not people.
Either-or fallacy	Considering only two options when there are more possible	"Either you support prayer in schools or you are an atheist."	Never set up an either-or argument. Be inclusive when offering options.
Slippery slope	Arguing that a small event sets off a chain reaction to disaster	"If you allow for an increase in taxes, the government will just want more."	Always consider the middle ground as an end result. Do not be overly dramatic.
Begging the question	Assuming the conclusion of the argument in a premise	"Women shouldn't be allowed to join men's sports teams. The teams are for men only."	Make sure your premises lead to your claim and the claim is independent of the premises.
Non sequitur	Not connecting an argument's conclusion to the premises	"Stephanie drives a large truck, so she must own cattle."	Be sure every step of your argument leads to the next and connects to the claim.
Appeal to tradition	Assuming something is best or correct because it is traditional	"Of course this detergent is best. This formula hasn't changed for 40 years."	Base claims on solid evidence and use tradition only to supplement evidence.
Ad populum	Arguing a claim is accurate because many people believe it	"Lots of people text while driving and don't wreck. As long as I'm careful, nothing will happen."	Use popular opinion only to support other forms of evidence.

15
THE PERSUASIVE SPEECH

Introduction

Jade is enrolled in an Introduction to Public Speaking class, and her next speech is due in a few weeks. The assignment states:

> The general purpose of this speech is to persuade. The topic of your speech should be a noteworthy current issue with meaning for and the potential to influence the lives of your audience. To meet this goal, you must analyze your classmates and select a topic that they connect with enough so that you might create, reinforce, or change their attitudes, beliefs, or values and/or bring them to action.

> The time limit is nine minutes. At least three sources are required for this speech (you will most likely need more to do an effective job). You must hand in a printed copy of the preparation outline as your ticket to the lectern the day of your speech. Remember to be natural, enthusiastic, engaging, confident, and sure. Use effective vocal qualities and body language.

Jade is a bit concerned about the complexity of creating a persuasive speech and finding the right topic. She is excited about engaging her classmates in a debate about a current topic. She remembers something her instructor said: "The complexity of creating a persuasive speech may be a daunting chore at first, but taking it one step at a time will make it a doable task."

This chapter will help you and Jade walk through the process of creating a persuasive speech. This process is not fundamentally different from that of any other type of speech. So relax and enjoy the energy and impact you can have with persuasion.

CHAPTER 14: Tools for Persuading   256

CHAPTER 15 CONTENTS

What Is the Creative Process for Persuasive Speaking?   280

How Do You Choose and Research a Persuasive Topic?   282
1 Get to Know the Audience and Situation   282
2 Create a Persuasive Idea Bank   283
3 Select and Narrow Your Persuasive Topic   284
4 Determine the Best Type of Persuasive Speech   285
5 Identify Your Specific Purpose   286
6 Identify Your Central Idea   287
7 Create a Working Outline   288
8 Conduct Your Research   289

How Do You Construct the Persuasive Outline?   290

How Do You Organize a Persuasive Speech?   292
1 Recognize Your Organizational Strategy   292
2 Commit to a Strategy   293
3 Construct Main Points   294
4 Organize Support Materials into Arguments   294
5 Compose Your Introduction and Conclusion   295

How Should You Prepare to Present or Evaluate a Persuasive Speech?   304
1 Put Your Speech on Its Feet   304
2 Evaluate the Message and Presentation   305

PART 7 Review   306

What Is the Creative Process for Persuasive Speaking?

Influencing others through a speech is a remarkable task requiring you to be diligent and ethical in some ways that differ slightly from those of informative speaking. This chart briefly outlines the five basic activities you will use to create an effective persuasive speech. Remember, being creative is not a linear process, so move back and forth between each activity as you mold your speech.

1 STARTING

→ 2 RESEARCHING

HOW DO YOU CHOOSE AND RESEARCH A PERSUASIVE TOPIC?

→ See page 282

Know who you are speaking to as well as where, when, and why you are speaking.

Select the persuasive topic that best fits you, your audience, and the occasion. Craft a central idea that defines what you want to persuade the audience of, keeping in mind the audience's relationship to the topic.

Understand how to evaluate, choose, and use a variety of support materials. Good persuasion requires a wide variety of accurate, current, complete, and suitable materials.

Find support materials through the Internet, the library, interviews, and surveys.

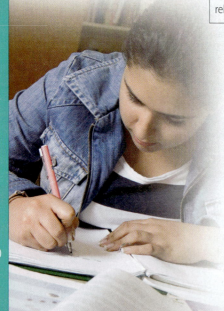

3 CREATING

HOW DO YOU CONTRUCT THE PERSUASIVE OUTLINE?

→ See page 290

Start with a working outline, create a preparation outline, and include a source page. Create a delivery outline.

HOW DO YOU ORGANIZE A PERSUASIVE SPEECH?

→ See page 292

Identify your main points. Use an organizational strategy appropriate for a persuasive speech, and carefully construct your arguments.

Gain the audience's attention and set up your speech in the introduction. Sum up, suggest an audience response, and end with impact in the conclusion.

4 PRESENTING

HOW SHOULD YOU PREPARE TO PRESENT OR EVALUATE A PERSUASIVE SPEECH?

→ See page 304

Use language that is familiar, concrete, and appropriate. Use vivid language and unique speech devices to appeal to your audience logically and emotionally.

Practice your delivery so that you are natural, enthusiastic, confident, and engaging.

Consider using presentation aids to help your audience understand evidence and follow arguments.

5 LISTENING & EVALUATING

Be an active and effective listener who can overcome barriers to listening and who shares responsibility in the persuasive process.

Determine the effectiveness and appropriateness of a speech's topic, support materials, organization, and language. Evaluate the speaker's delivery and ethics.

Be a critical thinker.

How Do You Choose and Research a Persuasive Topic?

1 **Get to Know the Audience and Situation**

2 **Create a Persuasive Idea Bank**

3 **Select and Narrow Your Persuasive Topic**

4 **Determine the Best Type of Persuasive Speech**

5 **Identify Your Specific Purpose**

6 **Identify Your Central Idea**

7 **Create a Working Outline**

8 **Conduct Your Research**

1

Get to Know the Audience and Situation

Taking the time to know your audience and the situation is even more significant with the persuasive speech than with the informative speech.

Think about what you are trying to do. You are going to attempt to change, influence, or reinforce the attitudes, beliefs, values, and/or behaviors of an audience. If you do not know where your audience stands on your topic, how the situation will influence them, or what their needs are, you cannot expect to persuade them.

Use the review checklist below to help you analyze your audience and situation. Later in this chapter, you (and Jade from the introduction) will also learn how to target the group you aim to appeal to the most.

➔ See Chapter 1 for more on how to analyze your audience and the situation.

REVIEW CHECKLIST for Audience and Situation Analysis

❏ What are the personal traits (age, race, gender, etc.) of my audience? Are there additional characteristics to consider, such as nationality or disabilities?

❏ What are their needs and knowledge level?

❏ What are their attitudes, beliefs, values, and behaviors related to my topic?

❏ Why is the audience here?

❏ What are the event details (location, time, etc.)?

❏ What are the audience's expectations because of the occasion?

❏ How do these factors influence my topic or type of persuasive speech?

2
Create a Persuasive Idea Bank

You know your general purpose is to persuade, so you need to create an idea bank full of topics that are debatable—in other words, there are two or more different opinions people may hold about each topic. Use the method from Chapter 2 to create your idea bank. This bank can contain words only, but phrases may be more beneficial because they allow you to consider some of the multiple points of view.

→ See Chapter 2 for more information on creating an idea bank.

Databases like EBSCOhost, CQ (Congressional Quarterly) Researcher, CQ Weekly, and Opposing Viewpoints Resource Center or newspapers and magazines like the *New York Times*, your local newspaper, *Time* Magazine, and *The Week* are all great places to locate current persuasive topics. Jade decided to go to the Opposing Viewpoints Resource Center database on her library Web site and to look through the local city newspaper. You can see Jade's idea bank on page 284, where she has begun to narrow it down to her final topic.

Below is an example of what you might see in a database like EBSCOhost.

In the EBSCOhost database, you can search for a specific topic or use a general keyword like "controversy." This example uses the Visual Search function.

Categories related to the search— such as U.S. Supreme Court cases— can offer current, debatable topics.

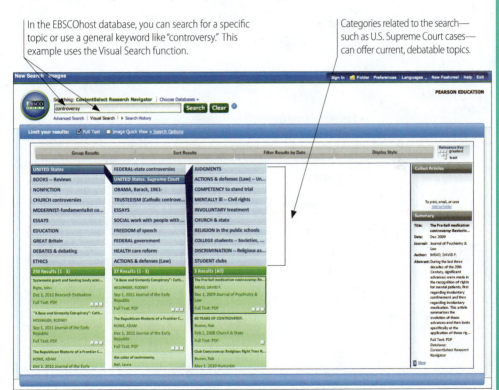

3

Select and Narrow Your Persuasive Topic

Once you have a list of broad topics and some that begin to narrow toward a viewpoint, you may still not know which is best for you, your audience, and the situation. Use the process from Chapter 2 to further narrow your idea bank. For a persuasive speech, especially consider these questions:

- Are there topics that are just not persuasive enough? Is there any way to make them persuasive?
- Will the audience be neutral, negative, or positive? Will they have an extreme reaction? How does this impact my focus?

→ See Chapters 2 and 14 for more questions to help you narrow your topic.

Before you commit to a topic, do some preliminary research. If locating current quality information on the topic is difficult, you may want to select another topic or change the viewpoint of the one you are researching.

→ Part 2 gives detailed guidance on researching.

Being a local resident and interested in equal rights, Jade was excited about almost every topic in her bank. So, as shown below, she began to systematically consider the topics and to eliminate the ones that did not seem to be the best choices.

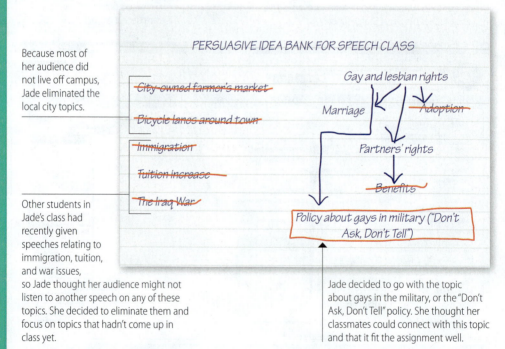

Because most of her audience did not live off campus, Jade eliminated the local city topics.

Other students in Jade's class had recently given speeches relating to immigration, tuition, and war issues, so Jade thought her audience might not listen to another speech on any of these topics. She decided to eliminate them and focus on topics that hadn't come up in class yet.

PERSUASIVE IDEA BANK FOR SPEECH CLASS

City-owned farmer's market

Bicycle lanes around town

Immigration

Tuition increase

The Iraq War

Gay and lesbian rights

Marriage   Adoption

Partners' rights

Benefits

Policy about gays in military ("Don't Ask, Don't Tell")

Jade decided to go with the topic about gays in the military, or the "Don't Ask, Don't Tell" policy. She thought her classmates could connect with this topic and that it fit the assignment well.

4
Determine the Best Type of Persuasive Speech

A persuasive speech is a speech to convince, stimulate, or actuate. To determine the best type of persuasive speech, consider the response you want from your audience.

TYPE OF PERSUASIVE SPEECH	DESIRED AUDIENCE RESPONSE	EXAMPLES
To convince	To convince my audience to change their attitudes, values, or beliefs	A speech arguing that outsourcing harms the U.S. economy, presented to a group of CEOs
To stimulate	To stimulate the attitudes, values, or beliefs my audience already holds	A speech arguing that it is important for the United States to help rebuild Haiti, presented to members of the Red Cross
To actuate	To move my audience to action	A speech arguing to vote for medical marijuana use, at a rally supporting a medical marijuana initiative

Also consider the characteristics of your target audience. The **target audience** is the primary group of people you are aiming to appeal to. You cannot appeal to everyone in the audience, but you can appeal to a portion of them and, hopefully, the majority. Use the target audience checklist on this page to reflect again on your audience analysis.

Muzafer Sherif and Carl Hovland, in their book *Social Judgment*, explain why it is important to know where your audience stands in relationship to a given topic. Their **social judgment theory** states that your persuasion will be easier, tolerated more, and potentially longer lasting if your audience can tie in what you are persuading about to what they find most acceptable, or what are called their **attitudinal anchors**. For example, if your audience is primarily conservative, they will likely favor conservative ideas; a liberal audience will likely favor liberal ideas.

Be careful not to negatively stereotype, but instead use the theory to potentially predict a reaction. Jade, for example, thinks her audience's age (mostly early 20s) may suggest millennial traits like openness to diversity, and she knows that many of the students have ties to the military. But she does not know for sure how her audience feels about this topic and she wants them to support changing a policy, so she will give a speech to *convince*.

CHECKLIST for Target Audience Analysis

❏ Who are the members of my audience?

❏ How do they feel about my topic?

❏ What is their relationship to my topic?

❏ Will I primarily be creating, reinforcing, or changing attitudes, values, or beliefs?

285

5

Identify Your Specific Purpose

If you remember the discussion in Chapter 2 about the specific purpose, you will remember that it is a single statement combining your general purpose, your audience, and your objective. Let's return to Jade's speech to see how she created her specific purpose.

You already know that Jade's topic is the military's "Don't Ask, Don't Tell" policy. Jade's assignment requires that she do a persuasive speech, and she knows that she personally wants to eliminate the policy. Given this information and the focus of her target audience, Jade decides to go with a claim of policy speech targeting an audience that would be willing to accept, or at least consider, a change to the "Don't Ask, Don't Tell" policy. As she wrote her specific purpose, she remembered that it should include the general purpose, her audience, and her objective in giving the speech.

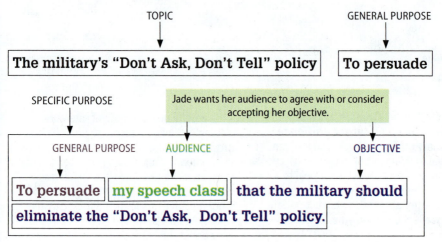

TOPIC

GENERAL PURPOSE

The military's "Don't Ask, Don't Tell" policy

To persuade

SPECIFIC PURPOSE

Jade wants her audience to agree with or consider accepting her objective.

GENERAL PURPOSE   AUDIENCE   OBJECTIVE

To persuade **my speech class** **that the military should eliminate the "Don't Ask, Don't Tell" policy.**

REVIEW CHECKLIST for Evaluating a Persuasive Specific Purpose

❏ Does my specific purpose contain my general purpose, an audience reference, and my objective?

❏ Is my specific purpose an infinitive statement beginning with "to persuade"?

❏ Is it a statement, not a question?

❏ Is it clear and concise, with only one speech topic?

❏ Does it relate well to me, the audience, and the situation?

6
Identify Your Central Idea

When you construct the central idea for a persuasive speech, you are constructing one concise sentence that states the core claim you want to make. It may also hint at your speech's main points. The central idea evolves from the objective in your specific purpose and relates to what you know about your audience. Jade's looked like this:

If Jade's Specific Purpose Is...	Jade's Central Idea Could Be...
To persuade my speech class that the military should eliminate the "Don't Ask, Don't Tell" policy.	**As citizens of a democratic society, we need to support the elimination of the "Don't Ask, Don't Tell" policy.**

At this point, it should be easy to see the overarching proposition that your speech—and Jade's speech—is trying to answer. Remember, all persuasive speeches support a proposition of fact, value, or policy. Jade's speech seeks to support a proposition of policy.

OVERARCHING PROPOSITION	GUIDING QUESTIONS	EXAMPLES OF PERSUASIVE CLAIMS
Proposition of fact	What is accurate or not? What will happen or not?	The military plan in Afghanistan will bring down terrorism.
Proposition of value	What has worth or importance? What is good, wise, ethical, or beautiful?	Animal theme parks are cruel.
Proposition of policy	What procedures, plans, or course of action needs to be terminated or implemented? (This question can ask the audience to just agree or to act.)	The "Don't Ask, Don't Tell" policy should be eliminated.

➜ See Chapter 2 for more on focusing your speech topic.

REVIEW CHECKLIST for Evaluating a Persuasive Central Idea

❏ Is the central idea persuasive in nature?
❏ Does my central idea focus on one speech topic?
❏ Is it a statement, not a question?
❏ Is it clear and concise?

❏ Can I do this in the time allotted?
❏ Is it unique?
❏ Is it worth persuading the audience of and worth the audience's time?

7

Create a Working Outline

Before embarking on your major research, create a working outline to guide you. At this stage, your working main points might be questions you think need to be answered, or they could simply be phrases that relate to subtopics. Later, when you get to your preparation outline stage, you want your main points to be concise and complete declarative sentences, not questions.

Your central idea might hint at possible main points. Also, your preliminary research should offer some insights and ideas.

Jade's central idea did not offer insight into her main points. However, her own curiosity about the history and details of the policy inspired two good points. When she conducted the preliminary research on her topic, she noticed discussions about how the policy has been used and the problems it presents. She created four working main points (see below) that would eventually lead to her final main points and potential strategy.

→ Chapter 5 explains working and preparation outlines in detail.

Remember, you may use questions for the main points in the working outline but should use declarative sentences for your main points in the preparation outline.

Working outline for "Don't Ask, Don't Tell" speech

TOPIC: The military's "Don't Ask, Don't Tell" policy

GENERAL PURPOSE: To persuade

SPECIFIC PURPOSE: To persuade my speech class that the military should eliminate the "Don't Ask, Don't Tell" policy.

CENTRAL IDEA: As citizens of a democratic society, we need to support the elimination of the "Don't Ask, Don't Tell" policy.

I. What is the history of gays in the military?

II. What does the "Don't Ask, Don't Tell" policy stipulate?

III. How has the policy been used?

IV. What are the problems with the policy?

REVIEW CHECKLIST for Working Main Points

❏ Does each main point cover only one key idea?

❏ Are my main points similarly constructed (are they parallel)?

❏ Am I roughly balancing the time spent on each point?

❏ Do my main points relate back to my central idea?

8

Conduct Your Research

Depending on your topic, your central idea, and the arguments you are using to support your claim, different types of support materials will be more effective than others. You can use facts, definitions, testimony, examples, and statistics. Good persuasion will require most of these.

For your arguments to be strong, effective, and ethical, your support materials must be:

- *Accurate:* Are your materials verifiable? Are you using information as it was originally intended (not twisting it for effect)?

- *Current:* Is the information the most current?

- *Complete:* Do you have enough material to make your argument? Does it give a complete picture? Did you consider all alternatives, including opposing ones?

- *Trustworthy:* Can you trust the evidence and the source? Can they be verified? Are they unbiased? If they came from the Internet, where anyone can create a site and information can easily be changed, are they correct?

- *Suitable:* Is your material appropriate for this topic, audience, or occasion?

To create an effective persuasive speech, research as many angles as possible. Most debatable topics have more than two issues, solutions, or viewpoints. Your job is to understand as much as you can about them and present the viewpoint or solution you think is best. Complex topics require good detective work, and you will not find all the answers in one place. Here are a few tips:

- The Internet gives you access to material that can be current or be an archive for older but important material. For example, Jade found that many government reports related to her topic dated back to the Clinton era.

- You can often locate current statistics on the Web, and many professional organizations (expert testimony) are present there. Jade even found a recording of a National Public Radio interview with the author of one of her sources.

- Although some items you locate in the library can be found on the Internet as well, the library item can often be viewed in its original form for verification. For example, Jade found a lot of references to a book (*Unfriendly Fire*) but needed the actual book to verify quotations.

- There are numerous items in a library that you cannot locate on the Internet. For example, even though databases are electronic, you often need to go through a library to access their contents.

- Interviews can give you access to testimony that is often not available in print—especially expert testimony, which can significantly support a claim.

- Survey data can help you gauge the current reactions or beliefs of a group.

→ See Part 2 if you need help with research.

> ### REMEMBER
>
> - Prepare to research—think about the options out there and what you might need.
> - Use a consistent note-taking system—don't forget to include citation information.
> - Know your appropriate style manual or where to consult one if you need it.

How Do You Construct the Persuasive Outline?

Constructing an effective preparation outline is imperative if you want to create a persuasive speech that your audience can follow, that you can follow as you speak, and that can persuade others. At this stage in the process, you want to create a preparation outline consisting of an introduction, a body, a conclusion, and a source page.

Later sections in this chapter will help you with the parts of an outline and how to organize each. For now, remember that a successful preparation outline will:

- Record the topic, specific purpose, and central idea
- Use full sentences
- Cover only one issue at a time
- Develop the introduction and conclusion
- Use correct outline format
- Use balanced main points
- Employ subordination
- Plan out formal links
- Use proper citations

Your outline should follow either a format similar to the one on the next page or a format your instructor suggests.

→ See Part 3 for an extended discussion of how to construct an outline.

CONFIDENCE BOOSTER

Effective outlines are like insurance policies. They give you the confidence that your speech has a strong introduction and conclusion as well as a well-organized body filled with convincing arguments.

Student name   Class
Date   Instructor name

Topic: The military's "Don't Ask, Don't Tell" policy
Specific purpose: To persuade my speech class that the military should eliminate the "Don't Ask, Don't Tell" policy.
Central idea: As citizens of a democratic society, we need to support the elimination of the "Don't Ask, Don't Tell" policy.

INTRODUCTION
     Attention-getter
     Credibility material
     Relevance to audience
     Preview of speech

(Link from introduction to first main point)

BODY
     I.   The U.S. military's ban on gays has a long, negative history.
         A.   Subpoint
         B.   Subpoint
             1.   Subpoint of B
             2.   Subpoint of B
             3.   Subpoint of B

(Link between first and second main points)

     II.   Second main point
         A.   Subpoint
         B.   Subpoint
             1.   Subpoint of B
             2.   Subpoint of B
         C.   Subpoint

(Link between second and third main points)

     III.   Third main point
         A.   Subpoint
             1.   Subpoint of A
                a. Subpoint of 1
                b. Subpoint of 1
             2.   Subpoint of A
         B.   Subpoint
         C.   Subpoint

(Link between third and fourth main points)

     IV.   Fourth main point
         A.   Subpoint
             1.   Subpoint of A
                a. Subpoint of 1
                b. Subpoint of 1
             2.   Subpoint of A
         B.   Subpoint
         C.   Subpoint

(Link to conclusion)

CONCLUSION
     Summary statement
     Audience response statement
     WOW statement:
             Works Cited

Jade begins working on her outline by filling in this template.

Jade begins to fill in her main points, making sure they are full, declarative sentences and cover only one idea at a time. She will make sure to have only one sentence per outline symbol and fill in the support material.

Jade doesn't know yet how many subpoints each of her main points will have. For now, she leaves a variety of subpoint placeholders in her outline.

Although Jade started with a template that only showed three main points, her speech will have four. She includes a place for the fourth point in her outline.

How Do You Organize a Persuasive Speech?

1 Recognize Your Organizational Strategy

2 Commit to a Strategy

3 Construct Main Points

4 Organize Support Materials into Arguments

5 Compose Your Introduction and Conclusion

Recognize Your Organizational Strategy

Many beginning speakers look to chronological and topical strategies for persuasive speeches, but although these tend to be easier to construct, they are not the best choices. Some instructors prohibit their use for a persuasive speech, in favor of more effective strategies. The common persuasive strategies are:

- Causal: ordered by cause-to-effect or effect-to-cause
- Comparative: ordered by contrasting two or more things
- Problem–solution: ordered by demonstrating and solving a problem
- Monroe's motivated sequence: ordered by demonstrating and solving a need

To select the right strategy, think about your speech type, overarching proposition, general purpose, topic, and audience. Your central idea can offer clues. For example, suppose your central idea is:

Recycling is a great solution to solid waste disposal problems because it decreases landfill usage, conserves natural resources, and saves money.

Guided by the first part of this sentence, you might use the problem–solution strategy to highlight the problem of solid waste disposal and the solution of recycling.

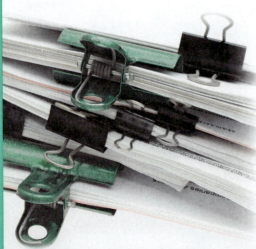

2

Commit to a Strategy

Committing to a strategy begins with selecting the best one, but the act of commitment also requires you to strictly adhere to that strategy. As a beginning speaker, it is easy to stray from your point or randomly connect thoughts together. Select your strategy and write your main points so that they stick to the strategy. Periodically, you should return to Chapter 6, where the strategies are explained in detail, and make sure you are following yours.

WHAT FACTORS SHOULD YOU CONSIDER WHEN SELECTING A STRATEGY?	STRATEGIES
Speech to stimulate	
Audience viewpoint needs reinforcement	Topical, chronological, Monroe's motivated sequence, or problem–solution
Speech to convince	
Audience is apathetic or uninformed and needs to create a viewpoint	Chronological, topical, problem–solution, comparative, Monroe's motivated sequence, or causal
Audience viewpoint needs to change because they disagree or are conflicted	Comparative, problem–solution, or causal
Speech to actuate	
Audience needs motivation to act.	Most of the strategies work for this type, but Monroe's motivated sequence is often the best
Overarching proposition for your speech	
Proposition of fact	Chronological or topical
Proposition of value	Comparative or topical
Proposition of policy	Topical, problem–solution, comparative, causal, or Monroe's motivated sequence

Jade selected and committed to the problem–solution strategy. She will spend most of her speech outlining the problems she feels are most important to proving that the policy needs to be changed, and then she will offer her simple solution in the conclusion—to lift the ban.

→ See Chapter 6 for a detailed explanation of these strategies.

REVIEW CHECKLIST for Selecting an Organizational Strategy

❑ Am I using a strategy that will work for my general purpose to persuade?

❑ Does my topic suggest a strategy? For example, if my specific purpose calls for my audience to accept a defined result, could the problem–solution strategy be best?

❑ What is my audience's relationship with the viewpoint of my speech?

3
Construct Main Points

Depending on how you constructed your central idea or which strategy you selected, one or both of these might hint at the main points you will need to cover in the speech. Strategies like Monroe's motivated sequence have certain steps that become main points and determine the focus of those main points. To create effective main points:

- Use full sentences to focus your main points into complete thoughts.
- Introduce only one idea in each main point.
- Write your main points in parallel form.
- Use declarative sentences.
- Adhere to coordination.

→ See Chapter 6 for a detailed explanation of these guidelines.

Although Jade's central idea did not suggest exact main points, her continued research helped her focus. Her working outline questions pointed to problems with the ban and hinted at lifting the ban as the best solution. Her working main points evolved into these main points:

I. The U.S. military's ban on gays has a long, negative history.
II. The U.S. military had several false, unnecessary reasons for implementing the ban.
III. The U.S. military's ban has cost us a lot.
IV. The U.S. military has several allies that have lifted their ban on gays with no significant problems.

Jade's speech has three main points presenting the problem and a fourth one that sets up the solution.

4
Organize Support Materials into Arguments

In the persuasive speech, your arguments will become the subpoints supporting your main points. Chapter 14 offers you guidance on choosing appeals and types of arguments, but ultimately, you will make these decisions based on what you want to accomplish, your audience's relationship to the speech, and the needs of the organizational strategy.

For example, in the body of her speech, Jade will use inductive reasoning because she has a lot of facts, statistics, examples, and testimony showing that the "Don't Ask, Don't Tell" policy is more harmful than good.

As you know from Chapter 14, there are many ways to organize the arguments within your speech. Jade will order her arguments chronologically because most are related to past practices and decisions.

Two additional models can help you decide how to arrange persuasive arguments:

- The **primacy model** suggests that you put your strongest arguments first in the body of the speech. The idea is that you are more likely to persuade if you win over your audience early. This method is best if your audience opposes your viewpoint.

- The **recency model** is the reverse of primacy. Here, you begin with the weakest argument and end with the strongest. If your audience is unfamiliar with your topic, is apathetic, or already agrees with you, this method is best.

There is no one set way to approach creating arguments, and the more you do it, the better you will get.

5

Compose Your Introduction and Conclusion

A persuasive speech needs a strong introduction and conclusion. See excerpts from Jade's speech below and the complete text on pages 296–303. An introduction for a persuasive speech should focus your audience's attention toward what you intend to claim about your topic.

This should be a "wow" moment.	**INTRODUCTION**
	► **ATTENTION-GETTER:** The U.S. military has long been known as a force to be reckoned with. . .We have been taught to treat our veterans with respect and reverence. . .to honor the sacrifices that servicemen and servicewomen have made for people they do not even know, and a country they are willing to die for.
State why you should give this speech.	
	► **CREDIBILITY MATERIAL:** I had a great-grandfather who fought in World War I, and both of my grandfathers fought in World War II. . .My father was a career airman and my brother, who is currently in Iraq, wants to make it a career as well. . .I am proud of my family's military history.
Give them a reason to listen.	
	► **RELEVANCE TO AUDIENCE**: From previous conversations we have had in this class, I know many of you have a connection to the military, be it a family member or friend . . .
Give them a road map.	► **PREVIEW OF SPEECH:** . . .[W]e need to support the elimination of the "Don't Ask, Don't Tell" policy. In the next few minutes, we will look at the history of the ban, the reasons for the ban, what the ban costs us, and what our allies do. I will demonstrate why this policy is such a problem and offer support for what I see as the best solution.

The persuasive speech's conclusion should leave your audience knowing your viewpoint and give them one more push to accept it or be influenced by it.

What do you want them to do?	**CONCLUSION**
	► **AUDIENCE RESPONSE STATEMENT:** In conclusion, I offer no fancy solution. It is simple. The United States needs to lift this ban.
What should they remember?	► **SUMMARY STATEMENT:** Research has shown that gays in the military are not a threat to our security. Research has shown that gays in the military are not a threat to "privacy, cohesion, and effectiveness" (Frank, *Unfriendly Fire* 113). If nothing else, the ban is too costly and unfair. . .
Dazzle them one more time.	► **WOW STATEMENT:** U.S. Congressman Barney Frank said it best: "Saying we can't have gay people in the military because heterosexuals won't like them, regardless of how they behave, is like saying we can't have black people around because white people won't like them. That was wrong and this is wrong" (Frank, *Unfriendly Fire* 61). Let's get rid of "Don't Ask, Don't Tell" and replace it with "Don't Discriminate, Don't Turn Away."

PREPARATION OUTLINE FOR A PERSUASIVE SPEECH

Jade Hunter   COMM 110
November 17, 2009   Dr. Davis

Topic: The military's "Don't Ask, Don't Tell" policy

Specific purpose: To persuade my speech class that the military should eliminate the "Don't Ask, Don't Tell" policy.

Central idea: As citizens of a democratic society, we need to support the elimination of the "Don't Ask, Don't Tell" policy.

INTRODUCTION

Attention-getter: The U.S. military has long been known as a force to be reckoned with. The U.S. military has often stepped up to protect this great land we call home or stepped out to save the day for many other countries, many times. We have been taught to treat our veterans with respect and reverence. We put magnets on our cars to support our troops and have a holiday with parades and ceremonies to honor the sacrifices that servicemen and servicewomen have made for people they do not even know, and a country they are willing to die for.

Jade evokes an appeal to mythos by discussing respecting veterans as a civic duty.

Credibility material: I had a great-grandfather who fought in World War I, and both of my grandfathers fought in World War II. My mother and father met when he was an airman and she a nurse in the Vietnam War. My father was a career airman and my brother, who is currently in Iraq, wants to make it a career as well. The military is deeply seated in my family. My family is proud of its military history. I am proud of my family's military history.

She uses repetition for emphasis and to build emotional appeal.

Relevance to audience: From previous conversations we have had in this class, I know many of you have a connection to the military, be it a family member or friend who served in the past or one who is currently serving in Iraq or Afghanistan. In many cases, the military has been a positive experience and helped our family members and friends through difficult times, such as getting a job to take care of family or getting a college education or other training. Some have even made a career out of the military, meeting the standards of excellence, following the rules, and giving decades of their lives to service.

Here, Jade appeals to the importance of the military, fulfilling an audience need.

Preview of speech: However, there is part of this equation that I am not proud of. I am not proud that there are men and women who do meet the standards, who do follow the rules, and who are putting their lives on the line for this country or have already given decades of their lives in service, but who were or may be discharged with no thank you, no privileges, no financial security in their later years, or no funding for an education because of an archaic law. That law is the basis of the current "Don't Ask, Don't Tell" policy preventing openly gay individuals from entering or continuing service in the military. Today, I want to persuade you that as citizens of a democratic society, we need to support the elimination of the "Don't Ask, Don't Tell" policy. In the next few minutes, we will look at the history of the ban, the reasons for the ban, what the ban costs us, and what our allies do. I will demonstrate why this policy is such a problem and offer support for what I see as the best solution.

(**Link:** First, let's look at the problems associated with the gay ban in the military.)

BODY

I.   The U.S. military ban on gays has a long, negative history.

   A.   Nathaniel Frank, in *Unfriendly Fire: How the Gay Ban Undermines the Military and Weakens America*, historically traces the military's homosexual intolerance to World War I.

      1.   In 1917, the military revised the Articles of War, making the act of sodomy, when committed as part of an assault, a military crime.

      2.   Three years later, a second revision "made consensual sodomy a crime in the military" (5).

      3.   However, this policy became the basis for the Navy, too, in "shocking" and "indefensible" investigation tactics to rid the Navy of unwanted sexual perversion—homosexuals (5).

         a.   Chief Machinist's Mate Ervin Arnold stated that he could spot "degenerates" a mile away by their clothing, walk, and effeminate manner.

         b.   The U.S. Senate eventually censured the Navy.

   B.   According to a 1947 *Newsweek* article republished in the book *Gay Rights*, the recruitment practice of asking "Are you a homosexual?" started during World War II (Burns 25).

      1.   If the recruit answered "yes," the recruit was usually referred to a psychiatric center.

      2.   This was a period of time in our history when being gay was viewed as abnormal and dangerously associated to communism (Burns 25).

Jade uses inductive reasoning with specific case support in A and B to sustain her first main point.

3. According to Frank, in 1949, the Department of Defense created a single policy throughout the branches of the military.
   a. "The new regulation stated: 'Homosexual personnel, irrespective of sex, should not be permitted to serve in any branch of the Armed Forces in any capacity, and prompt separation of known homosexuals . . . is mandatory'" (Frank, *Unfriendly Fire* 9).
   b. Each branch was asked to give homosexuality indoctrination lectures to ferret out the gays (9).
4. In 1950, Congress created the Uniform Code of Military Justice and made "unnatural carnal copulation" between heterosexuals or homosexuals in the armed forces punishable by five years of hard labor and dishonorable discharge without pay (9–10).
5. In 1981, the Carter administration created a ban on gays and lesbians in uniform by stating that "homosexuality is incompatible with military service" (10).
6. Another article in the book *Gay Rights*, titled "The Military's 'Don't Ask, Don't Tell' Policy Cannot Be Justified" and written by Rhonda Evans, states that when Bill Clinton ran for president in 1992, part of his platform was to repeal the ban on gays in the military, allowing them to serve without fear (Burns 149).
   a. A total repeal was not supported, and the compromise was the "Don't Ask, Don't Tell" policy, which is a compilation of regulations, directives, and a federal law.
   b. The Department of Defense issued a directive in 1994, stating: The Department of Defense has long held that, as a general rule, homosexuality is incompatible with military service because it interferes with the factors critical to combat effectiveness, including unit morale, unit cohesion, and individual privacy. Nevertheless, the Department of Defense also recognizes that individuals with a homosexual orientation have served with distinction in the armed services of the United States. Therefore, it is the policy of the Department of Defense to judge the suitability of persons to serve in the armed forces on the basis of their conduct. Homosexual conduct will be grounds for separation from the military services. Sexual orientation is considered a personal and private matter, and

When directly quoting, Jade puts the material in quotation marks or indents it further (see subpoint 6b).

This subpoint appears to break the "only one issue/sentence to an outline component" rule. However, Jade is simply incorporating a lengthy quotation. Follow your instructor's guidelines for how to do this.

homosexual orientation is not a bar to service
entry or continued service unless manifested by homosexual
conduct (Burns 150).

c. However, by the time the directive was implemented,
Congress passed its own legislation weakening the distinction
between conduct and the status of being gay by setting the
grounds for "discharge as engaging in, attempting to engage
in homosexual acts off-duty or not" (Burns 151).

d. The Pentagon's policy includes the "don't ask" provision, but
the law passed by Congress does not (Frank, *Unfriendly Fire* xii).

e. Furthermore, personnel can be "outed" by someone else.

f. According to Frank, "the government's conclusion was that
banning open gays from the military is necessary to preserve
privacy, cohesion, and effectiveness" (*Unfriendly Fire* 113).

g. Only 44 percent of Americans in 1993 supported gays serving
openly in the military (Dropp and Cohen).

(**Link:** Now that we have a historical context for the ban, let's look at why this ban is
a problem.)

II. The U.S. military had several false, unnecessary reasons for implementing
the ban.

A. In *Unfriendly Fire*, Frank discusses several studies suggesting that gays
pose no more risk to the military than do heterosexuals.

1. In 1957, the secretary of the Navy appointed a panel to investigate
the ban.

a. The results of this investigation are known as the Crittenden
report.

b. The researchers found that homosexuality posed no greater
security risk and that certain heterosexual relations were
considered more threatening (118).

2. The 1993 Rand study, commissioned by then-Secretary of Defense
Les Aspin, involved 75 social scientists who "analyzed the policies
of other countries' military, and the police and fire departments of six
U.S. cities" ("Changing").

a. The researchers studied all kinds of different data on group
cohesion, sexual harassment, leadership, health concerns, and
public opinion.

Again, Jade uses inductive reasoning in this second main point.

Even though these are in chronological order, Jade uses the theory of recency here as well by spending more time on 2 (continued on page 300), which is the better of the two arguments.

299

b. Frank states that the Rand report cost the taxpayers $1.3 million but barely made it out of the Rand office because it concluded that the gay ban could be lifted with little effect.

c. On the Rand Web site, rand.org, you can find a more detailed summary of the findings, but I find three of their seven main findings interesting.

　i. Acknowledged homosexuals very seldom challenge the norms or customs of the organization.

　ii. Anti-homosexual sentiment does not disappear but is more moderate than expected.

　iii. Effectiveness of the organization had not been diminished ("Changing").

B. Even public opinion polls strongly suggest that Americans no longer think the ban is necessary.

1. In their *Washington Post* article "Acceptance of Gay People in Military Grows Dramatically," Kyle Dropp and Jon Cohen report that 75 percent of Americans support dropping the ban.

2. That is up from 62 percent in 2001 and 44 percent in 1993, when President Clinton first tried to end the ban.

(**Link:** From only these two studies and one poll, we are starting to see that the reasons for having the ban are not necessarily valid. But that is not enough; let's turn to discovering how this ban greatly costs the United States.)

III. The U.S. military's ban has cost us a lot. ◄

A. More than 35,000 people have been discharged because of the policy from 1994 to 2007 (Frank, *Unfriendly Fire* 169).

B. As Frank puts it so poignantly, "This translates to a cost of $364 million, or 2,500 loaded, armored Humvees that could have been sent overseas" (*Unfriendly Fire* 169).

C. "Who are these discharged soldiers?" is another cost-oriented way to look at this.

1. The loss of any well-qualified soldier is costly no matter what their specialty is; but, according to Frank's interpretation of reports from the Government Accountability Office and other sources, 757 of these people were in "critical operations" (*Unfriendly Fire* 220).

Jade makes sure that she gives enough information to direct her audience to this Internet source.

Again, Jade uses inductive reasoning. This consistency will help her audience follow the logic she is using.

a. "These included voice interceptors, interrogators, translators, explosive ordnance disposal specialists, signal intelligence analysts, and missile and cryptologic technicians" (Frank, *Unfriendly Fire* 220).

b. Now, as Frank suggests in his book, there is no magic bullet for fighting radical Islamic violence (*Unfriendly Fire* 220).

c. However, it does seem important that we keep people who can speak the language (Arabic).

d. For example: On September 10, 2001, the National Security Agency intercepted two very brief messages in Arabic.
    i.   "Tomorrow is zero hour."
    ii. "The match is about to begin" (*Unfriendly Fire* 215; Grace).

e. These messages were not translated until September 12, 2001.

f. Although not enough information was intercepted to predict 9/11, it does give you pause to think: What if there was enough and these were translated a day late?

g. From 1994 to 2005, at least 54 Arabic speakers with the high level of training that the military requires have been fired because of the "Don't Ask, Don't Tell" policy (*Unfriendly Fire* 220).

2. Lt. Col. Victor Fehrenbach's story was published by *Stars and Stripes*, an independent news source for the U.S. military community (Shane).

    a. For 18 years, he was an F-15 pilot and had such achievements as serving in Kosovo, Iraq, and Afghanistan.

    b. In May 2009, he was grounded, and he now stands to lose his military pension two years before his retirement because his sexuality was discovered.

(Link: So, is there a solution to the ban? Well, let's look at what our allies do.)

IV. The U.S. military has several allies that have lifted their bans on gays with no significant problems.

    A. According to Frank in his book and a commentary on CNNPolitics.com, 24 foreign countries, close allies to the United States—including Britain, Canada, and Australia—have lifted their bans on gays with no significant problems (Frank, "Allow"; *Unfriendly Fire* 137).

Jade employs an appeal to need (safety) in subpoints a to g.

This story appeals to emotions and mythos.

Arguing by analogy, Jade uses Frank's information to compare the United States to some allies.

1. Australia and Canada lifted their bans in 1992 (Frank, *Unfriendly Fire* 137).
2. In 2000, Britain lifted its ban (148).

B. Research conducted in Britain, Israel, Canada, and Australia by the Palm Center at the University of California, Santa Barbara, found that persons or professional organizations related to the issue had not observed "any impact or any effect at all that undermined military performance, readiness, or cohesion, nothing that led to recruitment problems, or increased HIV health issues among the troops" (*Unfriendly Fire* 148).

1. The Palm Center reports that in Australia, complaints regarding sexual orientation issues comprise less than 5 percent of the total complaints received of incidents related to sexual harassment, bullying, and other forms of sexual misconduct ("The Effects").
2. During the year after the lift, "there was 'not a single . . . case of resignation, harassment or violence because of the change in policy,' the center says. 'The issue . . . has all but disappeared from public and internal military debates' in Canada'" (Price).
3. "In 1995, two-thirds of the men in Britain's all-volunteer armed forces said they would not be willing to serve if the gay ban were lifted. The gay ban ended in January 2000, and a grand total of three people actually resigned. With recruitment levels 'buoyant,' the policy change is 'hailed as a solid achievement' by the Ministry of Defense" (Price).
4. So impressed by these results, in 2006, Britain's Royal Air Force hired the Stonewall Group, a homosexual advocate alliance, to attract more gay and lesbian recruits.
5. Also, they enacted a policy that provided equal survivor benefits to same-sex partners (Frank, *Unfriendly Fire* 149).
6. As political scientist and director of the Center for the Study of Sexual Minorities in the Military at the University of California, Santa Barbara, Aaron Belkin states about lifting the ban in these countries: "It has no effect on unit cohesion. It has no effect on military performance. It has no effect on recruitment. It has no effect on any of the indicators of military capability" (Price).

Jade uses effective statistics in this section.

(**Link:** If countries similar to the United States, such as Britain, Canada, and Australia—countries we already fight side by side with—lifted the ban with no problems, so could the United States.)

302

CONCLUSION

Audience response statement: Therefore, I offer no fancy solution. It is simple. The United States needs to lift this ban.

Summary statement: Research has shown that gays in the military are not a threat to our security. Research has shown that gays in the military are not a threat to "privacy, cohesion, and effectiveness" (Frank, *Unfriendly Fire* 113). If nothing else, the ban is too costly and unfair. Even polls demonstrate that a sizeable majority of American citizens are ready to make this wrong a right.

WOW statement: U.S. Congressman Barney Frank said it best: "Saying we can't have gay people in the military because heterosexuals won't like them, regardless of how they behave, is like saying we can't have black people around because white people won't like them. That was wrong and this is wrong" (Frank, *Unfriendly Fire* 61). Let's get rid of "Don't Ask, Don't Tell" and replace it with "Don't Discriminate, Don't Turn Away."

Jade returns to the appeal to mythos she first employed in the introduction—belonging to a democratic society and respecting veterans.

Works Cited

Burns, Kate, ed. *Gay Rights*. Detroit: Thomson Gale, 2006. Print.

"Changing the Policy toward Homosexuals in the U.S. Military." *Rand: Objective Analysis. Effective Solutions*. Rand, 2000. Web. 25 Nov. 2009.

Dropp, Kyle and Jon Cohen. "Acceptance of Gay People in Military Grows Dramatically." *Washington Post*. Washington Post, 19 July 2008. Web. 25 Nov. 2009.

"The Effects of Including Gay and Lesbian Soldiers in the Australian Defense Forces: Appraising the Evidence." *Palm Center: Blueprints for Sound Public Policy*. Palm Center, 1 Sept. 2000. Web. 25 Nov. 2009.

Frank, Nathaniel. "Allow Gays to Serve Openly in Military." *CNNPolitics*. Cable Network News, 16 Apr. 2009. Web. 25 Nov. 2009.

—. *Unfriendly Fire: How the Gay Ban Undermines the Military and Weakens America*. New York: St. Martin's, 2009. Print.

Grace, France. "9/10 Message: 'Tomorrow Is Zero Hour.'" *CBSNEWS*. CBS Worldwide, 20 June 2002. Web. 25 Nov. 2009.

Price, Deb. "Gays in Military Succeeds Abroad." *The Detroit News*. 19 Feb. 2001. Palm Center, 2009. Web. 25 Nov. 2009.

Shane, Leo. "Pilot Facing Discharge under 'Don't Ask, Don't Tell' Policy." *Stars and Stripes*. Stars and Stripes, 23 May 2009, Mideast ed. Web. 25 Nov. 2009.

Jade follows the proper MLA citation style for the "Works Cited" section.

How Should You Prepare to Present or Evaluate a Persuasive Speech?

1 Put Your Speech on Its Feet

2 Evaluate the Message and Presentation

1

Put Your Speech on Its Feet

Now it's time to put your persuasive speech on its feet, by carefully choosing your language, polishing your delivery, and, if appropriate, preparing and practicing with presentation aids.

Effective language is a must if you intend to persuade. Emotive and stylistic language helps your audience follow your arguments, remember them, and be emotionally moved.

→ Chapter 8 covers language usage.

Practice your speech from the preparation outline the first few times, but then use a delivery outline. Your delivery should be powerful, direct, and enthusiastic, to suggest a high level of confidence and trust. Rehearse your speech until you can get through it several times without major errors or glitches.

→ See Chapter 5 to create a delivery outline and Chapter 9 for more delivery hints.

Presentation aids are often necessary for a persuasive speech, to help your audience understand facts and figures or to follow the logic of an argument. Keep in mind that aids should support your speech and not be added on just because you can make them.

Jade planned a slideshow. During the introduction, she used photos and brief video to reinforce military and country pride. During the body of the speech, she used slides with tables, quotations, or photos. Near the end, her slideshow remained on a photo of Lt. Col. Fehrenbach until her last sentence, when she advanced to a slide with the American flag while saying her ending phrase, "Don't Discriminate, Don't Turn Away!"

→ Chapter 10 offers details on creating presentation aids for your speech.

Evaluate the Message and Presentation

When persuasion is the goal, critical listening is key. For example, suppose you disagreed with Jade that the gay ban should be removed. Did you suspend judgment to consider the facts she presented? Did she address your concerns? As a speaker, you must use an effective organizational strategy, correct evidence, and persuasive proofs to persuade successfully. As an audience member, listen critically for these aspects. Does the speech meet its persuasive goal? Is the speaker's delivery persuasive?

Use this checklist, or guidelines provided by your instructor, to evaluate persuasive speeches.

CHECKLIST FOR EVALUATING THE PERSUASIVE SPEECH

TOPIC
.... Speech accomplished purpose to persuade
.... Topic appropriate to speaker, audience, and occasion
.... Interesting topic

INTRODUCTION
.... Gained attention and interest
.... Established credibility
.... Indicated relevance to audience
.... Declared central idea
.... Previewed speech

BODY
.... Main points clear and obvious to the audience
.... Points follow an appropriate organizational strategy
.... Main points appropriately researched and supported
.... Used effective proofs/arguments
.... Main points supported with appropriate presentation aids when necessary
.... Oral citations included throughout speech
.... Linked parts of speech

CONCLUSION
.... Contained a summary statement
.... Offered an audience response statement
.... Effectively comes to closure (WOW statement)

PRESENTATION
.... Language was clear, concise, and appropriate
.... Gestures/body movements were effective
.... Consistent and effective eye contact
.... Used vocal variety/emphasis/volume/rate
.... Used appropriate delivery style
.... Spoke with enthusiasm
.... Spoke with conviction and sincerity
.... Good use of delivery outline
.... Presentation aids appropriate to speech topic (if applicable)
.... Used presentation aids throughout entire speech (if applicable)
.... Used professional presentation aids (if applicable)
.... Speech met time requirements

The above list can also help guide you as you create and practice a speech.

→ See Part 5 for more about listening to and evaluating a speech.

PRACTICING ETHICS

As a member of a democratic society, you must be willing to ask the hard questions to ensure your safety and the safety of others: Is this true? Who stands to gain? Are these sources unbiased?

Part 7: Review

CHAPTER 14 REVIEW QUESTIONS

1. Define persuasion and explain how attitudes, beliefs, values, and behaviors relate to the persuasive process.
2. What should a persuasive speech do?
3. List and explain the traditional and modern forms of appeal.
4. Explain the three traits and the three levels of ethos.
5. What are the parts of an argument? Explain how they work to form an argument.
6. Briefly explain the three types of warrants.
7. List and explain the five types of arguments.
8. What are faulty arguments? Select three of the fallacies discussed in the chapter and explain them. Include an example in your explanation.

CHAPTER 15 REVIEW QUESTIONS

1. Explain the three types of persuasive speeches. Include an example in your explanation.
2. What is the social judgment theory, and how does it relate to selecting a persuasive topic?
3. What factors should you consider when selecting an organizational strategy for a persuasive speech?
4. Explain how the primacy and recency models can help you organize an argument.

TERMS TO REMEMBER

Chapter 14
persuasion (257)
proposition of fact (259)
proposition of value (259)
proposition of policy (259)
appeals (260)
coercion (261)
pathos (262)
mythos (263)
ethnocentrism (263)
ethos (264)
logos (265)
Cognitive Dissonance Theory (268)
Expectancy-Outcome Values Theory (269)
Elaboration Likelihood Model (269)
argument (270)
claim (270)
evidence (270)
warrants (271)
argument by deduction (272)
syllogism (272)
enthymeme (273)
argument by induction (274)
argument by analogy (275)
argument by cause (275)
argument by authority (275)
fallacy (276)

Chapter 15
target audience (285)
social judgment theory (285)
attitudinal anchors (285)
primacy model (294)
recency model (294)

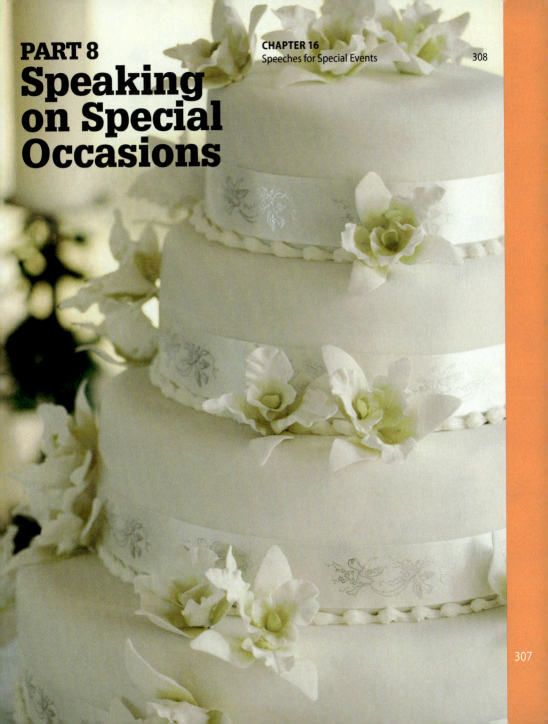

PART 8
Speaking on Special Occasions

16
SPEECHES FOR SPECIAL EVENTS

Introduction

Garrett has been best friends with Joe since grade school. In high school they played basketball on the same team, hunted quail, and took road trips together; in college they were roommates. When Joe began dating Stephanie, Garrett was happy his friend had found a great match.

Several months ago, Joe asked Stephanie to marry him and asked Garrett to be his best man. When Garrett told his dad, his father noted that Garrett would be expected to give a toast at the wedding reception. Wanting to do his best for Joe and Stephanie's event, Garrett gave his toast a lot of thought before the wedding.

First, he jotted down a few thoughts. His notes included how important Joe and, now, Stephanie are to him and a few stories that might make the toast fun or interesting. Because many of the audience members will not know him, Garrett decided to begin by briefly defining his relationship to Joe. Garrett then selected one favorite story and carefully crafted a toast that would honor the newlyweds. He practiced it several times in front of his dad to make sure it seemed from the heart and would flow well.

This chapter will help you give speeches in situations like Garrett's. During your lifetime, you may find yourself giving a wedding toast, commemorating someone's life work, or paying tribute to a friend. These are special occasion speeches, and much of what you have read in previous chapters will help you here as well. This chapter will offer additional insights about speaking at special events.

CHAPTER 16 CONTENTS

What Is the Creative Process for Special Occasion Speaking? 310

What Are Special Occasion Speeches? 312
1 Speeches to Celebrate 313
2 Speeches to Commemorate 313
3 Speeches to Inspire 313
4 Speeches to Entertain 313

How Do You Write a Special Occasion Speech? 314
1 Determine the Purpose of the Occasion 314
2 Clarify the Type of Special Occasion Speech 315
3 Analyze the Audience 315
4 Focus on a Central Idea 316
5 Research Your Speech 316
6 Create Your Outline 317
7 Practice the Speech 317
8 Evaluate the Special Occasion Speech 317

What Are the Types of Special Occasion Speeches? 318
1 Eulogy or Tribute 318
2 Speech of Introduction 319
3 Toast or Roast 320
4 Speech of Award Presentation 321
5 Speech of Award Acceptance 321
6 After-dinner Speech 322
7 Speech of Inspiration 323

PART 8 Review 324

What Is the Creative Process for Special Occasion Speaking?

Speeches for special occasions are some of the most creative you will ever present. They bring public speaking into your daily life to celebrate, commemorate, inspire, and amuse audiences during extraordinary times. This chart briefly outlines the five basic activities you will use to create an effective special occasion speech. Remember, being creative is not a linear process, so move back and forth between each activity as you mold your speech.

1 STARTING

DETERMINE THE PURPOSE AND TYPE OF SPEECH

➜ See pages 314–315

Know your audience as well as where, when, and why you are speaking. Select the topic that best fits you, your audience, and the occasion. Let the special occasion determine which type you should give.

ANALYZE THE AUDIENCE

➜ See page 315

Get to know who will be in the audience. Special occasion speeches can be culturally specific and tied to a particular audience.

FOCUS ON A CENTRAL IDEA

➜ See page 316

State in one sentence what you want the overall theme or message to be.

2 RESEARCHING

RESEARCH YOUR SPEECH

➜ See page 316

Research for accurate, current, complete, and suitable materials about your audience, topic, and special occasion.

Because of the personal nature of most special occasion speeches, you might locate much of your speech material from your own personal experience and relationship with the people, place, or event being celebrated.

3

CREATING

CREATE YOUR OUTLINE

→ See page 317

Create a preparation outline so that you are sure to have an introduction, body, and conclusion.

Use an organizational strategy appropriate to the special occasion speech.

Create a delivery outline if appropriate.

4

PRESENTING

PRACTICE YOUR SPEECH

→ See page 317

Use language that is familiar, concrete, and appropriate.

Practice your delivery so that you are natural, enthusiastic, confident, and engaging.

Use presentation aids *only* when appropriate and effective for the specific occasion.

5

LISTENING & EVALUATING

EVALUATE THE SPECIAL OCCASION SPEECH

→ See page 317

Determine the speech's effectiveness and appropriateness for the occasion and the audience.

Be an active and effective listener when helping someone with a speech.

What Are Special Occasion Speeches?

1 Speeches to Celebrate

2 Speeches to Commemorate

3 Speeches to Inspire

4 Speeches to Entertain

A *special occasion speech* has the general purpose to celebrate, commemorate, inspire, or entertain. The speaker's intent is to mark the occasion by making it a time to rejoice, honor, arouse, or amuse.

The special occasion is unique in that it often seems like you are bringing public speaking into the home or heart. The special occasion speech intertwines public speaking with your personal life, as the opening toast example demonstrates. Although you could be asked to give a special occasion speech because of who you are professionally, some aspect of the special occasion speech is usually tied to the daily lives of the speaker and/or the audience.

Special occasion speeches accentuate the extraordinary events in life, marking rites of passage, celebrating new beginnings, paying tribute to those you admire or love, and sometimes even entertaining your audience.

> *Let us celebrate the occasion with wine and sweet words.*[1]
>
> PLAUTUS

1
Speeches to Celebrate

Speeches to celebrate will honor or highlight a person, group, institution, place, or event. You may give a speech to celebrate at such events as weddings, anniversaries, retirements, banquets, welcome sessions, and birthdays. The speaker should praise the subject(s) of the special occasion and adhere to the expected customs of the group hosting the event. The tone of your speech should emulate the personality of the person, group, institution, place, or event being celebrated.

2
Speeches to Commemorate

Speeches to commemorate pay tribute to or remember a person, group, institution, place, or event. Unlike the speech to celebrate, which honors the event of the moment (an eleventh birthday), speeches to commemorate reside more in the past, or future, such as a speech marking the tenth anniversary of the September 11 attacks or the death of Senator Ted Kennedy. In both of these examples, the events really being remembered are September 11, 2001, and the past life of Senator Kennedy. The focus of the speech to commemorate can touch thousands or be closer to home, as with the death of a local police officer or a family member. This type of speech should reflect the personality of the person or the tone of the group, institution, place, or event being commemorated, and it should consider the needs of the audience as well as the cultural expectations of the speaking event.

3
Speeches to Inspire

Speeches to inspire are created to motivate, stir, encourage, or arouse the audience. Commencement speeches, keynote addresses, inaugural speeches, sermons, and daily devotionals are often examples of speeches to inspire. Inspirational speeches may reflect the personality and professional status of the speaker, but the main considerations are the needs of the audience and the expectations of the speaking event.

4
Speeches to Entertain

Speeches to entertain all have the general goal to amuse, delight, and engage the audience for the purpose of enjoyment, with a bit of wisdom or tribute thrown in depending on the special occasion. Speeches given at banquets, award dinners, and roasts are often speeches to entertain. The speeches are expected to be cheery, playful, light, and usually optimistic but may have an underlying serious message that can be informative or persuasive.

PRACTICING ETHICS

Special occasion speeches are very culturally specific and embedded. Make yourself aware of protocol and cultural expectations. Be audience centered.

How Do You Write a Special Occasion Speech?

1 Determine the Purpose of the Occasion

2 Clarify the Type of Special Occasion Speech

3 Analyze the Audience

4 Focus on a Central Idea

5 Research Your Speech

6 Create Your Outline

7 Practice the Speech

8 Evaluate the Special Occasion Speech

1

Determine the Purpose of the Occasion

You can create a special occasion speech much like you would an informative or persuasive speech. The primary difference is that this speech is determined by the occasion more than almost anything else. With most speeches, you first focus on understanding your audience. With the special occasion speech, you start by determining your purpose.

When you are invited to deliver the speech, ask about the purpose of the occasion. If the person inviting you is not able to answer your questions, seek out someone directly related to the occasion. You should ask:

What is the purpose of the event (meeting, conference, or ceremony)?
Knowing the focus or theme of the event can help you determine your topic. Does the event or its audience come with specific expectations or wishes? Should the speech celebrate, commemorate, inspire, or entertain?

Who will be in the audience?
At the least you want to know general characteristics, special needs, and how many.

Where will I speak?
How big is the space? Will there be a lectern and/or microphone?

Will someone introduce me? Will there be other speakers?
If so, you may want to try to coordinate with others so you don't cover the same information.

How long should I speak?
Know what the organizers expect.

→ See Chapter 1 for more on how to analyze the situation.

2

Clarify the Type of Special Occasion Speech

Now you want to determine if you should give a speech to celebrate, commemorate, inspire, or entertain, and also the specific type of special occasion speech. In general, the type of speech you give will match up to one of the following general purposes.

TYPE OF SPEECH	GENERAL PURPOSE
Toast or roast	Speech to celebrate
Introduction	
Award presentation or acceptance	
Eulogy or tribute	Speech to commemorate
Speeches of inspiration, such as sermons, commencement addresses, or motivational talks	Speech to inspire
After-dinner speech	Speech to entertain

Although the lines between these purposes seem to blur, you will only have one purpose for each type of speech. For example, a eulogy is a speech to commemorate but can celebrate a life. Your general purpose is to commemorate; your speech's tone is celebratory.

→ See "What Are the Types of Special Occasion Speeches?" (pages 318–323) for more information on each.

3

Analyze the Audience

As with any speech, you need to understand your audience's beliefs, values, and attitudes by investigating their personal, psychological, and social traits.

The person inviting you to speak can have insight, and talking with audience members before the event can offer you information. Researching the general demographics of groups represented in the audience can also be helpful. For example, a college commencement speech included this:

> When I asked the university's staff to tell me a bit about you, they told me that 65 percent of the students graduating today are African American . . . I remembered that . . . most low-income and first-generation students, as well as students of color, are less likely to attend four-year institutions and persist through degree completion.

> Do you know how many U.S. residents hold a bachelor's degree as of 2009? According to the Census Bureau, only 30 percent . . . If you are black, that number drops to 19 percent, and 13 percent if you are Hispanic. Today, you will increase those numbers—you should be proud. . . .

This speaker merged information she gathered from the college staff with facts and statistics to inspire her audience.

TIP: Clarifying the Speech Type

You should pay attention to how the person offering you the invitation to speak talks about the speech event. His or her description of the event or topic might give you clues to the type of speech expected.

4

Focus on a Central Idea

Central ideas for longer special occasion speeches, such as a keynote address or nomination speech, will be similar to those of informative or persuasive speeches. Shorter special occasion speeches, such as toasts or award acceptance speeches, will focus more on a theme. For example, if you return to Garrett's wedding toast, his central idea is:

Special people deserve special people in their lives.

Although this central idea does not tell you exactly what Garrett will say, it establishes a theme. With this central idea, Garrett is ready to brainstorm for the main points he wants to make and to craft the toast.

If you are giving a longer special occasion speech and have your central idea, take the time to draft working main points and a working outline to guide your research.

Later in this chapter are specific suggestions for what to include in each type of special occasion speech. For now, you might use these questions as you draft potential main points:

- What were the first ideas that came to mind when you were invited to give the speech?

- If you were invited because of your expertise or profession, how might that focus your content?

- What might the audience know about you that would help you focus?

- If you had to select three things for your audience to remember, consider, believe, or enjoy, what would they be?

→ See Chapter 2 for how to craft a central idea.

5

Research Your Speech

Depending on the type of special occasion speech you are giving, your research may be more personally reflective (from within your own experience) or you may need to do more formal research. For a wedding toast, you will use your own knowledge and experience of the couple, but for an award presentation, you might need to research the history of the award and the recipient. Some speeches to inspire, such as a commencement speech, can require a lot of research, depending on the main points covered.

Here are some specific questions that might guide your research.

- Are there special issues related to the occasion that require detailed understanding of a person, group, institution, place, or event? What do you need to know and tell your audience about this person, group, institution, place, or event?

- What types of materials (quotations, statistics, facts, etc.) might you need to locate related to your *topic* to celebrate, commemorate, inspire, or entertain this audience?

- What types of materials (quotations, statistics, facts, etc.) related to your *audience* might you need to help them celebrate, commemorate, be inspired, or be entertained?

→ See Part 2 for more on how to conduct research.

6
Create Your Outline

Outlining is as important to the special occasion speech as it is to the informative or persuasive speech, to help you avoid rambling or forgetting important parts.

Even the shortest special occasion speech will include an introduction, a body, and a conclusion. However, you may condense the parts into one, two, or three sentences. Use links to connect key points and to lead your audience through the speech. The chronological, topical, spatial, and comparative strategies are most common in special occasion speeches.

INTRODUCTION
   Attention-getter
   Credibility material
   Relevance to audience
   Preview of speech

Short speeches may incorporate all of these in one sentence.

BODY
   I. First main point
   II. Second main point
   III. Third main point

Very short speeches may have only one main point.

CONCLUSION
   Summary statement
   Audience response statement
   WOW statement

Should reflect the mood of your audience and speech.

For long speeches, create a delivery outline. Deliver shorter speeches, such as a toast, without notes—although you might review an outline privately beforehand.

→ See Part 3 for how to outline, organize the speech body, and construct introductions and conclusions.

7
Practice the Speech

Most special occasion speeches will be delivered extemporaneously. More formal and longer speeches, such as commencement or keynote addresses, might be delivered from a manuscript, as time and details are usually important considerations.

But most special occasion speeches, because they are a part of everyday life, need to come from the heart rather than a piece of paper. Rehearse until your delivery sounds confident and natural.

8
Evaluate the Special Occasion Speech

Unless you are giving special occasion speeches as part of a class assignment, they are rarely formally evaluated. However, you still want to make sure you have covered the necessary parts, used appropriate organization, and crafted a speech appropriate to the audience, topic, and occasion.

CHECKLIST for Evaluating a Special Occasion Speech
- ❏ Does my introduction include an attention-getter, credibility material, statement of relevance, and preview?
- ❏ Does the body of my speech have an appropriate organizational strategy and supported main points?
- ❏ Is my language clear, vivid, and appropriate?
- ❏ Does my conclusion include a summary, an audience reaction statement, and a WOW ending?
- ❏ Is the length of my speech appropriate?
- ❏ Is my delivery dynamic and enthusiastic? If appropriate, am I delivering the speech extemporaneously? Do I maintain almost constant eye contact?

What Are the Types of Special Occasion Speeches?

1 Eulogy or Tribute

2 Speech of Introduction

3 Toast or Roast

4 Speech of Award Presentation

5 Speech of Award Acceptance

6 After-dinner Speech

7 Speech of Inspiration

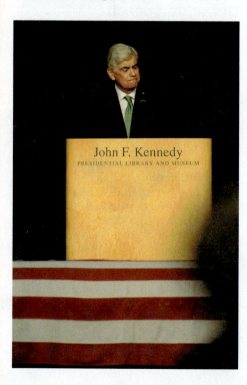

John F. Kennedy
PRESIDENTIAL LIBRARY AND MUSEUM

1

Eulogy or Tribute

The word **eulogy** derives from the Greek word *eulogia,* meaning "praise" or "good word," and is a speech presented after a person's death, at ceremonies like funerals.

A **tribute** commemorates lives or accomplishments of people, groups, institutions, or events and can be given with the recipient present or posthumously (after death). Tributes are often given at award ceremonies or dinners.

SPECIAL GUIDELINES

- Your focus should be to commemorate and celebrate the life of the honoree.
- Although eulogies and tributes should be brief (under 10 minutes), determine what is expected.
- For a eulogy, your purpose is to celebrate the deceased and to comfort the living. Stay in control of your emotions and pay attention to the needs of the audience. Be positive, but genuine.
- For a tribute, your purpose is to honor achievements. Vividly describe them, and use them to inspire the audience.

EXAMPLE

In 2009, Senator Chris Dodd eulogized Senator Edward M. Kennedy at a memorial service. He began:

> Tonight, we gather to celebrate the incredible American story of a man who made so many other American stories possible, my friend Teddy Kennedy.

His speech was a moving mix of celebration, humor, history, and inspiration. You can locate and watch it on YouTube.

2
Speech of Introduction

A *speech of introduction* presents an event's next or main speaker to the audience. This type of speech might also set out to welcome the audience; establish the tone, mood, or climate of the event; and/or build a level of excitement.

SPECIAL GUIDELINES

- Research the background of the speaker so that you can give a brief overview of his or her accomplishments and credentials. Review the speaker's résumé if you can. You might also talk with the event organizer or conduct a mini-interview with the speaker prior to the introduction. Do not wait until the last minute to research. You need time to prepare, and the speaker needs the time before the speech to get ready as well.

- Briefly preview the speaker's title and topic if appropriate. You should work this out ahead of time with the speaker. Do not give your own speech on the topic.

- Introductions should be short. The audience has come to hear the featured speaker.

- Your final words should ask the audience to welcome the speaker and include his or her name. For example, "Please join me in welcoming the CEO of AirBound, Joyce English."

EXAMPLE

The great screen and stage star Rosalind Russell once said, "Acting is like standing up naked and turning around very slowly." Luckily, if that is true, our next speaker isn't afraid of baring it all for his craft. It is my honor tonight to introduce a man who has graced our stage and hearts for years. He was here the day they placed the first coat of paint on the stage floor and opened the box office for our first production of *Hamlet*, where he had the leading role. He has acted in 35 main stage productions and 15 reading-hour productions and directed 18 plays over the years. Tonight, he is going to celebrate the history of the 18th Street Playhouse. He not only knows our history, he is our history. Please join me in giving a warm welcome to our founder, Leonardo Garrick.

This speaker started with a quotation as an attention-getter and humorous transition to the featured speaker. She then gives a brief preview of the accomplishments and connection to this audience before giving his title and name.

CONFIDENCE BOOSTER

Most special occasion speeches relate to affirmative topics, and their audiences usually want to listen. Even eulogies are positive in that they affirm the life of someone special to the audience, and you wouldn't be giving the eulogy if you weren't a positive part of that experience. Use that affirmative spirit to override your nervousness or lack of confidence. Decide beforehand to make your speech a powerful and positive experience for you and your audience.

3

Toast or Roast

A ***toast*** is a ritual expressing honor or goodwill to a person, group, institution, or event, punctuated by taking a drink. You may offer a toast at events such as New Year's Eve, weddings, births, housewarmings, graduation dinners, and retirement parties.

A **roast** is a humorous tribute to a person. The event and the speech are both called a roast. The protocol involves a series of speakers, all joking or poking fun at the honoree, often with a few heartwarming moments.

SPECIAL GUIDELINES

- Reflect the tone and purpose of the event.
- Speak mostly about the honoree.
- Be positive, appropriate, and gracious.
- Mix your humor with heartfelt meaning.
- Know the protocol for the event (e.g., wedding toasts usually follow an order—father of the bride or host of the reception, best man, maid of honor, and groom).
- Be brief and adhere to your time limit, especially at a roast. A toast should be three to five minutes or less.
- Praise, honor, and compliment. It is the honoree's day to shine and be happy.
- Tailor remarks to mirror the values, beliefs, and attitudes of the honoree and those close to him or her. Anything you say will be recorded in their memories and potentially on video.
- Stand, if possible, when you offer a toast or roast.

EXAMPLE

Garrett, the best man you met in the chapter's introduction, wrote this toast.

> May I have your attention, please? Wow, what an amazing day and celebration. For those who don't know me, I'm Garrett Cooper, Joe's shadow. We met in grade school and will leave this life as best friends. We have played ball, chased after quail, and hitchhiked across this great land together.
>
> On one of our trips, I learned a lot about how calm, cool, and trainable Joe could be. We were camping out under the stars in Washington state when we awoke to a large female moose straddling Joe's body, literally, and staring straight into his eyes. I'm there in my sleeping bag, wondering what her breath smells like and if she will bite or lick his face. Joe had to be wondering what her plans were for him in that compromising position. He didn't move. I didn't move. She checked us out for what seemed like an eternity and sauntered off eventually. We learned that day to stay calm and cool and let the ladies have their way. Stephanie, you owe that moose a lot.
>
> Joe, you better be glad you saw Stephanie first. She is one special catch and deserves the best. Too bad for her, she saw you first. No, seriously, I wish you two many years of happiness and a lifetime of joy. Special people deserve special people in their lives. Today, two very special people begin a lifetime of happiness and joy together. Congratulations, Joe and Stephanie! (toast)

TIP: Responding from the Audience

As an audience member to a toast, if you pick up your glass at the beginning of the toast, don't put it down until the end. You should always raise your glass and sip some liquid, or you will appear impolite or seem to suggest that you don't agree with the toast.

4

Speech of Award Presentation

You will give a **speech of award presentation** when you are announcing the recipient(s) of an award, prize, or honor.

SPECIAL GUIDELINES

- If it is not obvious to the audience, explain who you are and why you are giving the award. This should be very brief because the award is not about you.
- Explain the significance of the award.
- Compliment and recognize all of the nominees as a group.
- Highlight or explain why the individual or group is receiving the award.
- Be brief—no longer than five minutes and usually much shorter.
- If possible, physically hand the award to the recipient.

EXAMPLE

It is my honor and privilege to present the fifth annual St. Vincent Award. Ester St. Vincent worked in our elementary schools for more than 40 years. Outside the classroom, she dedicated much of her life to civic duty. She was a volunteer at the local soup kitchen and the hospital, taught adults to read, and took in countless animals until they could make it on their own.

This award was established in 2006 . . . Each year, we give the award to a local community member who carries on Ms. St. Vincent's spirit, sense of civility, and duty . . . This year's recipient grew up here, works as a nurse practitioner in our community, volunteers to maintain the city gardens, helps give medical care to the homeless, and has organized several successful fundraisers. The 2011 recipient of the St. Vincent Award is Eliana Lee.

5

Speech of Award Acceptance

A **speech of award acceptance** is the response you give when receiving an award, prize, or honor.

SPECIAL GUIDELINES

- Be prepared if you know you will or might receive an award.
- Be respectful of the event and give your speech from the heart. Be humble.
- Thank the person or group giving you the honor.
- Thank those close to you and/or those who have contributed greatly to your success. Limit this list to the most significant people, and avoid a long list (three to five works best).
- Know when to stop. Do not go on and on. Be as brief as possible (usually three to five minutes).

EXAMPLE

Thank you, Mayor Craig, for your kind words . . . I would also like to thank the award committee and the other nominees. I am truly humbled . . . Growing up here, I have loved this small town and its people—the people who made me who I am today. It took people like Ms. St. Vincent and my family to show me that I could be whatever I wanted, and I thank them for pushing and lifting me. They inspired me to do the same for others.

Almost every day when I would walk home from school or my dad's store, Ms. St. V, as we called her, would be on her way to help . . . No cause was too small or too large in Ms. St. V's eyes. Her motto was "Keep movin' forward and smile!" Thank you for this honor.

6

After-dinner Speech

Despite the name, an **after-dinner speech** can be given any time you need to give a speech with the general purpose to entertain but with a relevant message. After-dinner speeches tend to be longer than other special occasion speeches and are usually specific to the audience and/or the occasion.

SPECIAL GUIDELINES

- Start preparing the speech early. An after-dinner speech is one of the more difficult speeches to create because you are trying to entertain and deliver a relevant message at the same time.

- Tailor the speech to the occasion and the audience. Analyze your audience and situation to learn what might be appropriate or expected.

- Be focused and structured. You still need an introduction, a body, and a conclusion. Decide if your message is meant to inform or to persuade your audience.

- Be creative but avoid doing standup. You were asked to do a speech, not a comedy routine.

- Be dynamic. Use a lot of eye contact and speak extemporaneously.

- Know your time limit and stick to it.

- Practice. To be entertaining, effective timing and delivery are musts.

EXAMPLE

The following section comes from an after-dinner speech given by student Brendan Chan for a student organization. In the speech, Brendan pokes fun at how we feel about pennies and offers a solution to our "love/hate" relationship with this unit of currency.

> Next, we waste our resources producing pennies. The most obvious resource wasted is the metal that goes into making pennies. And guess what? That metal isn't even copper! It's zinc, the tawdry harlot of the alloys. Even their metallic makeup is lies! Whatever happened to Old Honest Abe?! The consulting company PSFK quotes Harvard economist Gregory Mankiw on its Web site on June 9, 2009, who said "The purpose of the monetary system is to facilitate exchange, but . . . the penny no longer serves that purpose." My peeps, pennies just aren't worth it! With the elimination of the physical penny, we could save the amount of time it would take to deal with pennies in everyday transactions, and save the metal for more pressing matters. Check it—metal is everywhere, so why waste it? Man, that's heavy. Heavy metal . . . .

PRACTICING ETHICS

When your goal is to entertain, avoid using language, jokes, or examples that are potentially insensitive to religion, race, gender, ethnicity, sexual orientation, age, or even political persuasion.

7

Speech of Inspiration

A *speech of inspiration* strives to fulfill a general purpose to motivate, encourage, move, or arouse an audience in a positive manner. Religious sermons, commencement addresses, motivational talks in the workplace or locker room, and nomination speeches at rallies, as well as keynote and welcoming addresses at conventions, are all speeches of inspiration. These speeches aim to awaken an audience's feelings, such as pride, perseverance, spirituality, and the search for excellence. The effectiveness of this type of speech is rooted in the speaker's ethos and appeal to audience pathos. Vivid language and storytelling are often key.

SPECIAL GUIDELINES

- Select a topic, theme, or subject that reflects the expectations, mood, and tone of the event.
- Know your audience and what would inspire them.
- Talk about something that inspires you. If you are not inspired, your audience will not be, either. Let your passion be inspirational.
- Appeal to your audience's pathos via stories (especially true ones), extended examples, or anecdotes. Use strong examples of what is or could be.
- Use vivid language, repetition, alliteration, metaphor, and other speech devices, and focus on connotative (emotional) usage.

    → See Chapter 8 for more on effective language usage.

- Draw on the power of inspirational people by quoting them at key moments.
- Use a vocal flow and rhythm that builds in intensity. Rally the audience's emotions with your delivery style. Be very dynamic.
- End with a significant WOW moment.

EXAMPLE

This devotional was given on the radio by the Rev. John Yonker.

> An old story tells about a teacher who held up a sheet of clean, white paper. "What do you see?" he asked the children. "A piece of paper," they told him. He then took a pen and drew a small black dot on the paper. "Now, what do you see?" he asked. "A dot," they all responded. "A dot?" he asked. "Why do you see the dot and not the rest of the paper?"
>
> Sometimes, life goes the same way. With each new sunrise, God gives us a clean sheet of paper, but we often let some small incident ruin it for us. A disagreement, a lost earring, an unkind word, a disruptive phone call—these trivialities become the dot we concentrate on instead of the rest of the paper.
>
> This is John Yonker at First Christian Church, reminding you to hang onto your perspective. Don't let one tiny ink spot blind you to a whole sheet of white paper!

Part 8: Review

CHAPTER 16 REVIEW QUESTIONS

1. What is a special occasion speech? Include in your answer an explanation for each of the four general purposes of a special occasion speech.

2. What should you consider when determining the purpose of the special occasion speech?

3. How do you research for a special occasion speech?

4. What are some helpful hints for practicing a special occasion speech?

TERMS TO REMEMBER

Chapter 16

special occasion speech (312)
speeches to celebrate (313)
speeches to commemorate (313)
speeches to inspire (313)
speeches to entertain (313)
eulogy (318)
tribute (318)
speech of introduction (319)
toast (320)
roast (320)
speech of award presentation (321)
speech of award acceptance (321)
after-dinner speech (322)
speech of inspiration (323)

NCA Student Outcomes for Speaking and Listening

The National Communication Association (NCA), in its 1998 report "Speaking and Listening Competencies for College Students," describes the speaking and listening skills students need in order to "communicate more effectively at school, in the workplace, and in society."

The following pages (326–339) provide a quick reference to key places *DK Speaker* addresses the outcomes and abilities from Part One of the NCA's "Expected Student Outcomes for Speaking and Listening: Basic Communication Course and General Education."

NCA defines speaking and listening as follows:

Speaking is the process of transmitting ideas and information orally in a variety of situations. Effective oral communication involves generating messages and delivering them with attention to vocal variety, articulation, and nonverbal signs.

Listening is the process of receiving, constructing meaning from, and responding to spoken and or nonverbal messages. People listen in order to comprehend information, critique and evaluate a message, show empathy for the feelings expressed by others, or appreciate a performance. Effective listening includes both literal and critical comprehension of ideas and information transmitted in oral language.

CONTENTS

Speaking Competencies: Basic Skills   326

Speaking Competencies: Delivery Skills   332

Listening Competencies: Literal Comprehension   334

Listening Competencies: Critical Comprehension   336

NCA information that appears on pages 325–339 comes from the National Communication Association, "Speaking and Listening Competencies for College Students" (Washington, D.C.: NCA, 1998), 7–12. Reprinted with permission of NCA, www.natcom.org.

Note: NCA's outcomes for interpersonal competencies are not included here.

Speaking Competencies: Basic Skills

In order to be a **competent speaker,** a person must be able to compose a message and provide ideas and information suitable to the topic, purpose, and audience. Specifically, the competent speaker should exhibit the following competencies by demonstrating the abilities included under each statement on pages 326–331.

Determine the purpose of oral discourse.

ABILITIES

- Identify the various purposes of discourse.
- Identify the similarities and differences among various purposes.
- Understand that different contexts require differing purposes.
- Generate a specific purpose relevant to the context when given a general purpose.

REFER TO…

Part 1 STARTING

Overview
Overview of public speaking, *2–19*

Chapter 2
Identify the general purpose of your speech, *36*
Identify the specific purpose of your speech, *42–43*

Part 6 SPEAKING TO INFORM

Chapter 13
The informative speech, *228–253*

Part 7 SPEAKING TO PERSUADE

Chapter 15
The persuasive speech, *278–305*

Part 8 SPEAKING ON SPECIAL OCCASIONS

Chapter 16
Speeches for special events, *308–323*

Choose a topic and restrict it according to the purpose and the audience.

ABILITIES

- Identify a subject that is relevant to the speaker's role, knowledge, concerns, and interests.
- Narrow the topic, adapting it to the purpose and time constraints for communicating.
- Adapt the treatment of the topic to the context for communication.

REFER TO...

Part 1 STARTING

Chapter 1
Getting to know your audience and situation, *20–33*

Chapter 2
How do you select a topic? *36–39*
How do you narrow your topic? *40–41*
How do you create a central idea? *42–47*

Part 6 SPEAKING TO INFORM

Chapter 13
How do you choose and research an informative topic? *234–239*

Part 7 SPEAKING TO PERSUADE

Chapter 15
How do you choose and research a persuasive topic? *282–289*

Part 8 SPEAKING ON SPECIAL OCCASIONS

Chapter 16
How do you write a special occasion speech? *314–317*

Fulfill the purpose of oral discourse.

ABILITIES

Formulate a thesis statement.
- Use a thesis as a planning tool.
- Summarize the central message in a manner consistent with the purpose.

REFER TO...

Part 1 STARTING

Chapter 2
How do you create a central idea (thesis statement)? *42–47*

Part 6 SPEAKING TO INFORM

Chapter 13
Identify your central idea, *237*

Part 7 SPEAKING TO PERSUADE

Chapter 15
Identify your central idea, *287*

Part 8 SPEAKING ON SPECIAL OCCASIONS

Chapter 16
Focus on a central idea, *316*

Fulfill the purpose of oral discourse (continued).

ABILITIES

Provide adequate support material.
- Demonstrate awareness of available types of support.
- Locate appropriate support materials.
- Select appropriate support based on the topic, audience, setting, and purpose.

REFER TO...

Part 2 RESEARCHING

Chapter 3
Locating support materials, *52–73*
Chapter 4
Selecting and testing support materials, *74–93*

Part 4 PRESENTING

Chapter 10
Using presentation aids, *178–201*

Part 6 SPEAKING TO INFORM

Chapter 13
Conduct your (informative speech) research, *239*

Part 7 SPEAKING TO PERSUADE

Chapter 15
Conduct your (persuasive speech) research, *289*

Part 8 SPEAKING ON SPECIAL OCCASIONS

Chapter 16
Research your speech, *316*

Fulfill the purpose of oral discourse (continued).

ABILITIES

Select a suitable organizational pattern.

- Demonstrate awareness of alternative organizational patterns.
- Demonstrate understanding of the functions of organizational patterns, including:
  - clarification of information
  - facilitation of listener comprehension
  - attitude change
  - relational interaction

Select organizational patterns that are appropriate to the topic, audience, content, and purpose.

REFER TO...

Part 3 CREATING

Chapter 5
Outlining your speech, *96–121*
Chapter 6
Organizing the speech body, *122–135*

Part 6 SPEAKING TO INFORM

Chapter 13
How do you organize an informative speech? *242–245*

Part 7 SPEAKING TO PERSUADE

Chapter 15
How do you organize a persuasive speech? *292–295*

Part 8 SPEAKING ON SPECIAL OCCASIONS

Chapter 16
Create your outline, *317*

Fulfill the purpose of oral discourse (continued).

ABILITIES

Demonstrate careful choice of words.

- Demonstrate understanding of the power of language.
- Select words that are appropriate to the topic, audience, purpose, context, and speaker.
- Use word choice in order to express ideas clearly, to create and maintain interest, and to enhance the speaker's credibility.
- Select words that avoid sexism, racism, and other forms of prejudice.

Provide effective transitions.

- Demonstrate understanding of the types and functions of transitions.
- Use transitions to:
  - establish connectedness
  - signal movement from one idea to another
  - clarify relationships among ideas

REFER TO...

Part 3 CREATING

Chapter 7
Introducing and concluding your speech, *136–149*

Part 4 PRESENTING

Chapter 8
Using language successfully, *152–161*

Part 6 SPEAKING TO INFORM

Chapter 13
Put your speech on its feet, *252*

Part 7 SPEAKING TO PERSUADE

Chapter 14
Highlight emotive and stylistic language, *261*
What are faulty arguments? *276–277*
Chapter 15
Put your speech on its feet, *304*

Part 8 SPEAKING ON SPECIAL OCCASIONS

Chapter 16
What are the types of special occasion speeches? *318–323*

Part 3 CREATING

Chapter 5
What can you use to link your speech parts together? *114–115*

NCA STUDENT OUTCOMES FOR SPEAKING AND LISTENING

Speaking Competencies: Delivery Skills

The **competent speaker** must also be able to transmit messages by using delivery skills suitable to the topic, purpose, and audience. Specifically, the competent speaker should exhibit the following competencies by demonstrating the abilities included under each statement on pages 332–333.

Employ vocal variety in rate, pitch, and intensity.

ABILITIES

- Use vocal variety to heighten and maintain interest.
- Use a rate that is suitable to the message, occasion, and receiver.
- Use pitch (within the speaker's optimum range) to clarify and to emphasize.
- Use intensity appropriate for the message and audible to the audience.

REFER TO...

Part 4 PRESENTING

Chapter 9   Pitch, rate, volume, pause, variety, *164–166*

Articulate clearly.

ABILITIES

- Demonstrate knowledge of the sounds of the American English language.
- Use the sounds of the American English language.

REFER TO...

Part 4 PRESENTING

Chapter 9   Pronunciation, articulation, dialect, *166–167*

Employ language appropriate to the designated audience.

ABILITIES

- Employ language that enhances the speaker's credibility, promotes the purpose, and [promotes] the receiver's understanding.
- Demonstrate that the use of technical vocabularies, slang, idiomatic language, and regionalisms may facilitate understanding when communicating with others who share meanings for those terms but can hinder understanding in those situations where meanings are not shared.
- Use standard pronunciation.
- Use standard grammar.
- Use language at the appropriate level of abstraction or generality.

REFER TO...

Part 4 PRESENTING

Chapter 8   How can you use language effectively? *156–161*
Chapter 9   Pronunciation, dialect, *166–167*

Part 6 SPEAKING TO INFORM

Chapter 13   Put your speech on its feet, *252*

Part 7 SPEAKING TO PERSUADE

Chapter 15   Put your speech on its feet, *304*

Employ language appropriate to the designated audience (continued).

Part 8 SPEAKING ON SPECIAL OCCASIONS

Chapter 16
What are the types of special occasion speeches?
318–323

Demonstrate nonverbal behavior that supports the verbal message.

ABILITIES

- Use appropriate paralanguage (extraverbal elements of voice such as emphasis, pause, tone, etc.) that achieves congruence and enhances the verbal intent.
- Use appropriate kinesic elements (posture, gesture, and facial expression) that achieve congruence and enhance the verbal intent.
- Use appropriate proxemic elements (interpersonal distance and spatial arrangement) that achieve congruence and enhance the verbal intent.
- Use appropriate clothing and ornamentation that achieve congruence and enhance the verbal intent.

REFER TO...

Part 4 PRESENTING

Chapter 9
What are the elements of vocal delivery? *164–167*
What are the elements of physical delivery? *168–171*

Part 5 LISTENING & EVALUATING

Chapter 11
How can you help your audience listen more effectively? *212–213*

Part 6 SPEAKING TO INFORM

Chapter 13
Put your speech on its feet, *252*

Part 7 SPEAKING TO PERSUADE

Chapter 15
Put your speech on its feet, *304*

Part 8 SPEAKING ON SPECIAL OCCASIONS

Chapter 16
Practice the speech, *317*

Listening Competencies: Literal Comprehension

In order to be a **competent listener,** a person must be able to listen with literal comprehension. Specifically, the competent listener should be able to exhibit the following competencies by demonstrating the abilities included under each statement on pages 334–335.

Recognize main ideas.

ABILITIES

- Distinguish ideas fundamental to the thesis from material that supports those ideas.
- Identify transitional, organizational, and nonverbal cues that direct the listener to the main ideas.
- Identify the main ideas in structured and unstructured discourse.

REFER TO…

Part 3 CREATING

Chapter 5	Use balanced main points, *104*
	Employ subordination, *104*
	Transitions, signposts, internal previews, internal reviews, *114–115*
Chapter 6	How do you make a speech out of a strategy? *130–135*

Part 4 PRESENTING

Chapter 9	What are the elements of vocal delivery? *164–167*
	What are the elements of physical delivery? *168–171*

Part 5 LISTENING & EVALUATING

Chapter 11	Listening, *204–215*
Chapter 12	The speech message, *222–223*

Identify supporting details.

ABILITIES

- Identify supporting details in spoken messages.
- Distinguish between those ideas that support the main ideas and those that do not.
- Determine whether the number of supporting details adequately develops each main idea.

REFER TO…

Part 2 RESEARCHING

Chapter 4	Selecting and testing support materials, *74–93*

Part 3 CREATING

Chapter 5	Employ subordination, *104*
Chapter 6	How do you make a speech out of a strategy? *130–135*

Part 5 LISTENING & EVALUATING

Chapter 11	Listening, *204–215*
Chapter 12	The speech message, *222–223*

Recognize explicit relationships among ideas.

ABILITIES

- Demonstrate an understanding of the types of organizational or logical relationships.
- Identify transitions that suggest relationships.
- Determine whether the asserted relationship exists.

REFER TO...

Part 3 CREATING

Chapter 5 Transitions, signposts, internal previews, internal reviews, *114–115*
Chapter 6 What organizational strategies can you use in your speech? *124–129*

Part 5 LISTENING & EVALUATING

Chapter 11 Listening, *204–215*
Chapter 12 The speech message, *222–223*

Part 6 SPEAKING TO INFORM

Chapter 13 How do you organize an informative speech? *242–245*

Part 7 SPEAKING TO PERSUADE

Chapter 14 Appeal to logos, *265*
         What are the parts of an argument? *270–271*
         What are the different types of arguments? *272–275*
Chapter 15 How do you organize a persuasive speech? *292–295*

Recall basic ideas and details.

ABILITIES

- Determine the goal for listening.
- State the basic cognitive and affective contents, after listening.

REFER TO...

Part 5 LISTENING & EVALUATING

Chapter 11 Listening, *204–215*
Chapter 12 The speech message, *222–223*

Listening Competencies: Critical Comprehension

The **competent listener** must also listen with critical comprehension. Specifically, the competent listener should exhibit the following competencies by demonstrating the abilities included under each statement on pages 336–339.

Attend with an open mind.

ABILITIES	REFER TO...
• Demonstrate an awareness of personal, ideological, and emotional biases. • Demonstrate awareness that each person has a unique perspective. • Demonstrate awareness that one's knowledge, experience, and emotions affect listening. • Use verbal and nonverbal behaviors that demonstrate willingness to listen to messages when variables such as setting, speaker, or topic may not be conducive to listening.	**Part 1 STARTING** **Chapter 1** Attitudes, beliefs, values, *22–23* What specific traits do you need to investigate? *24–27* **Part 5 LISTENING & EVALUATING** **Chapter 11** What can prevent effective listening? *210–211* As an audience member, how can you listen more effectively? *214–215* **Chapter 12** Evaluating speeches, *216–225*

Perceive the speaker's purpose and organization of ideas and information.

ABILITIES	REFER TO...
• Identify the speaker's purpose. • Identify the organization of the speaker's ideas and information.	**Part 1 STARTING** **Chapter 2** Identify the general purpose of your speech, *36* **Part 3 CREATING** **Chapter 6** What organizational strategies can you use in your speech? *124–129* **Part 5 LISTENING & EVALUATING** **Chapter 11** Listening, *204–215* **Chapter 12** Evaluating speeches, *216–225*

Discriminate between statements of fact and statements of opinion.

ABILITIES

- Distinguish between assertions that are verifiable and those that are not.

REFER TO…

Part 2 RESEARCHING

Chapter 4
Facts, *76*
What do you evaluate in your support materials? *86–87*

Part 7 SPEAKING TO PERSUADE

Chapter 14
Support a proposition of fact, value, or policy, *259*
What are the traditional appeals used to persuade? *262–265*
What are the modern appeals used to persuade? *266–269*

Distinguish between emotional and logical arguments.

ABILITIES

- Demonstrate an understanding that arguments have both emotional and logical dimensions.
- Identify the logical characteristics of an argument.
- Identify the emotional characteristics of an argument.
- Identify whether the argument is predominantly emotional or logical.

REFER TO…

Part 7 SPEAKING TO PERSUADE

Chapter 14
What are the traditional appeals used to persuade? *262–265*
What are the modern appeals used to persuade? *266–269*
What are the parts of an argument? *270–271*
What are the different types of arguments? *272–275*
What are faulty arguments? *276–277*

Detect bias and prejudice.

ABILITIES

- Identify instances of bias and prejudice in a spoken message.
- Specify how bias and prejudice may affect the impact of a spoken message.

REFER TO…

Part 4 PRESENTING

Chapter 8
Be appropriate (with language), *159*

Part 7 SPEAKING TO PERSUADE

Chapter 14
What are the traditional appeals used to persuade? *262–265*
What are the modern appeals used to persuade? *266–269*
What are faulty arguments? *276–277*

NCA STUDENT OUTCOMES FOR SPEAKING AND LISTENING

Recognize the speaker's attitude.

ABILITIES

- Identify the direction, intensity, and salience of the speaker's attitude as reflected by the verbal messages.
- Identify the direction, intensity, and salience of the speaker's attitude as reflected by the nonverbal messages.

REFER TO...

Part 4 PRESENTING

Chapter 8
What makes language so important? *154–155*
Chapter 9
What are the elements of physical delivery? *168–171*

Part 5 LISTENING & EVALUATING

Chapter 11
As an audience member, how can you listen more effectively? *214–215*
Chapter 12
The speaker's presentation, *222–223*

Synthesize and evaluate by drawing logical inferences and conclusions.

ABILITIES

- Draw relationships between prior knowledge and the information provided by the speaker.
- Demonstrate an understanding of the nature of inference.
- Identify the types of verbal and nonverbal information.
- Draw valid inferences from the information.
- Identify the information as evidence to support views.
- Assess the acceptability of evidence.
- Identify patterns of reasoning and judge the validity of arguments.
- Analyze the information and inferences in order to draw conclusions.

REFER TO...

Part 2 RESEARCHING

Chapter 4
What do you evaluate in your support materials? *86–87*

Part 5 LISTENING & EVALUATING

Chapter 12
The speech message, *222–223*

Part 7 SPEAKING TO PERSUADE

Chapter 14
What are the parts of an argument? *270–271*
What are the different types of arguments? *272–275*
What are faulty arguments? *276–277*

338

Recall the implications and arguments.

ABILITIES

- Identify the arguments used to justify the speaker's position.
- State both the overt and implied arguments.
- Specify the implications of these arguments for the speaker, audience, and society at large.

REFER TO...

Part 5 LISTENING & EVALUATING

Chapter 11
As an audience member, how can you listen more effectively? *214–215*

Part 7 SPEAKING TO PERSUADE

Chapter 14
What are the parts of an argument? *270–271*
What are the different types of arguments? *272–275*

Recognize discrepancies between the speaker's verbal and nonverbal messages.

ABILITIES

- Identify when the nonverbal signals contradict the verbal message.
- Identify when the nonverbal signals understate or exaggerate the verbal message.
- Identify when the nonverbal message is irrelevant to the verbal message.

REFER TO...

Part 4 PRESENTING

Chapter 9
What are the elements of physical delivery? *168–171*

Part 5 LISTENING & EVALUATING

Chapter 11
Listen critically, *215*
Chapter 12
The speaker's presentation, *222–223*

Employ active listening techniques when appropriate.

ABILITIES

- Identify the cognitive and affective dimensions of a message.
- Demonstrate comprehension by formulating questions that clarify or qualify the speaker's content and affective intent.
- Demonstrate comprehension by paraphrasing the speaker's message.

REFER TO...

Part 5 LISTENING & EVALUATING

Chapter 11
Listen actively, *214*

Glossary

abbreviation A shortened form of a word or phrase, used to represent the full form. (Chapter 8)

acronym A word formed from the initials or other parts of several words. (Chapter 8)

after-dinner speech A speech usually given with the general purpose to entertain but with a relevant message. (Chapter 16)

analogy A way of explaining the unfamiliar by comparing and contrasting it to what is familiar. (Chapter 4)

appeals The means by which speakers prove or establish the arguments they are making. (Chapter 14)

appearance A person's physical choices of dress and grooming practices. (Chapter 9)

appreciative listening Listening for recreation or enjoyment. (Chapter 11)

arbitrary The relationship between a word and what it stands for is random, subjective, or coincidental. (Chapter 8)

argument A reason or a series of reasons given to support an assertion. (Chapter 14)

argument by analogy The conclusion that something will be accurate for one case if it is true for another similar case. (Chapter 14)

argument by authority An argument dependent on the ethos and authority of others whose testimony you use to support a claim. (Chapter 14)

argument by cause An argument that demonstrates a relationship between two events or factors by focusing on the premise that one caused the other to occur. (Chapter 14)

argument by deduction Constructed by offering a series of general statements that then prove the specific claim/conclusion is correct. (Chapter 14)

argument by induction Predicting probability, this argument reasons from specific cases to a general statement. (Chapter 14)

articulation How completely and clearly you utter a word. (Chapter 9)

attending The phase of hearing when a person pays attention to a particular sound. (Chapter 11)

attention-getter An opening statement that grabs the audience's interest. (Chapter 7)

attitudes Learned persistent psychological responses, predispositions, or inclinations to act one way or feel a particular way toward something. (Chapters 1, 14)

attitudinal anchors The viewpoints an audience finds most acceptable. (Chapter 15)

audience The person or persons receiving the speaker's message and contributing feedback. (Overview, Chapter 1)

audience analysis A systematic investigation of the characteristics that make the audience unique. (Chapter 1)

audience centered A speech that grabs the audience's attention and recognizes their unique characteristics and viewpoints. (Chapter 1)

audio clips Recordings of only sound. (Chapter 10)

background The speaker's and audience's identities and life experiences. (Overview)

bar graphs Visual aids consisting of vertical or horizontal bars that represent specific sets of data. (Chapter 10)

behaviors The unconcealed actions or reactions people have, often in response to stimuli, related to their attitudes, beliefs, and values. (Chapter 14)

beliefs The ideas a person accepts as plausible, based on interpretation and judgment. (Chapters 1, 14)

blatant plagiarism Occurs either when speakers take an entire speech or document and present it as their own or when speakers take parts of information from other sources and link the parts together, creating an entire speech out of someone else's words. (Overview)

blog A Web site or Web page that contains regular postings by its author(s) and allows visitors to post comments. (Chapter 3)

body The central portion of the speech made up of the main points, the multiple layers of subordinate points, and links. (Chapter 5)

brainstorming The act of free associating from one word or concept to another. (Chapter 2)

brief examples Specific instances illustrating a single general notion. (Chapter 4)

causal strategy Used when the audience needs to understand the cause and effect or consequences of something, by either leading up to a particular result or backtracking from the effect to the cause. (Chapter 6)

central idea The concise, single sentence summarizing and/or previewing what a speaker will say during a speech. (Chapter 2)

central processing Occurs when an audience is motivated to think critically about a topic. (Chapter 14)

channel The means of getting the message across, such as a voice over the airwaves or visual messages in the form of nonverbal and visual aids. (Overview)

charts Visual summaries of complex or large quantities of information. (Chapter 10)

chronological strategy Used when moving through steps in a process or developing a timeline. (Chapter 6)

citations The credits for the original sources of the support materials used for a speech. (Chapter 4)

claim An assertion made in an argument. (Chapter 14)

clichés Overused words or phrases that have lost their effect. (Chapter 8)

closed-ended questions Questions that seek short, precise answers (such as "yes" or "no"). (Chapters 1, 3)

coercion The act of forcing a person, via threats or intimidation, to do something against his or her will. (Chapter 14)

Cognitive Dissonance Theory A theory emphasizing the human need to be in a harmonious state and that conflicting attitudes, values, beliefs, ideas, or behaviors can cause an inharmonious or dissonant feeling. (Chapter 14)

common ground The overlap within the speaker's and audience's identities and life experiences. (Overview)

communication apprehension Fears a speaker has about giving a speech. (Overview)

comparative advantage A strategy to convince an audience that one thing is better than another by comparing the two. (Chapter 6)

comparative strategy An organizational strategy using the practices of compare and contrast. (Chapter 6)

comparison The act of pointing out similarities between two or more ideas, things, factors, or issues. (Chapter 4)

conclusion The ending of the speech, which allows the speaker one last moment to reinforce the main ideas as well as "wow" the audience. (Chapters 5, 7)

connotative meaning The emotional and personal reaction a person may have to a word. (Chapter 8)

contrast The act of pointing out differences between two or more ideas, things, factors, or issues. (Chapter 4)

critical listening Listening carefully to a message to judge it as acceptable or not. (Chapter 11)

critical thinking The careful, deliberate determination of whether one should accept, reject, or suspend judgment about a claim or information and the degree of confidence with which one accepts or rejects it. (Chapter 11)

culture The learned patterns of beliefs, values, attitudes, norms, practices, customs, and behaviors shared by a large group of people that are taught from one generation to the next. (Chapters 1, 8)

databases Extensive collections of published works, such as magazine, newspaper, and journal articles, all in electronic form. They contain descriptions, citation information about the articles, and often the full text of the articles. (Chapter 3)

decoding The process of interpreting messages. (Overview)

definitions Brief explanations designed to inform the audience about something unfamiliar. (Chapter 4)

delivery outline An outline maintaining the structure of the speech while eliminating much of the detail. Used during the speech and contains delivery hints. (Chapter 5)

341

denotative meaning The accepted meaning of a word, which can be found in the dictionary. (Chapter 8)

description The stage of evaluation when the evaluators offer what they saw and heard. (Chapter 12)

descriptive statistics Numerical facts or data that describe or summarize characteristics of a population or a large quantity of data. (Chapter 4)

design principles Principles relating to the arrangement and placement of various elements of visual aids for optimum effect. (Chapter 10)

dialect The way a culture or subculture pronounces and uses language. (Chapter 9)

direct eye contact The act of a speaker briefly looking into an audience member's eyes. (Chapter 9)

drawings Maps, sketches, diagrams, plans, or other nonphotographic representations. (Chapter 10)

egocentrism The tendency for an audience to be interested in the topics that relate and matter to them, as well as their need for the speaker to recognize that they are a group of unique individuals. (Chapter 1)

Elaboration Likelihood Model Suggests that people process persuasive messages based on their commitment or involvement by either central processing or peripheral processing. (Chapter 14)

emblems Speech-independent or culturally learned gestures that have a direct verbal translation. (Chapter 9)

empathic listening Listening for the purpose of giving the speaker emotional support. (Chapter 11)

encoding The process of conveying messages. (Overview)

enthymeme A truncated syllogism that omits an obvious minor premise. (Chapter 14)

enunciation The ability to use distinctiveness and clarity while saying linked whole words. (Chapter 9)

environmental barriers Conditions within the speech location that interrupt the listener's ability to concentrate, such as movement, heat, cold, or hard seats. (Chapters 1, 11)

ethnicity Traits that stem from national and religious affiliations. (Chapter 1)

ethnocentrism The notion that one's culture is superior to other cultures. (Overview, Chapter 14)

ethos Appeal of reliability or credibility. (Chapter 14)

eulogy A speech presented after a person's death. (Chapter 16)

evaluation A detailed description of a speech's successes and/or the improvements needed, which is grounded in justified judgment. (Chapter 12)

evidence The material that proves a claim to be accurate. (Chapter 14)

examples Specific instances or cases that embody or illustrate points in a speech. (Chapter 4)

Expectancy-Outcome Values Theory A theory suggesting that people will evaluate the cost, benefit, or value related to making change in a particular attitude, value, belief, or behavior to decide if it is worth it or not. (Chapter 14)

expert testimony Firsthand knowledge or opinions from a specialist in a field related to the speech's topic. (Chapter 4)

extemporaneous speaking The speaker plans out, rehearses, and delivers the speech from a key-word/phrase outline in a conversational manner. (Chapter 9)

extended examples Detailed stories, narratives, illustrations, or anecdotes allowing the audience to linger on the vivid, concrete images the examples create. (Chapter 4)

external noise Any barrier to effective listening that originates outside of the listener's mind and body, often caused by environmental or linguistic barriers. (Chapters 1, 11)

facial expressions The use of facial features and muscles to convey a speaker's internal thoughts and feelings. (Chapter 9)

facts Verifiable bits of information about people, events, places, dates, and times. (Chapter 4)

fallacy A faulty argument or error in logic. (Chapter 14)

faulty syllogism A flawed argument in which the major premise, minor premise, and/or conclusion is not factual. (Chapter 14)

feedback The verbal or nonverbal messages encoded by the audience and decoded by the speaker. (Overview)

figurative analogy Compares and contrasts two essentially different things. (Chapter 4)

fillers Unnecessary sounds, words, or phrases that serve no purpose and do not add to the understanding of the message, such as the word "um." (Chapters 8, 9)

First Amendment U.S. Constitutional amendment establishing freedom of speech by stating, "Congress shall make no law... abridging the freedom of speech, or the press...." (Overview)

flowcharts Charts that diagram step-by-step development through a procedure, relationship, or process. (Chapter 10)

follow-up questions New questions the interviewer produces based on the interviewee's answers to questions during an interview. (Chapter 3)

general purpose The unrestricted aim of a speech. (Chapter 2)

gestures The use of the body or parts of it (hands, arms, eyes, or head) to convey a message or feeling during a speech. (Chapter 9)

graphs Visual representations of numerical information that demonstrate relationships or differences between two or more variables. (Chapter 10)

hearing Occurs when sound waves strike the eardrum and spark a chain reaction that ends with the brain registering the sound. (Chapter 11)

hits A list of Web pages, files, and images related to the term entered into a search engine. (Chapter 3)

hypothetical examples Examples based on the potential outcomes of imagined scenarios. (Chapter 4)

idea bank A list of general words and phrases that could be potential speech topics. (Chapter 2)

identification The human need and willingness to understand as much as possible the feelings, thoughts, motives, interests, attitudes, and lives of others. (Overview)

identity Made up of a person's beliefs, values, and attitudes. (Chapter 1)

illustrators Gestures that are speech-dependent or closely linked to what is being said, which help demonstrate the message. (Chapter 9)

impromptu speaking A delivery method where the speaker has little or no preparation or rehearsal prior to the speech. (Chapter 9)

inferential statistics Draw conclusions about a larger population by making estimates based on a smaller sample of that population. (Chapter 4)

inflection Varying the pitch of one's voice to demonstrate enthusiasm, excitement, concern, and dedication to the topic. (Chapter 9)

informative listening Listening that concentrates on language and detail as well as remembering the knowledge gained by listening for insight or comprehension. (Chapter 11)

informative speaking Gives the audience completely new knowledge, skills, or understanding about a topic or increases their current knowledge, skills, or understanding. (Chapter 13)

internal noise Any physiological or psychological barrier to effective listening that originates within the body or mind of the listener. (Chapters 1, 11)

internal previews Links to what is next in the speech. (Chapter 5)

internal reviews Links that summarize the information just stated in the previous section of a speech. (Chapter 5)

interviews Information-gathering sessions where one person asks the other a series of prepared questions. (Chapters 1, 3)

introduction The opening of a speech used to grab the audience's attention and focus in on the topic. (Chapters 5, 7)

jargon The technical or specialized vocabulary used among members of a profession. (Chapter 8)

judgment The stage of evaluation where the evaluator offers what was good or not about a speech. (Chapter 12)

justification The stage of evaluation where the evaluator explains why something was good or not about a speech. (Chapter 12)

lay testimony Testimony from a peer or an ordinary person, other than the speaker, who bears witness to his or her own experiences and beliefs. (Chapter 4)

line graphs Visuals with numerical points plotted on a horizontal axis with one variable and on the vertical axis with another; the points are then connected to make a line. (Chapter 10)

linguistic barriers Barriers to listening that occur when the verbal and nonverbal messages from the speaker are unfamiliar or misunderstood by the listener. (Chapters 1, 11)

links Words, phrases, or sentences that make a logical connection between the parts of the body of the speech and/or thoughts. (Chapter 5)

listening The conscious learned act of paying attention and assigning meaning to an acoustic message. (Chapter 11)

literal analogy Compares and contrasts two like things. (Chapter 4)

logos Appeals to the audience's ability to reason through statistics, facts, and testimony to reach a conclusion. (Chapter 14)

main points The essential ideas or claims about a topic that comprise the body of a speech. (Chapters 2, 5)

manuscript speaking The delivery method used when a speaker reads directly from a word-for-word copy of the speech. (Chapter 9)

Maslow's hierarchy of needs The theory that humans have a hierarchical set of needs that must be met, starting with the lower, more basic needs and progressing to the higher, less basic needs. (Chapters 1, 14)

mean An average of a set of numbers. (Chapter 4)

median The middle value in a set of numbers arranged in increasing order. (Chapter 4)

memorized speaking A delivery method where the speaker delivers a speech from memory exactly as written. (Chapter 9)

message The verbal and nonverbal ideas encoded by the speaker and decoded by the audience. (Overview)

mode The number that occurs the most in a set of numbers. (Chapter 4)

models Three-dimensional representations. (Chapter 10)

monotone A vocal quality that is constant in pitch that can be distracting and boring. (Chapter 9)

Monroe's motivated sequence A five-step strategy that motivates an audience to action based on their needs. (Chapters 6, 14)

movement The use of motion and space during a speech. (Chapter 9)

multimedia The combination of multiple presentation aids (still images, graphs, text, sound, and video) into one choreographed production. (Chapter 10)

mythos Appeals to the audience's sense of their history in the larger culture and their need to be a member of that culture; draws upon feelings of patriotism, pride, and valor. (Chapter 14)

no-citation plagiarism Occurs when speakers fail to give source credit to a specific part of their speech that has been taken from another source. (Overview)

noise Any unwanted pleasant or unpleasant barrier that prevents listening and/or interferes with the message and/or feedback. (Overview, Chapter 11)

objective The part of the specific purpose that describes the outcome or behavior the speaker wants the audience to experience or adopt. (Chapter 2)

open-ended questions Questions that allow for discussion and longer responses. (Chapters 1, 3)

oral evaluations Brief verbal overviews describing what the evaluator saw and felt about a speech. (Chapter 12)

organizational charts Illustrate the structure or chain of command in an organization. (Chapter 10)

parallelism The arrangement of words, phrases, or sentences in similar patterns. (Chapter 6)

paraphrasing Restating material in a simpler format using the speaker's own words. (Chapter 4)

pathos Appeals to emotions. (Chapter 14)

pause Slowing down the speaking rate or stopping during a speech for effect. (Chapter 9)

peripheral processing The act of the audience dismissing a speech because they believe the message to be irrelevant, uninteresting, or too complex to pay close attention. (Chapter 14)

personal testimony The speaker's experience or point of view. (Chapter 4)

personal traits Audience demographics, or traits such as age, gender, sexual orientation, household type, education, occupation, income, and disabilities. (Chapter 1)

persuasion A deliberate attempt, by the speaker, to create, reinforce, or change the attitudes, beliefs, values, and/or behaviors of the listener. (Chapter 14)

photographs Two-dimensional photographic representations. (Chapter 10)

physiological barriers Internal noise such as hunger, sickness, disabilities, and pain that can interrupt the listening process. (Chapters 1, 11)

pictographs Bar graphs that use pictures instead of bars. (Chapter 10)

pie graphs Circular graphs with sections representing a percentage of given quantity. (Chapter 10)

pitch How high or low a person's voice is in frequency, which is determined by how fast or slow the vocal cords vibrate. (Chapter 9)

plagiarism Intentional or accidental use of all or a portion of the words, ideas, or illustrations created by someone else without proper credit. (Overview)

popular sources Publications written for general readers. (Chapter 4)

population The larger group of individuals represented by a small survey group. (Chapter 3)

posture A speaker's body position and stance during a speech. (Chapter 9)

preparation outline The detailed, full-sentence outline of a speech. (Chapter 5)

presentation aids Two- or three-dimensional visual items, video footage, audio recordings, and/or multimedia segments that support and enhance a speech. (Chapter 10)

prestige testimony Firsthand knowledge or opinions from a person known for his or her popularity, fame, attractiveness, high-profile activities, and/or age. (Chapter 4)

primacy model Suggests that the speaker should put the strongest arguments first in the body of the speech to persuade the audience early in the speech. (Chapter 15)

primary sources Original sources of information, such as photographs, autobiographies, and letters. (Chapter 4)

problem–solution strategy An organizational strategy in persuasive speeches demonstrating a problem and advocating a solution. (Chapter 6)

pronunciation The standard way or commonly accepted way to make a word sound. (Chapter 9)

proposition of fact An assertion made in a persuasive speech central idea to prove something factual. (Chapter 14)

proposition of policy An assertion made in a persuasive speech central idea that seeks to prove a need for a new or different policy. (Chapter 14)

proposition of value An assertion made in a persuasive speech central idea that seeks to make a value judgment. (Chapter 14)

psychological barriers Internal noise in the form of emotional conditions that may prevent the listener from focusing on and absorbing a message. (Chapters 1, 11)

psychological traits The needs and motivations of the audience. (Chapter 1)

quotations A form of support material where the speaker directly uses words or passages written by someone else. (Chapter 7)

race The biological differences of humankind based on physical markers, such as color or texture of hair, color of skin and eyes, shape of facial features, and bodily build and proportions. (Chapter 1)

rate The speed at which a person speaks. (Chapter 9)

rationale The stage of evaluation where the evaluator offers a rationale or norm for his or her judgment. (Chapter 12)

reasoning The rational thinking that humans do to reach a conclusion or to justify beliefs or acts. (Chapter 14)

receiving The physiological process of hearing. (Chapter 11)

recency model The speaker begins with the weakest argument and finishes with the strongest to persuade the audience. (Chapter 15)

remembering The final stage of hearing, in which the listener retains information. (Chapter 11)

responding The phase of hearing when a response is given to the sounds that have been processed. (Chapter 11)

rhetorical questions Questions that the speaker does not expect the audience to answer, which are used for effect rather than to gain knowledge. (Chapter 7)

roast A humorous tribute to a person. (Chapter 16)

sample The surveyed portion of a larger population. (Chapter 3)

schemes Speech devices or language techniques that manipulate word order or repeat sounds, words, phrases, sentences, or grammatical patterns. (Chapter 8)

scholarly sources Sources written for readers who are specialists in their academic or professional fields. (Chapter 4)

search engines Specific tools used to locate information on the Web. (Chapter 3)

secondary sources Sources that build upon other (often primary) sources, by citing, reviewing, quoting, and/or paraphrasing the other materials or sources. (Chapter 4)

signposts Words or phrases that signal to the audience where they are with regard to related thoughts or what is important to remember. (Chapter 5)

situation The location and time in which the process of communication takes place. (Overview)

social judgment theory States that the speaker's persuasion will be easier, tolerated more, and potentially longer lasting if the audience can tie the persuasion to what they find most acceptable. (Chapter 15)

social traits Relate to how the audience is affected by or identifies with other groups of people. (Chapter 1)

sources Any books, magazines, journals, blogs, Web sites, e-mail, interviews, or other such resources that contribute information to the creation of a speech. (Chapter 3)

spatial strategy An organizational strategy recognizing space as a method of arrangement. (Chapter 6)

speaker The person who initiates and is responsible for most of the message. (Overview)

special occasion speech A speech given to celebrate, commemorate, inspire, or entertain. (Chapter 16)

specific purpose A single statement combining the general purpose, a specific audience, and the speaker's objective. (Chapter 2)

speeches to celebrate Honor or highlight a person, group, institution, place, or an event by praising the subject of the occasion. (Chapter 16)

speeches to commemorate Pay tribute to or remember a person, group, institution, place, or an event. (Chapter 16)

speeches to entertain Have the general goal to amuse, delight, and engage the audience for the purpose of enjoyment with a bit of wisdom or tribute thrown in. (Chapter 16)

speeches to inspire Speeches that motivate, stir, encourage, or arouse the audience. (Chapter 16)

speech of award acceptance The response a speaker gives after receiving an award, prize, or honor. (Chapter 16)

speech of award presentation A speech given to announce the recipient(s) of an award, prize, or honor. (Chapter 16)

speech of inspiration A speech that strives to motivate, encourage, move, or arouse an audience in a positive manner. (Chapter 16)

speech of introduction A speech that introduces the next or main speaker. (Chapter 16)

speech to describe A speech that describes an object, a person, an animal, a place, or an event. (Chapter 13)

speech to explain A speech that explains a concept or issue. (Chapter 13)

speech to instruct A speech that teaches or demonstrates a process. (Chapter 13)

speech to report An oral report or briefing. (Chapter 13)

standard of balance The subpoints under the main point in a speech should be nearly equal to each other in length and weight. (Chapter 6)

statistics Numerical facts or data that are summarized, organized, and tabulated to present significant information about a given population. (Chapter 4)

stereotyping The false or oversimplified generalizing applied to individuals based on group characteristics. (Chapter 1)

strategy A plan designed to achieve a goal, particularly concerning the relationship and arrangement of a speech's main points. (Chapter 6)

subpoints Subordinate points that offer information to support and relate back to the main points of a speech. (Chapter 5)

support materials Any information that helps explain, elaborate, or validate a speech topic. (Chapter 3)

surveys Series of questions used to collect quantifiable information from a population. (Chapters 1, 3)

syllogism The classical form of deductive reasoning, featuring major and minor premises and a conclusion. (Chapter 14)

symbolic A word that represents what it is referring to either by association, resemblance, or convention. (Chapter 8)

tables Visuals consisting of numbers or words arranged in rows, columns, or lists. (Chapter 10)

target audience The primary group of people the speaker is appealing to. (Chapter 15)

testimony Firsthand knowledge or opinions held by someone. (Chapter 4)

toast A speech expressing honor or goodwill to a person, institution, group, or an event that is punctuated by taking a drink. (Chapter 16)

topical strategy Used when there is a strong inherent or traditional division of subtopics within the main topic. (Chapter 6)

transactional process The fluid process of communication where the speaker and the listener participate equally by giving and receiving information to and from one another. (Overview)

transitions Words or phrases signaling movement from one point to another and how the points relate to each other. (Chapter 5)

tribute A speech that commemorates the lives or accomplishments of people, groups, institutions, or events, either with the recipient present or posthumously. (Chapter 16)

tropes Language techniques that embellish or enhance ordinary words. (Chapter 8)

understanding The phase of the listening process in which meaning is applied to a sound. (Chapter 11)

values The enduring principles related to worth or what a person sees as right or wrong, important or unimportant. (Chapters 1, 14)

variety The fluctuation, change, or adjustment of a speaker's volume, pitch, rate, and pauses. (Chapter 9)

video clips Footage from television, movies, or any other type of video. (Chapter 10)

volume How loud or soft the speaker's voice is. (Chapter 9)

warrants Assumptions that act as links between the evidence and the claim in an argument. (Chapter 14)

347

Web sites Consist of multiple, unified pages beginning with a home page, created and maintained by an individual, group, business, or organization. (Chapter 3)

working main points The early drafts of a speaker's main points that are subject to change during the course of research. (Chapter 2)

working outline A brief, usually handwritten, outline of the body of the speech, used to guide the research during the early stages of creating a speech. (Chapters 2, 5)

written evaluations Assessments given in written form. (Chapter 12)

Bibliography

Aristotle. "De Anima." Trans. J. A. Smith. *The Basic Works of Aristotle.* Ed. Richard McKeon. New York: Random, 1941. 554–581. Print.

—. "De Caelo." Trans. J. L. Stocks. *The Basic Works of Aristotle.* Ed. Richard McKeon. New York: Random, 1941. 404. Print.

—. "Rhetorica." Trans. W. Rhys Roberts. *The Basic Works of Aristotle.* Ed. Richard McKeon. New York: Random, 1941. Print.

Burke, Kenneth. *A Rhetoric of Motives.* Berkeley: U of California P, 1969. viii. Print.

Carson, Rachel L. *Under the Sea-Wind: A Naturalist's Picture of Ocean Life.* 1st ed. New York: Simon, 1941. xiii. Print.

Conan Doyle, Arthur. *The Hound of Baskervilles.* New York: Grossett, 1902. 36. Print.

Corbett, Edward J. and Robert J. Connors. *Classical Rhetoric for the Modern Student.* 4th ed. New York: Oxford UP, 1999. 62–71. Print.

Duarte, Nancy. *Slide:ology: The Art and Science of Creating Great Presentations.* Sebastopol: O'Reilly, 2008. 13, 83. Print.

Festinger, Leon. *A Theory of Cognitive Dissonance.* Stanford: Stanford UP, 1957. Print.

Fishbein, Martin and Icek Ajzen. *Belief, Attitude, Intention, and Behavior: An Introduction to Theory and Research.* Reading: Addison-Wesley, 1975. 6. Print.

Lancaster, Lynne C. and David Stillman. *When Generations Collide.* New York: Harper, 2002. 18–32. Print.

Legal Information Institute. "First Amendment." *United States Constitution.* Cornell U School of Law, n.d. Web. 17 Aug. 2010.

Maslow, Abraham. *Motivation and Personality.* New York: Harper, 1954. 80–106. Print.

Monroe, Alan H. *Principles and Types of Speeches.* Chicago: Scott, 1935. Print.

Moore, Brooke Noel and Richard Parker. *Critical Thinking.* 4th ed. Mountain View: Mayfield, 1995. 4. Print.

Pelias, Ronald J. and Tracy Stephenson Shaffer. *Performance Studies: The Interpretation of Aesthetic Texts.* Dubuque: Kendall, 2007. 181–195. Print.

Petty, Richard. E. and John T. Cacioppo. *Communication and Persuasion: Central and Peripheral Routes to Attitude Change.* New York: Springer-Verlag, 1986. Print.

Population Reference Bureau. "Traditional Families Account for Only 7 Percent of U.S. Households." *PRB,* Population Reference Bureau, n.d. Web. 22 Oct. 2010.

Sagan, Carl. *The Demon-Haunted World: Science as a Candle in the Dark.* New York: Random, 1996. 209–217. Print.

Sherif, Muzafer and Carl I. Hovland. *Social Judgment: Assimilation and Contrast Effects in Communication and Attitude Change.* New Haven: Yale UP, 1961. Print.

Sleep Disorders Center. "Relaxation Techniques." *University of Maryland Medical Center.* University of Maryland Medical Center, 3 Aug. 2010. Web. 10 Aug. 2010.

Syrus, Publius. *The Moral Sayings of Publius Syrus, A Roman Slave.* Trans. Darius Lyman, Jr. Cleveland: L. E. Barnard. 1856. 43. Print.

Toulmin, Stephen Edelston. *The Uses of Argument.* New York: Cambridge UP, 1958. 94–145. Print.

Toulmin, Stephen, Richard Rieke, and Allan Janik. *An Introduction to Reasoning.* 2nd ed. New York: Macmillan, 1984. 129–175. Print.

United States Census Bureau. "An Older and More Diverse Nation by Midcentury." *U.S. Census Bureau Newsroom.* U.S. Department of Commerce, 14 Aug. 2008. Web. 7 June 2009.

Notes

OVERVIEW

1. David G. Myers and Malcolm A. Jeeves, *Psychology through the Eyes of Faith* (San Francisco: Christian College Coalition, 1987), 139, Print.

CHAPTER 4

1. Ed. Robert I. Fitzhenry, *The Harper Book of Quotations*, 3rd ed. (New York: Harper, 1993), 398, Print.

CHAPTER 8

1. Martin Luther King, Jr., "I Have a Dream," Lincoln Memorial (Washington: 28 Aug. 1963), Speech.

2. Sojourner Truth, "Ain't I a Woman?" Women's Convention (Akron: May 1851), Speech.

3. Patrick Henry, "Give Me Liberty or Give Me Death," St. John's Henrico Parish Church (Richmond: 25 Mar. 1775), Address.

4. Hillary Clinton, "Women's Rights Are Human Rights" (Beijing: 5 Sept. 1995), Speech.

CHAPTER 9

1. Although commonly attributed to Aristotle, this quotation originates from Will Durant's summation of Aristotle's ideas in *Ethics,* book II, chapter 4 and book I, chapter 7. See Will Durant, *The Story of Philosophy: The Lives and Opinions of the World's Greatest Philosophers* (New York: Pocket, 1991), 76, Print.

CHAPTER 11

1. Rachel Naomi Remen, *Kitchen Table Wisdom: Stories that Heal* (New York: Berkley, 2006), 143, Print.

CHAPTER 16

1. Titus Maccius Plautus, Ed. Ferruccio Bertini, *Asinaria* (Padova: R.A.D.A.R., 1968), 104, Print.

Credits

PHOTOGRAPHS

TABLE OF CONTENTS: outside flap (top) ImageSource/ AGE Fotostock; (bottom) Ladi Kirn/Alamy; **inside flap** Anders Sellin/Alamy; **inside front cover** ERProductions Ltd/Glow Images

FRONT MATTER: i (top) Corbis Premium RF/Alamy; (bottom) Bon Appetit/Alamy; **vi** © Oliver Knight/Alamy; **vii** Columbia College/Kaci Smart; **ix** CJG - Technology/Alamy

OVERVIEW: 1 ImageSource/AGE Fotostock; **2** imagebroker/ Alamy; **4** Realistic Reflections/Alamy; **6** Image Source/Alamy; **8** Columbia College/Megan Pettegrew-Donley; **10** Columbia College/Kaci Smart; **12** Oliver Knight/Alamy

CHAPTER 1: 20 Jeff Greenberg/AGE Fotostock; **22** (top) Glowimages/AGE Fotostock; (bottom) Jeff Greenberg/ AGE Fotostock; **23** (left) Jim West/AGE Fotostock; (right) CLEO Photo/Alamy; **24** INSADCO Photography/Alamy; **28** Walter Zerla/AGE Fotostock; **30** Paul Bradbury/Alamy; **32** Peter Cavanagh/Alamy

CHAPTER 2: 34 StockbrokerXtra/AGE Fotostock; **36** Mark Sykes/Alamy; **40** David Crausby/Alamy; **42** Anderson Ross/ AGE Fotostock; **48** Beaconstox/Alamy

CHAPTER 3: 51 Ladi Kirn/Alamy; **52** Dorling Kindersley, Ltd.; **54** CJG - Technology/Alamy; **60** Dan Dunkley/Alamy; **66** Tetra Images/Alamy; **68** © Kristian Peetz/Alamy; **70** Gala_Kan/Shutterstock; **72** Stanley Marquardt/Alamy

CHAPTER 4: 74 Hill Street Studios/AGE Fotostock; **76** © ImageDJ/Alamy; **82** Paul Bradforth/Alamy; **86** © Geoffrey Kidd/Alamy; **88** Royalty Free/AGE Fotostock; **90** © [apply pictures]/Alamy

CHAPTER 5: 95 Anders Sellin/Alamy; **96** Zoonar/I Poleshchuk/ AGE Fotostock; **98** © Joe Fairs/Alamy; **100** Micah Hanson/ Alamy; **106** tbkmedia.de/Alamy; **114** Helen Sessions/Alamy; **116** Giovanni Guarino STOCK/Alamy; **118** © Fancy/Alamy

CHAPTER 6: 122 Raymond Forbes/AGE Fotostock; **124** Hill Street Studios/AGE Fotostock; **130** Amana Images Inc./Alamy

CHAPTER 7: 136 Carmo Correia/Alamy; **138** MARKA/ Alamy; **140** Tono Balaguer/AGE Fotostock; **142** Koichi Saito/ Amanaima/AGE Fotostock; **144** Paul Bradforth/Alamy; **146** Peter Casolino/Alamy; **148** Mick Sinclair/Alamy

CHAPTER 8: 151 Amana Images Inc./Alamy; **152** Keystone Pictures USA/Alamy; **154** Spencer Grant/AGE Fotostock; **156** David Grossman/Alamy

CHAPTER 9: 162 ERProductions Ltd/Glow Images; **164** Paul Burns/Glow Images; **168** PhotosIndia/Glow Images; **169** Clu/iStockphoto; **170** (top and bottom) © RubberBall/Alamy; **171** (top left) Lifestylepics/Alamy; (top right) Myrleen Pearson/Alamy; (bottom left) Corbis RF/AGE Fotostock; (bottom right) Myrleen Pearson/Alamy; **172** © Sean Nel/iStockphoto; **174** Number 7/Alamy

CHAPTER 10: 178 PhotoSpin, Inc/Alamy; **180** (left) Image Source/Alamy; (right) © Hugh Threlfall/Alamy; **181** (left) Corbis RF/Alamy; (right) Dorling Kindersley, Ltd.; **182** (map and diagram) Dorling Kindersley, Ltd.; **183** (left and right) Dorling Kindersley, Ltd.; **184** (left and right) Dorling Kindersley, Ltd.; **185** cambpix/Alamy; **186** Dave & Les Jacobs/Glow Images; **188** Image Source/Alamy; **191** aberCPC/Alamy; **192** Stock Connection Blue/Alamy; **193** (top and bottom) Dorling Kindersley, Ltd.; **194** (all top) Dorling Kindersley, Ltd.; (bottom) Chromorange/ Ohde Christian/WoodyStock/Alamy; **196** Adam Borkowski/ Fotolia; **200** Chris Schmidt/iStockphoto

CHAPTER 11: 203 The National Trust Photolibrary/Alamy; **204** Radius Images/Alamy; **206** imagebroker/Alamy; **208** imagebroker/Alamy; **210** Blend Images/Alamy; **212** fStop/Alamy; **214** Hill Street Studios/Getty Images

CHAPTER 12: 216 vario images GmbH & Co.KG/Alamy; **218** Image Source/AGE Fotostock; **222** Fotosearch/AGE Fotostock; **224** Chris Ryan/AGE Fotostock

CHAPTER 13: 227 Mitch Diamond/Alamy; **228** Westend61 GmbH/Alamy; **230** Art Directors & TRIP/Alamy; **232** Zute Lightfoot/Alamy; **234** Fancy/Alamy; **240** Kevin Britland/ Alamy; **242** Elenathewise/Fotolia; **252** Inspirestock Inc./Alamy

CHAPTER 14: 255 Corbis Premium RF/Alamy; **256** A.Sarti/AGE Fotostock; **258** chrisstockphotography/ Alamy; **262** Florian Kopp/AGE Fotostock; **266** Peter Glass/Alamy; **270** Alex Havret/AGE Fotostock; **272** Mike Hill/Alamy; **276** Ken Welsh/Alamy

CHAPTER 15: 278 Jeff Greenberg/Alamy; **280** Ian Shaw/ Alamy; **282** Ian Shaw/Alamy; **290** Steve Skjold/Alamy; **292** Mettafoto/Alamy; **304** Simon Jarratt/Corbis/ Glow Images

CHAPTER 16: 307 Bon Appetit/Alamy; **308** Design Pics Inc./Alamy; **311** Andres Rodriguez/Alamy; **312** Charles Dragazis/Alamy; **314** Tetra Images/Alamy; **318** C.J. Gunther/ PSG/Newscom

TEXT

OVERVIEW: 5 Martin Luther King, Jr., quotation, Reprinted by arrangement with The Heirs to the Estate of Martin Luther King Jr., c/o Writers House as agent for the proprietor New York, NY. Copyright 1963 Dr. Martin Luther King Jr; copyright renewed 1991 Coretta Scott King

CHAPTER 3: 58 and 59 Columbia College screenshots, Screenshot copyright © 2012 by Columbia College. Reprinted with permission. **61** University of Colorado screenshot, University of Colorado Boulder Libraries Catalog. http://ucblibraries.colorado.edu/#Chinook. Copyright © Regents of the University of Colorado; **63** JSTOR screenshot, Screenshot copyright © 2012 by JSTOR. Reprinted with permission; **67** dissonance definition, Definition of dissonance from LONGMAN DICTIONARY OF AMERICAN ENGLISH, 4th Edition. Copyright © 2012 by Pearson Education Limited. Reprinted with permission.

CHAPTER 8: 153 Martin Luther King, Jr., quotation, Reprinted by arrangement with The Heirs to the Estate of Martin Luther King Jr., c/o Writers House as agent for the proprietor New York, NY. Copyright 1963 Dr. Martin Luther King Jr; copyright renewed 1991 Coretta Scott King

CHAPTER 10: 198 Microsoft PowerPoint screenshot, Microsoft® PowerPoint® 2008 for Mac. Version 12.2.3 © 2007 Microsoft Corporation. Reprinted with permission.

Chapter 15: 283 EBSCO screenshot, copyright © 2012 by EBSCO Publishing. Reprinted with permission.

BACK MATTER: 325 "NCA Student Outcomes for Speaking and Listening" from SPEAKING AND LISTENING COMPETENCIES FOR COLLEGE STUDENTS. Copyright © 1998 by National Communication Association. Reprinted with permission.

Index

A

Abbreviation, 156
Acronym, 156
Action, in Monroe's motivated
    sequence, 129, 167
Actual items, 180
After-dinner speech, 322
Age
    generational trends, 25
    as personal trait, 24, 71, 159,
        234, 282, 322
    as characteristic of prestige
        testimony, 77
Ajzen, Icek, 269
Alliteration, 161
American Psychological
    Association (APA)
    citations, 73, 117, 120–121
    style manual, 73, 99
Analogy
    argument by, 275
    figurative, 89, 275
    literal, 89, 275
    overview, 89
Anecdotes
    as attention-getters, 141
    as "WOW" statements, 146
APA. See American Psychological
    Association
APA citations
    examples of, 73
    in outlines, 117
    source page, 120–121
Apologizing, 176
Appeals. See also Persuasion
    persuasive speech, 260, 262–269
    practicing ethics with, 262, 268
Appeals, modern
    to commitment, 269
    to gain, 269
    to harmony, 268
    to need, 266–267
    overview, 260, 266
    persuasion and, 266–269

Appeals, traditional
    to ethos, 264
    to logos, 265
    to mythos, 263
    overview, 260, 262
    to pathos, 262–263
    persuasion, 262–265
Appearance, 168
Appreciative listening, 208
Arbitrary words, 154
Argument. See also Persuasion
    creation checklist, 275
    faulty, 276–277
    organizing support materials
        into, 294
    overview, 270
    premises, 272
Argument format
    draw conclusion, 265
    make statement, 265
    offer support materials as
        evidence, 265
Argument parts
    claim, 270, 271
    evidence, 270, 271
    warrants, 271
Argument types
    argument by analogy, 275
    argument by authority, 275
    argument by cause, 275
    argument by deduction, 272–273
    argument by induction, 274
    overview, 272
Aristotle, 262, 263, 264
Articulation, 167
Assonance, 161
Assumptions, 271. See also Warrants
Attention-getters
    effective, 140–141
    facts and statistics as, 140
    humor in, 141
    overview, 138, 140
    questions as, 141
    quotations as, 140

stories, narratives, illustrations, or
    anecdotes as, 141
    "WOW" statements and, 146
Attention, in Monroe's motivated
    sequence, 129, 267
Attitudinal anchors, 285
Audience. See also Situation
    adaptation during speech,
        32–33
    analysis for informative
        topic, 234
    analysis for persuasive
        topic, 282
    attitudes, 22, 257
    behaviors, 257
    beliefs, 23, 257
    captive versus voluntary, 29
    central idea appropriateness
        for, 47
    challenges as "WOW"
        statements, 147
    choosing presentation aid type
        for, 187
    in communication process,
        10, 11
    egocentrism, 21
    feedback from, 11, 213, 217,
        221, 224
    identity of, 23, 257
    intercultural, 156
    introduction capturing
        attention of, 138
    introduction relevance to, 139
    investigating specific
        traits of, 24–27
    knowing your, 12, 14, 21–31
    knowledge of informative
        topic, 243
    listening to, 212
    locating information
        about, 30–31
    personal traits, 24–25, 159
    persuasive speech and free
        decisions of, 261

Audience (continued)
  psychological traits, 26
  question-and-answer session, 177
  respect for gender of, 25
  response and persuasive speech
    types, 258, 285
  response statement in conclusion,
    148, 149
  response to toast, 320
  size, 27
  social traits, 27
  special occasion speech
    analysis of, 315
  speech evaluation by, 224
  target, 285
  values, 23, 257
Audience analysis
  brainstorming in, 30
  confidence booster, 22
  interview, 31
  overview, 21
  research, 30
  survey, 31
Audience-centered public speaking
  identification and empathy in, 4
  overview, 4, 21
Audio clips, 185
Authoritative warrants, 271
Authority, argument by, 275
Award acceptance speech, 321
Award presentation speech, 321

B
Background
  in communication process,
    10, 11
  pattern design principle
    and, 193
Balance design principle, 194
Bar charts, 183
Bar graphs, 183
*Belief, Attitude, Intention, and
  Behavior* (Fishbein
  and Ajzen), 269
Blogs, 57
Body language. *See* Physical delivery

Body of speech. *See* Speech body
Books, 64
Brainstorming
  in audience analysis, 30
  in idea bank creation, 37

C
Cacioppo, John, 269
Causal strategy, 125, 127
Cause
  argument by, 275
  effect-to-, 275
  -to-effect, 275
Central idea
  appropriateness for audience and
    event, 47
  creating, 42–47
  criteria for mechanically sound,
    46–47
  elements of, 45
  evaluating, 41, 46–47, 237, 287
  identifying, 41, 44–45, 237, 287
  informative speech identification
    of, 237
  in outlines, 100
  overview, 41, 44
  persuasive speech identification
    of, 287
  proposition types and, 259, 287
  refining, 46
  special occasion speech focus
    on, 316
  specific purpose and, 42–45
  working main points and, 49
Central processing, 269
Chalkboards, 188
Channel, in communication
  process, 10, 11
Charts
  bar, 183
  flip, 190
  flow, 182
  organizational, 182
  overview, 182
  pie, 184
Chronological strategy, 125, 126

Circle graphs, 184
Citations. *See also* APA citations;
    MLA citations; Oral citations
  in outlines, 105, 116–117
  overview, 90
  plagiarism avoidance and, 9,
    116, 247
  practicing ethics with proper, 117
  source page, 118, 119–121
Claim
  of argument, 270, 271
  evidence, warrant, and, 271
  of fact, 270
  of policy, 270
  of value, 270
Classroom peers, speech evaluation
  by, 225
Clichés, 158
Closed-ended questions, 31, 68
Coercion, 261
Cognitive Dissonance Theory, 268
Color harmony, 193
Color unity, 193
Commitment, appeal to, 269
Common ground, in communication
  process, 10, 11
Communication
  improvements from speech
    evaluation, 221
  process, 10–11
Communication and Persuasion
  (Petty and Cacioppo), 269
Communication apprehension, 6.
  See also Speech anxiety
Comparative advantage, 128
Comparative strategy, 125, 128
Comparison, 89
Concluding transitions, 114
Conclusion
  audience response statement in,
    148, 149
  checklist, 149
  creating one last impact with, 145
  developing, 101
  eliciting response with, 145
  functions of, 144–145
  informative speech, 245

introduction and, 144
organization of, 148–149
outline, 99, 101
overview, 99, 137, 144, 148
persuasive speech, 295
in public speaking creation
    phase, 13, 16
sample student, 149
signaling ending with, 145
summary statement in, 145,
    148, 149
three parts of, 148–149
"WOW" statements in, 137,
    145–147, 148, 149
Confidence
audience's effective listening and
    speaker's, 212
speech evaluation as building, 221
Confidence boosters, 6
audience analysis, 22
body training, 7
deep breathing, 7
effective listening, 213
guided imagery, 7
informative speech, 231
introduction, 143
language, 160
organizational strategy, 125
outline, 99, 290
parallelism, 133
persuasive speech, 260
practicing speech, 176
presentation aid, 201
pride in speech, 82
public speaking creative
    process, 231
research, 67
special occasion speech, 319
speech evaluation, 220
support materials, 87
topic selection, 37
vocabulary, 160
Connective transitions, 114
Connotative meaning, 154
Contemporary media, 190
Contrast, 89
Coordination, of main points, 132–133

Creativity, in public speaking, 5.
    See also Public speaking creation
    phase; Public speaking creative
    process
Credibility. See also Ethos
from character, 264
from charisma, 264
from competency, 264
ethos and, 264
introduction's building of, 139
material for introduction, 142–143
Critical listening
characteristics of, 215
practicing ethics through, 209
Critical thinking
characteristics of, 215, 220
practicing ethics through, 209, 220
skills and speech evaluation, 220
Culture
appropriate language, 8, 155
audience's effective listening
    and, 213
cyber-, 155
delivery and, 167, 169, 170
diversity, 156
humor and, 141
identity and, 27, 155, 263
intercultural audiences, 156
as social trait, 27
Cyber-cultures, 155

D

Databases. See also Library
    databases
for locating current persuasive
    topics, 283
Deduction, argument by, 272–273
Definitions, 76
Delivery. See also Physical delivery;
    Vocal delivery
effective, 163
informative speech, 252
of introduction, 139
overview, 163
persuasive speech, 261, 304
in presentations, 13, 17
special occasion speech, 317

Delivery methods
extemporaneous speaking, 172
impromptu speaking, 173
manuscript speaking, 173
memorized speaking, 173
Delivery outline
overview, 112
preparing, 175
student sample, 112–113
tip for holding, 175
Demographics, 24, 31, 70, 71, 315.
    See also Personal traits
Demonstration speech,
    chronological strategy, 126
Denotative meaning, 154
Design principles
balance, 194
emphasis, 194
overview, 192
pattern, 193
rhythm, 195
unity, 193
Dialect, 167
Disabilities, 24, 25
Diversity
cultural, 27, 155, 156, 213
ethical public speaking and
    respecting, 8, 25, 27
and language, 156
and presentation aids, 179
Drawings, 182

E

Education, 24, 25
Effective listening
active, 214
checklists, 213, 215
confidence booster, 213
critical, 215
good note taking and, 215
helping audience's, 212–215
noise barrier to, 32, 210–212
overcoming barriers to, 18
overview, 205
prevention of, 210–211
Elaboration Likelihood
    Model, 269

Emblems, 170
Empathic listening, 208
Emphasis design principle, 194
Enthymeme, 272, 273
Enunciation, 167
Environment, and audience's effective listening, 33, 211, 212
Equipment checking, 200
Ethical public speaking. *See also* Practicing ethics
 citations and plagiarism avoidance in, 9, 116
 freedom of expression and, 9
 reliable evidence, logic and reasoning in, 9
 respecting diversity in, 8
 understanding ethics, 8
Ethics. *See also* Practicing ethics
 in public speaking, 139
 in support materials, 86, 289
 understanding, 8
Ethnicity
 language and, 8, 167, 322
 as social trait, 27
Ethnocentrism
 avoidance, 8
 mythos and, 263
Ethos, 139. *See also* Credibility
 appeal to, 264
 credibility and, 264
 derived level of, 264
 initial level, 264
 terminal level of, 264
Eulogy, 318
Evaluation. *See also* Speech evaluation; Support materials evaluation
 of central idea, 41, 46–47, 237, 287
 of online sources, 55
 overview, 219
 of presentation, 252–253, 304–305
 of specific purpose, 42, 236, 286
 of speech message, 222, 223, 253
 of working main points, 48

Event, and central idea appropriateness, 47
Evidence, 53. *See also* Support materials
 of argument, 270, 271
 ethical public speaking using reliable, 9
 support materials as, 265, 270
 warrant, claim, and, 271
Examples
 brief, 78–79
 extended, 78–79
 hypothetical, 78–79
 overview, 78
Expectancy-Outcome Values Theory, 269
Extemporaneous speaking, 172
Extemporaneous speech, 5
Extemporaneous speech preparation
 day before speech, 177
 day of speech, 177
 delivery outline in, 175
 final dress rehearsal in, 176
 overview, 174
 practicing multiple times, 176
 preparing for questions in, 177
 presentation aids in, 175
 reading preparation outline aloud, 175
 rehearsals in, 174, 176
External noise
 adapting to, 33
 as environmental barrier, 33, 211
 as linguistic barrier, 33, 211
 overview, 33, 211
Eye contact, 169

F

Facial expressions, 170
Fact, 76
 as attention-getter, 140
 claim of, 270
 proposition of, 259, 287
Fallacies
 overview, 276
 types of, 277

Feedback
 audience, 11, 213, 217, 221, 224
 in communication process, 10, 11
 encoding and decoding, 11
 giving, 214, 215, 224, 225
 nonverbal, 207, 213
 verbal, 207, 213
Festinger, Leon, 268
Fillers
 overview, 158
 removing vocal, 165
First Amendment (U.S. Constitution), 9
Fishbein, Martin, 269
Flip charts, 190
Flowcharts, 182
Follow-up questions, 69
Fonts
 balanced, 194
 pattern design principle and, 193
 readable size, 194
Formal outlines, 108. *See also* Preparation outline
Freedom of expression, and ethical public speaking, 9
Full-sentence outlines, 108. *See also* Preparation outline

G

Gain, appeal to, 269
Gender
 neutral language, 159
 offensive language and, 8
 as personal trait, 24, 71, 234, 282, 322
 respect for audience's, 25
General purpose
 idea bank creation by exploring, 38
 identifying, 36
 overview, 36
Gestures, 170
Gone and *went* usage, 157
Government resources, 66

Grammar errors
  common, 157
  misplaced modifier, 157
  pronoun errors, 157
  subject/verb agreement, 157
  went versus gone, 157
Graphs
  bar, 183
  line, 183
  overview, 183
  pictographs, 184
  pie, 184
  as presentation aid type,
    183–184

H
Handouts, 189
Harmony, appeal to, 268
Hearing, 206–207
Hovland, Carl, 285
Humor
  in attention-getters, 141
  practicing ethics with, 147
  in "WOW" statements, 147

I
Idea. *See also* Central idea
  main point use of one, 132
Idea bank
  creation for informative
    topic, 235
  creation for persuasive topic, 283
  overview, 37
  for presentation aids, 195
Idea bank creation
  brainstorming in, 37
  exploring general purpose
    in, 38
  topic idea searching in, 37
Identity
  of audience, 23, 257
  cultural, 27, 155, 167, 263
Illustrations
  as attention-getters, 141
  as "WOW" statements, 146
Illustrators, 170
Image unity, 193
Impromptu speaking, 173

Inclusive language. *See* Language,
  appropriate
Income, 24, 25
Induction, argument by, 274
Inflection, 164
Informative listening, 209
Informative speaking
  creative process for, 230–231
  overview, 229, 232–233
  practicing ethics with, 232
Informative speech
  confidence booster, 231
  creating working outline
    for, 238
  creation phase of, 231
  evaluation of, 231, 252–253
  five activities for creating,
    230–231
  identifying central idea of, 237
  outline, 240–241, 246–251
  overview, 229
  preparation of presentation
    and evaluation of, 252–253
  preparation outline, 240–241,
    246–251
  presentation of, 231, 252–253
  research of, 230, 239
  sample student preparation
    outline for, 241, 246–251
  starting phase of, 230
  support materials, 239, 244
Informative speech organization
  committing to organizational
    strategy, 242–243
  composing introduction and
    conclusion in, 245
  constructing main points
    in, 244
  recognizing organizational
    strategy, 242
  support materials organization
    in, 244
Informative speech types
  determining best, 236
  organizational strategy types for,
    242–243
  speech to describe, 233
  speech to explain, 233

speech to instruct, 233
speech to report, 233
Informative topic
  audience and situation
    analysis, 234
  audience knowledge of, 243
  best informative speech
    type for, 236
  choosing, 234–235
  creating informative idea bank
    for, 235
  identifying specific purpose
    of, 236
  research of, 239
  selection and narrowing, 235
Inspiration, speech of, 313, 323
Instructor, speech evaluation
  by, 224
Internal noise
  adapting to, 33
  overview, 33, 211
  as physiological barrier, 33, 211
  as psychological barrier,
    33, 211
Internal reviews, 115
Internal summaries, 115
Internet. *See also* Web sites
  accessing libraries through,
    58–59
  blogs, 57
  evaluating sources from, 55
  government resources, 66
  reference works, 67
  search engines, 54–55
  support materials location
    and, 54–58, 66–67
Interviews
  audience analysis, 31
  checklist, 69
  conducting, 69
  finding people for, 68
  follow-up questions, 69
  open-ended and closed-ended
    questions, 31, 68
  overview, 68
  practicing ethics with, 69
  preparing for, 68
  support materials for, 68–69

Introduction
attention-getters, 138, 140–141, 142–143
building credibility early with, 139
capturing audience's attention with, 138
checklist for, 143
conclusion and, 144
confidence booster, 143
credibility material, 142–143
delivery of, 139
developing, 101
four parts of, 142–143
functions of, 138–139
informative speech, 245
introducing topic in, 139
launching into, 138
organization of, 142–143
outline, 99, 101
overview, 99, 137
persuasive speech, 295
previewing speech with, 139, 142–143
in public speaking creation phase, 13, 16
relevance to audience, 139, 142–143
sample student, 143
"WOW" statements referring to, 147
Introduction speech, 319

J
Jargon, 156
Journals, 65

K
Knowledge
in public speaking, 5
support materials selection and personal, 82

L
Language. See also Grammar; Words
appealing to senses, 160
appropriate, 159
clear, 156

confidence booster, 160
correct, 157
culturally appropriate, 155, 167
distinctive, 160–161
effective, 156–161
embellishing, 161
gender-neutral, 159
importance of, 154–155
meaning of, 154
offensive, 8
oral style, 158
overview, 153
persuasive speech, 261
power of, 155
quotations showing power of, 153
specific, 158
speech devices use in, 161
successful usage in presentations, 13, 17, 153–161
unbiased, 159
Lecterns, 171
Libraries
books, 64
catalogs, 61
government resources, 66
Internet access of, 58–59
journals, 65
magazines, 65
newspapers, 64
offerings of, 60–67
overview, 60
reference works, 67
Library databases
multiple-subject, 62
overview, 62
searching, 62–63
specialized, 62
tips for using, 62
Line graphs, 183
Links
outline planning of formal, 105
overview, 99
preparation outlines and effective, 115
Listening. See also Critical listening; Effective listening
barriers to, 32, 33, 210–212, 215
to audience, 212

goals, 208
hearing and, 206–207
overview, 205, 206
in public speaking creative process, 13, 18
Listening process
attending phase, 207
hearing in, 206–207
overview, 206
receiving phase, 207
remembering phase, 207
responding phase, 207
understanding phase, 207
Listening types
appreciative listening, 208
critical listening, 209, 215
empathic listening, 208
informative listening, 209
overview, 208
Logic, 265
ethical public speaking using reliable, 9
Logos, appeal to, 265

M
Magazines, 65
Main points. See also Working main points
as complete sentences, 132
coordination of, 132–133
creating, 132–133
as declarative sentences, 132
discovery and organizational strategy, 123–135
informative speech, 244
one idea per, 132
organizational strategy and, 130–131
outline format of, 102
outline use of balanced, 104
overview, 48, 99
parallelism of, 133
persuasive speech, 294
standard of balance use with, 135
Manuscript speaking, 173
Maslow, Abraham, 266
Maslow's hierarchy of needs, 26, 266, 267

Mean, 81
Meaning, of language, 154
Media
contemporary, 190
multimedia, 185
as presentation aid, 185,
190–191
traditional, 191
video and audio, 185
Median, 81
Memorized speaking, 173
Message
audience's effective listening
and effective, 212
in communication process,
10, 11
encoding and decoding, 11
evaluation of speech, 222,
223, 253
Microphone use, 165
Misplaced modifier, 157
MLA. See Modern Language
Association
MLA citations
examples of, 73
in outlines, 117
source page, 120–121
Mode, 81
Models, 181
Modern Language Association (MLA)
citations, 73, 117, 120–121
style manual, 73, 99
Modifier, misplaced, 157
Monotone, 164
Monroe, Alan, 129, 266
Monroe's motivated sequence
strategy, 125, 129, 266, 267
Movement, in physical
delivery, 171
Mumbling, 167
Mythos, appeal to, 263

N
Narratives
as attention-getters, 141
as "WOW" statements, 146
Need, in Monroe's motivated
sequence, 129, 267

Needs
appeal to, 266–267
Maslow's hierarchy of, 26,
266, 267
physiological, 26, 266, 267
safety, 26, 266, 267
self-actualization, 26, 266, 267
self-esteem, 26, 266, 267
social, 26, 266, 267
Newspapers, 64
Noise
adapting to, 33
in communication process,
10, 11
effective listening and, 32,
210–212
external, 33, 211
internal, 33, 211
overview, 210
speech adaptation to, 32–33
Note taking. See also Research notes
effective listening by good, 215
research, 72–73

O
Objective, of specific purpose,
41, 42
Occupation, 24, 25
Offensive language, 8
Online sources evaluation, 55
Open-ended questions, 31, 68
Oral citations
checklist, 93
collecting necessary content for,
90–91
contents of, 91
creation and delivery of, 92–93
overview, 90
samples of, 93
Oral evaluation, 217
Oral style, 158
Organization
of conclusion, 148–149
of introduction, 142–143
persuasive speech, 260
problems and solutions, 135
in public speaking, 5
Organizational charts, 182

Organizational strategy
confidence booster, 125
discovering main points and,
130–131
for main points, 123–135
overview, 123, 124–125
selecting, 130
speech body, 123–135
speech making from, 130–135
for subpoints, 134
Organizational strategy types
causal, 125, 127
chronological, 125, 126
comparative, 125, 128
for informative speech types,
242–243
Monroe's motivated sequence,
125, 129, 266, 267
for persuasive speech types,
292–293
problem–solution, 125, 128
spatial, 125, 127
topical, 125, 126
Outline. See also Delivery outline;
Preparation outline; Working
outline
APA citations in, 117
balanced main points in, 104
body of speech, 99
checklists, 119, 240
citations in, 105, 116–117
conclusion, 99, 101
confidence boosters, 99, 290
covering one issue at
a time in, 101
creating effective, 100–105
formal links in, 105
full sentences in, 100
informative speech, 240–241,
246–251
introduction, 99, 101
MLA citations in, 117
overview, 97
parts of, 98–99
persuasive speech, 290–291,
296–303
in public speaking creation
phase, 13, 16

Outline (*continued*)
  source page, 99
  special occasion speech, 317
  subordination in, 104
  topic, specific purpose, and
    central idea in, 100
  types, 100, 106–113
Outline format
  alignment of points, 103
  main points, 102
  overview, 102
  pattern of symbols, 102
  subpoints, 103

P

Parallelism
  confidence booster, 133
  distinctive language using, 161
  of main points, 133
Paraphrasing, 88
Pathos, appeal to, 262–263
Pattern design principle, 193
Pause, vocal, 165
Peers, speech evaluation by, 225
Pelias, Ron, 219
Peripheral processing, 269
Personal knowledge, in support
  materials selection, 82
Personal traits, 24–25, 159
Persuasion. *See also* Appeals;
  Argument
  coercion compared to, 261
  modern appeals, 266–269
  overview, 257
  practicing ethics with, 257,
    261, 276
  traditional appeals, 262–265
Persuasive speaking
  creative process for, 280–281
  overview, 280
Persuasive speech
  appeals, 260, 262–269
  choosing, 282–284
  confidence booster, 260
  creating working outline
    for, 288
  creation phase of, 281

evaluation of, 281, 304–305
five activities for creating,
  280–281
identifying central idea of, 287
outline, 290–291, 296–303
overview, 257, 279
preparation of presentation and
  evaluation of, 304–305
preparation outline, 290–291,
  296–303
presentation of, 281, 304–305
research of, 280, 289
sample student preparation
  outline for, 291, 296–303
starting phase of, 280
support materials, 260, 289, 294
Persuasive speech functions
  acknowledge audience's freedom
    to decide, 261
  different appeal types use, 260
  emphasize powerful and direct
    delivery, 261
  highlight emotive and stylistic
    language, 261
  highly structured organization
    use, 260
  narrow listeners' options, 258
  rely on varied and valid support
    materials, 260
  seek response, 258
  support proposition of fact, value,
    or policy, 259, 287
Persuasive speech organization
  committing to organizational
    strategy, 293
  composing introduction and
    conclusion in, 295
  constructing main points in, 294
  primacy model, 294
  recency model, 294
  recognizing organizational
    strategy, 292
  of support materials into
    arguments, 294
Persuasive speech types
  audience response and choice of,
    258, 285

to convince, 285
determining best, 285
organizational strategy types for,
  292–293
speech to actuate, 258, 285
speech to convince, 258, 285
speech to stimulate, 258, 285
Persuasive topic
  audience and situation
    analysis, 282
  best persuasive speech
    type for, 285
  creating persuasive idea bank
    for, 283
  databases for locating
    current, 283
  identifying specific purpose
    of, 286
  research of, 289
  selection and narrowing, 284
Petty, Richard, 269
Photographs, 181
Physical delivery
  appearance, 168
  checklist, 171
  elements of, 168–171
  eye contact, 169
  facial expressions, 170
  gestures, 170
  movement, 171
  posture, 171
Physiological needs, 26, 266, 267
Pictograms, 184
Pictographs, 184
Pie charts, 184
Pie graphs, 184
Pitch, 164
Plagiarism
  blatant, 9, 73
  no-citation, 9, 73
  overview, 9
Plagiarism avoidance
  citations and, 9, 116, 247
  overview, 9
Points. *See also* Main points;
  Subpoints
  outline alignment of, 103

Policy
claim of, 270
proposition of, 259, 287
Popular sources, 84
Posters, 189
Posture, 171
PowerPoint, 196
basics, 197–199
slide design, 199
Practicing ethics
with appeals, 262, 268
through asking hard
questions, 305
copyright law observance, 197
through critical listening, 209
through critical thinking,
209, 220
honesty and reliability in, 128
with humor, 147
with impromptu speaking, 173
with informative speaking, 232
with interviews, 69
with speech goal to entertain, 322
personal traits and, 25
with persuasion, 259, 261, 276
plagiarism avoidance, 9
with presentation aids,
181, 185
with proper citations, 117
with special occasion speech,
313, 322
with support materials, 87
with topic selection, 39
in word selection, 155
Practicing speech
confidence booster, 176
multiple times, 176
presentation aids, 200
special occasion speech, 317
speech anxiety and, 7
Premises, 272
Preparation outline
effective links in, 115
format and template, 108, 241, 291
informative speech, 240–241,
246–251
overview, 108

persuasive speech, 290–291,
296–303
reading aloud, 175
sample student, 241, 246–251,
291, 296–303
student sample, 109–111
tip, 175
Presentation. See also Delivery;
Language
appropriate techniques, 5
evaluation of, 252–253, 304–305
of informative speech, 231,
252–253
of persuasive speech, 281,
304–305
phase of public speaking creative
process, 13, 17
slide use in, 199
of special occasion speech, 311
speech delivery, 13, 17
speech evaluation standards for,
222–223
successful language use in, 13, 17,
153–161
Presentation aids
backup plan for, 201
checking assignment for, 186
checklist, 201
choosing, 186–187
confidence booster, 201
crafting effective, 192–195
design principles, 192–195
equipment checking, 200
idea bank for, 195
overview, 179
passing around, 201
planning time for, 192
practicing ethics with, 181, 185
preparing, 175
proofreading, previewing, and
practicing, 200
purpose of, 186
successful use of, 200–201
time needed to create, 195
"Touch, Turn, Talk Method" use
with, 201
using, 13, 17

Presentation aid display
choosing, 187
timing for, 201
Presentation aid display methods
advanced technology, 190–191
chalkboards and whiteboards, 188
contemporary media, 190
flip charts, 190
handouts, 189
posters, 189
traditional media, 191
Presentation aid types
actual items, 180
audience and choosing, 187
charts and tables, 182
choosing, 187
drawings, 182
graphs, 183–184
media, 185
models, 181
photographs, 181
situation and choosing, 187
topic and choosing, 187
Presentation software
overview, 196
PowerPoint basics, 197–199
storyboarding, 197
tutorials, 196
using, 196–199
Preview, internal, 115
Previewing
presentation aids, 200
speech with introduction, 139,
142–143
Primacy model, of persuasive
speech organization, 294
Primary sources, 83
Problem–solution strategy, 125, 128
Pronoun errors, 157
Pronunciation, 166
Proofreading presentation aids, 200
Proofs, 260. See also Appeals
Proposition types
central idea and, 259, 287
of fact, 259, 287
of policy, 259, 287
of value, 259, 287

Psychological traits, 26
Public speaking. *See also* Speech;
  specific speaking topics
  appropriate presentation
    techniques, 5
  audience centered, 4
  benefits of, 3
  communication process, 10–11
  ethics in, 139
  knowledge, creativity and
    organization in, 5
  overview, 2–19
  qualities for success in, 4–5
Public speaking creation phase
  of informative speech, 231
  introduction and conclusion in,
    13, 16
  outlines in, 13, 16
  of persuasive speech, 281
  in public speaking creative
    process, 13, 16
  of special occasion speech, 311
  speech body organization in,
    13, 16
Public speaking creative process.
  See also Listening; Presentation;
  Public speaking creation phase;
  Public speaking starting phase;
  Research; Speech evaluation
  confidence booster, 231
  creation phase of, 13, 16
  for informative speaking, 230–231
  listening and evaluation phase
    of, 13, 18
  overview, 12–19
  for persuasive speaking, 280–281
  presentation phase of, 13, 17
  research phase of, 12, 15
  for special occasion speaking,
    310–311
  starting phase of, 12, 14
  steps of, 19
Public speaking fear. *See* Speech
  anxiety
Public speaking starting phase
  of informative speech, 230
  knowing your audience and
    situation, 12, 14

of persuasive speech, 280
in public speaking creative
  process, 12, 14
selecting topic and purpose, 12, 14
of special occasion speech, 310
Purpose. *See also* General purpose;
  Specific purpose
  of presentation aids, 186
  selecting, 12, 14, 35

Q
Questions. *See also* Rhetorical
  questions
  as attention-getters, 141
  closed-ended, 31, 68
  follow-up, 69
  open-ended, 31, 68
  practicing ethics through asking
    hard, 305
  preparing for, 177
  response-evoking, 141
  in surveys, 70, 71
  topic selection using focus and
    research, 39
Question-and-answer (Q and A)
  session, 177
Questionnaires, 31
Quotations
  as attention-getters, 140
  effective use of, 88
  from famous speeches, 153
  showing power of language, 153
  as "WOW" statements, 146

R
Race, as social or personal trait,
  27, 71, 234, 282
  language and, 8, 159, 322
Rate, vocal, 164
Reasoning, 265. *See also* Argument
  ethical public speaking using
    reliable, 9
Recency model, of persuasive
  speech organization, 294
Reference works, 67
Rehearsals
  final dress, 176
  overview, 174

Religion, 8, 23, 27, 71, 322
Repetition, 161
Research. *See also* Support materials
  audience analysis, 30
  confidence booster, 67
  of informative speech, 230, 239
  of informative topic, 239
  overview, 53, 75
  of persuasive speech, 280, 289
  of persuasive topic, 289
  phase and support materials
    selection and evaluation,
    12, 15
  phase of public speaking creative
    process, 12, 15
  of special occasion speech,
    310, 316
  support materials location,
    12, 15
Research notes
  methods, 72
  style manuals and, 73
Rhetoric (Aristotle), 88, 262
Rhetorical questions
  as attention-getters, 141
  as "WOW" statements, 147
Rhythm design principle, 195
Roast, 320

S
Safety needs, 26, 266, 267
Sample, explanation of, 71
Satisfaction, in Monroe's motivated
  sequence, 129, 267
Schemes
  alliteration, 161
  assonance, 161
  overview, 161
  parallelism, 161
  repetition, 161
Scholarly sources, 84
Search engines
  hits, 54
  overview, 54–55
  search term tips, 54
Secondary sources, 83
Self-actualization needs, 26,
  266, 267

Self-esteem needs, 26, 266, 267

Sentences. *See also* Subject sentence
  main points as complete, 132
  main points as declarative, 132
  outline use of full, 100

Sexual orientation, 24, 25, 159, 322

Shaffer, Tracy Stephenson, 219

Sherif, Muzafer, 285

Signposts, 115

Situation. *See also* Audience
  analysis for informative
    topic, 234
  analysis for persuasive topic, 282
  choosing presentation aid types
    for, 187
  in communication process, 10, 11
  knowing your, 12, 14, 28–31
  locating information about, 30–31
  occasion, 29
  place and audience size, 28
  time, 29

Slides, 199

Social Judgment (Sherif and
    Hovland), 285

Social judgment theory, 285

Social needs, 26, 266, 267

Social traits, 27

Sources. *See also* Online sources;
    Support materials
  overview, 53
  personal, 53
  popular, 84
  primary, 83
  scholarly, 84
  secondary, 83
  selection, 82–85

Source citation. *See* Citations

Source page
  citations, 118, 119–121
  creating, 118–121
  format, 119
  outline, 99
  overview, 99

Spatial strategy, 125, 127

Speaker
  in communication process, 10, 11
  confidence and audience's
    effective listening, 212

Speaking. *See* Public speaking

Special occasion speaking
  creative process for, 310–311
  overview, 310

Special occasion speech
  analyzing audience of, 315
  confidence booster, 319
  creation phase of, 311
  evaluation of, 311, 317
  five activities for creating, 310–311
  focusing on central idea of, 316
  outline, 317
  overview, 309, 312
  practicing, 317
  practicing ethics with, 313, 322
  presentation of, 311
  research of, 310, 316
  starting phase of, 310
  writing, 314–317

Special occasion speech purpose
  to celebrate, 313
  to commemorate, 313
  determining, 314
  to entertain, 313
  to inspire, 313, 323

Special occasion speech type
  after-dinner speech, 322
  clarifying, 315
  eulogy or tribute, 318
  speech of award
    acceptance, 321
  speech of award presentation, 321
  speech of inspiration, 313, 323
  speech of introduction, 319
  toast or roast, 320

Specific purpose
  central idea and, 42–45
  evaluating, 42, 236, 286
  examples of, 43
  guidelines for composing, 43
  identifying, 41, 42–43, 236, 286
  informative topic identification
    of, 236
  objective of, 41, 42
  in outlines, 100
  overview, 41, 42
  persuasive topic identification
    of, 286

Specific topic, 40

Speech. *See also* Public speaking;
    specific speech topics
  confidence booster of
    pride in, 82
  devices, 161
  expansion using subpoints, 134
  extemporaneous, 5
  linking parts of, 114–115
  organizational strategy for
    making, 130–135

Speech anxiety. *See also* Confidence
    boosters
  communication apprehension as, 6
  overcoming, 6–7
  practice and, 7, 101
  techniques for controlling, 6
  tip, 5

Speech body
  outlines, 99
  overview, 99

Speech body organization. *See also*
    Organizational strategy
  overview, 123
  in public speaking creation phase,
    13, 16
  strategy, 123–135

Speech evaluation
  by audience, 224
  checklists, 218, 317
  by classroom peers, 225
  communication improvements
    from, 221
  confidence booster, 220
  as confidence building, 221
  considerations, 222–223
  criterion-based, 222
  effective, 218, 219
  as good thing, 218–219
  guidelines for useful
    feedback, 225
  importance of, 218–221
  of informative speech, 231, 252–253
  by instructor, 224
  oral, 217
  overview, 217
  of persuasive speech, 281,
    304–305

Speech evaluation (*continued*)
  in public speaking creative
    process, 13, 18
  sample form, 223
  of special occasion speech,
    311, 317
  standards for speaker's
    presentation, 222–223
  teaching of critical thinking
    skills, 220
  written, 217
  by yourself, 224
Speech preparation. *See*
    Extemporaneous speech
    preparation
Statistics
  as attention-getters, 140
  common measurements, 81
  descriptive, 80
  inferential, 80
  overview, 80
  using, 80
Stereotyping, 24, 25, 159
Stories
  as attention-getters, 141
  as "WOW" statements, 146
Storyboarding, 197
Strategy. *See* Organizational strategy
Style
  oral, 158
  written, 158
Style manuals. *See also* American
    Psychological Association;
    Modern Language Association
  overview, 99
  research notes and, 73
Subject sentence, 41, 44. *See also*
    Central idea
Subject/verb agreement, 157
Subordinate points, 99. *See also*
    Subpoints
Subordination, in outlines, 104
Subpoints
  expanding speech with, 134
  organizational strategy, 134
  outline format of, 103
  overview, 99, 134

Supporting points, 99. *See also*
    Subpoints
Support materials. *See also*
    Evidence; Sources
  confidence booster, 87
  as evidence, 265, 270
  informative speech, 239, 244
  interview, 68–69
  overview, 53
  persuasive speech, 260, 289, 294
  practicing ethics with, 87
  purposes of, 89
  surveys and, 70–71
Support materials evaluation, 239
  accuracy in, 86
  checklist, 72
  completeness in, 86
  currency in, 87
  from online sources, 55
  in research phase, 12, 15
  suitability in, 87
  trustworthiness in, 87
Support materials location
  Internet and, 54–58, 66–67
  libraries and, 58–67
  overview, 53
  in research phase, 12, 15
Support materials selection
  personal knowledge in, 82
  primary *vs.* secondary sources
    in, 83
  in research phase, 12, 15
  scholarly *vs.* popular
    sources in, 84
  topic needs in, 85
Support materials testing. *See*
    Support materials evaluation
Support materials types
  definitions, 76
  examples as, 78–79
  facts, 76
  statistics, 80–81
  testimony, 77
Support materials usage
  analogy, 89
  comparison, 89
  contrast, 89

  direct, 89
  effective, 88–89
  purposes, 89
  of quotations and
    paraphrasing, 88
Surveys
  audience analysis, 31
  conducting, 70–71
  creating, 70–71
  overview, 70
  population, 70
  questions in, 70, 71
  sample, 71
  support materials and, 70–71
Syllogism, 272, 273
Symbolic words, 154
Symbols, and pattern design
    principle, 193

T
Target audience, 285
Testimony
  expert, 77
  lay or peer, 77
  overview, 77
  personal, 77
  prestige, 77
Text
  emphasizing, 194
  placement, 195
Theme, 41, 44. *See also* Central idea
A Theory of Cognitive Dissonance
    (Festinger), 268
Thesis statement, 41, 44. *See also*
    Central idea
Time transitions, 114
Titles, emphasis using, 194
Toast, 320
Topic. *See also* Informative topic;
    Persuasive topic
  choosing presentation aid type
    for, 187
  introduction of, 139
  needs in support materials
    selection, 85
  in outlines, 100
  specific, 41

Topical strategy, 125, 126
Topic selection
  confidence booster, 37
  creating idea bank in, 37–38
  focus and research questions
    for, 39
  identifying general purpose
    in, 36
  informative topic, 235
  overview, 12, 14, 35
  persuasive speech, 284
  practicing ethics with, 39
  topic narrowing in, 40–41,
    235, 284
Toulmin, Stephen, 271
Traditional media, 191
Transitions, 99. *See also* Links
  overview, 114
Tribute, 318
Tropes, 161
Unity design principle, 193
The Uses of Argument
  (Toulmin), 271

V

Value
  claim of, 270
  proposition of, 259, 287
Variety, vocal, 166
Verb/subject agreement, 157
Video clips, 185
Viewpoint transitions, 114
Visualization, in Monroe's motivated
  sequence, 129, 267

Vocabulary, confidence
  booster, 160
Vocal delivery
  articulation, 167
  checklist, 167
  dialect, 167
  elements of, 164–167
  microphones and, 165
  pause, 165
  pitch, 164
  pronunciation, 166
  rate, 164
  removing vocal fillers, 165
  variety, 166
  volume, 165
Volume, vocal, 165

W

Warrants
  of argument, 271
  authoritative, 271
  evidence, claim, and, 271
  motivational, 271
  substantive, 271
Web sites
  commercial, 56
  nonprofit organization, 56
  overview, 55
  personal, 57
Went and *gone* usage, 157
Whiteboards, 188
Words. *See also* Language
  arbitrary, 154
  connotative meaning of, 154

denotative meaning of, 154
  practicing ethics in selection of,
    155
  symbolic, 154
Working main points
  categories and key ideas, 49
  central idea and, 49
  checklists, 238, 288
  constructing, 49
  evaluating, 48
  overview, 48
Working outline
  creating informative speech,
    238
  creating persuasive
    speech, 288
  overview, 41, 48, 106
  sample student, 107
  working main points of, 48–49,
    238, 288
"WOW" statements
  attention-getters and, 146
  challenges to audience
    as, 147
  in conclusions, 137, 145–147,
    148, 149
  humor in, 147
  quotations as, 146
  referring to introduction in, 147
  rhetorical questions as, 147
  stories, narratives, illustrations,
    or anecdotes as, 146
Written evaluation, 217
Written style, 158